Rituals of Race

Carter G. Woodson Institute
Series in Black Studies

ARMSTEAD L. ROBINSON
General Editor

Rituals of Race

AMERICAN PUBLIC CULTURE
AND THE SEARCH FOR RACIAL DEMOCRACY

Alessandra Lorini

University Press of Virginia

Charlottesville & London

THE UNIVERSITY PRESS OF VIRGINIA

© 1999 by the Rector and Visitors
of the University of Virginia
Printed in the United States of America

First published 1999

∞ The paper used in this publication meets the minimum
requirements of the American National Standard for Information
Sciences—Permanence of Paper for Printed Library Materials,
ANSI Z39.48-1984.

Library of Congress Cataloging-in-Publication Data
Lorini, Alessandra, 1949–
    Rituals of race : American public culture and the search for
racial democracy / Alessandra Lorini.
        p.   cm. — (Carter G. Woodson Institute series in Black
studies)
    Includes bibliographical references and index.
    ISBN 0-8139-1870-7 (cloth : alk. paper). — ISBN 0-8139-1871-5
(pbk. : alk. paper)
    1. United States—Race relations—Political aspects. 2. United
States—Social life and customs—1865–1918. 3. Festivals—
Political aspects—United States—History. 4. Pageants—Political
aspects—United States—History. 5. Exhibitions—Political
aspects—United States—History. 6. Popular culture—Political aspects—United States—History. 7. Afro-Americans—Civil rights—
History—19th century. 8. Afro-Americans—Civil rights—History—20th century. 9. Democracy—United States—History.
I. Title. II. Series.
E185.61.L675   1999
305.8'00973—dc21   98-33171
                                                            CIP

To the memory of my father,
Umberto Lorini

Contents

Illustrations

Preface

When I was a fifteen-year-old high school student in Florence, the city where I was born, the only progressive teacher at my otherwise ultraconservative school gave a lecture on the American Civil War that profoundly touched my feelings. That lecture, centered on slavery and abolitionism, gave me new values and a new sense of reality. There was nothing in my daily experience of my art-city, where homogeneity was the norm, from which I could understand the meaning of freedom and of slavery, and that the American Civil War was a turning point of the modern world.

That lecture slept in my mind for three years. But at the end of the 1960s I heard the radical language of abolitionism in the words of the Parisian students in May 1968, a language they shared with the American students protesting against the Vietnam War, with the Italian workers struggling for control over their workplaces and their lives, with women fighting against patriarchy, with environmental activists' early warnings on the internal destructive forces of consumption society. That high school lecture came back to my mind and never left.

Over the years I spent in the United States as a graduate student and researcher in American cultural history, I witnessed the explosion of trendy academic debates in poststructural fashion that paralleled the creation of women's studies and black studies departments at American universities. I witnessed the growing market of gender and race knowledge, and the attention the media gave to the entrance of a number of women and black individuals into academia.

This positive aspect of creating new jobs went hand in hand with the growing essentialization of collective identities. Yet racism, sexism, and class exploitation were still undisturbed in American society at large. I came to realize that the tension between the universalist call for human rights and social justice, on the one hand, and postmodern fragmentation of knowledge and the culture of global market, on the other, challenged the human scientist who had become aware that there was no such thing as a neutral point of observation, that a researcher's identity was the complex product of feelings about gender, class, and race. This challenge has led non-neutral human scientists to reframe universalist values of freedom, equality, and justice in a postmodern context of democratization of differences. This challenge has opened a perspective of socially active scholarship and redefinition of the human scientist as "public intellectual," whose role, as Cornel West states in *Keeping Faith: Philosophy and Race in America,* would be "to fuse the best of the life of the mind from within the academy with the best of the organized forces for greater democracy and freedom from outside the academy" (103). This does not mean to play the role of opinion maker in the mass media market but to have the capacity to address issues expanding the boundaries of democracy in our postmodern global world. Among these crucial issues are the retrieval of conflictual views of democracy and the market, and the exploration of conflictual definitions of political activism for the new millennium. These two issues, when combined, constitute a challenging search for the twenty-first century, a quest that cannot be separated from a structural economic change in the production and distribution of wealth.

The political culture of the 1960s has shaped my notion of participatory democracy, which this book explores as the never fully expressed potential of American public culture. Unlike in other western countries, public culture in the United States has always been the ground where irreconcilable differences could confront and negotiate their space. Far from being a neutral ground, public culture is a contested space in which collective or subjective identities fight for recognition. Public culture is also broader than political culture as it can include politically conflictual contents. Furthermore, public culture is broader than the notion of public sphere, a concept, take from Jurgen Habermas's *Structural Transformation of the Public Sphere* (Cambridge: Poly Press, 1989), that is more connected to representative democracy.

American public culture is shaped by race, gender, and class tensions crossing the civil society. It shows power and empowerment, definitions of inclusion in and exclusion from the nation. As a contested ground, public culture reflects the tensions between institutions and movements. It is a space where conflictual definitions of democracy can converse. This conversation occurs in the language of rituals whose symbolic contents reveal political and economic power and conflicts of gender, race, and class.

The word "ritual" has a religious connotation. Yet when associated with race, public culture, and democracy, it takes the broader meaning of collective symbolic behavior, a practice that connects individuals to a social body. From this perspective, *Rituals of Race* is a story of political interracial alliances in public events from Reconstruction to World War I. How individuals or groups expressed the language of these alliances in public events sheds light on what I call the search for participatory democracy.

In participatory democracy, individuals and groups are directly involved in political choices affecting change in their lives. How individual or group participation occurs in public events defines the question of inclusion in or exclusion from the boundaries of democracy. Rituals of empowerment express individual and group symbolic behavior asking for recognition of values in opposition to existing distribution of political and economic power.

Civil society can be defined as those spaces of social interaction not included in the state or the economy. In American political and social history, spaces of civil society have been the black civil rights, feminist, labor, antinuclear, peace, and environmental movements. The question of how movements whose goal is the expansion of the boundaries of democracy gain recognition is the question of a participatory democracy in which politics is reappropriated of its ethical components by establishing the principle of "democratic equivalence" of group recognition, as political scientist Chantal Mouffe puts it in *Dimensions of Radical Democracy: Pluralism, Citizenship, Community* (New York: Verso, 1992). Mouffe discusses the question of creating "a chain of equivalence among democratic struggles, and therefore the creation of a common political identity among democratic subjects" (225).

By connecting American public culture to the search for participatory democracy, the story of struggles for liberty and equality becomes the story not of abstract principles but of living forces expanding the boundaries of democratic inclusion. African-American struggles for freedom and equality have profoundly affected the search for participatory democracy in the United States. Public culture, broadly defined, is the theater where the tensions of African-American struggles have articulated the conflictual discourses of group integration and separation. The history of interracial alliances has generated forms of public culture within unexpressed and radical potentials of democracy.

"The uplift of women is, next to the problem of the color line and the peace movement, our greatest modern cause. When, now, two of these movements—women and color—combine in one, the combination has deep meaning," W. E. B. Du Bois wrote in 1920 in *Darkwater: Voices from within the Veil* (New York: Schocken Books, 1969, 181). Although the word "uplift" is heavily charged with paternalist and patriarchal connotation, as shown in such recent scholarship as Kevin K. Gaines's *Uplifting the Race: Black Leadership, Politics, and Culture in the Twentieth Century* (Chapel Hill: Univ. of North Carolina Press, 1996), it gives ethical meaning to political battles. Great causes are those in which ethics and politics are reconciled. Battles against sexism, racism, and war are still "our greatest modern cause" on the agenda for the new millennium.

Historians have conventionally divided the period of American history from 1865 to 1918 into three ages: Reconstruction, Gilded Age, and Progressive Era. But looking at the period as a whole offers a better opportunity to understand change in public culture in a postmodern perspective, that is, as a contested ground of inclusion and exclusion of racial, gender, and class differences. From the end of the Civil War to World War I, an "invented tradition" or mainstream ideology of national reconciliation supported unified economic interests in the North and South and the beginning of the U.S. imperialism at the turn of the century. As Eric Hobsbawm explains in his introduction to *The Invention of Tradition* (Hobsbawm and Terence Ranger, Cambridge: Cambridge University Press, 1983), "'Invented tradition' is taken to mean a set of practices, normally governed by overtly or tacitly accepted rules and of a ritual or symbolic nature, which seek to inculcate certain values and norms of behaviour by repetition, which automatically implies continuity with the past" (1).

In the name of national reconciliation, African-American human rights were sacrificed. The appeal of expanding markets coincided with a political definition of American democracy molded around the myth of individual economic success in a free country. National celebrations made this ideology pervasive by producing a public culture in which patriotism and economic success defined the boundaries of inclusion in and exclusion from American democracy. Yet the erasure of civil and political rights achieved during Reconstruction did not stay uncontested, for the values of participatory democracy entered public culture. As party politics had become a business of rewards that progressive administrators attempted to moralize, groups of men and women in the civil society created autonomous spaces of opposition in the realm of public culture and in so doing broadened its definition. The bleak records of the Progressive Era on African-American human rights paralleled the growing mobilization in the civil society of a variety of agencies. Inspired by a universal definition of human progress, civil organizations fought for the inclusion of differences of gender, race, and class in that definition by building difficult alliances whose complex and ambiguous political language was charged with current scientific explanations of human differences. The assumption of "inferiority" of the "Negro race" became a dominant theme in public culture in both subtle and explicit ways. African-American public figures, whose very existence dismissed the pseudoscientific "inferiority," brought into the theater of public culture different political languages and interracial alliances.

The story of rituals of race this book tells is the story of conflicts over memory of historical events that shaped collective identities. National reconciliation celebrated the erasure of the abolitionist memory from the Civil War and made the reunified country a racialist democracy. The institutionalization of scientific discourses on "race" justified exclusion and segregation of the "separate but equal formula" the Supreme Court legitimized in 1896. At the same time, the oppositional language of a color-blind Constitution made all individuals potentially equal without considering that existing economic and social conditions were a barrier for equality of opportunities. The myth of a color-blind economic success was the obverse of the myth of a color-blind Constitution.

This book is the story of public culture made by gender-differentiated interracial alliances of individuals whose public roles as activists, scientists, academics, community workers, and organizers shaped both the ideology of "national reconciliation" and the search for participatory democracy. Individual biographies show that a person could be both radical on certain issues and conservative on others or could change views over time. But the thread that connects public figures like Frederick Douglass, Ida Wells-Barnett, W. E. B. Du Bois, Jane Addams, Franz Boas, Mary Ovington, and several other public intellectuals or intellectual activists included in this book, despite great differences in background and world view, is that they brought into public culture, at different times in their lives, battles for great causes. Although several of them did not hold radical views, their passionate involvement in the great causes of human rights, social justice, and world peace linked their battles with the search for participatory democracy.

This story of rituals of race from the Civil War to WWI as the story of broadening democratic spaces through public culture, ambitious as it seems, does not have any pretense of completion or of giving the final answer to the controversial issue of race, gender, and class alliances for a participatory democracy. This book simply adds complexity to the understanding of the tension between group integration and separation, between assimilation and cultural pluralism, in American democracy by exploring in an interdisciplinary perspective public events seen through the lenses of those intellectuals who lived them.

The main argument connecting these events is that interracial alliances over African-American integrationist and separatist strategies have been the engine for the search for participatory democracy in America. The study of tensions between individual achievements and group responsibility, the myth of economic success, and the value of solidarity in African-American strategies sheds light on potential expansion of the boundaries of democracy for the twenty-first century.

This book works on a broad definition of public culture that includes parades and demonstrations, festive national and local events, international exhibitions, association meetings, debates generated on periodical literature, the theater, the movies and other forms of commercial culture, and community pageants. Each chapter examines a selection of public events chronologically and thematically. My selection of these events of public culture among the thousands from Reconstruction to World War I, in both the North and South, has followed the criteria of national impact of each event on definitions of race and democracy. Most of the events took place in New York since what occurred in that city assumed a national connotation.

Chapter 1 explores parades as rituals of race in the national metropolis from the aftermath of the Civil War to the late 1870s by focusing on enlistment of black soldiers in the Union army, interracial alliances between the Union League Club and African-American leaders, dissonance between the idea of loyalty and that of freedom, and between representations of race and gender relations, and the strengthening of the political culture of national reconciliation by the 1880s.

Chapter 2 deals with two of the great international exhibits of the 1890s as public theaters of national reconciliation. The Chicago World's Columbian Exposition of 1893 was conceived as a six-month mass celebration of the idea of linear progress from simplicity to complexity. Against the pervasive message of progress, the fair delivered in explicit and subtle ways the idea that slavery had helped Africans to become civilized in America, which enraged black activists Ida Wells and Frederick Douglass. The Atlanta Cotton States and International Exposition of 1895 celebrated an idealized interracial economic cooperation between the white rulers and the black masses of the New South by proclaiming Booker T. Washington as the national Negro leader. Besides celebrating the national reconciliation that developed from the ashes of Reconstruction, racial science displays at international expositions as-

sured the "average" American that Anglo-Saxons were a superior race
and could build empires. Fairs helped the fostering of an expansionist
public culture that found expression in the Spanish-American War of
1898.

Academic conferences as part of American public culture and interracial alliances among social scientists as public intellectuals are explored in chapter 3. By following W. E. B. Du Bois from his paper on
conservation of races at the American Negro Academy in 1897 to his Atlanta University conference of 1906 in which Franz Boas gave the commencement address exhorting his listeners to be proud of their African
ancestors, the chapter deals with the notion of active social science as a
weapon of social change. It compares the intellectual alliance between
Du Bois and Boas to the one between Booker T. Washington and sociologist Robert E. Park and explores how the quest for radical democracy
emerged from the theater of public culture at the New York National
Negro Conference leading to the formation of the interracial National
Association for the Advancement of Colored People (NAACP). Those
"believers in democracy" who gathered to revive the spirit of abolitionism created a public event at which social scientists as public activists announced their latest findings to finally dismiss the question of Negro inferiority.

By going behind the scenes of the National Negro Conference, chapter 4 explores the rituals of interracial alliances, the issue of power in the
struggle for racial equality, and the tensions of gender, race, and class
as experienced by Ida Wells-Barnett, Mary White Ovington, W. E. B.
Du Bois, and other founders of the NAACP. The public event closing the
chapter is the birth of the *Crisis,* the NAACP magazine edited by Du Bois
as a journal of militant social science.

Chapters 5 and 6 deal with meanings of racial uplifting to the world
of musical show business and to the National Negro Business League,
respectively. Both chapters end with riots, in New York in 1900 and in
Atlanta in 1906, in which white mobs assaulted black persons despite
how respectable these targets looked. Chapter 5 delves into the rituals
of the African-American musical theater, whose forms of empowerment
for black men and women differed from other economic fields. Chapter
6 studies social rituals of class differentiation within the New York black
community and the tension between moral uplifting and the mounting
materialistic culture of economic success. The chapter examines the
early annual meetings of the National Negro Business League, which
embodied the ideology of a color-blind market as a means of social advancement and which was Booker T. Washington's attempt to connect
all colored men and women engaged in business.

Chapter 7 looks at different pageants as rituals of race. Based on pageants in New York, the chapter explores events that had an impact on the whole nation and showed the conflict between the quest for radical democracy and versions of public culture. The Hudson-Fulton Festival of 1909, the staging of Du Bois's pageant *The Star of Ethiopia* for the fiftieth anniversary of Emancipation in 1913, the first public showing of D. W. Griffith's epic movie *The Birth of a Nation* in 1915 and the NAACP campaign against it, the staging of Percy MacKaye's masque *Caliban of the Yellow Sands* for the tercentennial commemoration of the birth of Shakespeare in 1916, the African-American "Silent Parade" of 1917 as a response to the East St. Louis massacre, and the black soldiers' parade of 1918 were expressions of the rich and conflictual public culture as the contested space for recognition of differences in postmodern American democracy.

The unifying theme of this book's narrative is public culture, broadly defined, as a conflictual space in which gender, race, and class alliances are made and remade in the ongoing battle for expansion of the boundaries of democracy. My major argument is that African Americans and their Euro-American allies in the battle for human rights and democracy played a central role in shaping public culture according to the values of participatory democracy.

When I read Edward Carr's *What Is History?* in the early 1970s, I was struck by the image of the historian looking at history as a marching procession. The historian, according to Carr, is simply one of those obscure figures moving in that procession, whose point of observation of the past is determined by his or her position in that march. I would also add that the historian's gender affects the point of observation and the description of advancement, arrest, change, and continuity in the past. In writing this book, I felt that my way of looking at American public events from the Civil War to World War I had been profoundly influenced by my experience as a woman who came of age in the early 1970s and whose radical notion of democracy shaped her later intellectual choices and her research subjects as a professional historian.

I owe many debts on both sides of the Atlantic Ocean for my research trips and intellectual inspiration. It was thanks to several grants I received from the Consiglio Nazionale delle Ricerche, the Fulbright Commission, the Woodrow Wilson Foundation, the Graduate Schools of Arts and Science of Columbia University, and the Dipartimento di Storia of the University of Florence that my graduate studies in New York were made possible. I had the great opportunity to study with Herbert Gutman of the Graduate Center of City University of New York, who warmly encouraged me to pursue social and cultural history and from whom I learned the enthusiasm of combining research and historical imagination. When I went to Columbia University and framed the research project for my doctoral dissertation, I received the most encouraging support, stimulating advice, and helpful criticism from Eric Foner, whose teaching and scholarship have deeply influenced me. Foner has followed the ambitious project of this book over the years and helped me to find direction when I was overwhelmed. I am also grateful to Elizabeth Blackmar, who always found the time to engage me in challenging discussions of my work.

During the decade I spent in the United States, I had the opportunity to meet other first-rate scholars who discussed and criticized my work. I am particularly in debt to Thomas Bender for his insightful criticism of my dissertation and to David Blight, who read drafts of this book and warmly encouraged me. I thank Henry Louis Gates Jr., Cornel West, and the fellows at the Du Bois Institute, Harvard University, for their friendship and stimulating reception of my work, and Catherine Clinton for having inspired the title of this book. I also need to extend special thanks to Jeannette Hopkins, whose insightful, severe yet constructive criticism of my manuscript at an early stage helped me enormously through the revisions. I am similarly grateful to Jane Curran, whose talent, generosity, and enthusiasm have turned her excellent copyediting into a very rewarding experience for the author. I also want to acknowledge Julie Falconer at the University Press of Virginia for her skilled assistance in turning my manuscript into a book.

In this book I use the terms "Negro" and "colored people" as I find them in my sources. Although in my interpretations I give preference to "African Americans" and "black Americans," today's commonly accepted terms, in discussing documents I leave the original language intact. As these terms connote change in black Americans' racial perceptions over time, their different usage should be maintained as the expression of change in individual and group identity.

Rituals of Race

Parades in New York City

Rituals of Loyalty and Freedom

Well the nation may forget, it may shut its eyes to the past . . . but
the colored people of this country are bound to keep the past in lively
memory till justice shall be done to them. FREDERICK DOUGLASS

Colored Troops Marching under Loyal Banners

Early on 5 March 1864, the Twentieth Regiment U.S. Colored Troops
left the camp at Riker's Island, New York harbor, and were transported
to Twenty-sixth Street, East River, where they disembarked, formed a
regimental line, and with loaded muskets and fixed bayonets marched
to Manhattan's Union Square.[1] They proceeded through a large crowd
of spectators and at one o'clock arrived in front of the Union League
clubhouse in Union Square, where flag presentation ceremonies had
been arranged. A vast crowd of citizens "of every shade of color, every
phase of social and political life," filled the square and streets, and every
door, window, veranda, tree, and housetop that commanded a view of
the scene was peopled with spectators.[2] In Union Square, on a platform,
stood "the ladies of the members," and across the street on another platform stood the members of the prestigious Union League Club.

The colored troops lined up on the square with their "burnished rifle
barrels, white gloves, white gaiters, polished boots," and Charles King,
the president of Columbia College, presented the colors: "I am proud
of the opportunity to stand before you as the representative of the Loyal
Women who have united in the patriotic purpose of presenting to you a

regimental flag." Having defined his public role as a "representative" of the ladies, King continued to speak on their behalf to the black soldiers. These "loyal women," he said, promised to provide "careful ministration for the sick and the wounded" and to supply charity and welfare to the families of the soldiers. The role of the ladies so defined, the president addressed the black soldiers as "emancipators of your own race, while acting as the defenders and champions of another." The black soldiers were in arms, King said, "not for the freedom and law of the white race alone, but for universal law and freedom."[3] The flag—a regimental banner showing a conquering eagle, a broken yoke, and the armed figure of liberty—was presented, together with a stand of colors, by the "ladies of the members," who had provided them at their own expense. An address, signed by 189 women prominent in New York society, was read on their behalf by President King:

> We, the Mothers, Wives, and Sisters of the members of the New York Union League Club, by whose liberality and intelligent patriotism, and under whose direct auspices, you have been organized into a body of National Troops for the defense of the Union, earnestly sympathizing in the great cause of American free nationality, and desirous of testifying, by some public memorial, our profound sense of the sacred object and the holy cause, in behalf of which you have enlisted, have prepared for you this Banner, at once the emblem of freedom and faith, and the symbol of woman's best wishes and prayers for our common country, and especially for your devotion thereto. When you look at the Flag and rush to battle . . . remember that it is also an emblem of love and honor from the daughters of this great metropolis to her brave champions in the field, and that they will anxiously watch your career, glorying in your heroism, ministering to you when wounded and ill, and honoring your martyrdom with benedictions and with tears.[4]

The physical presence of the ladies in a public ceremony had a high symbolic meaning, given the prevailing disapproval of women taking part in public demonstrations.[5] In view of the explosion of racist feelings in the city following the draft riot of July 1863, this public event was an important statement about class, race, and gender relations and the use of public space in one of the most exclusive areas of the city. The symbolic meaning of this use of the public space is further enhanced when other details of the celebrations are taken into account.

The stand of colors was given to Colonel Bartrum, the white officer in charge of the regiment, who, upon receiving the banner, praised his regiment "composed of a race hitherto despised, of a race almost hopelessly sunk in degradation, by a system of slavery" and labeled coward by "those among us who sympathize with the traitors now in arms against us." Praising the courage that black soldiers had already shown during the war, he thanked the "noble women" on behalf of his soldiers. The latter, after the flag presentation ceremonies were over, moved to the refreshment tables of "corpulent cans of coffee and fat baskets of sandwiches" furnished by the club, while the members, their ladies, and the officers (who were white) lunched at Jaunch's or Delmonico's or Maison Dorée. Black soldiers, who were not asked to give any public speech about their real motivation for volunteering in the Union army, were reported to have eaten "heartily." When the bugle blew, the soldiers fell into line for their march to a transport bound for New Orleans. The procession advanced in the following order: Police Superintendent Kennedy (a heroic figure during the July riots), one hundred policemen, the members of the Union League Club, colored friends of the recruits, the Governor's Island Band, and the Twentieth Regiment United States Colored Troops.[6]

The black soldiers' use of the public ceremonial space of the city was portrayed by the press as a strongly physical presence. According to the *New York Tribune*, the black soldiers made "a fine appearance in their blue uniforms, white gloves and white leggings. They are earthy and athletic fellows." Contrary to the worst expectations of those who thought blacks incapable of discipline, the *Tribune* reported that not one of the members of this completely "African regiment" disobeyed orders, "no one broke ranks to greet enthusiastic friends, no one manifested the least inclination to leave the service, and their marching was very creditable."[7]

Was the march a "truly magnificent demonstration, and a triumphant sign of progress," as the *Tribune* defined it? Scholars of civic ceremonies of the nineteenth century find the parade the characteristic genre of American public life in the context of rapid urban growth. Mary Ryan, who has studied American parades as representations of social order, defines an individual parade as a "peculiar text" by "multiple authors" and therefore susceptible to "multiple interpretations." From the perspective of retrieving white women in public, Ryan has convincingly shown that civic ceremonies are telling events in which the meaning attributed to sexual difference clearly emerges.[8] In the case of the Twentieth Regiment, it can be argued that the parade was coauthored by the members of the Union League, the silent ladies, and the black soldiers.

The *New York Times*, strongly in favor of black enlistment for the Union cause, stressed the fact that after only seven months from the draft riots, many of those colored men who had their homes assaulted by the

mob were now marching "in the honorable garb of United States soldiers, in vindication of their own manhood, and with the approval of a
countless multitude." The *Times* also remarked that these black men
were saving from conscription the same number of those who attacked
them during the riots. That was "a noble vengeance."[9]

Whose noble vengeance was it? A close look at the story of the Twentieth Regiment reveals an unbalanced alliance between the white elite
of the New York Union League Club, whose purpose was to show how
loyal merchants and intellectuals could be to the Union cause by raising
and displaying a regiment of black soldiers a few months after the draft
riots, and black leaders who saw in African-American participation in
the Union army the first step toward full citizenship. For Henry Highland Garnet, Frederick Douglass, Martin Delany, and almost all leading
black abolitionists who joined in the task of recruiting black troops for
the Union army, 5 March 1864 was a proud day.

The meaning African-American leaders gave to enlistment differed
from the intent the New York Republican conservative elite had in raising and displaying a colored regiment. This alliance showed that its
components did not give "loyalty" the same meaning.

The concept of loyalty in time of war is a very ambiguous one, as
George Fredrickson has shown. The Union League Club's concept of
loyalty served the interests of conservative nationalism. On the other
hand, Frederick Douglass turned the idea of loyalty into a radical issue
for black freedom since he saw enlistment in the Union army as an opportunity for black people to express their American nationalism and
achieve American citizenship, as David Blight points out: "A yearning to
belong might be combined with the right to fight in a struggle that
blacks could view as their very own."[10] Douglass's notion of loyalty did
not mean saving the Union with slavery; it meant saving the Union by
abolishing slavery.

"Let me sound once more the trump of war," thundered Douglass,
the powerful public speaker, abolitionist, and former fugitive slave, in
April 1863 from Rochester, New York, where he lived and edited the
Douglass' Monthly. "We should have blast on blast from that trumpet,"
the most convinced recruiter among the black leaders wrote in biblical
terms, "till thrilled with its notes every brave black man of the North, capable of bearing arms, shall come forth, clad in complete steel, ready to
make the twin monsters, slavery and rebellion, crumble together in the
dust." The eye of the nation, Douglass continued, was on the black man,
who was called to show his courage and to fight for the government
and, consequently, for "nationality." It was true that Congress had given
in to prejudice by establishing that colored men could not rise higher

than company officers, but Douglass encouraged young black men to enter the army anyway and be courageous. He was confident that if they deserved promotion, sooner or later they would inevitably get it. Douglass was strongly convinced that whoever looked upon a conflict between right and wrong—a point he constantly made in his later speeches—and did not "help the right against the wrong, despises and insults his own nature, and invites the contempt of mankind." There was no space for neutrality: "Manhood requires you to take sides. . . . there is nothing in your *color* to excuse you from enlisting in the service of the republic against its enemies."[11] It was time to change the reputation black people had "of being not a brave people, but a patient, docile, and peaceful people" by fighting against the rebels.

By 1862 the war took on an antislavery character that pushed Lincoln to give his approval to black enlistment and issue the Emancipation Proclamation of 1 January 1863. The more difficult the military situation became, the more willing northerners were to employ black soldiers to defend the Union. In the summer of 1863, the War Department authorized the governors of several northern states to recruit Negro regiments to fill their state troop quotas. At the end of October 1863, there were fifty-eight regiments of colored troops in the Union army with a total of 37,482 men, including white officers.[12] But in New York black enlistment did not proceed.

At the beginning of 1863, many northern governors had already authorized recruitment of colored regiments, given the growing difficulty in raising state quotas of troops in an unexpectedly demanding war. A few weeks after the Emancipation Proclamation, the secretary of war authorized the governor of Massachusetts, John A. Andrew, to enlist black volunteers. Abolitionist Andrew spearheaded the recruitment of the first Negro regiment in the North, the celebrated Massachusetts Fifty-fourth. The governor appointed a supervisor of enlistments to collaborate with well-known black leaders as recruiting agents. Led by young Colonel Robert Gould Shaw, a member of a wealthy and refined New England abolitionist family, and made up of black men who in great number were free people of color and to a lesser extent were fugitive slaves, the Massachusetts Fifty-fourth suffered a valiant defeat in the assault of Fort Wagner near Charleston, South Carolina, on 18 July 1863. Following the lead of Massachusetts, Rhode Island and Pennsylvania recruited their black regiments in the summer of 1863. In New York State the opposition of Democratic governor Horatio Seymour, whose election in 1862 was the result of his open opposition to the Emancipation Proclamation, delayed the enlistment of black troops.[13]

In the spring of 1863, New York's black leaders were still recruiting for the Massachusetts Fifty-fourth. On 27 April a large recruiting meeting was held at Shiloh Church, chaired by the Reverend Henry Highland Garnet and addressed by Frederick Douglass. In spite of the eloquent appeals of both speakers, at the end only one young man came forward to enlist. More appeals followed, and Douglass declared he felt "ashamed," but no one volunteered. At that point a Mr. Johnson from the audience explained that young men hesitated to enlist not because of cowardice but because of respect for their manhood. If the government would grant them all the rights of citizens and soldiers, Johnson said, he was convinced that within twenty days he would be able to bring not just one man but five thousand men to enlist.

By the end of July 1863, the month in which occurred both the sacrifice of the Massachusetts Fifty-fourth and the killing of a number of innocent black people by mob action during the draft riots, Douglass stopped promoting enlistment. In a letter to Major G. L. Stearns of 1 August 1863, he expressed his will to "leave to others the work of persuading colored men to join the Union Army." He could no longer do it, as he felt "that colored men have much overrated the enlightenment, justice and generosity of our rulers at Washington." Douglass thought that he had somewhat contributed to "that false estimate." When Jefferson Davis announced that colored prisoners would be either returned to slavery or killed—in other words, they would be treated not as soldiers but as felons—black people still had faith that President Lincoln and his advisers would do something to protect them. But no word came from the president when free men from Massachusetts "were caught and sold into slavery in Texas." And no word was said, Douglass continued, when courageous black soldiers fighting at Fort Wagner "were captured, some mutilated and killed, and others sold into slavery." According to Douglass, "the case looks as if the confiding colored soldiers had been betrayed . . . by the very Government in whose defense they were heroically fighting."[14] Even though Douglass stopped his active promotion of enlistment, he nevertheless continued to support the idea of blacks fighting for the Union and their freedom.

Although Douglass could count on the Reverend Henry Highland Garnet's commitment to recruitment, black New Yorkers did not come forward. Unlike former fugitive slave Douglass, who thought his life represented the way America should go beyond racism to form a society based on universal human rights and who advocated black integration, New Yorker Henry Garnet was among those black abolitionists who in the 1850s espoused the cause of emigration to Africa or the Caribbean. After the passage of the Slave Fugitive Act and the Dred Scott decision, Garnet, together with Martin Delany, the founder of black nationalism, became very pessimistic about the realization of black equality in the United States. Unlike Douglass, who grew up with no family ties, Garnet escaped with his family from a Maryland plantation in 1824 at the age of nine and grew up in New York's African-American community, where he received the best education available at that time for a black youth. Garnet belonged to a new generation of free Negroes who broke with the cautious manners of the previous generation in the struggle for racial equality. Largely inspired by West Indian emancipation, the new generation became more radical and more independent from white abolitionists.[15]

By the early 1840s, moving away from what he considered apolitical Garrisonianism, Garnet became an eminent exponent of political abolitionism, an eloquent speaker for the cause of Negroes' full citizenship on the basis of historical, religious, and economic considerations. In 1843 Garnet was ordained minister of the Presbyterian church in Troy, New York. He made his church an important station of the Underground Railroad, set up a grammar school, as he believed education was the key to black progress, preached temperance, and urged African Americans to leave the cities and gain economic independence by owning farms. Yet, when the Civil War broke out, Garnet joined Frederick Douglass, the most ardent advocate of integration of black Americans, in recruiting colored soldiers for the Union army. "We should be fighting a double battle," Douglass thought, "against slavery at the South and against prejudice and prescription at the North." Of the 179,000 black soldiers who served in the Union army, 141,000 were former slaves from the South and 33,000 were free blacks from northern states, with the remainder from Canada, the Caribbean, or Africa.[16]

In June 1863 the War Department established that black troops were to be paid ten dollars a month, from which three dollars were taken to cover clothing, instead of thirteen dollars, as common white soldiers received. Protests spread everywhere black troops were recruited. When on 13 July antidraft riots broke out in New York City, in which a dozen blacks were lynched by mobs, military discrimination could no longer be patiently accepted in the hope of attaining equality in the war aftermath.

It was at that juncture that the recently formed Union League Club decided to raise money for a New York Negro regiment. Together with the Association for Promoting Colored Volunteering, led by Henry Highland Garnet, the Union League Club formed the Joint Committee on Volunteering. By December the committee had raised $18,000 and proceeded to recruit Negroes for the Twentieth Regiment to fill the state's draft quota.

How can this unlikely joint venture be explained? What was the purpose of the Union League Club? "The Union League Club of New York
is the child of the United States Sanitary Commission," Unitarian minister and commission secretary Henry W. Bellows wrote in later years.
That body was not "a merely humanitarian or beneficent association,"
Bellows assured. The commissioners, all residents of New York, "were
men with strong political purpose" who believed in "the value of a great
common national life." They saw love for the national cause and the national soldier as an antidote for state feelings and local pride. How was
the Sanitary Commission related to the idea of a Union League Club?
According to Bellows, it was Professor Wolcott Gibbs, a distinguished
chemist, who suggested that the idea of education in nationality on
which the Sanitary Commission was founded needed to find expression
in a club "devoted to the social organization of the sentiment of loyalty
to the Union."[17]

That the idea of loyalty should take the form of a club became clear
in January 1861, soon after the secession of South Carolina, when Fernando Wood, the city's Democratic mayor, proclaimed in a speech to
the New York Common Council that a dissolution of the Union seemed
inevitable, and that it was New York's right to declare itself a free city, independent of both the state and national governments. With "the
brethren of the Slave States," the mayor continued, "we have friendly relations and a common sympathy." New York's ships went everywhere in
the Union, and so did New York's capital, energy, and undertakings.
The city therefore needed to keep itself in friendly relations with every
section, Wood candidly remarked. As citizens of a free city, New Yorkers
could live "free from taxes, and have cheap goods nearly duty free," the
mayor concluded.[18]

Sympathetic feelings for the South were well spread in the city. The
northern metropolis was the financial center for the South, counting
just a few important banks and even fewer factories. New York banks financed the cotton crops of the South, New York shippers freighted
them to the English midlands, and New York wholesalers sold the South
the tools, wagons, and machinery for its plantations. Fancy retail stores
in New York furnished the elegant plantation houses and dressed southern ladies. So connected with the South was New York's economy that
feelings spread in the city that the collapse of the slave economy would
drag New York's economy down with it.

The urge to suppress the growth of the pro-secession feeling in New
York led to the formation of the Union League Club, as did the election
in 1862 of Governor Horatio Seymour, who publicly declared the war
unconstitutional. Furthermore, recognition of the Southern Confeder-

acy by the Pope, Louis Napoleon, and the English Tories emboldened New York's secessionist forces. The idea of founding a patriotic club to oppose these forces was passed on to Frederick Law Olmsted, the "father" of Central Park, for its concrete materialization.[19]

The day after the Democratic victory in New York Olmsted elaborated on his political philosophy of loyalty and provided organizational details. The club he envisioned would be formed by men who, like the members of the Sanitary Commission, were loyal to the founding fathers of the country. These men of highest quality were, in Olmsted's mind, "the hereditary, natural aristocracy." This gentlemen-only club in which they would gather "would be a club of true American aristocracy," a club "which shall not be felt by an English gentleman to be the mere ape and parrot of a European gentry." Having established the principle within the boundaries of the nineteenth-century male-dominated public sphere, Olmsted then proceeded to elaborate a rigid method by which the club would close its doors to whoever did not have "blue blood." Members were to be selected "one by one, with great caution." He thought of three classes of men: men "of substance" and established high social position, including men of "good stock or of notably high character," such as men of letters and science and men with "old colonial names"; "clever men" in the arts who had made their mark; and "promising young men," especially those "innocent rich young men" who did not understand what their place would be in American society. Olmsted clearly dissociated "standing" from wealth and imagined the club members as a group of New Yorkers supporting themselves entirely from their offices and their ideas. He envisioned what historian Thomas Bender has called the "metropolitan gentry," who aimed at replacing politicians in directing the country.[20]

Olmsted himself belonged to the first generation of urban professionals. At the opening of the war Olmsted, a landscape architect, was the clever and efficient director of New York's Central Park project. He was also well known for his reportage on the slave states for the *New York Times* in the 1850s. His letters from the South did not include any abolitionist argument on the moral sin of slavery and its dehumanizing effects but framed instead an antislavery appeal on the grounds of its obsolescence as an economic system. Olmsted's appeal had a tremendous impact on the development of a free-labor ideology for the new Republican Party.[21]

Actions at the founding meeting of the Union League Club in January 1863 followed Olmsted's recommendations. It was proposed that the club should not simply "cultivate a profound national devotion, as distinguished from State or sectional feeling," but should also strive to

"elevate and uphold the popular faith in republican government; to dig-
nify politics as a pursuit and a study; to awaken a practical interest in
public affairs in those who have become discouraged; to enforce a sense
of the sacred obligations inherent in citizenship; and, finally, to bring to
bear upon national life all that a body of earnest and patriotic men can
accomplish by unified effort."[22]

In *Historical Sketch of the Union League of New York,* Henry Bellows recalled the riots of July 1863, when colored people in New York "were
pursued with an ignorant but bloody hatred by the populace of the city."
The riots, in Bellows's view, "took the place of the insurrection planned
by the enemy, with its sympathizers in New York City." Many members of
the Union League Club were actively involved in sustaining the military,
civil, and municipal officers in crushing the rioters. Acton and Kennedy,
the leaders of the New York City police, belonged to the Union League
Club.[23]

The draft riots of July 1863 were a turning point in the Union
League Club's campaign for nationalism and loyalty. The members, bar-
ricaded in the club's building in Union Square during the rioting, decided to equip a regiment of colored troops and send them to the front.
To challenge public sentiment, the members also decided "they would
march these freedmen through the city streets."[24]

Recruitment for the Union army became an important expression of
the Union League Club's active national loyalty. The members donated
$18,000 to be used in the recruitment of colored regiments. Early in
November 1863 seven Union League members were appointed to the
Committee on Volunteering. On 22 November the committee sent a
letter to Governor Horatio Seymour asking permission to raise a regiment of companies of colored men in New York State. They added that
thanks to the influence of the Union League Club, "composed as it is of
five hundred of the wealthiest and most influential gentlemen of the
city," the raising of a considerable body of colored troops in New York
would be easily accomplished, giving, in so doing, a considerable contribution toward the filling of the state quota. A few days later Governor
Seymour answered that the matter of organizing Negro regiments was
entirely the concern of the War Department in Washington, and that he
had no power to authorize such recruitment. Then the Committee on
Volunteering decided to apply directly to the secretary of war.[25] On 3
December 1863, authorization was granted. The letter from the War
Department made clear that no bounties would be paid to these troops
and that they would receive one ration and ten dollars per month, three
dollars of which would cover clothing. It also designated the regiment as
the Twentieth Regiment U.S. Colored Troops, whose prescribed numb-

er of (white) commissioned officers would be appointed by the president and whose site of rendezvous would be Riker's Island in the New York harbor. The Committee on Volunteering immediately communicated the received authorization to Governor Seymour but received no reply. Not wasting any time, the committee immediately contacted "prominent colored men in this city and solicited their co-operation." Given the difficulties black leaders encountered in recruiting, they were glad to have such a powerful ally on their side.

The Committee on Volunteering sent a circular to every New York town in which they asked officials to induce colored men to enlist in the Twentieth Regiment, explaining that the volunteers would receive more bounty in hand than elsewhere and they would be protected against discrimination by the influential New York Union League Club.[26] Two hundred colored men were rapidly drafted and sent to Riker's Island. They were among those parading on 5 March 1864 and greeted by the "loyal women" in Union Square.

Before the Committee on Volunteering took exclusive responsibility for recruitment, many colored men had been deceptively enlisted by other agents to fill the state quota. Many recruits were defrauded of their bounties, some men were drugged before enlisting, and others were deceived regarding the service expected of them.[27] Investigation by the committee revealed that the recruitment agents at General Spinola's headquarters in Lafayette Hall stopped colored men on the streets, promised them jobs as coachmen, gave each a glass of drugged liquor, and then had them sign enlistment papers. The *New York Tribune* reported that old men over sixty were forced to enlist, young boys were kidnapped on their way to or from school, and men with incurable diseases were accepted. However, the Democratic *New York Herald* defended General Spinola's practices by arguing that other states followed similar practices and that the quota had to be filled anyway.

Crowded public meetings at African-American churches exposed these deceptive practices. The Reverend Henry Highland Garnet and other eminent black clergymen signed and distributed throughout the state circulars explaining the amount of bounties and wages paid to colored men and the rights of their families to relief. On behalf of the Committee on Volunteering, Garnet visited Riker's Island.

The volunteers included men from the British West Indies, Haiti, Canada, Maryland, Virginia, Kentucky, and the American West, yet the majority of recruits came "from the respectable, industrious and hard-working classes of our own State and City," including some who had been driven out of their homes by the mob during the riots of July 1863.

On 2 and 3 March 1864, arrangements were made for fourteen hundred women, children, and other family members of the volunteers to visit Riker's Island. Three regiments had been raised by then, and the first, the Twentieth, was ready to leave. On 5 March the Twentieth Regiment paraded, marking "an era of progress in the political and social history of New York," as the *New York Times* put it. Vincent Colyer, the general superintendent of recruiting for the Committee on Volunteering, had two thousand copies of the written remarks of the "loyal ladies" distributed among the parading soldiers and their friends. He also distributed one thousand copies of the *Anglo African* containing the complete muster roll of the regiment, with the name of each soldier and mailing address of his nearest relative.[28]

This parade was meant to send a clear message to the conservative groups of the middle and upper classes that had supported the riots: the members of the Union League Club established that acceptance of black emancipation was one of the requirements for entry into the best circles of the upper society.[29] At a symbolic level, the men of the Union League Club and their silent ladies created a patronizing alliance between the white upper classes and free blacks in the name of the Union. The values that characterized this alliance were those of an elite of an "intelligent, cultivated, gentlemanly caste," who thought of the future of northern capitalism in terms of "free labor" and state control. Their direct antagonists were the slave society, immigrant Catholic laborers, and the Democrats who supported both groups. The notion of moral "uplifting" appealed to leaders of the black community who saw in this alliance a step toward the real emancipation of the respectable of their race.[30]

One of the most telling aspects of this alliance, however, was the creation of a public ceremonial space in which differences of race and gender were clearly defined and accepted. The ritual symbolically brought together white women and black men in the same ceremonial space. White women appeared as symbolic figures who preserved a cohesive notion of the republican order by maintaining authority over their separate sphere. Black women, organized in an association with the financial support of the Union League Club to provide assistance to the recruits, in a letter to the club members expressed their gratefulness for "the noble acts of those patriotic ladies who presented our troops with elegant stands of colors and cheered them by their presence on the days of their departure." As mothers, wives, and sisters of those heroic men, they had every reason to believe that "our men will show by their valor and courage on the field that the kindness and encouragement of the ladies of New York were not vainly bestowed."[31]

There was no question about the actual exclusion of "the ladies of New York" from public speaking. Their presence was kept at a symbolic level, as a cathartic instrument of purification of the public space. Yet, these ladies, kept silent during the ceremony, were actively involved in the work of the U.S. Sanitary Commission. In November 1863 Henry Bellows, the president of the Sanitary Commission, had gathered at the Union League clubhouse about one hundred of the most "patriotic women" of New York to plan a metropolitan fair. The ladies organized it and realized more than one million dollars for the care and nursing of the wounded of the Union army.[32] Fund-raising was part of the unprecedented and extraordinary mobilization of over two hundred thousand middle-class women in the North. Besides their voluntary work for the Sanitary Commission, these women were the body and soul of the freedmen's aid movement to help keep liberated slaves from falling into destitution. Most of the teachers who went south to teach the former slaves were women.[33]

The provocative shock effect of the joint presence of white women and black men in the public ceremonial space succeeded with the conservative Democratic *Herald,* which in a mocking fashion called the ceremony the "inauguration of miscegenation." The paper made vitriolic comments on the different treatment that "the brave boys" of Maine, Vermont, Massachusetts, New Jersey, and many other regiments of white soldiers received in the city: "we gave none of them such a reception as our first families gave this regiment of negroes. Aristocracy sides with aristocracy, and so our best society neglected the common white trash and reserved their utmost courtesies for the refined, cultivated and chivalric recruits from Sullivan street, Broadway Alley and the Five Points."[34]

It was the symbolic marriage between the lowest of the Five Points—the degraded area of Manhattan near today's Federal Plaza—and the upper classes of Fifth Avenue that the *Herald* mocked. The paper derisively stated that "the daughters of Fifth Avenue" had made a promise of marriage to the black men, for they had called the flag "an emblem of love and honor from the daughters of this great metropolis to her brave champions." If these promises were not to be broken, according to the *Herald,* the phrase "love and honor" needed only the word "obey" to become equivalent to a marriage ceremony. The anti-Republican paper claimed this article, entitled "Fifth Avenue and the Five Points—Practical Movements toward Miscegenation," was a response to a "mysterious pamphlet" the paper declared it had received, which affirmed the superiority of the "negro race," declared the degradation of the Irishman who had "sunk below the level of the most degraded negro," and pushed forward racial intermingling with "healthy, loving, warm-blooded negroes" as "essential to American progress." The *Herald* feared that what it termed "a silly pamphlet" endorsing radical abolitionist issues outlined the future direction of American society: giving social and political rights to blacks, men and women, and sharing "hearts and homes" with blacks. According to the *Herald,* Wendell Phillips, Henry Ward Beecher, William Lloyd Garrison, Angelina G. Weld, Sarah M. Grimke, Lucretia Mott, and Horace Greeley endorsed a radical view of abolitionism and agreed with the content of the pamphlet. Citing the example of a William Wells Brown, "a negro and ready to marry a white heiress off hand," the *Herald* seemed to focus on a fear of miscegenation as a form of protection from a threat of a Republican conspiracy whose visible signs were in the ceremonies that the Union League Club staged for the black recruits. The anti-Republican paper used the word "degeneration" in connection with the fear of miscegenation and similarly ridiculed Charles King, who "degenerated from journalist to a professor" and "retired into that asylum for good society people of weak intellects—Columbia College."

If the symbol of marriage between "the aristocracy of the Five Points and the aristocracy of Fifth Avenue" evoked the fear of political exclusion from the conservative Democratic *Herald,* what did it actually mean to black men and women? Black men were called to fight to preserve, in a way, their subordinate role in the northern industrial society by responding to the silent appeal of its first ladies. Black soldiers were depicted as physically entering the public space, with their earthy manners and their good qualities of obedience and subordination. They were given citizenship in the republic as long as they accepted their subordinate and segregate status and promised to morally uplift themselves according to the values of the progressive white elite. But there was no real connection between the world of the white elite and that of the black soldiers. The Union League people ate at the best restaurants of the city, where the most respectable free blacks were not allowed, and the black soldiers devoured sandwiches with their earthy appetite. Gender difference within the black community was also enhanced by this public use of the city space. Black women followed their men, who were parading for their manhood. Like white women, their presence in public space assumed a highly symbolic value. Their being pushed to the background of the public ceremonial space, however, purified their status. The black women were perceived as the mothers, wives, sisters, and daughters of citizens and not as the symbol of miscegenation that the slave woman represented.

After the Twentieth Regiment, the Union League raised the Twenty-sixth and the Thirty-first Regiments of colored troops. The three regiments were reported to have behaved courageously in battle, but half the men lost their lives. During World War I the New York Union League Club paraded another black regiment going, this time, to

France to "make the world free for democracy," at a time when the
lynching of black people was no longer an exclusively southern practice. By then the Union League Club no longer represented the "aristocracy" of the city's public culture or black people's exclusive ally. It
was still an exclusive all-male, loyal Republican club, but the merchant
princes of the early years had given way to members whose fortunes
came from the railroads, manufacturing, and Wall Street.[35]

The ghost of the draft riots haunted New York's elite for a long time.
Scholarship has shown that the riots cannot be regarded simply as a
one-dimensional episode of Irish ethnic hatred, white working-class racism, Confederate-sympathizing or Peace Democrat treason, or poor
New Yorkers' resentment of the inequities of the Conscription Act, although each of these themes was present in those bloody riots. The riots
of 1863 assaulted the symbols of the new order created by the Republican Party and the Civil War. After the conscription office, rioters attacked government offices, factories, and the elegant homes of the Republican elite; they burned the Colored Orphan Asylum, the symbol of
the alliance between the Fifth Avenue aristocracy and the Five Points,
and expressed a genocidal will toward black residents.[36]

The role that black soldiers played in the Civil War extended beyond
showing they were courageous human beings. Their service, which
meant to them more than saving the Union, influenced the debate on
equality before the law and black suffrage, which arose in the aftermath
of the Civil War. Eric Foner has told the story of those talented and ambitious black men who, after serving in the army, became political
leaders of radical Reconstruction in the South.[37]

Celebrating the Union Victory
and the Cooper Union Mass Meeting

On 6 March 1865, the Empire City witnessed one of the most "enthusiastically unanimous exhibitions of public rejoicing." The city celebrated
the victories of the Union with a military and civic procession attracting
an extremely large public. If the Union League's staging of the presentation of colors and the parade of black soldiers shaped the postslavery
moral order, the gigantic celebration of 1865 created a public culture
based on the unity of moderate Democrats and Republicans and their
common faith in the progress of capitalism in the Union. The organizers of the celebration, "the citizens of New York engaged in the pursuits of commerce," wrote Abraham Lincoln a letter of congratulations
for the success of the national forces.

Only white men paraded in the military, civic, and industrial procession, which extended for almost seven miles, lasted almost six hours,

and gathered almost two million spectators. The huge parade filled downtown and midtown Manhattan with colors and those exotic tricks that in the second half of the nineteenth century characterized American mass political events. In accordance with the tradition of the great Barnum Circus, two elephants and two camels closed the long military and civic procession. Each division had its own color: blue for the military, black for the civic and industrial displays, and red for the New York City Fire Department. The display of the units of the all-white Union army was impressive, but even more stirring was the civic portion of the parade in which marched all trades and select ethnic associations. The latter were represented by "Teutonic fellow citizens," five hundred singers of the Allgemeine Saengerbund, forty people of the Robert Blum Mutual Aid Union of Germans, and two hundred people of the Italian Benevolent Society. In the same division marched one thousand people, including one hundred singers of the Mechanics' and Artisans Association of Social Reformers, the Nineteenth Ward Republican Club, and the Total Abstinence Association.[38]

The division representing the industrial order was a powerful display of that northern and western business world that had made downtown Manhattan its administrative center. It was a fragmented world of small and big business presented to the public as symbolically united in a spectacular circus performance. Among hundreds of industrial *tableaux vivants* were displays by the Singer Company, with sewing machines being operated by company employees; the great American Tea Company, with a ten-horse truck; Steinway and Sons, with 450 workmen demonstrating the manufacture of a piano along the route; L. Schepp, with a four-horse truck decorated with flags and loaded with coffee, tea, and spices, from which packages of coffee were handed out; Perkins, Stern & Company, promoting the interests and products of California by distributing thousands of bottles of wine to the ladies; Eureka Segar Machine, with a two-horse truck producing ten thousand cigars that were freely handed out to the people on the route; and Leslie, Ellioy & Company, with two four-horse wagons portraying the manufacture of polar refrigerators and gas and kerosene stoves. The tradespeople's parade was closed by Hannibal, the "Mammoth War Elephant," and Tippoo Sahib, a performing elephant.[39] The trade division was followed by the new fire department, with two thousand men in uniform, steam engines, hoses, and hook and ladder companies. The display of this professionally organized body marked the end of the era of volunteer firemen as the popular heroes of white working-class New York.[40]

The giant procession ended in Union Square. A reception was held at a palace, the Maison Dorée, whose large rooms were packed with visitors. The ladies outnumbered the gentlemen and welcomed the soldiers and the committeemen "with cheers and waving their cambric handkerchiefs."[41] Unlike the ladies at the Union League Club parade of colored soldiers, who had appeared in public during the ritual, women at the Maison Dorée had no role and were just an ornamental appendix.

In Union Square Major General John A. Dix gave a long speech on the cause of the Union and the victorious struggle "to preserve unbroken the national compact." The Honorable Edward Pierrepont remarked that the Union was a necessity because American citizens were "of one language, of one blood, and of the same religion." He observed that the North, with its material wealth, was open to trade and emigration from the world, while there was no immigration to the South, where the slaves were fleeing to northern lines: "half sleeping in the dull brain of the negro has lain some sense of his rights, and some shadowy tradition that his deliverance was to come from the North." According to Pierrepont, it was fortunate that "Sherman's cannon wakes up the negro."[42]

No one mentioned the black soldiers fighting for the Union or the bloody draft riots of the previous July. It would have been out of place in a celebration of the Union's victories and the development of capitalism. As one speaker put it, the events celebrated on that day were "the victories on land and water, the achievements of science and arts, the advancement in agriculture and commerce." All these events had educated the nation: "the mass has been rendered homogeneous, all sorts and conditions of men have met and have been subjected to the same discipline and endured the same hardships and trials in camp and on the battlefield." Someone else made clear that the end of slavery was not the reason for rejoicing: "If by the advancing of the Union army in restoring law and constitutional authority, bondmen are liberated and the tutelage of the superior over all the inferior race is terminated, let it be." The cause of abolitionism was detestable, for the Union "is a government of white men, and should not and shall not be destroyed for the sake of the African." Another participant congratulated those who had come together, not as Republicans or Democrats to celebrate a party triumph, or as New Yorkers to celebrate a local festival, but as American citizens to rejoice in the reunification of the republic.[43]

In the evening this public of American citizens at Union Square was treated to a spectacular display of fireworks announced by a rapid discharge of rockets of every hue, color, and shade. Among the illuminated designs representing the Union forces, the most cheered was one in which the word "Sumter" appeared with the rebel flag floating over it, and then an explosion tore the rebel flag to pieces, its place being taken

by the old Stars and Stripes. As in the festivals of the early republic, fireworks that celebrated the past, present, and future of the new Union
showed an American flag with mottoes such as "One Country, One
People, One Destiny" and the names of "Grant, Thomas, Sherman, Porter, Sheridan," and "Atlanta, Nashville, Savannah, Charleston and Will-
mington." On the opposite side of the square, fireworks represented the
American coat of arms, with a wheel of Chinese, Egyptian, and radiant
fires, closing with the figures of Justice and Liberty and the motto "Union Forever." Then representations of battle scenes followed.[44]

This celebration was a reenactment of early republican traditions that
a committee of wealthy citizens felt compelled to promote.[45] The message was the unification of all people in one big reconciled nation, beyond party differences. To a cheerful crowd, the ending of the war signi-
fied the appearance of American progress and industrial development.
It was a celebration of the new federal government and its industrial order, staged as a spectacular political pageant of the triumph of the North
in which black Americans, however, were not called upon to participate.

During the war the North became very prosperous. Railroads, essential for transportation of troops and supplies, made astonishing earn-
ings. The combined boom of the railroads and the meat-packing industry, for feeding the troops, made the city of Chicago, which had the
most important slaughterhouses and railroad system in the country, the
first commercial center of the Midwest. By the early 1890s Chicago challenged and defeated New York's attempt to host the World's Columbian
Exposition. The new industrial bourgeoisie tied its interests to the Republican Party and the national state. The Union efforts needed the
mobilization of enormous financial resources.[46]

From an economic point of view, the celebration of the Union victories symbolized the triumph of the industrial bourgeoisie, the expansion of markets, the development of new forms of industrial organization, and the growth of the railroad system in the country. New York's
old commercial elite was now witnessing the emergence of a powerful
class of industrialists and railroad owners, a class of professional and
white-collar workers, and a working class of wage earners that replaced
independent craftsmen. Eric Foner has shown how labor relations,
party politics, attitudes toward the South, and every single aspect of life
in the North was profoundly affected by Reconstruction.[47]

In his presidential address of 1866, John Jay, the new president of the
New York Union League Club, caught the meaning of this profound
change and offered a bridge to the South. He observed that under the
new economic influences the most enlightened men of the South were
proposing a new "policy of freedom and justice." This new class, Jay be-

lieved, would secure the prosperity of the South and "the happiness of both whites and blacks by harmony between the races." Almost forecasting the alliance between the "New South" and black leader Booker T. Washington in the last decade of the century, Jay emphatically asserted that "the importance of those races to each other is large and mutual."

According to Jay, Alexander H. Stephens, the South's wartime vice president, was an example of the South's profound ideological change. Jay was impressed by a speech Stephens delivered to the legislature of Georgia early in 1866 in which he advised the South to accept the result of the war and to seek "happiness and prosperity" in the Union and "cordial relations as equal citizens between those who so recently were masters and slaves." Jay stated that Stephens accepted the idea of the freedmen's equality before the law "in the possession and enjoyment of all rights of personal liberty and property." Jay defined "enlightened" as someone like Stephens who, after serving a brief period of imprisonment in Boston, was reelected to Congress in 1873 and died ten years later as the governor of Georgia. Jay thought that the Union League Club could help these enlightened people by opening its doors "to Southern gentlemen coming to New York, who however deeply involved they may have been in the Rebellion, are now prepared not only to acquiesce in the result of the war and the abolition of slavery, but to assist in the work of reconstruction upon the basis of universal education and equal right." This social intermingling in the elegant rooms of the Union League Club would emphasize a common consciousness of "a deep and earnest desire that no sectional strife may again disturb our peace" and that the South and the North "may be more closely bound than ever before, in the bonds of a common interest and mutual affection."[48] Although Jay's presidential speech offered an "aristocratic" version of the emerging ideology of national reconciliation as an alliance of the "enlightened men" of the North and the South, as demanded by the tradition of the Union League Club, a mass meeting of the "citizens of New York" held at Cooper Union in February 1866 gave a different version.

Cooper Union, a building located in downtown Manhattan that was donated in 1859 by industrialist engineer Peter Cooper "for the advancement and diffusion of the knowledge of arts and sciences," by 1866 had become the most important gathering place of what Thomas Bender calls the "civic culture" of New York City.[49] The mass meeting of 22 February of that year was called to support President Andrew Johnson's annual message to Congress and his veto of the Freedmen's Bureau Bill. Some of those merchants and other eminent citizens who were involved in planning the celebration of the Union victory in March 1866 appeared among the organizers of the Cooper Union event as well. What was the meaning of this mass meeting in New York in support of President Johnson, the Unionist Democrat from Tennessee and former vice president who took office after Lincoln's assassination?

An advocate of state's rights, Johnson aimed his program of Reconstruction at restoring the political power of southern whites by giving them the authority to define the legal status of the freedmen and by offering forgiveness to former rebels. In the summer of 1865, the Freedmen's Bureau, which had been authorized to take possession of land seized under the confiscation laws and to lease it to the freedmen, was forced by Johnson to release the eight hundred thousand acres of land taken from Confederate supporters during the war and to return it to the now pardoned owners. The Republican Congress assumed that the president would sign the Freedmen's Bureau and the Civil Rights Bills, but Johnson vetoed the Freedmen's Bureau Bill, finding it unconstitutional and financially unaffordable. He also thought the bill was morally unsound, implying that providing assistance to the freedmen would lead them to a life of laziness instead of working for a living. Johnson's veto "voiced themes that to this day have sustained opposition to federal intervention on behalf of blacks," Eric Foner observes.[50] The modernity of Johnson's politics also appears in the powerful effect his veto had on reuniting northern and southern whites' interests under a pervasive ideology of national reconciliation in the name of which all political achievements of blacks during Reconstruction would be erased by the turn of the century.

Johnson won support from conservative business interests in the North that were represented at the mass meeting held at Cooper Union. The "citizens of New York" approved of Johnson's annual message to Congress and his veto message concerning the Freedmen's Bureau Bill, and they wished "to promote harmony in the public councils of the country." The call for this meeting, signed by several thousand people, received an extraordinary response. The gathering of people was so huge that even the large facilities of Cooper Union could not accommodate them. The hall was decorated with portraits of President Johnson, flanked by those of Generals Grant and Sherman, and many American flags. The chair of the committee arranging the meeting was George Opdyke, a strenuous supporter of Johnson's policy, which he found "at once so just, so wise, so salutary and so comprehensive as to embrace all classes and all interests of our common country."[51] The list of the unanimously elected vice presidents of the meeting, presided over by Francis B. Cutting in the presence of Secretary of State William H. Seward, included more than 150 of the most well known New York merchants, manufacturers, bankers, academics, and intellectuals.

The meeting discussed the different views prevailing in the executive and legislative branches of government. The "task of pacification" was the main point addressed by keynote speaker David Dudley Field. In Field's view, the only element of disturbance to prevent accomplishing this task was "the political condition of freedmen." He found that both the president and Congress agreed on the fact that the freedmen were entitled to the "civil rights of any other class of citizens," namely the rights of person and property, the right to sue and testify. There was no question that *equality before the law* was what freedmen should get. But the divisive question was whether they should be given political rights. Field summarized the four arguments of those in favor of the freedmen's suffrage: the elective franchise was a natural right; every person had the title to participate in the enactment of laws; blacks gave their help in suppressing the rebellion and therefore had to be endowed with the privilege of participating in the government of the country they helped to save; and suffrage was the only safeguard of colored people for preserving their freedom and civil rights. Those who opposed the freedmen's suffrage, with whom Field sympathized, maintained that in respect to the states, whether those involved in the rebellion or those loyal to the Union, the federal government did not have any right to interfere with the question of the elective franchise; and that wherever there was a large number of ignorant and debased blacks, it was unwise and dangerous to grant them suffrage. Field, in supporting Johnson's policy, expressed his agreement with those who thought granting suffrage to freedmen would be an interference of the federal government on the states: "New York has no more right to say who shall or shall not vote in Virginia, than Virginia has to say who shall or shall not vote in New York." He also thought that having fought for the country did not necessarily give blacks the right to govern it, or to participate in its government: "If it were otherwise, every brave boy, from sixteen to twenty-one, who fought in the Union ranks . . . should have a vote, instead of waiting for years to participate in the government to which he is subjected." Like minors, blacks could bear arms but were considered mentally immature for suffrage. By the first decade of the twentieth century, the argument of "immaturity" became the authoritative language of social scientists.

After resolutions in support of President Johnson were passed, Secretary of State William Seward addressed the mass meeting. A conservative Republican, he opened with a joke on the difference between the president as "a man of nerve" in the executive chair in Washington and the "nervous men"—obviously the Radical Republicans—in the House of Representatives. He attacked the Radical Republicans' proposal to force the rebel states to give political rights to the freedmen or face the penalty of a reduction in the states' representation. As in the parable of the prodigal son, in Seward's view the rebel states had been humiliated enough and should be readmitted at the "family's table" with no further disgrace. Seward thought President Johnson was right in arguing that since "harmonious relations between the States and the Union" had been restored, the Freedmen's Bureau was not only unnecessary but also "unconstitutional, demoralizing and dangerous," and therefore it should be abolished.

The audience then "greeted with very great applause" another conservative Republican: New York congressman Henry J. Raymond, the founding editor of the *New York Times*. Raymond confessed that although it was painful for him to take a different view "on great public questions" from those "personal and political friends" with whom he had interacted in the recent past, he did so because he believed "that the interests of the country required different action from that which they were counseling me to take." He strongly believed that from the day the war began to the day it ended no authority ever declared any other purpose in waging it than "to preserve the integrity of the Union and maintain the supremacy of the Constitution of the United States." Taking distance from his former friends who were Radical Republicans in Congress, Raymond told his fellow citizens that "the path of wisdom, the path of safety and the path of patriotism lies in quite another direction." He resented the language with which the "friends of the bill" spoke of the president's veto. He was disturbed by their assumption that the president's disapproval of the bill would leave all freedmen "at the absolute will and mercy of the late rebels among whom they live." For Raymond, that language revealed "an entire misapprehension of the facts in the case." He believed that the president, far from willing to leave the freedmen unprotected in the exercise of their civil rights, was mainly concerned with the danger that the federal government would usurp the rights of the states. According to Raymond, the president simply proposed to restore the Union by the practical method of admitting "loyal representatives of loyal constituents" to take their seats in Congress. On the other hand, "Congress proposes to exclude them, but it proposes nothing else."[52]

The mass meeting at Cooper Union endorsed the president's veto of the Freedmen's Bureau Bill containing the radical proposal to confiscate land and give it to the former slaves. Many words were spent on the necessity of pushing the freedmen to work under their former masters, but none was spoken in favor of changing the rules of the plantation discipline. The gentlemen gathered at Cooper Union did not understand, or did not want to understand, that Johnson did not intend to grant civil rights to black people. Thanks to the support received from the North, the president also vetoed the Civil Rights Bill. This time Johnson's veto message called the granting of civil rights to black people a discrimination against whites: "the distinction of race and color is by the bill made to operate in favor of the colored race against the white race."[53] Johnson's argument is very close to those made in recent attacks on affirmative action in the name of a color-blind Constitution. But unlike today, during Reconstruction the racist argument underlying the president's veto did not win. Early in April 1866 the Republican Congress overrode the president's veto to pass this important legislation that enormously expanded federal authority over black civil rights. In July 1866 Radicals approved over the president's veto a second Freedmen's Bureau Bill, which gave the bureau authority to intervene when state officials denied blacks their rights.

The period of Reconstruction in the North witnessed an acceleration of the campaign against racial segregation of the antebellum period. Laws banning segregation in public transportation were passed in 1865 in Massachusetts, in 1873 in New York, and in 1874 in Kansas. During those years school segregation was legally prohibited in Michigan, Connecticut, Rhode Island, Iowa, Minnesota, Kansas, Colorado, and Illinois. In Chicago, Cleveland, and Milwaukee, school boards ran integrated schools and employed a few black teachers. New York Republicans, after the election of Radical Reuben Fenton as governor, made an attempt to eliminate the state's property qualification for black voters. African-American churches, newspapers, and public meetings pressed for the end of discriminatory laws and for access to public facilities such as schools and transportation.[54] These extraordinary advancements in the political, civil, and social rights of blacks in the North did not immediately mean economic advancement. The majority of the colored population in northern cities remained in poverty, lived in inferior housing, performed unskilled jobs, and were subjected to the pressure of the growing waves of European immigration and to discriminatory practices by both employers and unions. Nevertheless, the political advancement of this minority group, which in the North was no more than two percent of the whole population, unleashed forces and hopes that change would come soon.[55] The impact of the Fourteenth and Fifteenth Amendments, which defined the constitutional frame of the Republican "unfinished revolution," gave a new meaning to black freedom and created new complex alliances and fractures between black leadership and white reformers.

Race, Class, Gender, and Suffrage

On 8 April 1870, about five thousand black men took part in a procession in Manhattan that marched from Thirty-fourth Street down to Union Square, between two lines of African Americans of both sexes. Black
women filled the city's streets to cheer their husbands, brothers, fathers,
and sons celebrating the Fifteenth Amendment with "an imposing affair."[56]

In Union Square "a noticeable and praiseworthy tribute of respect
was paid to the Father of His Country" by all the men in the procession,
who reverently raised their hats as they passed the bronze equestrian
statue of George Washington.[57] It was a symbolic gesture that created a
ceremonial space linking the history of black people to American egalitarian principles. The black men who marched behind a banner with
the motto "We Ask Nothing But a Fair Race in Life" felt they had finally
been recognized as the sons of the symbolic father of a great democratic
tradition, which they would now make even stronger. The order of their
march enhanced the moral achievements of African-American community organizations. Black military club members, in U.S. Army uniforms, were followed by members of a number of benevolent associations and masonic lodges in full regalia. From the early nineteenth
century, the New York black community had developed a tradition of a
rich variety of associations and distinctive institutions whose members
paraded at special events like this. Besides the number of African-American Methodist and Baptist churches that played an extremely important role as gathering places for large abolitionist meetings, black New
Yorkers, like other "free people of color" in northern cities, had self-
supported benevolent societies. In 1870, approximately 600 colored
men belonged to the six lodges of the Society of the Good Samaritans,
850 were associated with the Society of Love and Charity, and 120 were
members of the Society of the Sons of Wesley; others joined the Saloon
Men's Society, the Coachmen's Benevolent Society, the Young Men's
Christian Benevolent Society, and the Mutual Relief Society. At the same
time, approximately 2,000 colored women in the city were members of
the Daughters of Esther, the Daughters of Wesley, the Female Persever-
ance, the Ladies' Mutual Relief, the Ladies' Loyal League, and the
Daughters of Zion. Colored men also had fourteen lodges of colored
Freemasons, with 750 members, and four lodges of the Grand United
Order of Odd Fellows, with 350 members. All these associations, with
their different resources and aims, made strenuous efforts in the battle
for human recognition and freedom of the black community and constituted an important piece of New York's public culture.[58]

In Union Square the procession was greeted by a large crowd. Among the speakers was the Reverend Henry Highland Garnet, who emphasized the great difference between the crowd that was cheering the black people that day and the mob that in 1863 attacked and murdered blacks in the same square. He evoked the memories of those horrible days of the draft riots and that day of rejoicing on which black people were called "Fellow Citizens" of African descent.[59]

The ratification of the Fifteenth Amendment also brought a new perspective to the difficult alliance between black workers and organized labor. On 9 April 1870, the day after the parade celebrating the Fifteenth Amendment, the *Workingman's Advocate* offered a new class-based definition of "loyalty": "The proper sphere of the black man is by the side of his white citizen brethren, in a duel to the death with the odious money tyranny, which entertains for each an equal love." Tammany Hall and the Union League Club were "no more the friends of the white than of the black workingman," the article continued, and the perpetuation of their "soulless regime" depended on their capacity "to enforce a continuance of this blind battle of prejudices, purposely generated by the political excesses of each." Loyalty did not mean simply "an ever-present readiness to resist those who would take up arms against a wicked regime" but the duty of the citizen to be a "careful, honest and logical inquirer" into the causes of the alleged grievances. Then, if the grievances really existed, loyalty meant "to apply the political remedies, always accessible, and always efficacious." The article concluded that a loyal people "is a people at peace," whereas a disloyal people was one "which goes to war with unholy prejudices."[60]

In Frederick Douglass's view, the question of black suffrage gave a broader meaning to the word "loyalty": "If I were in a monarchical government . . . where the few bore rule and the many were subject, there would be no special stigma resting upon me, because I did not exercise the elective franchise. . . . But here, where universal suffrage is the . . . fundamental idea of the Government, to rule us out is to make us an exception, to brand us with the stigma of inferiority."[61]

In the North, only Radical Republicans actively campaigned to convince public opinion that black suffrage was the logical consequence of emancipation. Since they saw in the North's victory the triumph of Republicanism and free labor ideology, Radicals insisted that freedmen be given the same economic opportunities as white laborers, and they were also instrumental in the passage of the Civil Rights Act of 1866 and the Fourteenth and Fifteenth Amendments.[62] Campaigning for the political rights of black Americans, however, also meant preventing black people from moving North by improving their conditions in the South, as Republican lawyer Robert G. Ingersoll flatly put it in 1868: "It would be unwise to allow the negro to vote in Illinois and not in the South. The result of that would be to make Illinois a negro Mecca. They would come here in droves. Allow them to vote everywhere and then they would remain where they are and where the climate suits them."[63]

Similarly, Horace Greeley, the editor of the *New York Tribune,* gave his support to the enfranchisement of black males by arguing that the citizens of New York State could afford to be just and could not pretend to be afraid of blacks who, by nature, shunned the northern regions of the country: "I have no doubt that, under the beneficent rule of freedom, they will gradually gravitate toward the tropics, where they belong. They will go there because it is their nature to go there; and they will become still fewer here in proportion to our whole population."[64]

It was not until March 1870, when three-fourths of the states had ratified the Fifteenth Amendment, that black males in New York secured the franchise on an equal basis with white males. They celebrated the adoption of the Fifteenth Amendment with a parade on 8 April 1870. The Fifteenth Amendment was a victory for Radical Republicans. The Democrats denounced it as a conspiracy for black equality and for transforming the United States into a centralized nation.[65] The amendment prohibited disfranchisement on the grounds of race, color, or previous condition of servitude, but it totally ignored women's suffrage. It was over the Fifteenth Amendment that the difficult but crucial alliance between the cause of feminism and the cause of abolitionism came to an end. Historian Ellen Du Bois and other scholars have extensively analyzed this fracture.

The angry reaction of suffragists Susan B. Anthony and Elizabeth Cady Stanton is well known. They vigorously opposed the amendment, dissolved the American Equal Rights Association they had founded with Frederick Douglass, and accepted the support of millionaire Democrat George Train for their feminist cause. From the pages of the *Revolution,* the new feminist newspaper financed by Train, Stanton thundered that "It would be better to be the slave of an educated white man than of an ignorant black one" and went as far as to imply that extending the right to vote to black men meant a license to rape. Raising the issue of class together with race and campaigning for an "educated suffrage, irregardless of sex or color," Stanton declared she would prefer "Bridget and Dinah at the ballot box to Patrick and Sambo," namely the poor Irish and the poor Negro. However, other leading white feminists like Lucy Stone and Julia Ward Howe did not think that the world would collapse if black men, whose leadership strongly favored women's suffrage, went to the ballot box first. On the other hand, not all black women supported the Fifteenth Amendment enthusiastically. Sojourner Truth, for example, was afraid that giving more power to black men would aggravate the oppression of black women.[66] Nevertheless, the majority of black women did support an amendment that excluded them from its benefits. According to black feminist Frances Ellen Harper, black women could support the Fifteenth Amendment because the greatest obstacle to the improvement of their condition was not black men but white racism, including the racism of white women. Furthermore, by giving their support to the Fifteenth Amendment, black women did not lose interest in their suffrage. They felt that in order to continue their own battle, the rights of black men had to be granted. Women's struggle, they thought, was meaningless if the black race had no rights. Frederick Douglass, who had always been a sincere supporter of women's suffrage, at the 1869 meeting of the American Equal Rights Association explained the greater urgency of black men's suffrage: "When women, because they are women, are hunted down through the cities of New York and New Orleans; when they are dragged from their houses and hung upon lamp posts; when their children are torn from their arms, and their brains dashed upon the pavement; when they are objects of insult and outrage at every turn; when they are in danger of having their homes burnt down over their heads; when their children are not allowed to enter schools; then they will have an urgency to obtain the ballot equal to our own."[67]

Douglass also remarked that all this was true for black women, not because they were women, but because they were black. By using these strong words, Douglass wanted to dispute Stanton's stand against the idea of the "Negro man's hour" that justified the dropping of women's suffrage by the Republicans: "The world never hears us say 'this is the woman's hour,' for in the world of work, as in politics, we demand the equal recognition of the whole people."[68] At a meeting in 1868, Douglass accused Stanton of discrediting the freedmen and comparing negatively "the daughters of Jefferson and Washington and the daughters of bootblacks and gardeners," for her attempt to advance the cause of women's rights "on the back of defenseless slave women." By cheering the parade for the Fifteenth Amendment, New York's black women seemed to agree with him.

These post–Civil War parades represented the forces unleashed by the abolition of slavery that profoundly affected the country's future. These forces, however, did not move in the same direction. Although unity was the common theme of these public rituals, they offered different versions of it. The celebration for the Union victory of 1864 outlined an industrial order in which the political ideology of the free labor of a republic of small producers would give way to a more complex class ideology. The ideal unity that the parade for the Fifteenth Amendment celebrated was the entrance of black men into American citizenship as the fulfillment of a Republican egalitarian principle.

Racial and class biases nullified Stanton's radical point of "equal recognition of the whole people," for she did not give equal emphasis to differences of race and class in the battle for political rights. Douglass pointed out her biased language. Yet his argument in favor of the "Negro man's hour" gave more relevance to political compromise than equal recognition of all differences. As both requests for suffrage became mutually exclusive, the old abolitionist alliance between women and black rights collapsed. Parades and public events revealed the shaky ground on which race, gender, and class alliances were built in the aftermath of the Civil War.

National Holidays and the Memory of the Civil War

Since the early 1870s, thanks to the country's developed railroad system, reunions of the "Blue" and the "Gray"—Union and Confederate veterans—celebrating the harmonious reconciliation between the North and the South became frequent festive events. Historian Michael Kammen points out that one important consequence of these reconciliatory celebrations was "a blurring of specific historical memories into mythical sagas that were at least partially spurious." What was forged in this period was "a capacity for amnesia" concerning the meaning of a recent past that had profoundly divided the country. By 1888 Memorial Day celebrations had become so popular "as the occasion for military and civic display," the *New York Times* reported, that the day "has usurped the place formerly held by the Fourth of July."[69]

In his final memoir, Frederick Douglass remembered with pride the invitation he received from the Department of New York of the Grand Army of the Republic, a national body that had sponsored Memorial Day observances since 1868, to give an address for the celebration in Union Square on 30 May 1878. Although it was a rainy and windy day, the veterans paraded from Decoration Day's headquarters at the Delmonico Building, on the corner of Fourteenth Street and Fifth Avenue, to Union Square. At 9 a.m., "the crowd grew denser and denser," Douglass recalled, around the statues of Abraham Lincoln and the Marquis de Lafayette. After the authorities' opening remarks, Douglass approached the platform, and the crowded square became silent. As soon as he raised his hand to point to the statue of Lincoln—a gift from the Union League Club to the city in 1870—the crowd "broke into enthusiastic shouts."[70]

Douglass's speech was applauded, while the crowd's waving of regimental flags from the war indicated that the meaning of loyalty was still alive. With his powerful rhetoric Douglass remembered "the heroic deeds and virtues of the brave men who volunteered, fought and fell in the cause of Union and freedom," and stated that New York was "the grand centre where these patriotic legions rallied." It was to these "brave and noble spirits" whose memory will "never perish," Douglass said, that Memorial Day, "the homage of the loyal nation, and the heartfelt gratitude of emancipated millions," was dedicated. Although he declared himself in favor of peace and emphasized that he was not there "to fan the flame of sectional animosity, to revive old issues, or to stir up strife between races," he felt compelled to remind his audience that "we are still afflicted by the painful sequences both of slavery and of the late rebellion." Peace was good, but liberty, law, and justice should come first. This was why in pursuing the policy of pacification "we must not be asked to say that the South was right in the rebellion, or to say the North was wrong." Douglass's argument was crystal clear: "We must not be asked to put no difference between those who fought for the Union and those who fought against it, or between loyalty and treason." By using this rhetoric, Douglass emphasized the memory of the Civil War as "a war of ideas, a battle of principles and ideas which united one section and divided the other," a war between "the old and the new, slavery and freedom, barbarism and civilization." Hence there was "a right side and a wrong side in the late war, which no sentiment ought to cause us to forget."[71]

But by 1888 Memorial Day was clearly celebrating both sides, with no distinction between right and wrong side and no memory of the Civil War as a war of ideas. Celebrations included solemn services, grave decorations of both Union and Confederate soldiers, peppy parades, yachting, and athletic events. On Memorial Day of 1888, New York City organized a parade that showed the highest spirit of national reconciliation: the Confederate grays of Richmond marched amidst the federal blues, and the Sons of Veterans, "white and colored," marched together.[72]

That year George Washington's birthday had also been celebrated in New York as a reunifying event. "Effervescent with enthusiasm, the Solid Southerners of New York dined at the Hotel Brunswick last evening in honor of Washington, the solid South and the reunited Union," the *New York Times* reported. Among eminent northern gentlemen invited to the dinner was Mayor Hewitt, who gave an electrifying speech. "I have heard your fight spoken of as the lost cause," he said, but "the South never knew what it was to live and prosper until it lost its cause." The "resurrection" of the South was making the region "the garden of this land, which is filling it with wealth, wealth won by the labor of freemen and not of slaves." The mayor told his hosts that "the irrepressible conflict" was now taking a new dimension: it was the conflict between the manufacturing states of the North and the South. He predicted that by the turn of the century the southern states of the Union would win that conflict. "It was the North that lost by the outcome of the rebellion, not you," the mayor concluded in front of his electrified audience. Similarly Colonel John Calhoun, who acted as chair of the meeting, remembered that some thirty years before, William Seward, then secretary of state, had proclaimed that the irrepressible conflict between the North and the South was over when the cause of that conflict, slavery, was ended. But it was not so, Calhoun said. "And we tonight, of the South and for the South, in our turn now proclaim to the North another irrepressible conflict, an everlasting strife between the sections as to which section shall contribute most to the prosperity and the glory of our common country, and in this struggle, by the help of God, we mean to beat the North if we can."[73]

Memorial Day reunions and other celebrations of national holidays forged the spirit of reconciliation of a reunified country whose sections had now found a common goal in economic growth. This ideology of national reconciliation, born from the ashes of Radical Reconstruction, was strengthened by the great national celebration of the centennial of the Declaration of Independence in Philadelphia in 1876. Among the dignitaries seated on the platform at the opening ceremonies of the Centennial Exposition was Frederick Douglass together with President Ulysses Grant, the secretary of state, members of Congress, governors, and representatives of foreign countries. Douglass had trouble in reaching the platform to take his assigned seat. Police officers refused him admittance: to them it was inconceivable that a "nigger" would be allowed access to that ceremonial platform. Fortunately a U.S. senator who knew Douglass was near the entrance, saw the black man in trouble, and helped the most famous orator in the country get past the police line.

When the black leader reached the platform, he was loudly cheered. But the greatest speaker in the nation had not been invited to speak— he was invited just to be seen. The Centennial Exposition's aim was to bring the whole nation together for the first time after the Civil War. Black people were not included in its exhibits as it was commonly thought they could not show any proficiency in the arts and sciences. Frederick Douglass's invitation was the result of a political compromise between members of the Centennial Commission.[74] He was therefore invited to be visibly silent. It was a humiliation, indeed, for a powerful speaker.

Douglass would probably have said that the North was making too many concessions to the South at the expense of black citizens, as he had asserted in a speech he gave in 1875 at the centennial of the Pennsylvania Society for Promoting the Abolition of Slavery: "The Centennial of Seventy-Six stands for patriotism; ours stands for philanthropy. One stands for nationality; the other stands for universal humanity. One stands for what is transient; the other stands for what is permanent." Douglass pointed out that although the freedman had won the ballot, he was not given enough protection, education, and knowledge to make good use of it. In the South "schools were burned, teachers educating colored children shot down, black voters did not dare to deposit their votes for fear of their lives."[75]

Douglass was quite right to fear that the road to national reconciliation was paved only for whites. But he was already a man of the past who believed in and publicly fought for a collective memory of the Civil War that did not delete the fact that there were a wrong side and a right side, those who fought for slavery and those who fought for freedom. This is why Douglass was made visibly silent on the platform of the Philadelphia Centennial Exposition. The goal of the great celebration was the glorification of the present, not the explanation of the past. Educating the public to national reconciliation for the fulfillment of the country's "manifest destiny" to expand its democratic views together with its markets was a mission that the great international expositions of the 1890s and early 1900s presented to the American public. From this perspective there was no space for Douglass's struggle for a memory of the Civil War based on the spirit of abolitionists and the meaning that emancipation had for humanity. For Douglass, this was a memory of the past that would have brought vision into the present. History, like a weapon for the present, would have exhorted African Americans to fight for their civil rights and shun the violent South, where they were disfranchised, segregated, and lynched. It was a memory of the past that did not accept any compromise on freedom in the present. It was a memory of conflict, against a collective amnesia of a recent past.

The urban and industrial complexity created by the end of the Civil War caused intense social tensions and conflicts, the nature of which could no longer be explained by contemporary observers in terms of "free soil, free labor, free men." In 1877, at the height of the wave of railroad strikes, the *New York Times* warned that American cities were acquiring those "elements of vice and lawlessness which we had fondly hoped were confined to the older and less liberal countries of Europe." The socialist revolt, according to the *Times,* was no longer "a visionary peril here, when one great city after another falls without a blow under the control of a mob of reckless and law-defying men."[76] The waves of strikes in the 1870s and 1880s in most northern cities, culminating with the bomb and rioting in Haymarket Square in Chicago in 1886, swept away the image of the harmonious small-scale competitive capitalism of the antebellum North in which industrious "free laborers" could hope to become independent manufacturers.[77] New York, the northern metropolis, became the symbol of poverty, crime, political corruption, and social insurrection in a profoundly divided country. It was at that point that the idea of national reconciliation became a recurrent theme of American public culture.

2

International Expositions in Chicago and Atlanta

Rituals of Progress and Reconciliation

Chicago was the first expression of American thought as a unity.
HENRY ADAMS

Why are not the colored people, who constitute so large an element of the American population, and who have contributed so large a share to American greatness, more visibly present and better represented in this World's Exposition? IDA B. WELLS

The Chicago World's Columbian Exposition of 1893

Between 1865 and 1890, the expansion of the national rail network marked a profound transformation of the idea of public events. People could gather together from all over the country. The telegraphic wires made them capable of exchanging news and sending petitions and resolutions, thus transforming human communication.[1] Between 1876 and 1916, almost one hundred million people visited international expositions in Philadelphia, New Orleans, Chicago, Atlanta, Nashville, Omaha, Buffalo, St. Louis, Portland, Seattle, San Francisco, and San Diego.[2] The Chicago World's Columbian Exposition was the biggest of these events. It opened on 1 May 1893, five years after the Haymarket Square bomb and subsequent rioting and on the edge of a serious financial crisis, to deliver an optimistic message to the more than 27.5 million people who visited it (well over one-third of the U.S. population, according to the census of 1890) by the time it closed its gates on 31 October 1893.

The fair was designed to celebrate the triumph of American industrialization and commerce enlightened by applied social scientific knowledge and mechanical wonders like the electric light bulb and the long-distance telephone. It celebrated the extensive railroad system, the centralized government, the new academic institutions and free associations, and Columbus's voyage, as the full-sized replicas of the three caravels attested.

Why did Congress select Chicago, a midwestern city, as the site for a great international exposition celebrating the fourth centennial of Columbus's voyage? For William Dean Howells's utopian "Altrurian Traveller," Chicago was simply a "Newer York, an ultimated Manhattan, the realized ideal of largeness, loudness, and fastness, which New York has persuaded the American is metropolitan."[3] Yet the great fair was a source of optimism for Howells's fictional character Homos, as well as for several million visitors. They could hope that what they saw was an idealized American future based on the triumph of morality, industry, and progress.

"Progress" was a concept that events such as the Chicago World's Fair exemplified to the many by popularizing science and its authoritative language for the "average" citizen. As the *Chicago Tribune* stated in reporting a Fourth of July oration: "Selfish wealth and hopeless poverty combine to present the great problem of the age: for one leads on to inhumanity—the essence of despotism—and the other to sullen despair—the source of anarchy. This problem is to be solved by the average citizen—that plain, sturdy, self-reliant, ambitious man, who is known as the typical American." The fair was designed for this invented character. It was for the "Average People," learned the readers of *Cosmopolitan* magazine, "not for the few at the top or for the helpless lot in the gutter, but for the Average."[4]

The business and financial communities of New York and Chicago were the leading contenders for this colossal celebration designed for the average citizen, although other cities such as Minneapolis, Washington, D.C., and St. Louis had made proposals to Congress.[5] That the celebration of Columbus's voyage was a pretext for profit for businessmen and financiers was clear since neither New York, with its Dutch origins, nor Chicago, situated a thousand miles from the Atlantic, had anything to do with Columbus's landing in the West Indies. After the success of the Philadelphia Centennial Exposition in 1876, in which each visitor contributed on average $4.50 to the city's economy, proponents of the Columbian celebration, the major businessmen and financial giants of the respective cities, expected much greater returns. In New York, Chauncey Depew, the president of the New York Central Railroad, was among those who pushed, for good personal reasons, New York's candidacy. Similarly, Cornelius Vanderbilt, William Rockefeller, William Waldorf Astor, and other New York tycoons used their time, money, and political influence to obtain state and federal support for the fair. The Chicago financial community, including names such as Cyrus McCormick and George Pullman, was able to build an effective corporation and began to lobby in Congress several weeks before the New York delegation arrived. Meanwhile, a political fracture in the Republican Party and conflicts with Tammany Hall weakened New York's efforts in Congress. Discord had developed between Chauncey Depew, the leading Republican of the city and the strongest supporter of the fair, and Thomas Collier Platt, the leader of the state Republicans. In order to prevent the ascendency of Tammany or his rival, Depew, in the 1892 elections, Platt explicitly opposed the fair, thus ending New York's chances. Yet in August 1889 the popular publication *Harper's Weekly* had no doubt that New York was the most suitable place for the Columbian Exposition, given its great location, its commercial and manufacturing capabilities, and its transportation and accommodation facilities. William Waldorf Astor, the heir to the Astor family fortune, went as far as saying that if Chicago won, the fair would be simply an agricultural show and not a real international exposition. Backing New York's candidacy, he said that New Yorkers would make the fair "an historic exemplar of the last four centuries—to illustrate what has been achieved in civilization since the discovery of America." Chicago was, in Astor's view, "an inland and prosaic city."[6]

Whereas the New York financial community was strongly in favor of the fair, Republican politicians were becoming uneasy about the possibility that Tammany, the Democratic machine whose capacity for controlling elections and stealing public money was unquestionable, would control the millions of dollars appropriated for the fair. Later in 1889 even the enthusiasm of *Harper's Weekly* had chilled. By this time the magazine did not find New York "in the true sense a public-spirited city" because its population was "too heterogeneous to generate public spirit." There was also the difficult question of finding a suitable site for the fair without disturbing the landscape of Frederick Law Olmsted's Central Park. In September 1889, however, the Committee on Site reached the conclusion that the site would have to be Central Park, or at least part of it, or the city would have to give up its candidacy for the international fair. According to the *New York Times,* a large number of people in the city agreed that it was better not to host the fair at all than to choose

Central Park as its site. However, according to the *Times,* which was the leading paper of the city, this was not the opinion of the majority who believed, as did the *Times* editorial board, that "the interest of the city has been so deeply aroused, its pride so awakened, and its heart so firmly set upon having the fair that its people would consent, though with some reluctance, to the use of their pleasure ground, when they were once convinced that the choice of any other site would imperil the success of the enterprise." Reluctant people should be convinced that "wherever the great exposition is held its attractions will draw within the gates everybody in the city and in the country who has an interest in human progress."[7]

For Frederick Olmsted, the idea of an international fair in his Central Park was compatible with his notion of democracy, which included social progress associated with urbanization, the transportation revolution, economic growth, and technological development under the direction of a centralized government. When his influential role in the U.S. Sanitary Commission during the Civil War ended, Olmsted went back to his profession of landscape architecture and undertook extensive projects including Prospect Park in Brooklyn, Riverside and Morningside Parks in Manhattan, the grounds surrounding the Capitol in Washington, D.C., the layout of Boston's extensive system of parks and parkways, and, in California, the campus of Stanford. Ironically, after New York lost the battle for the world's fair, it was Olmsted, at the culminating point of his career, who designed the Columbian Exposition grounds in Chicago, introducing into Jackson Park an extraordinary chain of lagoons, wooded islands, and cultivated shrubbery in harmony with his conception of public recreational facilities.

By 1890 the only leading New York Republican who was still an enthusiastic supporter of the bid for the Columbian Exposition was Chauncey Depew, the president of the New York Central Railroad. When in January of that year Democratic governor David Bennett Hill gave his blessing to the New York campaign for the Columbian exhibit, Depew and the city committee of one hundred went to Washington for the Congressional hearing. After St. Louis and Washington, D.C., had presented their arguments, the New York delegation was the third to be heard, before Chicago's.

Depew presented the various arguments favoring New York as the site of the exposition: its proximity to Europe, its large population, its financial and industrial leadership, the availability of transportation, and its climate. Although the Washington hearing went extremely well for the New York delegation, the fair bill was defeated in the state legislature because of Platt's fear that the selection of New York might reestablish Tammany's supremacy in 1892, the year of presidential elections.[8]

On 20 February the House of Representatives discussed the report of its world's fair committee. The two major antagonists, New York and Chicago, had their spokesmen. Those speaking for New York argued that the city had a $15 million commitment that would eliminate the need for federal funds and offered excellent accommodation facilities for one million visitors a day, splendid museums and galleries, easy access from Europe, and a site of 309 acres available near Central Park.

Those who spoke in favor of Chicago claimed to have in mind the whole nation—and in particular, the West. They said that Chicago was the most convenient place for the millions of people the fair would attract, and that it was an "American city" and therefore more representative than "foreign" New York. Chicago won. "The New York fair died of politics," Depew commented. On 28 April 1890, President Harrison signed the bill for the World's Columbian Exposition to be held in Chicago.[9]

New York lost the battle because of its local politicians; Chicago won because it embodied the new ideal of the American city and because it could count on twenty-four railroad terminals. Yet it was New Yorker Frederick Olmsted who designed the fair's landscape, and it was New York architects who created the classical style of the white buildings of the exposition known as the "White City."

The fair opened in May 1893, delayed for the completion of construction of numerous buildings, but dedication ceremonies were held 12 October 1892. On that day schoolchildren all over the country celebrated Columbus's voyage of "discovery" and recited, for the first time, the Pledge of Allegiance to the U.S. flag. With endorsement from presidential candidates Cleveland and Harrison, educator Francis J. Bellamy arranged for American schoolchildren to pledge "allegiance to my flag and the Republic for which it stands, one Nation indivisible with Liberty and Justice for all."[10]

More than one hundred thousand people participated in the opening ceremonies in Chicago. New York Republican Chauncey Depew, the major supporter of New York's campaign, was among the official speakers. The fair was to celebrate "the emancipation of man," he said, inviting the whole world to come and see what America was about. The only problem he foresaw was that current policies of unrestricted immigration could undermine the future of the country. The New York daily and monthly press extensively covered the Chicago World's Columbian Exposition. The New York business community had lost a big opportunity but did its best to regain its power at the fair.

Depew's rhetorical phrase that the fair celebrated "the emancipation of man" did not refer to the emancipation of black Americans. Only one generation after slavery, African Americans initially looked at the Chicago World's Fair as a great opportunity to show their progress in such a short time. However, as soon as it became clear that no committee in charge of organizing the various parts of the fair included any black member in a position of authority, these hopes that the Chicago fair might serve as a forum for showing black people's achievements since emancipation quickly disappeared. Organization committees did not accept the idea of racially separate exhibits and instead encouraged individual black Americans to participate in state exhibits, but many state committees did not accept any proposal coming from African Americans. At that point blacks had the choice of accepting the small concessions made to them or not participating at all. Black spokespersons sharply disagreed among themselves on what should be done to oppose the discrimination they encountered at each organizational level of the fair.

The main goal of these great international expositions was to give millions of people a shared experience of faith in the progress of American society. President McKinley, shortly before he was murdered at the Pan-American Exposition in Buffalo in 1901, declared that expositions were the "timekeepers of progress." To McKinley, progress was a forward movement of America's economic expansion in order to open new markets and search for new supplies and natural resources. This was what expositions celebrated: "They record the world's advancement. They stimulate the energy, enterprise, and intellect of the people and quicken human genius. They go into the home. They broaden and brighten the daily life of the people. They open mighty storehouses of information to the student."[11]

When one looks at the kind of information that international expositions gave to the millions who attended, one is struck by the extraordinary and entertaining mix offered of science, arts, religion, zoological gardens, circus entertainment, minstrel show, and Wild West show. Educating the public to have faith in American progress through the medium of fairs was an attempt to unify the country by building consensus on scientific, economic, and technological achievements. The underlying themes of these colossal extravaganzas were optimism and faith in a reconciled country. Yet African-American progress did not coincide with the progress of the country. The spread of lynching, disfranchisement, and segregation of black people in the South characterized the experience of this group in post-Reconstruction America.

Black Americans, evidently, were not included among the "average people" the Chicago World's Fair addressed, as their proposed exhibits, which would have encouraged African Americans to visit the fair, were turned down by the organizers. Those blacks who ventured to go to Chicago became the target of satire in *Harper's Weekly*. The magazine printed a series of cartoons portraying a highly caricatured black family unsuccessfully trying to make sense of the fair. In one of these cartoons the "Johnson family," while visiting the Kentucky building, meets Mr. Johnson's former master, who asks him what he is doing at the fair. A deferential Mr. Johnson answers: "Well, sah, I's lak a noble shoe dat's been blacked—'bout time I's getting some polish!"[12] "Polishing" as a metaphor for "becoming civilized" gives the sense that black Americans achieving a middle-class lifestyle were still considered "niggers," not fully human. But what happens when such common stereotypes become authoritative scientific views?

"Perhaps one of the most striking lessons which the Columbian Exposition taught," read a caption in a souvenir book entitled *Oriental and Occidental*, "was the fact that African slavery in America had not, after all, been an unmixed evil, for of a truth, the advanced social condition of American Africans over that of their barbarous countrymen is most encouraging and wonderful." This was what a visitor could learn after visiting the Midway Plaisance ethnological exhibit, organized under the supervision of Harvard ethnologist Frederic Ward Putnam. Here, together with "authentic" Native American, Chinese, Samoan, and Arab villages, a savage Dahoman group showed the debasing origins of "American Africans." Midway Plaisance, located on a narrow strip of land that was a perfect site for displaying simulated villages of different groups of humanity, provided an opportunity for popularizing the science of anthropology as the explanation of progress according to racial lines. "The late P. T. Barnum should have lived to see this day," the *New York Times* commented on the opening of Midway Plaisance. A powerful mix of entertainment and evolutionary anthropology, the Midway Plaisance exhibit of Native Americans was attacked by Emma Sickles, a member of Putnam's staff, in a letter of protest she wrote to the *New York Times*. The young anthropologist accused the exhibit of representing Native Americans as savages whose animal nature could be tamed only by government agencies. She maintained that every means had been used "to keep the self-civilized Indians out of the Fair."[13]

Although Putnam was eager to include all different races in his portrayal of American civilization, his desire to popularize anthropology was even greater. Historians of anthropology have included the "museum process" among the forms of popularization of anthropology during the late nineteenth century. As far as Native Americans were concerned, scientists who agreed to put them on display at events like world's fairs, Wild West shows, and ethnological exhibits helped to destroy Native American history.[14] Midway Plaisance was a theater in which this process of dehistoricization of Native Americans, Africans, and other "primitive" people took place.

Literary critic Denton Snider visited Midway Plaisance and described it as "a sliding scale of humanity." In this "living museum of humanity," which "moved in harmony with the thought of evolution," the Teutonic and Celtic races were at one end, followed by the Mohammedan world and Asia. Then, he wrote, "we descend to the savage races, the African of Dahomey and the North American Indian," preceded by the semi-civilized Javanese and Samoans. "There is nothing difficult for the mind to comprehend," the New York Times reported, as Midway Plaisance was designed for the "average visitor." The Dahoman village, with its mud-daubed huts on which animal figures were scraped and its war dance on a central platform, was supposed to give "a real glimpse of Negro Africa," while the narrow, crooked streets of Cairo, with its bazaars, booths, and shops on both sides, its donkeys and camels, and its school with children reciting the Koran aloud, were meant to lecture large crowds on human variety.[15]

Even the "below average" visitor could easily perceive that the African Dahomans, with their rumored cannibalism and their wild war dances, were the most savage and threatening of all groups. An article in Frank Leslie's Popular Monthly immediately elaborated on this straightforward message by detecting in the sixty-nine Dahomans a "barbaric ugliness." The skin of these savages was "blacker than buried midnight," and their sensibility was "as degraded as the animals which prowl the jungles of their dark land." All these qualities reminded Edward McDowell, the author of the article, of "many characteristics of the American Negro." After describing the idolatrous forms of worship performed by the Dahomans, who, according to McDowell, danced around a pole on which was perched a human skull or images of reptiles, lizards, and other crawling things, he concluded that the American Negro "has learned the language of civilization, and by its teachings has been raised above the deplorable level of his less fortunate kinsman."[16]

Ironically this exotic, scary, and negative image of Africa was played against any attempt African Americans made to live according to the values of the American Declaration of Independence or to use the protection of the constitutional amendments. Poignantly, another cartoon in Harper's Weekly showed our Mr. Johnson visiting the Dahoman village and shaking hands with one of the savages. His wife shouts at him:

"Ezwell Johnson, stop shakin' hands wit that heathen! You want the hull fair ter t'ink you's found a poo' relation!"[17]

If the exhibitions at the Chicago fair were organized to please the average visitor, the number of academic and institutional meetings held on its grounds attested to the importance of the event to the American intellect. The list of conferences and congresses "expected to have a great influence on the thought of the nineteenth century," according to an exposition officer, was in fact extraordinary and covered all branches of art, science, literature, and religion.[18]

It was at the meeting of the American Historical Association held at the Columbian Exposition that historian Frederick Jackson Turner propounded his celebrated "frontier thesis."[19] Like Turner's thesis, which became the most relevant interpretation of American history for the following fifty years, the Chicago World's Fair celebrated the idea of a linear progression of American society from simplicity to complexity. Turner made the West the symbol of reunification for the country and made slavery disappear as a fundamental cause of the Civil War. By seeing the frontier as "the line of the most rapid and effective Americanization" and the place of birth of "a composite nationality for the American people," Turner offered a unified account of the American past that fitted the need of national reconciliation at the time when the country was experiencing economic depression, labor conflicts, and racial discrimination. Turner's thesis, like the Columbian Exposition, gave America an idea of national coherence, a forward mission in which there was no place for social conflicts. The myth of creative individualism inherited by the frontier pioneers was a powerful force of unification.

Similarly, leading ethnologist Otis T. Mason, the curator of ethnology of the National Museum of Natural History, explained the meaning of racial progress to those attending the International Conference of Anthropology, which met both at the Chicago Art Institute and on the fairgrounds. A strong believer in evolution, Mason explained that one major characteristic of civilized communities was "a reverence for the government, called patriotism, and from this, combined with the love of one's native land, comes a strong motive in holding the people of a nation together." Savages lacked this characteristic, Mason argued. Consequently the Smithsonian's ethnological exhibit would display the industries of western Africans and African Americans to allow visitors to compare their respective levels of cultural achievement and to understand that the current political and economic situation of American blacks was an outgrowth of their "savage" heritage.[20]

It was therefore extremely important, as Frederick Douglass and
black journalist Ida Wells argued, for African Americans to attend the
Chicago World's Fair and openly fight against its pervasive message that
slavery had actually helped Africans to become more civilized in America. Douglass and Wells were among those black spokespersons who
thought the Chicago World's Fair was an important interracial forum to
inform a large public about their achievements in this country during
their short period of freedom. Both Douglass and Wells recognized the
important role the world's fair played as a channel of popularization of
evolutionary ideas about race and progress.

A Radical View of the "White City"

When the elderly Frederick Douglass visited Midway Plaisance and saw
the fake African village, he sadly commented, "as if to shame the Negro,
the Dahominas are also here to exhibit the Negro as a repulsive savage."
Douglass's loyalty to the Republican party won him in 1889 a diplomatic
appointment as American consul to the black republic of Haiti, a position that allowed him to participate at the Chicago World's Columbian
Exposition as the representative of the Haitian exhibit. At the Haitian
building Douglass was joined by journalist Ida Wells. Had it not been for
the republic of Haiti, "Negroes of the United States would have had no
part nor lot in any official way in the World's Fair," Ida Wells-Barnett
later commented in her autobiography.[21]

Wells arrived in Chicago as soon as she returned from her successful
anti-lynching campaign in England. An excellent organizer, she managed to raise in a few weeks $500 to publish a booklet entitled *The Rea-
son Why the Colored American Is Not in the World's Columbian Exposition*. "I
called the representative women of Chicago together, and asked their
help in arranging a series of Sunday afternoon meetings at different
churches—Mr. Douglass to preside and I to speak," she recalled in her
autobiography. Thanks to this women's network, Wells and Douglass
spoke to crowded meetings at the city's black churches. Ten thousand
copies of the book were printed, not in three languages (English,
French, and German) as originally planned, but just in English with a
preface in the other two languages due to the shortness of time and
funds. In the preface a visitor to the fair could read that "the exhibit of
the progress made by a race in 25 years of freedom as against 250 years
of slavery would have been the greatest tribute to the greatness and pro-
gressiveness of American institutions."

Not all African-American papers agreed with the propriety of fund-
raising for the booklet and with its content. Those supporting the Doug-
lass-Wells initiative *(Cleveland Gazette, Afro-American Advocate, Philadelphia*

Tribune, Richmond Planet, Topeka Call) found it worthy of financial support because the whole race would benefit from the widest diffusion of the booklet. Other papers, like the *Methodist Union,* did not admit the existence of open racial discrimination at the Chicago World's Fair and condemned the undertaking by arguing that blacks were going to the Chicago Exposition "as American citizens" and not "as an odd race." Although there was discrimination, the *Indianapolis Freeman* attested, it should not be publicly admitted to foreign visitors, and complaining too much about it would increase white hostility in the United States. Some other black papers condemned the booklet on the grounds that black people should not waste their money on it, and that the funds for the booklet should be used to finance an orphanage instead.[22]

The booklet, a collection of essays written by several black authors and edited by Ida Wells, with an introductory chapter by Frederick Douglass, radically attacked national reconciliation and the organizers of the Chicago fair that celebrated this concept. It also expressed a radical view of what it meant to African Americans to be "fairly represented" at the World's Columbian Exposition. It went beyond the issues of black Americans' exclusion from policy-making committees, of their having separate exhibits of agricultural and industrial skills, or of showing Negro music, dances, and poetry to a large interracial public or integrating any form of individual black talent in state exhibits. Douglass's introduction stressed "the moral depths, darkness and destitution from which we are still emerging" and explained "the grounds of the prejudice, hate, and contempt in which we are still held by the people, who for more than two hundred years doomed us to this cruel and degrading condition." "Slavery" was still the reason why African Americans were excluded from the World's Columbian Exposition. Readers could become aware of the "outrages upon the Negro in this country" narrated in the booklet, although "they will seem too shocking for belief." Douglass thought that the authors of the volume "will be censured" because its publication occurred when America stood in front of the world "as a highly liberal and civilized nation." But the timing was right for African Americans because the important services they had offered in order to suppress the rebellion and save the Union, which for a time "created a sentiment of gratitude by their loyal white fellow citizens," were now forgotten. This memory was erased by the passage of time and also by the restoration of friendship between the North and the South, Douglass wrote. Thus, he concluded, "what the colored people gained by the war they have partly lost by peace."[23] By 1893 Douglass had lost confidence in the Republican Party, in political compromises made on the ashes of Reconstruction, and in the survival of a collective memory of the Civil War as a war of ideas. In 1883 the U.S. Supreme Court had struck down the Civil Rights Act of 1875 and had "sacrificed" Reconstruction amendments for national reconciliation. The booklet Douglass introduced offered visitors to the fair a documented account that national reconciliation was proceeding at the expense of black people. Its gloomy picture was a pessimistic antidote to the fake optimism of the average citizen that the World's Columbian Exposition was celebrating.

The booklet told the story of a crescendo of abuses to their human dignity that black people experienced in the southern states after Reconstruction because constitutional amendments were largely nullified. Exposition visitors who read the book learned that the result of voter registration under the educational and poll tax provision of the new Mississippi Constitution made black registered voters decrease from 130,278 in 1880 to 22,024 in 1892. This dramatic disfranchisement was accomplished "by political massacres, by midnight outrages of the Ku Klux Klans, and by state legislative enactment." The reader unfamiliar with southern facilities for travelers also learned that laws concerning segregated transportation for "colored persons" did not grant equality. Usually half of the smoking car of a train was reserved as the "colored car." Ida Wells, who had the experience of being violently forced off a train because she refused to travel in this type of car, informed the reader that into these separate facilities were crowded "all classes and conditions of Negro humanity, without regard to sex, standing, good breeding, or ability to pay for better accommodation." White men could pass through these "colored cars" and ride on them if they were pleased to do so, "but no colored woman, however refined, well educated or well dressed may ride in the ladies, or first-class coach . . . unless she is a nurse-maid traveling with a white child." The only equal treatment was the train fare.[24]

To some visitors who had just visited Midway Plaisance, seen the savage Dahomans, and learned about their cruel rituals, the reading of detailed descriptions of southern lynching mobs, performing the most barbarous and cruel acts on their colored victims, must have been rather shocking. Relying on her own documented research originally published in the *New York Age* in 1892 and on her recent tour of England to present her book *Southern Horrors* for English public opinion, Wells produced an extraordinary amount of data on lynching and examples drawn from the national press. The booklet reported extracts from the *Memphis Commercial* of 23 July 1892 giving a detailed account of a mob torturing and killing a black man accused, with no evidence, of harassing two white women. The growing violence against the poor man culminated with the burning of his naked body in a big fire. The following description must have proved horrifying to the visitors of the fair celebrating American progress and national reunion:

> It was a horrible sight, one which perhaps none there had ever witnessed before. It proved too much for a large part of the crowd and the majority of the mob left very shortly after the burning began. But a large number stayed, and were not a bit set back by the sight of a human body being burned to ashes. Two or three white women, accompanied by their escorts, pushed to the front to obtain an unobstructed view, and looked on with astonishing coolness and nonchalance. One man and a woman brought a little girl, not over 12 years old. . . . The comments of the crowd were varied. Some remarked on the efficacy of this style of cure for rapists, others rejoiced that men's wives and daughters were now safe from the wretch. Some laughed as the flesh cracked and blistered, and while a large number pronounced the burning of a dead body as a useless episode, not in all that throng was a word of sympathy heard for the wretch himself.

Wells explained that during the first years of freedom black men were lynched by masked mobs while exercising their right to vote. As that cause made lynching unpopular in public opinion, a new reason was given to justify this growing practice in the following decade. The Negro was charged with assaulting or attempting to assault white women, a charge, "as false as it is foul," Wells said, that robbed black people of the sympathy of the world by "blasting the race's good name." In the early 1890s lynchers no longer wore masks. Mobs acted "in broad daylight," with sheriffs, police, and state officials standing by. Lynchers and their supporters, the owners of telegraph wires and newspapers, wrote reports that justified lynching "by painting the Negro as black as possible," reports that public opinion accepted without question or investigation.

Wells explained to exhibition visitors a table published by the *Chicago Tribune* early in 1892 concerning the number of colored people murdered by mobs in the period 1882–91 (an increase from 52 in 1882 to 169 in 1891) and their alleged crimes. Wells's data showed that only one-third of nearly a thousand murdered black men were charged with rape, a crime punished with lynching only when blacks were accused by white women, accusations that were never proven. The same crime committed by either black or white men on black women was completely ignored even in the law courts. The fact that many lynchings occurred for no reason meant that the word of any white person against a black person was enough to stir a lynching mob. There were also many examples

of black women who were killed by furious mobs on a charge of poison-
ing white persons and later found completely innocent. Of the 241 persons lynched in 1892, 160 were people of African descent. Among these
were Wells's three friends, whose only guilt was their economic success
as grocery store owners in Memphis; they were three of the most well
known young men in a colored population of thirty thousand people.[25]
Ida Wells's early interpretation of lynching as a violent response by
whites to a fear of black economic achievement and upper mobility was
a rather accurate understanding of the nature of current racist stereotypes that were propagated by even those *Harper's Weekly* cartoons of the
"Johnsons," the caricatured black middle-class family visiting the Chicago World's Fair.

Wells's muckraking booklet completed its gloomy picture by telling
visitors why they could not see at the world's fair any evidence of the
progress African Americans had made since emancipation in the professions, education, the arts and literature, and the accumulation of
wealth, in spite of the high cost they were paying for national reconciliation. Chicago journalist Ferdinand L. Barnett—Ida Wells's future husband—explained the reason why the colored American was not at Chicago's Columbian Exposition by telling the reader the full story of how
the organizers had successfully managed to exclude any colored person
from decision-making committees. After the site selection, Congress decided that a National Board of Commissioners constituted by two representatives of each state, one for each territory, and ten at large would be
appointed by the president to organize the Chicago World's Fair. As
black people in the country numbered over seven and one-half million
and constituted the population majority of two southern states, there
had been hopes among African-American communities to obtain one
commissioner at large and at least one from the southern states. However, President Harrison "willfully ignored the millions of colored
people in the country and thus established a precedent which remained
inviolate through the entire term of Exposition work," Barnett declared. To those African Americans who suggested the establishment of
a Department of Colored Exhibits in the exposition to show "the products of skill and industry of race since emancipation," the National
Board of Commissioners answered that no separate exhibits were allowed. On the grounds that colored people were not united in asking
for a separate exhibit, even the Board of Lady Managers, in charge of
the Department of Women's Work at the fair, refused to accept any proposed African-American representative, as "it would be impolitic to recognize either faction." In Barnett's view, this was a bad excuse. Colored
people were not alone "in their failure to agree upon the same person,

to do a designated work." Thus the Board of Lady Managers rejected petitions from various "factions" of colored people and turned them over to the various state boards. Proposals for separate exhibits were not accepted on the grounds that colored people were citizens and that it was against the policy of the exposition "to draw any distinction between different classes of American citizens." Barnett recognized that this was a reasonable argument, but it was made, in this case, to cover the southern state boards' discrimination against colored people.

This issue of separate exhibits was rather controversial among African Americans as well. Those in favor argued that since state exhibits including colored people would be so few in number, African-American progress would go unnoticed. Opponents of separate exhibits held that "merit knows no color line" and that colored people should be willing to be measured by the same rule applied to other people. Barnett, however, questioned the rightness of the color-blind argument of the exposition authorities by using arguments similar to today's hot debate on affirmative action:

> exposition authorities had considered it best to act entirely without reference to any color line, that all citizens of all classes stood on the same plane, that no distinctions should be drawn between any classes and special work extended to none. . . . It may have been strictly just but it was certainly not equitable to compel the colored people who have been emancipated but thirty years to stand on the same plane with their masters who for two and one half centuries had enslaved them. Had the colored people of America enjoyed equal opportunities with the people they would have asked in the Exposition no favor of any kind.

Barnett informed unaware visitors to the fair that only a few years had passed since many states "made it a misdemeanor to teach a colored person to read." Thus in this case not only was the color-blind argument "inequitable," but it was also "a false and shallow pretense." If no distinctions were to be drawn in favor of colored people, then it would have been fair that none would be drawn against them. But that was not the case. After petitions from African Americans asking for representation on the fair's policymaking committees had been dismissed, the management of the exposition found it easy to exclude colored people from most clerical and remunerative jobs. Barnett reported many examples of colored people facing covert or open discrimination in the hiring process for hundreds of jobs connected with the fair. In that "wonderful hive of national industry," which represented an investment of thirty million dollars and which had thousands of employees, only two colored people held occupations higher than that of janitor, laborer, or porter. Barnett concluded that even though the World's Columbian Exposition was theoretically open to all Americans, the exposition was, literally and figuratively, a "White City," and in building this city "the Colored American was allowed no helping hand, and in its glorious success he has no share." This showed "the Nation's deliberate and cowardly tribute to the Southern demand 'to keep the Negro in his place.'"[26]

As a group, African Americans were certainly underrepresented at the Chicago World's Fair. As individuals, however, they made their voices heard in many conferences and state exhibits of this interracial forum. Frederick Douglass was in charge of the Haitian pavilion and also spoke, as a former Detroit citizen, during Michigan Days (held 13–14 September 1893); a few "exceptional" black women were invited by the Board of Lady Managers to address the World's Congress of Representative Women.

Fannie Barrier Williams was one of this select group. A distinguished lecturer and organizer, Williams had moved in the 1880s from New York State to Chicago, where she started the first training school for black nurses, was the first woman to be appointed to the Chicago Library Board, and was one of the few black members of the Chicago Women's Club. Williams strongly believed in interracial cooperation. Her style differed from that of Ida Wells, but she held the same view on lynching and white men's unpunished harassment of black women. Williams told the women's forum that black women were the victims of sexual immorality, not the perpetrators. She blamed slavery for "every moral imperfection that mars the character of the colored American." Williams openly attacked the myth of black promiscuity and warned white women that if they were so deeply concerned about morality, they should help to take measures to protect black women. She implied that white men were responsible for degrading the black race, not the black men who supposedly assaulted white women. "I do not want to disturb the serenity of this conference," Williams said, "by suggesting why this protection is needed and the kind of man against whom it is needed."[27]

Another exceptional black woman to address the women's congress was educator, writer, and poet Frances E. W. Harper. The daughter of free parents, she was born in Maryland, received an uncommon education at her uncle's school, and later moved to Philadelphia, where she became actively involved in the antislavery movement. After the Civil War she was among those educated northern women who traveled into the South to teach and offer other forms of social services to the former slaves. A member of the American Equal Rights Association, Harper addressed the World's Congress of Representative Women at the Chicago fair with a speech on women's political future: "If the fif-teenth century discovered America to the Old World, the nineteenth is discovering woman to herself," she said. Women had the opportunity to fill the world "with fairer and higher aims than the greed of gold and the lust of power." Harper felt that in women's hands were possibilities "whose use or abuse must tell upon the political life of the nation, and send their influence for good or evil across the track of unborn ages." She did not think the extension of the ballot "a panacea for all the ills of our national life," for the main need of the country, in her view, was not more voters but "better voters." Harper believed that the "upbuilding of national character" was in order, more than changing institutions. Speaking to all women, regardless of their color and class, Harper em-phasized the moral role that women should have in developing a na-tional consciousness and how they should "mould its character." She was not sure, however, that women were naturally so much better than men "that they will clear the stream by the virtue of their womanhood." In Harper's view, it was not gender per se but "through character that the best influence of women upon the life of the nation must be ex-erted." She concluded her speech by urging women to take an active step against the practice of lynching, the worst of evils in American pub-lic life. "How can any woman send petitions to Russia against the hor-rors of Siberian prisons if, ages after the Inquisition has ceased to devise its tortures, she has not done all she could by influence, tongue, and pen to keep men from making bonfires of the bodies of real or sup-posed criminals."[28]

The organizers of the Chicago World's Fair did not object to the par-ticipation of a number of African Americans in interracial forums as ex-ceptional individuals whose personal achievements elevated them far above the rest of a backward race. What African Americans were offered as a group was a "Colored American Day," scheduled for 25 August, as a day set aside for African-American music and speeches; similar celebra-tions for Swedish, German, Irish, and other nationalities had already been scheduled. Douglass promptly accepted the offer. Ida Wells did not—she felt it was not right for African Americans to be treated like foreign immigrants in the "American quilt." Wells was not alone in re-jecting the Colored American Day, or Jubilee Day. As the celebration ap-proached, former Congressman J. Mercer Langstone and the famous singer Matilda Sissieretta Jones, the "Black Patti," refused to participate, and a group of Chicago black ministers planned suburban excursions for that day to discourage attendance. On the other hand, the pro-moters assured that the celebration was going to be "refined, dignified, and cultured" and tried to obtain a large audience by getting Negro fraternal organizations involved. Ida Wells did not attend either of the highlights of Negro Day, the performance of the Jubilee Singers gospel group of Fisk University or the reading of Paul Dunbar's poem "The Colored American." Many years later Wells-Barnett wrote in her autobiography that when she read newspaper reports of Douglass's keynote speech the following day, she went "straight out to the fair and begged his pardon for presuming in my youth and inexperience to criticize him for an effort which had done more to bring our cause to the attention of the American people than anything else which had happened during the fair."[29]

According to the *Indianapolis Freeman*, "Jubilee Day," because of the division of opinion it caused among colored people, "was a dismal failure." Less than one thousand people attended, because the local colored people did not think it was the appropriate way to represent the advancement of the Negro race after emancipation. At the same time, the paper recognized that the day's great concerts were "a glittering success." It also found Douglass's speech the most impressive feature of that day.

When the elderly Douglass reached the platform together with Isabella Beecher-Hooker, the sister of Harriet Beecher Stowe, who wrote *Uncle Tom's Cabin,* and Henry Ward Beecher, "the applause was deafening." Douglass's words evoked his former speeches on the memory of slavery and the Civil War, on the right and wrong sides of the conflict. "Men talk of the Negro problem," he said, but he denied its existence. "The problem is whether the American people have honesty enough, loyalty enough, honor enough, patriotism enough to live up to their own Constitution." To those who thought the solution to the "Negro problem" was the removal of the Negro to Africa, he answered that "we Negroes have made up our minds to stay just where we are." Douglass reminded those whites who had forgotten that during the war Negroes were "eyes to your blind, legs to your lame, shelter to the shelterless among your sons." Now that African Americans numbered almost eight million people, he continued, a reckless effort was made "to blacken the character of the Negro and to brand him as a moral monster." Douglass pointed out that in fourteen states of the Union wild mobs had taken the place of law, and everywhere the Negro was excluded from almost every decent employment. Emphatically the orator asked the North that Negroes "be treated as well as you treat the late enemies of your national life," and he requested the North not to gratify the South at black people's expense. The North should look instead at the progress the Negro race had made in thirty years: "We have come up out of Dahomey into this. Measure the Negro. But not by the standard of the splendid civilization of the Caucasian. Bend down and measure him—measure him—from the depths from which he has risen."[30] These depths, as Douglass wrote in his introduction to *The Reason Why the Colored American Is Not in the World's Columbian Exposition,* were the depths of slavery.

Douglass's emphasis on national reconciliation at the expense of Negroes concerned the very issue that the Chicago World's Fair was meant to erase from public consciousness. The black leader, having celebrated the end of slavery and the hopes of Reconstruction and having fought for the memory of the Civil War over a blind reconciliation, did not live long enough to witness the Supreme Court decision of 1896, in the *Plessy v. Ferguson* case, that sanctioned reconciliation between the North and the South by establishing that racial segregation was constitutionally sound. Douglass died of a heart attack early in 1895—a few hours after he had given a speech on women's rights. By 1893 he had clearly seen the direction the country was taking, and he openly protested against it. So did Ida Wells. From this perspective Douglass's focus on memory and Wells's on lynching were complementary.

There was another black speaker, however, who gave a paper entitled "Progress of Negroes and Free Laborers" to the Labor Congress held at the Chicago World's Fair on 1 September 1893. His accommodationist philosophy on racial relations and black economic achievements was to win the respect of many whites and have the most profound impact on political alliances and organizational strategies of the black leadership from 1895 to 1915. This man, Booker T. Washington, spoke at a meeting chaired by the venerable Frederick Douglass. Washington would reach the status of national leader with his famous Atlanta speech of 1895, but by the time he spoke at the Chicago fair he was well known in the South as the successful school principal of the Tuskegee Normal and Industrial Institute for colored students, which he founded in 1881.

At the session of the Labor Congress in Chicago, Washington wanted to show what Negroes could do if they had the opportunity. He told the story of his Tuskegee Institute, which he and his fellow workers built "with nothing but determination to start an industrial school" on an abandoned cotton plantation. This self-sufficient project was well received, and "pupils flocked in." They cultivated the farm to produce their own food, started a sawmill for the building materials they needed, a brickyard, and a carpentry department, and worked at masonry and blacksmithing. Within twelve years the students had erected twenty-four buildings and were cultivating five hundred acres of land, manufacturing more than half a million bricks, operating a steam engine, and running a printing office for the needs of the whole county. Lacking room and sufficient resources, the school was forced to reject the applications of three hundred young black men and women. In his conclusive remarks, Washington stressed the "insatiable enthusiasm throughout the South among the colored young people for manual training."[31] Washington left Chicago as a local southern black leader. Two years later he became a nationally acclaimed public speaker by convincing a part of white America he had the right prescription to cure the "Negro problem" of the "New South."

Booker T. Washington's Speech at the Atlanta Cotton Exposition

Many New Yorkers who visited Atlanta during the Cotton States and International Exposition of 1895 found similarities between what had become the commercial capital of the New South and New York. Visitors from the northern metropolis agreed that it was not simply a question of commercial relations but the existence of a closer social bond. Atlanta was active, energetic, hustling—the most "modern" city in the South, according to the *New York Times*.[32] The world of international expositions and the transportation and communication revolution had made the country more unified.

On 18 September 1895, in late afternoon, President Grover Cleveland, former governor of New York, touched a golden button at Buzzard's Bay, his house in Massachusetts, and instantly gave life to the wheels of the machinery at the Cotton States and International Exposition in Atlanta, a thousand miles away. This symbolic gesture celebrated a sectionally reunified country: "Cannon blazed and thundered, 60,000 people cheered, a thousand flags fluttered from the tops of the many buildings, and the great South's industrial exposition was officially opened," the *New York Times* informed its readers. The parade of civic and military personnel that acted as an escort to the officials of the exposition and the guests was "the most imposing procession ever seen in the South."[33] When the parade reached the exposition grounds, the official party proceeded to the auditorium. Among the speakers at the opening ceremonies was the principal of the Tuskegee Institute of Alabama, Booker T. Washington.

The celebrated metaphor of the fingers and the hand at the climax of Washington's speech did not leave any space for misunderstanding. It was a speech that sanctioned the legitimacy of a political compromise on racial segregation in exchange for interracial economic cooperation between the white rulers and the black masses of the "Redeemed South."[34] If one looks closer at the public ceremonial space in which Washington delivered his famous speech, the shaking ground on which

the alliance between Washington and his white supporters was enthusiastically celebrated clearly emerges.

The Atlanta Cotton States and International Exposition of 1895 was
a southern attempt to celebrate national reconciliation by highlighting
the progress of the New South from the ashes of Reconstruction. Between 18 September and 31 December 1895, the exposition attracted
1,286,863 visitors.[35] It was the powerful spirit of reunion forged in those
Memorial Day parades and the meetings of Blue and Gray from North
and South in the 1880s that made the Atlanta event possible. The cotton exposition embodied the spirit of Henry Grady, the editor of the *Atlanta Constitution,* who became a major figure in the Georgia political
scene in the early 1880s and who traveled north to recruit capital for
the Redeemed South. In his northern speeches Grady could both praise
Abraham Lincoln as the "typical American" and proudly say that the
South had "nothing for which to apologize. . . . nothing to take back."
Grady told northern audiences that he was glad that "human slavery was
swept forever from the American soil, the American Union was saved
from the wreck of war." He was able to convince New York audiences
that the southerners were back to business instead of politics and that
they loved the new world they were creating. He believed that cooperation of the races was crucial for the New South. When Booker T. Washington became the principal of the Tuskegee Institute in Alabama in
1881, he began corresponding with the white leader, agreeing with
Grady that racial peace was the most important ingredient for the
South's economic progress, and that economic progress was crucial to
racial peace.[36] Racial harmony was what the New South needed to show
the country and the world by finding a solution for its "Negro problem."

In 1895 the Atlanta Cotton Exposition as a public ritual offered an
idealized solution: social segregation and use of the black labor force
for the development of the local economy with the agreement of black
leadership. The Atlanta fair, similar to other minor southern fairs at
that time, assigned an important role to African Americans to develop
domestic and foreign markets. Unlike the planners of the Chicago
World's Fair, the organizers of the Atlanta Exposition did not have any
doubt about establishing a separate Negro Department to show the
products of black industrial and technical schools. Visitors would be
given the impression of racial harmony, they thought, if the Negro Department showed that blacks, kept industrious in local business and
made to feel they cooperated in the economic growth of the South, did
not undermine white supremacy. At the same time, if blacks believed
that their success in finding new markets for their products was left to
them, the problem of class and race relations in the South would be

solved forever. A circular announcing the forthcoming Atlanta Cotton Exposition explained the reason why another international fair was needed so soon after the great Chicago World's Fair in terms of economic "overproduction"—that is, the "absolute necessity for an expansion of trade beyond the limits of the home market."[37]

The financial sponsors of the Atlanta Exposition were the business leaders who had gained power in southern cities in the late 1880s. By the early 1890s, these children of farmers, small-town merchants, and lawyers controlled banks, operated insurance companies, headed cotton firms, and found the *Atlanta Constitution* to be a newspaper supporting their undertakings.[38] The federal government appropriated $200,000 for exhibits as imposing as those of the gigantic Chicago World's Columbian Exposition. Atlanta symbolized the most successful southern city now asserting its importance to the nation and the world. By 1895 Atlanta had six city railroads and a population of one hundred thousand people.

Atlanta businessmen already knew Booker T. Washington's ideas. The Tuskegee principal regularly corresponded with many of them, expressing the views he made public at the Chicago World's Fair. There Washington had heavily criticized the southern sharecrop system and advocated its end through an intensive "manual training" of black workers. The same year, 1893, Washington was also invited to speak to an international meeting of Christian workers held in Atlanta. "I knew that the audience would be largely composed of the most influential class of white men and women," Washington later wrote in his autobiography, "and that it would be a rare opportunity for me to let them know what we were trying to do at Tuskegee, as well as to speak to them about the relations of the races." He took a train from Boston and reached Atlanta just in time to give a five-minute speech that was enthusiastically received by an audience of two thousand people, mostly southern and northern whites. Washington felt he had accomplished his object of "getting a hearing from the dominant class of the South."[39] After that speech he was repeatedly invited to give public addresses, mostly in the North, which was the largest source of funds for his industrial school. It was because of this public exposure that Washington was invited to deliver one of the opening addresses at the Atlanta Cotton States and International Exposition on 18 September 1895.

Impressed with Washington's ideas, the managers of the Atlanta Exposition chose him as one of the three black men (the other two were ministers) included in a delegation that went to Washington, D.C., to meet the House Appropriations Committee. The delegation spoke on behalf of the Atlanta Exposition Committee, composed of the most prominent men of Georgia, and appealed for $200,000 in federal funds. The last on the list of speakers, Washington told the congressional committee in the few minutes left at his disposal that he had "eschewed all participation in politics or political gatherings" and had advised his people to do the same. He explained that his goal was to persuade black people to aspire to "industry, thrift, intelligence and property" in order to gain the respect of whites; he concluded that the Atlanta Exposition "would present an opportunity for both races to show what advance they had made since freedom, and would at the same time afford encouragement to them to make still greater progress."[40] At the end of his speech, Washington was warmly congratulated by both the Georgia committee and the members of Congress. In a few days a bill was passed, and the success of the Atlanta Exposition was assured.

From the beginning of their work, the managers of the Atlanta Exposition did not have any doubt about having a separate Negro Department. They decided that a Negro Building would be designed by a white architect, but it would be constructed entirely by black workers. Although Washington was offered the post of heading the Negro Department at the exposition, he declined the offer because of his duties at Tuskegee and recommended schoolteacher and lawyer I. Garland Penn for that position. When the board of directors discussed the issue of "putting a member of the Negro race on for one of the opening addresses," Washington's name was the one they chose. Although several members of the committee in charge of the opening exercises had preferred to give blacks a separate space, they were reminded by Penn of the crucial speech Washington gave to the House Appropriations Committee. Thus the Tuskegee principal was invited to appear as one of the speakers at the opening ceremonies.[41]

As 18 September 1895, the opening day, approached, Washington felt both honored and nervous. He remembered his early years when he was a slave and his childhood spent "in the lowest depths of poverty and ignorance." He was the last of the major black leaders to be born in slavery. Growing up during Reconstruction in West Virginia, Washington was a child laborer in the salt works and coal mines and a houseboy for a leading white family. He became a student at Hampton Institute in Virginia, a school that applied the missionary method to black education, and he developed the Tuskegee Normal and Industrial Institute in Alabama in 1881 according to Hampton's principles. While anxiously preparing for his public address, Washington thought that only a few years had passed since "any white man in the audience might have claimed me as his slave." He also thought that it was quite possible that

some of his former owners "might be present to hear me speak." He felt
the heavy burden on him, as it was the first time "in the entire history of
the Negro that a member of my race had been asked to speak from the
same platform with white Southern men and women on any important
National occasion." He would be speaking "to an audience composed of
the wealth and culture of the white South, the representatives of my
former masters." There would also be a large number of influential
northern whites, such as those who had largely financed his industrial
school. Washington felt that his speech was so crucial that "by one sentence I could have blasted, in a large degree, the success of the Exposition." After rehearsing his speech with his wife and colleagues at Tuskegee, he felt more confident and ready to go to Atlanta to address
northern and southern whites and blacks together.

Early in the morning of 18 September, Washington was escorted by a
committee of local Negro dignitaries to take his place in a procession
that was to march to the exposition grounds at Piedmont Park for the
opening ceremonies. The presence of eminent black citizens in carriages was remarkable. Washington, Penn, Bishop Wesley J. Gaines, who
was with the Tuskegee principal on the committee sent to the congressional hearings, the black cotton manufacturer William C. Coleman
from North Carolina, and the Reverend Henry H. Proctor, minister of
the First Congregational Church in Atlanta, paraded together with several Negro military organizations. Washington was impressed that the
white officers in charge of the parade "seemed to go out of their way to
see that all of the coloured people in the procession were properly
placed and properly treated." Washington did not take notice that Negro carriages and marchers were in the rear of the parade. This rehearsal of the "separate but equal" formula lasted three hours. Finally,
the procession reached the packed auditorium. When Washington entered the large, racially segregated room, he heard cheers from the colored section of the audience and some from the white part. He was
aware that although many white people were there to hear his speech
out of curiosity, and others attended out of sympathy, a large part of the
white audience was there "for the purpose of hearing me make a fool of
myself."[42]

The great moment arrived. When former governor Rufus Bullock announced that "we shall now be favored with an address by a great Southern educator," the aroused crowd broke into a loud applause but chilled
when Washington stood on the platform, and white people realized
they were applauding a black man. Bullock went ahead and reassured
the crowd by introducing Washington as "a representative of Negro enterprise and Negro civilization." Then the Tuskegee principal gave his

famous speech. He praised the "magnificent Exposition" that would cement the friendship of the two races, and he heralded "a new era of industrial progress." He admitted that because of their ignorance and inexperience, freedmen "in the first years of our new life" thought that a
seat in Congress or the state legislature was more important than real estate or industrial knowledge, "that the political convention of stump
speaking had more attractions than starting a dairy farm or truck garden." He urged his race to "Cast down your bucket where you are. . . .
Cast it down in agriculture, mechanics, in commerce, in domestic service, and in the professions," as it was in the South that black people had
their chances. He was convinced that no race "can prosper till it learns
that there is as much dignity in tilling a field as in writing a poem." Thus
blacks had to start at the bottom, not at the top. Washington asked his
white listeners not to look "to the incoming of those of foreign birth
and strange tongue and habits for the prosperity of the South" but to
cast down their bucket "among the eight millions of Negroes whose
habits you know, whose fidelity and love you have tested in days when to
have proved treacherous meant the ruin of your firesides." These
people, Washington continued, "without strikes and labour wars, tilled
your fields, cleared your forests, builded your railroads and cities, and
brought forth treasures from the bowels of the earth, and helped make
possible this magnificent representation of the progress of the South."
Washington offered a terrific deal, given the subordinate role he left
to black people: "they will buy your surplus land, make blossom the
waste places in your fields, and run your factories," and "you and your
families will be surrounded by the most patient, faithful, law-abiding,
and unresentful people that the world has seen." Washington stressed
his point with his celebrated metaphor of the fingers and the hand, with
the fingers representing social activities, in which whites and blacks
could be segregated, and the hand representing economic unity, which
could be achieved regardless of the social segregation. Washington then
expressed his thanks for "the constant help that has come to our educational life, not only from the Southern states, but especially from
Northern philanthropists." His conclusive remarks that the wisest of the
Negro race understood that "agitation of questions of social equality is
the extremest folly," that no race "that has anything to contribute to the
markets of the world is long in any degree ostracized," and that "the opportunity to earn a dollar in a factory just now is worth infinitely more
than the opportunity to spend a dollar in an opera-house," made former governor Bullock rush across the platform to shake Washington's
hand, as did most people in the audience that day.[43] The fact that the
former governor was southern born, a former slaveholder, and a Con-

federate officer added to that warm handshake the pathos of reconciliation and brought the crowd's excitement to its highest peak.

Many papers in the country published Washington's speech in full,
and for months adulating editorials appeared on his remedy for class
and racial conflicts. The *Atlanta Constitution* welcomed the Tuskegee
principal's address as "a revelation" and "a platform upon which blacks
and white can stand with full justice to each other."[44] Northern papers
were similarly inspired. The *New York World* correspondent writing from
Atlanta was enthusiastic about the morning procession in which Negro
troops and white soldiers from Georgia and Louisiana marched as separate bodies in the same parade. It was the spirit of the New South at its
best. This correspondent was so inspired by Washington's oratory and
message that he portrayed an idolizing, unrealistic representation of
the black speaker:

> A Negro Moses stood before a great audience of white people and deliv-
> ered an oration that marks a new epoch in the history of the South. . . .
> tall, bony, straight as a Sioux chief, high forehead, straight nose, heavy
> jaws, and strong, determined mouth, with big white teeth, piercing eyes,
> and a commanding manner. . . . The sinews stood out on his bronzed
> neck, and his muscular right arm swung high in the air, with a lead-
> pencil grasped in the clinched brown fist. His big feet were planted
> squarely, with the heels together and the toes turned out. His voice rang
> out clear and true, and he paused impressively as he made each point.

Washington was not tall, bony, or even very straight, but these were
the details. This portrait created a powerful image of the leader of a
"moral revolution" in America. Then the New York reporter described
the "uproar of enthusiasm" from the multitude: "hand-kerchiefs were
waved, canes were flourished, hats were tossed in the air," and the "fair-
est women of Georgia stood up and cheered." It was as if "the orator had
bewitched them."[45] Northern public opinion had already built a monu-
ment to Washington. Frederick Douglass had died at the beginning of
1895, and a new black leader was born, the white press heralded. But
Douglass fought throughout his life for equal citizenship. Washington,
proclaimed a black leader by the white press, pursued the philosophy of
national reconciliation that Douglass had abhorred. Douglass was inspired by the Declaration of Independence, Washington by a belief in
the market as a color-blind institution.

A few days later President Grover Cleveland wrote Washington to
thank him for his address: "I have read it with intense interest, and I
think the Exposition would be fully justified if it did not do more than
furnish the opportunity for its delivery." Cleveland met Washington

when he visited the exposition and, to please the Tuskegee principal, spent a full hour at the Negro Building.[46]

Black public response to Washington's speech varied. Among the many who congratulated him was his old friend T. Thomas Fortune, who felt Washington would become the new Frederick Douglass. Other blacks who supported the speech, like W. E. B. Du Bois, would later become Washington's harshest critics. Du Bois, who in 1895 taught at Wilberforce University, wrote Washington to express his admiration for "your phenomenal success at Atlanta." Du Bois also sent a letter to the *New York Age* expressing his confidence that in Washington's speech "might be the basis of a real settlement between whites and blacks in the South, if the South opened to the Negroes the doors of economic opportunity and the Negroes co-operated with the white South in political sympathy."[47] It would not take Du Bois longer than five years to change his mind. The question of the economic approach to racial advancement was a crucial issue on which black leaders held different strategic views.

Washington believed that when the Negro in the South reached economic stability, he would be given access to "all the political rights which his ability, character and material possessions entitle him to." But Washington was also convinced that the Negro's free exercise of political rights would not come "through outside or artificial forcing" but would be accorded by the white southerners, who would also protect the Negro in the exercise of those rights. Washington was a rather optimistic man, as lynching and disfranchisement of black individuals who were honestly gaining economic success certainly did not create a picture of a hopeful future. This was one of the important points made by Ida Wells-Barnett's anti-lynching campaign. Although at this stage she would quite agree with Washington about the importance of gaining economic ground for black people, she did not think that this would please the whites. Consequently, she felt it was wrong to expect civil and political rights from whites as a reward. Wells-Barnett felt that economic achievement was a weapon to use against the status quo of racial discrimination. Historian Thomas Holt has argued that whereas Washington thought that blacks' economic success would gain whites' respect and acceptance, Wells-Barnett saw in economic success the key to imposing changes in white behavior.[48]

Obviously those African Americans who shared Washington's beliefs in the importance of participating at the Atlanta Exposition did their best to deny charges of discrimination against black visitors and encouraged black attendance by asking from the pages of the *Atlanta Constitution* that white employers give their black workers a day off to attend the opening ceremonies at the Negro Building on 21 October 1895.

The Negro Building was located at the southeastern corner of Piedmont Park, the fairgrounds. Black workers erected the structure with its large windows, squared pavilion, and central tower.[49] Here colored visitors could find their hospital facilities, an information service for their accommodations, and their restaurant. One side of the building exhibited a reconstruction of a plantation scene with a one-room log cabin, a log church, and equipment for cotton cultivation. The other side of the building housed a comfortable dwelling, a stone church, and various symbols of Negro progress in arts and literature in thirty years of emancipation. The exhibits represented fourteen states and included thirty models of inventions by colored people, such as Granville T. Woods's "underground electric propulsion and synchronous multiplied railroad telegraph," a medical formula and a set of surgical instruments owned by a colored woman of Chicago, a bust of Charles A. Sumner by a Negro sculptress, women's handwork (edibles, jellies, artificial flowers, etc.), and examples of woodwork. Negro educational institutions like Tuskegee and Hampton were well represented. The displays, in fact, showed what black industrial schools could produce.

The *New York Times,* like most national papers, gave extensive coverage to the Negro Building at the Atlanta Exposition and presented it as the symbol of the new race relations in the South. The paper published an interview with the New York recorder John W. Goff, who spent five days in Atlanta during a three-week tour of the South. He described Atlanta as "a Southern New York" and gave enthusiastic descriptions of the exposition. Goff found the Negro Building "an impressive lesson, especially to the Northerner," as it revealed "the usefulness of the Negro and his position in the New South." Most importantly, the exhibits showed the Negro "as the most prominent factor in the manual arts." Goff was impressed with "every conceivable specimen of his skill as a handicraftsman," producing such items "in the ordinary course of business from plants owned and operated exclusively by Negroes." This was evidence, according to the visitor, that in Atlanta the black man "has equal opportunities with his white brother, and he seems to take good advantage of the chance offered him." Reassured by such a superficial glance given to working conditions for blacks in the South, the northern paper concluded that "the Negro has had the greater chances for practical advancement here in the South than he has ever had, or than he could have, in any other part of the country." The Negro Building was there to show that this was true. In a previous article illustrating Negro exhibits in the making, the *New York Times* informed its readers that a good number had to be turned down for lack of room. "The work of the farm laborer, the carpenter, the mason, the machinist, and the mechanic in all branches of that phase of industry, will be shown here," together with the displays of "the many splendid institutions devoted to the education of the colored youth, especially those wherein the education is of manual training and on technical lines." In a following article covering the opening exercises at the Negro Building, the *New York Times* reported that "Negro Day brought the largest attendance the exposition has had."[50]

With a special ceremony the building was symbolically donated by I. Garland Penn to the president of the exposition, C. A. Collier. On the stage of the auditorium were a number of prominent people, including Daniel Nash Morgan, U.S. treasurer, Mayor Porter King, war correspondent James Creelman, Exposition President Collier, General J. R. Lewis, Booker T. Washington, and Penn. This young educator assembled all the exhibits, with the help of Washington, to "teach a strong lesson of the progress of the Negro people." One of the speakers underlined how "the progress of the Negro is not to be measured alone by his achievements, but also by the depths from which he has risen since his freedom." One after the other, speakers were greeted by the singing of several student choruses. When Penn's turn came, the Virginian educator stressed the main idea of Booker T. Washington's speech by linking the progress of the race to the progress of the South. Penn thought the exhibits at the Negro Building, largely the products of industrial and technical schools since emancipation, showed the possibilities, new aspirations, and endeavors of the Negro race, the magnitude of northern philanthropy, and the "largeness" of the South's generous "recognition of the race in the trade and other fields of labor." In a symbolic deliverance of the building to President Collier, Penn emphasized Washington's point of a common interest essential to prosperity: the New South and the New Negro "will work out their own salvation." Then it was President Collier's turn to respond. He thanked both Penn and Washington for making the whole exhibit such a success and stressed the importance of the event. "For the first time in the history of industrial expositions," Collier said, "we see here a building set apart and dedicated to the Negro race." He also emphasized the epochal meaning that at the inauguration of an international exposition a Negro orator figured "among those who were commissioned to speak of its significance and purpose." Consequently there was "no reason for any conflict between the two races which have by God's providence been thrown together here." Taken by his own words, President Collier concluded his portrait of idealized relations between the two races in the South by defining the progress of the Negro race since emancipation as "one of the marvels of history."[51]

Black public opinion, however, did not unanimously support these optimistic views of Booker T. Washington's philosophy. Many African Americans objected to the idea of having a Negro Building at the Atlanta Exposition. Some northern blacks agreed with John C. Buckner, a black Illinois legislator, that Congress should not give any financial support to business in the South, where black people were lynched and their constitutional rights abused. Others, like William S. Scarborough, a member of the National Philological Society, objected to the whole event and asked black people to shun the fair because their presence at the Atlanta Exposition would tacitly support segregation practices. Opposition also came from black Atlanta residents and from other parts of the South. Those who opposed the fair remarked that although black visitors were given access to every building, they could not purchase refreshments except at the Negro Building. Private exhibitors with restaurant concessions refused to admit black customers. In the auditorium, audiences were segregated. "The Fair is a big fake," a local black paper exclaimed. "Negroes have not even a dog's show inside the Exposition gates unless it is in the Negro Building." In responding to those African Americans from other parts of the country asking whether the fair was worthy of a trip to Atlanta, this local paper warned potential black visitors: "if they wish to feel that they are inferior to other American citizens, if they want to pay double fare on the surface cars and also be insulted, if they want to see on all sides: 'For Whites Only,' or 'No Niggers or dogs allowed,' if they want to be humiliated and have their man and womanhood crushed out, then come."[52]

Commissioner I. Garland Penn found these rumors of racial discrimination disturbing, for they undermined the positive image of the alliance between blacks and whites for their common interest in the New South. In a letter to the *Atlanta Constitution,* Penn dismissed as "wholly untrue" any allegation of discrimination by citing letters he had received from eminent black people who visited all fair buildings and went everywhere they wanted without being harassed. Penn was convinced that "men and conditions in the South are changing," and he blamed "malicious misrepresentation" of how black people were treated at the fair on those "many little men in our race who think it the greatest feat of a lifetime to be regarded as a defender of and a martyr for their race to the extent of keeping the breech between the Negro and the white man open by a total misrepresentation of even that which is good and great in the South." Penn concluded his letter by saying that the exposition organizers were "men of broad and liberal minds" who represented "the best elements of the new South."[53]

Penn's words, however, did not sound convincing to black visitors from the North. Editor T. Thomas Fortune went to Atlanta in the winter to visit the exposition. He wrote an article for the *New York Sun* in which he portrayed Atlanta as a "new" and "gawky" city where "prejudice of race" was "more general and pronounced than in any other city of the South." Fortune could not think of any civil, social, or political right to which black people were entitled. Under those circumstances, to expect the progress of the race was "to expect a stream to rise above its source." At the exposition Fortune came across many examples of white rural southerners of the type "who did most of the fighting in the war" and who did "most of the fighting now." This type of rural southerner, Fortune observed, was seldom elected to Congress but was a strong presence in state legislatures responsible for Jim Crow laws that segregated black people in public places, and at constitutional conventions that disfranchised black men. It was this type of southerner that led the "lynching party" and went unpunished. Although a friend and political ally of Washington's, Fortune felt he could be more outspoken than the Tuskegee principal because he lived and approached racial issues in the North.[54] Such differentiated responses to the question of black representation in public events further complicated integrationist and separatist strategies.

Fairs, Racial Science for the Average Man, and Empire

Fairs were effective instruments of dissemination of evolutionist ideas from academic circles to popular consumption. After the success of Chicago's Midway Plaisance, Atlanta tried to emulate the White City with its Midway Heights, where showmen controlled the ethnological display of "authentic" primitive types and the Buffalo Bill show. These exhibits of human types, whose layout differed only slightly from Chicago's, were patterned according to the Atlanta Exposition's goal of presenting the world of the New South as a classless society of proud Anglo-Saxons.

After Booker T. Washington's historical speech, the opening exercises of the Atlanta Exposition continued with the address of Judge Emory Speer of the U.S. District Court at Macon. He gave the longest speech in the name of the southern white man and announced that the race question simply did not exist. Gladly Speer informed his segregated listeners that blacks were not a threat to white civilization. He urged those whites who were still afraid of "Negro control" to think about the extraordinary "commanding nature of the Anglo-Saxon race." To avoid any misunderstanding on this point, Speer identified India as a good example. According to the judge, in India forty million "dark-skinned men" were overcome by "a handful of men of our race"

and led "on all paths of modern progress by the English Government as
readily as it controls a parish in Yorkshire or Kent." The South had the
largest number of the old Anglo-Saxon stock in the country and therefore could follow the English colonial model.[55]

· This language of the white man's burden was rather common at late
nineteenth-century international expositions both in Europe and the
United States. By delivering the ambiguous message of exporting American democracy to the rest of the world in the language of white supremacy, ceremonial rituals at the Chicago World's Columbian Exposition designed the leading role the United States would play in the world
in the new century. Both Alan Trachtenberg and Robert Rydell have
convincingly argued in their works that the Chicago World's Fair symbolized the U.S. imperial position, which the Spanish-American War
would consolidate within a few years.[56]

An example of this imperial position is the following description of
the Fourth of July celebration at Midway Plaisance in the *Frank Leslie's
Popular Monthly:*

> When the Stars and Stripes were loosed to the breeze cheer after cheer
> went up from people from all parts of the earth. Never before had such
> a cosmopolitan gathering saluted the emblem of our nation. A com-
> pany of artillery from England's standing army spoke her majesty's salu-
> tation from the cannon's mouth. Sixty Arabs, mounted on their gallant
> steeds, and ten camels in holiday attire, bore dusky wanderers from the
> desert. It was a day for strange people and queer sights. The five races
> of man were there. The American Indian was represented by a dozen
> tribal types. The Esquimau, in his suit of sealskin, thought the day quite
> warm. The Dahomeyan, the Nubian and the Soudanese, from the wilds
> of Africa, appeared in neglige attire. Japan, Java, and China lent their
> presence as Mongolians. The brown Polynesian, from the Samoan and
> Fiji Islands, whooped as the Malay only can. And last, but not least, the
> Caucasian of every land, complexion and religion, joined hands with
> his colored kinsman and cheered for that which Americans enjoy and
> which all men love, "Liberty."[57]

Anthropological exhibits explained to visitors this crucial role the
United States was going to play by expanding the boundaries of the old
theory of Manifest Destiny in the name of "Liberty." At Atlanta's Midway
Heights the visitor could see a Native American village, rebuilt with original lodges, which recalled the events of the early 1890s leading to the
massacre at Wounded Knee.[58] Many of the Sioux put on display had
been involved in the Ghost Dance movement and fought the U.S.
troops, the majority of whom were white soldiers, but there also were a

few colored regiments. The Smithsonian Institution continued its popularization of evolutionary anthropology at the Cotton Exposition by displaying backward types of humanity. The message was clear: the inferior (dark) races were lifted up by contact with the superior (white) race.

Racial science for the average man targeted by public events like the Chicago World's Fair and the Atlanta Cotton Exposition based its discoveries on the large amount of research on anthropometry that the U.S. Sanitary Commission carried out during the Civil War. Scientists working for the Sanitary Commission, devised by eminent New Yorkers Henry W. Bellows and Frederick Law Olmsted, agreed that the successful conduct of the war depended more on the health of the troops than on other factors. Consequently the extensive collection of body measurements they pioneered became the authoritative point of reference that framed late nineteenth-century popular racial attitudes. Historian of science John Haller aptly points out that "the war which freed the slave also helped to justify racial attitudes of nineteenth century society." The constitution of the anthropometric section of the Sanitary Commission followed congressional authorization of 1862 to employ people of "African descent" to suppress the rebellion, namely to form colored regiments that by the end of war had utilized 180,000 African-American men. American scientists saw in that opportunity a means to organize the most extensive investigation of racial differences. The Sanitary Commission based its survey on the statistical methodology of the Belgian philosopher Lambert A. J. Quetelet, whose mid-nineteenth-century theory of probability applied to moral and political science.[59] Quetelet's statistical methodology aimed at the creation of an average man and the examination of his physical, moral, and social relations.

During the Civil War the U.S. Sanitary Commission applied Quetelet's methods to characterize the average man among the varieties of men of British, Irish, German, Native American, and African ancestry composing the Union and the Confederate armies. Investigator Benjamin A. Gould, a member of the National Academy of Sciences and the president of the American Association for the Advancement of Sciences, was invited in 1863 to act as director of anthropometric statistics for the Sanitary Commission. Gould's reports to the commission established that "the external form of this average man may be legitimately adopted as a standard of beauty and a model of art." He argued, as Quetelet had shown, that "we may discover not merely the outward semblance of this abstract being, but his needs, capacities, intellect, judgment, and tendencies."

These broad generalizations were drawn from inadequate sampling of Negroes and Native Americans. During the first year the anthropometric section of the Sanitary Commission examined 8,004 white Union and Confederate troops. From 1864, after the formation of Negro regiments, until the end of the war, 10,876 white soldiers, 1,146 white sailors, 68 white marines, 2,020 full-blooded Negroes, 863 mulattoes, and 519 Indians were examined. The commission, by using instruments like the andrometer and the facial angle, measured and compared individuals of various nationalities, Negroes, and Indians according to body and head dimensions, physical strength, sight, teeth, and respiratory capacity. Evidence seemed to corroborate all preexisting racialist beliefs about the physiological inferiority of the mulatto to the original stocks and the racial inferiority of the Negro. The obvious conclusion was that racial mixing was wrong. Because the commission had established that a long head and neck and short arms were the desirable characteristics of the average man and had found these characteristics frequently among white soldiers, black soldiers were therefore considered closer to apes because they presented excessively long arms and short body length.[60]

After the war Sanford B. Hunt, a surgeon who had worked for the Sanitary Commission, published an article in the authoritative British *Anthropological Review* that was a copy of his report to the Sanitary Commission. His findings concerned black soldiers' capacity to learn tactics, level of intellect, personal hygiene, resistance to hunger and fatigue, diseases, courage, obedience, and other moral qualities. He found the Negro a good recruit because of his "well known" imitative faculty, his love of rhythmic movements, and his habit of obedience inherited from slavery. To test intellectual capacities of colored soldiers, Hunt relied on the size and weight of the brains of 405 dead soldiers (24 white and 381 black), whose autopsies showed that the brain of a full-blooded Negro weighed on average five ounces less than the brain of a white soldier. Although Hunt's results confirmed Samuel Morton's measurements of the 1850s, he reached different conclusions. Hunt suggested to regularly repeat Negro autopsies over time in the future to find whether longer exposure to the benefits of freedom and education would alter Negro brain size. Thus, he thought, the controversy between environmentalists and hereditarians would be finally resolved. As Hunt framed it, the question was: "Does the large brain by its own impulses create education, civilization and refinement, or do education, civilization and refinement create the large brain?"[61] Hunt left this broad question open to further investigation.

Starting in the 1870s, physicians and academic natural scientists oriented their research to suggest that not only was the Negro race physically inferior to the white, but since emancipation the growing mortality rate of the Negro race anticipated its future extinction. Historians of those investigations have definitively shown that scientists were influenced by surrounding social circumstances in which Negroes were progressively disfranchised, attacked by the Ku Klux Klan, and lynched in growing number. By defining Negroes as biologically inferior human beings, scientists provided a legitimization of racial prejudice.

According to William Lee Howard, a physician from Baltimore, as a result of emancipation the Negro man was "returning to a state of savagery," and his sexual madness and religious emotionalism were "innate" characteristics of the African. Howard argued that the attack of the Negro man on the Caucasian woman was also an irrepressible part of his African instinct. If emancipated Negroes did not possess the capacity of becoming civilized and educated, what should be done with them? Dr. Charles S. Bacon of Chicago did not think that several million black laborers in the South should be forced to migrate from the country because they were an important economic resource. His advice was to fully utilize the manual labor of the Negro while eliminating him as a political and social threat. The ballot was unnecessary for the Negro, he argued, because it "will not make a man moral, industrious, thrifty, or healthy." In 1870 Harvard natural scientist Nathaniel Southgate Shaler asserted that science had shown the mulatto to be physiologically inferior to both parents. He hoped that this type would soon cease to exist and would leave the South to the two pure-blood races. Shaler found the mulatto particularly unfit to compete in the struggle for existence: "From the white he inherits a refinement unfitting him for all work which has not a certain delicacy about it; from the black, a laxity of morals which, whether it be the result of innate incapacity for certain forms of moral culture or the result of an utter want of training in this direction, is still unquestionably a negro characteristic."

Twenty years later Shaler wrote that the highest proportion of blacks in the United States came from the Guinea coast inhabited by the least capable of all Africans. He found their facial expression partially human and partially "a remnant of the ancient animal who had not yet come to the careful stage of life." The Guinea type lacked intellectual abilities and was an example of a body dominating the mind. Shaler also found a minor presence of the Zulu type, a "vigorous, brave, alert" stock, whose straighter hair and facial expression suggested a mixture of Arabian blood. Unfortunately, he complained, this type was rare in the United States, but the best household servants under slavery belonged to the Zulu type. The Harvard scientist hoped that future anthropometrical studies would compare the mental and physical characteristics of the American Negro with his African ancestors: "it may be possible to determine if the two centuries of enforced labor and civilizing influences to which our American blacks have been exposed have had any effect on their mental development."[62]

The Chicago World's Columbian Exposition seemed to answer Shaler's request. Anthropometric research was done on a large scale on the fairgrounds, although not exclusively on Negroes. Besides the Midway Plaisance ethnological exhibit at the World's Fair, popularization of ethnology and anthropometric research was made available to visitors at the Anthropological Building, Department M, under the direction of Harvard ethnologist Frederick Ward Putnam with the assistance of the German-Jewish anthropologist Franz Boas. Looking for a stable job, the immigrant scientist accepted Putnam's invitation to act as his assistant in charge of physical anthropology and to organize a display on the tribes of the Northwest Coast, the object of Boas's study since his first fieldwork in that area in 1886. An important aspect of Boas's job was establishing connections with hundreds of schoolteachers, missionaries, and administrators to make arrangements for the measurement of over ninety thousand North American schoolchildren and seventeen thousand Native Americans. He also had to organize an extensive exhibit of the native tribes of the Northwest Coast.[63] At Department M, visitors could examine collections of ethnological and archaeological research and physical anthropology. They could admire a rich display of masks and dancing paraphernalia that Franz Boas had found in the Pacific Northwest. Visitors could then explore the laboratory and exhibit of physical anthropology. Here Boas and his assistants explained the use of a series of instruments such as anthropometric machines, craniometric instruments, and instruments for drawing skulls and outlines of the body forms. Visitors could watch other visitors while their cephalic index was measured.

It is ironic that Boas, who later made the most radical break with the evolutionists' comparative theory of stages of human development by dismissing the idea of race as the most significative source of differences in mental or social capacities of human groups, organized anthropological exhibits at the Chicago World's Fair that popularized racial biosocial science for the average visitor. But he needed a job, and he had already done extensive anthropometrical research. By the turn of the century, however, Boas began to challenge the false assumptions of racial inequality on which his colleagues had built their theories and shaped public opinion. Although Boas was a believer in objective scientific research, his priority was racial equality. Given this assumption, Boas oriented his scientific research accordingly. The importance of Boas's new paradigm of cultural explanation for human behavior over biological assumptions should not be undervalued at a time when racism was pervasive in the United States, racial segregation was imposed in the South by law, and eugenic remedies like sterilization of "defective," "degenerate," or "inferior" people were emerging as hereditarian solutions to social problems.

In the late 1890s and 1900s eminent individuals who had been quite liberal before the war turned against the Fifteenth Amendment, which called for racial integration, and publicly spoke in favor of racial segregation. Thomas Wentworth Higginson, for example, a former abolitionist who had commanded a Negro regiment during the Civil War, by 1909 believed that extending voting rights to Negro males was a mistake and that white communities would never give their consent to political supremacy of any colored race. Another example was Charles W. Eliot, the president of Harvard University, who in his later years gave his authoritative support to the growing eugenic movement, publicly denounced any form of mixing of racial stocks, and endorsed racial separation in the South.[64]

The U.S. Supreme Court, a year after Booker T. Washington's Atlanta speech, ruled with only one dissenting voice that "legislation is powerless to eradicate racial instincts" and made the majority view of national reconciliation based on racial separation constitutionally sound. It is ironic that the famous *Plessy v. Ferguson* decision was passed by a Supreme Court whose justices were largely northern Republicans, six of whom were Harvard Law School graduates, with the only dissenting voice that of Justice John Marshall Harlan from Kentucky. A veteran of the political battles of the Reconstruction era who had served on the Court for nearly twenty years, Justice Harlan compared the *Plessy* decision to the Dred Scott case and asserted that the Constitution was color-blind. This was what the plaintiff, Homer A. Plessy, who was seven-eighths Caucasian and one-eighth Negro, and his supporters held after he was arrested for entering a railroad car reserved for whites and refused to sit in a segregated coach for Negroes, as the Louisiana laws established in 1890. The American Citizens Equal Rights Association, a group that was organized by blacks in New Orleans to challenge the Louisiana law requiring railroads to provide "separate but equal" accommodations for blacks and that was represented by carpetbagger Albion Tourgee, a New York Radical Republican of the Reconstruction era in North Carolina, denied that the law's guarantee of equal facilities satisfied the requirements of the Fourteenth Amendment. Tourgee emphasized that the main purpose of the post–Civil War amendments was the eradication of caste and the establishment of a color-blind Constitution.

In his dissenting statement Justice Harlan declared that the 1896 ruling could not only "stimulate aggressions, more or less brutal and irritating, upon the admitted rights of colored citizens," but also could easily encourage the belief "that it is possible, by means of state enactments," to defeat the Thirteenth and Fourteenth Amendments. For Justice Harlan, the destinies of the two races in the country were "indissolubly linked together," and it was therefore in the interest of both that "the common government of all shall not permit the seeds of race hate to be planted under the sanction of law." Without denying that the white race was the dominant race in the country in prestige, achievement, education, wealth, and power, Harlan argued that "in view of the Constitution, in the eye of the law, there is in this country no superior, dominant, ruling class of citizens." The Constitution was "color-blind." Legitimating by law the seeds of race hate by ruling that "colored citizens are so inferior and degraded that they cannot be allowed to sit in public coaches occupied by white citizens" was unconstitutional in Harlan's view. To those who held that colored citizens had to pay equal fare for their separate "and equal" facilities, Harlan answered that the "thin disguise of 'equal' accommodations for passengers in railroad coaches will not mislead anyone, or atone for the wrong this day done." There was no question that segregated cars were, in the greatest majority of cases, unequal cars. But the Supreme Court ruled that these "separate but equal accommodations" satisfied the demands of the Fourteenth Amendment: "If the civil and political rights of both races be equal one cannot be inferior to the other civilly or politically. If one race be inferior to the other socially, the Constitution of the United States cannot put them upon the same plane."[65]

With southern segregation already accepted as the price of national reconciliation, the country did not pay much attention to the Supreme Court decision of 1896. There were crucial economic and political issues on the domestic front and a growing national interest in the escalation of tensions with Spain over Cuban independence. Domestic and foreign economic and political issues soon overlapped with the breaking out of the Spanish-American War of 1898. It was a great opportunity for the country to show the world that its national reconciliation had succeeded and that the United States could become the imperial power of the twentieth century. The response black Americans gave to the expansionist trend in foreign policy "dramatized the vacillation and contradiction born out of their unreconciled strivings," in historian Willard Gatewood's words.[66]

After the sinking of the *Maine* early in 1898, war became inevitable. Booker T. Washington saw in the coming war with Spain an opportunity for black Americans to show their loyalty to the country. Echoing Frederick Douglass's black enlistment campaign during the Civil War, Washington promptly informed the secretary of the navy that in the case of war he would recruit "at least ten thousand loyal, brave, strong black men in the south who crave an opportunity to show their loyalty to our land and would gladly take this method of showing their gratitude for the lives laid down and the sacrifices made that the Negro might have his freedom and rights." Many African Americans identified with the Cuban struggle. Antonio Maceo was the mulatto general whose fight against the Spanish forces inspired many black Americans. To them, colored Cubans' fight for freedom was similar to their struggle for full citizenship in the United States. Many others did not think that they should fight under the American flag since black people in the United States were denied civil and political rights, were segregated, and were lynched. An armed conflict with Spain, they argued, would not grant racial justice in the country. "Negro haters have declared that this is a white man's country," John Mitchell, the editor of a black paper in Richmond, thundered. If the black man was not "good enough to exercise the right of franchise," why should he be considered "good enough to exercise the right to enlist in the service of the United States," Mitchell argued.[67]

Four black regiments of the regular army, stationed in the American West since the Civil War, were the first to be sent to Cuba. The "Buffalo soldiers," as Native Americans of the Great Plains called the black cavalrymen sent out to "pacify" the West in the 1890s, and other black regiments were the first to be mobilized in 1898. Their white commanders, like most Americans, thought that their racial characteristics suited them to fight in tropical Cuba. Pulled out of Utah, Montana, and other western states, the black soldiers traveled south to embark for Cuba, cheered by racially mixed crowds. When they crossed Kentucky and Tennessee, they met the silence of staring whites and could not be welcomed by their black supporters, who were not allowed to get close to the train. The first battles fought by the black soldiers on Cuban soil in June of 1898 were successful and gave them national recognition. Their fame encouraged more than ten thousand black men from both the North and South to volunteer by the end of the summer, ready to participate in the invasion of Havana. Stationed in the South before embarkation, the black recruits from the North wrote home to tell their families what they saw and experienced: horrible details of lynchings, the humiliation of separate railroad cars, the prejudice "not so much against the ignorant Negro," a recruiting officer born a slave wrote his family in the North, "as it is against the intelligent, educated, taxpaying Negro . . . who is trying to be a man."[68] In Tampa, Florida, a riot broke out after some white volunteers took a two-year-old black boy from his mother's arms and used him, for fun, as a target in front of his hysterical mother. Out of vengeance, black soldiers in Tampa destroyed all those public places, such as saloons, cafes, and brothels, refusing service to colored soldiers.

The southern press reacted to the Tampa riot by remarking that the mobilization of black soldiers had been a mistake because it made them forget "their place." The *Atlanta Constitution* concluded that army discipline did not have any effect on Negro soldiers. Only three years had passed since the paper had enthusiastically supported Booker T. Washington's speech. Now it speculated that sending Negro troops to Cuba after "their wild and demoniac conduct . . . at Tampa" was a criminal act. Black troops should be sent back "to the Indian reservations" before they could attack "white Cubans."[69]

The four black regiments participated in the conquest of Santiago. In the assault at San Juan Heights, Colonel Theodore Roosevelt found himself leading the charge of his Rough Riders together with other cavalrymen and infantrymen, including Negro troops. "If it had not been for the Negro cavalry," a volunteer from Roosevelt's Rough Riders later declared, "the Rough Riders would have been exterminated." A black infantryman who witnessed the battle stated that without the "smoked Yankees," as the Spanish called the black soldiers, "the Rough Riders would not have dislodged the Spaniards by themselves." Yet instead of giving credit to the colored troops, Roosevelt, in a series of articles in *Scribner's Magazine* in 1899, when he was governor of New York, portrayed black soldiers as "particularly dependent" on white officers, lacking the capacity to lead, showing extreme panic under fire, and seeking safety in the rear lines during battles. He attributed all these bad military qualities to "the superstition and fear of the darkey, natural in those but one generation removed from the wildest savagery." Roosevelt was wrong, eyewitnesses reported. He had erroneously concluded that black soldiers were leaving their positions out of fear when in reality both black and white soldiers were transporting the wounded to the rear.[70]

Although in 1901, shortly after becoming president, Roosevelt shocked the country by inviting Booker T. Washington to dine with him at the White House, his contradictory and paradoxical racial views followed the tradition of Anglo-Saxon supremacy. As Roosevelt put it in 1894, it was "America's duty toward the people living in barbarism to see that they are freed from their chains, and we can free them only by destroying barbarism itself. . . . peace cannot be had until the civilized nations have expanded in some shape over the barbarous nations." When President William McKinley, a Union veteran, went to the South looking for support for the treaty with Spain, he declared before the

Georgia legislative assembly that "sectional feeling no longer holds back the love we bear each other." He then reviewed parades of Confederate veterans and stood for the playing of "Dixie."[71]

The Spanish-American War inscribed national reconciliation into popular imagination. Based on myths that the language of biosocial science legitimized Anglo-Saxon superiority, national reconciliation gave the country a solid identity and a way of handling the "dark races" of the world. By the turn of the century, the United States was well on the way to building an empire that dominated over primarily people of African, Indian, Polynesian, Japanese, and Chinese extraction. "The White Man's Burden," as Rudyard Kipling's poem aptly justified British colonialism, became an American burden. The poem, which first appeared in the United States in February 1899, defined the "white man's burden" as the Anglo-Saxon's duty to uplift the "new caught, sullen peoples, half-devil and half-child," who lived in the lands conquered by Western civilization. To Governor Roosevelt, the poem was "poor poetry but good sense from the expansionist standpoint."[72]

At the end of the Spanish-American War the United States faced the problem of dealing with Cubans, Filipinos, Puerto Ricans, the Polynesian peoples of Hawaii, and other groups outside the American continent. Cuba was not annexed but was left open to American business adventures. Puerto Rico was taken over by U.S. military forces, the Hawaiian Islands were annexed by a congressional resolution in July 1898, and Wake Island in the Pacific was occupied by American forces that also took Guam, the Spanish possession further west in the Pacific.

The most inflamed debate on U.S. expansionism occurred on the Philippines. President McKinley justified annexation on the grounds that "there was nothing left for us to do but to take them all and to educate the Filipinos, and uplift and civilize and Christianize them, and by God's grace do the very best we could by them." Opposition to "McKinley imperialism" was strong among African Americans. Booker T. Washington was against the annexation of the islands: "Until our nation has settled the Negro and Indian problems I do not believe that we have a right to assume more social problems," he declared in September 1898. When the hostilities between the colored followers of Filipino leader Aguinaldo and the American forces broke out, black American opposition to McKinley's policy became stronger. Ida Wells-Barnett included anti-imperialist notes in her anti-lynching campaign by asserting that the American administration should protect black citizens from lynching mobs before taking on the white man's burden in the Philippines. There were also some African Americans who thought that it would be beneficial for the natives of those Pacific islands to accept "the same boon that was offered the American negro in 1861—the opportunity to become subjects of a great and good government." Filipinos did not understand, some black Americans thought, that Americans were their "saviors," offering them the same future that Lincoln offered the Negro. But some black Americans were aware that white troops referred to Aguinaldo and his followers as "niggers." Some claimed that Aguinaldo and his companions opposed American control because they feared that Filipinos would be given the same bad treatment as Negroes received in the United States. Ironically, in the Senate the major anti-imperialist bloc came from southern senators, some of whom justified their opposition by agitating the ghost of Reconstruction. A senator from Arkansas, for example, declared that he would never vote "to force upon the inhabitants of the Philippine Islands, Malays, negroes, and savages though they may be, the curse of carpetbag government."[73]

Some Americans opposed imperialism by forming anti-imperialist leagues that joined in a coalition in Chicago, in October 1899, to approve the platform of the American Anti-Imperialist League. The individuals who gathered there held conflictual views on domestic politics but shared a common opposition to colonial expansionism. Supporters of the Anti-Imperialist League were political and business leaders, writers, and academics, and they held a wide range of views. Included were former president Cleveland, McKinley's Democratic opponent William Jennings Bryan, industrialist Andrew Carnegie, Secretary of the American Federation of Labor Samuel Gompers, writer Mark Twain, Harvard philosopher William James, and reformer Jane Addams. Some were responding to the brutal behavior of American troops in the Philippines, whereas others were afraid that the imperial expansion would bring an armament race leading to foreign alliances and future wars of intervention. This coalition signed a platform containing language, like that of the abolitionists, that was inspired by the Declaration of Independence: "We hold that the policy known as imperialism is hostile to liberty and tends toward militarism, an evil from which it has been our glory to be free. We regret that it has become necessary in the land of Washington and Lincoln to reaffirm that all men of whatever race or color are entitled to life, liberty, and the pursuit of happiness. . . . we earnestly condemn the policy of the present national administration in the Philippines. It seeks to extinguish the spirit of 1776 in those islands."[74]

At the turn of the century, anti-imperialist positions took international connotations. Although the new pan-African movement represented a broad political spectrum and was more concerned with ending European colonial rule, it progressively developed a strong criticism of the philosophy of the white man's burden. Among the African-American intellectuals involved since the first Pan-African Congress in London in July 1900 was thirty-two-year-old W. E. B. Du Bois. The fact that Ethiopian emperor Menelik II had defeated the Italian army at Adwa in 1896 had a prodigious meaning to African-American intellectual Du Bois. In the London conference of 1900 he addressed the "congress of men and women of African blood" with his prophetic speech "To the Nations of the World":

> The problem of the twentieth century is the problem of the colour line, the question as to how far differences of races, which show themselves chiefly in the colour of the skin and the texture of the hair, are going to be made, hereafter, the basis of denying to over half the world the right of sharing to their outmost ability the opportunities and privileges of modern civilisation. . . . If now the world of culture bends itself towards giving the Negroes and other dark men the largest and broadest opportunity for education and self-development, then this contact and influence is bound to have a beneficial effect upon the world and hasten human progress. But if, by reason of carelessness, prejudice, greed and injustice, the black world is to be exploited and ravished and degraded, the results must be deplorable, if not fatal, not simply to them, but to the high ideals of justice, freedom, and culture which a thousand years of Christian civilisation have held before Europe.[75]

3

Social Science as Public Culture

Rituals of Race at Academic Meetings

One could not be a calm, cool, and detached scientist while Negroes were lynched, murdered and starved. . . . Stepping . . . out of my ivory tower of statistics and investigation, I sought with bare hands to lift the earth and put it in the path in which I conceived it ought to go.
W. E. B. DU BOIS

The background of my early thinking was a German home in which the ideals of the revolution of 1848 were a living force.   FRANZ U. BOAS

When W. E. B. Du Bois Met Franz Boas

W. E. B. Du Bois framed his first racial definition of history at the founding meeting of the American Negro Academy in Washington, D.C., in 1897. His paper, entitled "The Conservation of Races," and the foundation of the American Negro Academy occurred the year following the Supreme Court decision on the constitutionality of racial segregation, and two years after Booker T. Washington's "Atlanta compromise." The principal of the Tuskegee Institute had stressed the importance of industrial education to solve any economic and moral problems of black people and had praised the virtues of slavery as an educational stage toward Christianity and citizenship. "We went into slavery without a language," Washington repeated on several occasions; "we came out speaking the proud Anglo-Saxon tongue."[1]

In strong disagreement with the Tuskegee Institute's idea of a limited industrial education for American blacks, the elderly Episcopal minister Alexander Crummell founded the American Negro Academy (ANA) as an elitist association of intellectual black men, with membership limited to "men of African descent." On 5 March 1897, in Washington, D.C., Crummell addressed eighteen African-American intellectual men who held legal or academic positions or who were ministers of Protestant denominations. Among these highly educated individuals were professor W. E. B. Du Bois, who had just moved to Philadelphia from Wilberforce, poet Paul Laurence Dunbar, and Francis Grimke, the Princeton-educated natural son of a South Carolina slaveholder. These men were assembled, Crummell said, to promote "the civilization of the Negro race in the United States, by the scientific processes of literature, art and philosophy." To Crummell, who spent most of his life in Liberia, progress, Christianity, and civilization had an identical meaning.[2]

By delivering his address, "The Conservation of Races," Du Bois offered a theoretical ground to justify the existence of the ANA. Still highly influenced by his German mentor Heinrich von Treitschke, with whom he had studied at the University of Berlin and who held the romantic nationalistic notion that history was made by the powerful wills of great men, and by his Harvard supervisor Albert Bushnell Hart, who held a racialist view of history, Du Bois declared in Hegelian terms: "The history of the world is the history, not of individuals, but of groups, not of nations, but of races, and he who ignores or seeks to override the race idea in human history ignores and overrides the central thought of all history." In his Hegelian scheme, great men were no more than representatives of racial ideals. Each "race"—that is, each "family of human beings, generally of common blood and language, always of common history, traditions and impulses, who are both voluntarily and involuntarily striving together for the accomplishment of certain more or less vividly conceived ideals of life"—had a "gift" to offer to humanity. This was the result of differences—"subtle, delicate and elusive, though they may be—which have silently but definitively separated men into groups."

Young Du Bois had learned from his Harvard and German teachers that white, Negro, and yellow were the three primordial examples of races. The historical examples of race groups were the Teutons, Slavs, English of Great Britain and North America, the so-called Romance nations, Negroes of Africa and the Americas, Semites, Hindus, and Mongolians. Whereas the English gave the world constitutional liberty and commercial freedom, the Germans contributed science and philosophy, and the Romance nations provided literature and art. Negroes, too, in Du Bois's view, possessed the cohesiveness of these "racial" groups, but their spiritual message had not been fully given to the world. The Egyptian civilization showed just a hint of that message, but the Negro race, like the yellow and Slavic races, was just starting to deliver its messages. Black people's "subtle sense of song" had given America, Du Bois held, "its only American music, its only American fairy tales, its only touch of pathos and humor amid its money-getting plutocracy." It was, therefore, black people's duty "to conserve their physical powers, intellectual endowments, spiritual ideals." As a race, black people "must strive by race organizations, by race solidarity, by race unity to the realization of that broader humanity which freely recognizes differences in men, but sternly deprecates inequality in their opportunities of development." Raising the dilemma of his double-consciousness of being an American and a Negro, Du Bois questioned himself: "Am I an American or am I a Negro? Can I be both? Or is my duty to cease to be a Negro as soon as possible and be an American? . . . Does my black blood place upon me any more obligation to assert my nationality than German, or Irish or Italian blood would?"[3]

The early Du Bois differed from Frederick Douglass, whose integrationist views urged African Americans not to form separate civil, social, political, and economic organizations whenever possible. "There can be but one American nation," Douglass believed, and "a nation within a nation" was an anomaly. For Du Bois, Negroes were Americans "not only by birth and by citizenship" but also by their political ideals, language, and religion. Nevertheless, he added that "farther than that our Americanism does not go." Negroes for young Du Bois were "members of a vast historic race that from the very dawn of creation has slept, but [was] half awakening in the forests of its African fatherland." Because of their nature, blacks had a mission to accomplish in the United States: "We are the first fruits of this new nation, the harbinger of that black to-morrow which is yet destined to soften the whiteness of the Teutonic to-day." Unlike Douglass, young Du Bois asserted, in what he called the American Negro Academy "Creed," that it was the duty of the "Americans of Negro descent" to maintain "their race identity," that it was feasible for the white and Negro races in America "to develop side by side in peace and mutual happiness, the peculiar contribution which each has to make to the culture of their common country." He advocated not "social equality" but "social equilibrium" between these races.[4]

Not all listeners at the ANA meeting agreed with Du Bois's thesis of preservation of racial endowments. William H. Ferris, a student of theology, argued that talented black people had to be recognized for human qualities that went beyond race and were embodied in civilization itself. He also attacked Du Bois's Hegelianism by arguing, not that men were great because they represented a race, but that because of their outstanding achievements they made their race great. William S. Scarborough, professor of classics at Wilberforce, the first African-American college, also raised the issue that it was hardly possible that two races living next to each other on equal terms did not intermingle. But ANA president Crummell defended Du Bois's "essentially good" paper and concluded that races, like families, were to exist because God had made them a category of human existence.[5]

At this point Du Bois offered a version of the "separate but equal" formula of race relations to which Washington would have subscribed. Du Bois was not too far from Washington's idea of "self-help" in advocating the formation of strong "racial organizations" for a racial battle against "immorality, crime and laziness among the Negroes themselves." Unlike Washington, however, Du Bois thought these evils were the heritage of slavery.

Du Bois still did not differentiate between the concepts of nation and race. In later years he wrote in his autobiography *Dusk of Dawn* that his early concept of race was "a matter of course without explanation or definition," as it was commonly thought in the nineteenth century. "Just as I was born a member of a colored family, so too I was born a member of the colored race. That was obvious and no definition was needed." By the time he gave the paper to the ANA, Du Bois had adopted the designation "Negro" for the race to which he belonged, a term he felt was "more definite and logical." The making of his racial theories, Du Bois admitted, was probably a process "largely unconscious." From his New England hometown he went to Fisk University in Nashville, Tennessee, a Negro college where racial equality was asserted and natural inferiority denied. There he became "a member of a closed racial group with rites and loyalties, with a history and a corporate future, with an art and philosophy." When he went to Harvard University, he began to face "scientific race dogma" in classes and student communities where the difference in the development of the white and the "lower races" was continually stressed, and where evolution was exemplified in a museum with a series of skeletons arranged from a little monkey to a chimpanzee to a Negro to a well-developed white man. In his classes the same concept was more subtly explained as a difference of brain weight and capacity in human groups and by the cephalic index, which was the ratio of the length to the width of the human head. At Harvard "the theory of race separation was quite in my blood," Du Bois recalled. Both at Harvard and at the University of Berlin, race "became a matter of culture and cultural history." The superior race was the white race, students were taught, the only race with a history. The best universities in America and Europe at that time did not offer any courses in Chinese or Indian history and culture, and in lectures "Africa was left without culture and without history." He recalled Heinrich von Treitschke in Berlin, who authoritatively thundered mulatto inferiority in his classes. Young Du Bois sensed the constant shift of proofs and arguments in racial discussions. He did accept evolutionary theories and the survival-of-the-fittest argument, "provided the interval between advanced and backward races was not made too impossible," but he was skeptical about brain weight, physical measurements, and social investigations. He was "in revolt" when racial arguments became a question of comparative culture: "I began to see that the cultural equipment attributed to any people depended largely on who estimated it." Then he realized that "race lines were not fixed and fast," that within the Negro group "there were people of all colors," that many of his colored friends objected to his extreme race loyalty, that he was not a "Negro" but a "mulatto," that he was not a southerner but a northerner, that his goal was to be "American" and not "Negro." Yet he still saw "inner racial distinction in the colored group" and resented the habit of light-colored people to shun the company of darker people as a defense mechanism to escape discrimination in public. After returning from Germany, where he experienced close contacts with white people, Du Bois felt that the "eternal walls between races did not seem so stern and exclusive." He began to stress the cultural aspects of race."[6]

There is no evidence that in 1897 Du Bois was aware of Franz Boas's steps toward cultural explanations of human differences. It is true that Boas by then "had not achieved a fully developed notion of the cultural determination of behavior as an alternative to the prevailing racial determinism," as historian of anthropology George Stocking points out. Yet the German-Jewish scientist had already begun to formulate the theories that within a few years would challenge current thoughts of racial hierarchies among both white and black social scientists. When in 1892 Boas was appointed chief assistant at the Chicago World's Exposition to supervise the Anthropological Building, he had already completed his intellectual journey from physics to geography to physical anthropology. The first Ph.D. in anthropology in the country was given at Clark University in Worcester, Massachusetts, under Boas, but he subsequently resigned from that university, along with most of the faculty, because of disagreements with President G. Stanley Hall. The exhibitions Boas organized for the fair's Anthropological Building left him profoundly unsatisfied. It was the idea of "exhibition" in itself, by pretending to recreate "authentic" cultures, that made Boas say at the end that he would never again play the role of a "circus impresario."[7]

Du Bois and Boas met in 1906 at Atlanta University, where the former was professor of social studies and invited Boas, by then full professor of anthropology at Columbia University, to address a conference on Negro physical characteristics. Their intellectual exchange and friendship lasted until Boas's death in 1942. In 1897, however, Du Bois seemed unaware of Boas's early efforts and did not make any reference to the anthropologist's work in the speech he gave on 19 November at the forty-fourth session of the American Academy of Political and Social Science in Philadelphia entitled "The Study of the Negro Problem." In this speech Du Bois made the plea, for the first time to an audience of white social scientists, that great universities such as Harvard and Columbia should join the University of Pennsylvania, where he taught at that time, to give financial support and use their resources for an extensive and comprehensive study of the Negro question at Tuskegee, Hampton Institute, or Atlanta University. He argued that the American Negro was worthy of objective investigation "for the great end of advancing the cause of science in general." If scholars missed such opportunity, Du Bois warned, "they hurt the cause of scientific truth the world over."[8]

What type of study did Du Bois encourage at this time? He strongly believed in scientific research as a sort of weapon inducing social change. He recalled in his *Autobiography*: "I was going to study the facts, any and all the facts, concerning the American Negro and his plight, and by measurement and comparison and research, work up to any valid generalization which I could. I entered this primarily with the utilitarian object of reform and uplift; but nevertheless wanted to do the work with scientific accuracy. Thus in my own sociology, because of firm belief in a changing racial group, I easily grasped the idea of a changing developing society rather than a fixed social structure."[9]

To Du Bois, the pursuit of scientific truths was the essential condition for bringing about an egalitarian society in the United States. What best exemplified Du Bois's scientific approach in 1897 was *The Philadelphia Negro: A Social Study*, which he published two years later. With this work Du Bois provided the empirical evidence of the class structure among African Americans that was either unknown or thought nonexistent by contemporary social scientists. Exceptional black people were generally considered oddities or the result of the white blood they had inherited. It was commonly assumed that there were only "bad" and "good" Negroes in an undifferentiated mass of black Americans. Du Bois's empirical investigation uncovered four classes of African Americans in several communities. The first class was the "aristocracy," which he described as a minority of "families of undoubted respectability, earning sufficient income to live well; not engaged in menial service of any kind." The second class was made up of the families of the "respectable working class," who had remunerative jobs and put their young children in school. The third group was the working poor, "honest although not always energetic or thrifty." Finally, there was the submerged "lowest class." This class differentiation was an important redefinition of racial differences.[10]

Du Bois's book was pathbreaking even from the point of view of sociological methods. At Harvard, philosopher William James had convinced Du Bois, although he was an outstanding student in the class, to leave the field of philosophy for sociology, since a Negro did not have much chance to earn a living as a philosopher in academia. It was James's pragmatism and Albert Bushnell Hart's research methods that turned Du Bois "from the lovely but sterile land of philosophical speculation, to the social sciences as the field for gathering and interpreting that body of fact which would apply to my program for the Negro." With his impressive research on the Philadelphia Negro, Du Bois conducted the highest level of social investigation of that time.[11]

In 1897 Du Bois reviewed a study by Frederick L. Hoffman, a German-born statistician working for the Prudential Insurance Company of America, entitled *Race Traits and Tendencies of the American Negro* (1896). A member of the American Academy of Medicine, the American Statistical Association, and the Royal Statistical Society of London, Hoffman predicted the extinction of African Americans in a few generations, as he found them progressively deteriorating physically and morally. This work on race characteristics of the American Negro summarized medical and anthropometric data on race relations in the United States accumulated during the nineteenth century. Hoffman synthesized a century of pre-Darwinian, evolutionist, and medical research and concluded that the efforts of the "higher races" to better the condition of the Negro or of any other "lower" race resulted in widening the differences between races. To Hoffman, it was highly evident that after thirty years of freedom the Negro and the Caucasian races were more "apart than ever in their political and social relations." He elaborated the large body of "indisputable evidence" that statisticians and physicians had gathered from the 1870s showing that the Negro had the lowest power of resistance "in the struggle for life." The evidence Hoffman provided included the anthropometric investigations reported by Benjamin A. Gould that the U.S. Sanitary Commission carried out during the Civil War and the study by Sanford B. Hunt on Negro soldiers. According to Hoffman's reading of the evidence, Negro soldiers showed "a higher mortality rate" than white soldiers under similar or even less difficult conditions. He looked at the Civil War anthropometric statistics, compared the war findings with later data concerning the same physical aspects investigated, and found clear signs of decline in the physiological capacities of the Negro since the Civil War. Hoffman also predicted that the natural increase of the colored population "will be less from decade to decade and in the end a decrease must take place." The German statistician concluded that miscegenation worked against the progress of both races: "the amalgamation of the two races through the channels of prostitution and concubinage, as well as through the intermarrying of the lower type of both races, is contrary to the interest of the colored race, a positive hindrance to its social, mental and moral development." Hoffman was convinced that, moral considerations put aside, "the physiological consequences alone demand race purity and a stern reprobation of any infusion of white blood."[12]

In reviewing Hoffman's study for the *Annals of the American Academy of Political and Social Science,* Du Bois attacked the German statistician's assumptions about the "physical constitution of the Negro," the anthropometrical data on which Hoffman based his findings on the deterioration of blacks, and his conclusions that the cause of the failure of many freedmen to improve their social conditions was the "lack of those race characteristics for which the Aryan is pre-eminent." For Du Bois, black people's progress in religious organization and in education was more relevant than what statistics showed about crime, poverty, and sexual immorality. Du Bois easily dismissed Hoffman's hereditarian argument on inferior racial characteristics and on the mulatto as an inferior type. He questioned Hoffman's uncritical use of the sources that led him to the absurd conclusion that the colored race was going downward to its extinction. Du Bois's counterargument introduced the category of class to explain contradictory social facts among blacks such as "increasing of intelligence and increasing of crime, increasing wealth and disproportionate poverty, increasing religious and moral activity and high rate of illegitimacy in births." These contradictory social facts, he held, did not pertain to the whole Negro race but to "its various classes, which development since emancipation has differentiated." It was a natural fact, observable in all races, that in the course of a single generation mental development "progressed farther than the moral."[13] It was racial prejudice that kept most black people in the lower ranks of society and not their race attributes. Presumably Du Bois was still unaware of Boas's work, but he was proceeding in the anthropologist's direction by stressing the importance of social aspects in the explanation of human differences. Whereas Boas's emphasis was on individual merit as the criterion of one's position in social hierarchy, Du Bois's emphasis was on race, which he conceived of as a socially differentiated group whose educated elite had the moral duty of uplifting the others.

At this stage of Du Bois's thought, the idea of racial uplifting was related to a cathartic meaning of knowledge. He was convinced that social science, by objectively classifying African Americans in highly differentiated subgroups, would defeat racial prejudice. A child of the Enlightenment, like many other liberal and radical progressives, Du Bois thought, and later wrote in his *Autobiography*, that the Negro problem was "a matter of systematic investigation and intelligent understanding," that the world "was thinking wrong about race, because it did not know," that the worst evil was stupidity, whose cure "was knowledge based on scientific investigation."[14]

In 1906 the Du Bois–Boas intellectual relationship materialized when Boas accepted Du Bois's invitation to address a conference at Atlanta University. In 1897, the year Boas became professor of anthropology at Columbia University, Du Bois moved to the capital of the New South to become professor of social science at the high-standard, racially integrated university, which was supported through northern philanthropy. Du Bois taught classes and became director of the Atlanta University Studies, whose results he presented at yearly conferences covering a wide range of subjects. Under Du Bois's leadership these conferences became a laboratory reflecting his notion of social science as a weapon, an active instrument for stimulating change in racial relations. Despite the small financial support he received, Du Bois's conferences covered questions of black education, health, business, church, family, and urbanization. Visitors applauded the efforts, but the city of Atlanta still banned black scholars, Du Bois included, from using its new public library, the largest in the South, and the Southern Education Board took action to encourage colored teachers in colored schools, social separation of races in the school system, and the making of colored schools almost exclusively industrial.

In the procession of scholars, social reformers, religious leaders, and eminent public figures who accepted Du Bois's invitations, Boas's turn came in 1906.[15] The Columbia professor did not address the whole eleventh Atlanta University conference on "The Health and Physique of the Negro American," as Du Bois had hoped, but accepted to give the final commencement speech on 31 May. Boas was more interested in giving his contribution as a public intellectual who fought a battle for racial equality than as a scientist whose methods of measuring racial differences had not yet fully defeated current racial beliefs of Negro inferiority. He therefore gave a speech on the value of African history and culture to strengthen black American identity: "I have accepted with pleasure the invitation to address you on this day, because I believe that the broad outlook over the development of mankind which the study of the races of man gives to us, is often helpful to an understanding of our everyday problems, and may make clear to us our capacity as well as our duty. I shall speak to you from the standpoint of the anthropologist, of one who has devoted his life to study of the multifarious forms of culture as found in different races."

With this opening statement, German-Jewish anthropologist Franz Boas addressed an assembly of black students, teachers, and professionals in attendance at Du Bois's eleventh Atlanta University conference. "The fundamental requirement for useful activity on your part," Boas announced, "is a clear insight into the capabilities of your own race." He offered an effective description of these insights to his audience, which was composed of "the more fortunate members" of the Negro race who had the opportunity to graduate from Atlanta University. The first useful insight was that the achievements of races could not be measured by what they had done in the short span of the last two thousand years, during which the European, the Chinese, and the East Indian had done more than any other racial group. One had to look back at the time when "mankind struggled with the elements, when every small advance that seems to us now insignificant was an achievement of the highest order, as great as the discovery of steam power or of electricity, if not greater." To these early advancements of humanity, the Negro race gave the highest contribution to the human race: "While much of the history of early invention is shrouded in darkness, it seems likely that at a time when the European was still satisfied with rude stone tools, the African had invented the art of smelting iron." Ancient Europe and China did not know iron at that time, but evidence found in the nineteenth century showed that the trade of blacksmith was all over Africa, where the natives had also developed agriculture and animal domestication in each village. "The evidence of African ethnology," Boas told his audience, "is such that it should inspire you with the hope of leading your race from achievement to achievement." Then he mentioned the powerful military organization of the Zulu whose armies swept southeastern Africa, the diplomatic skills of local chiefs who managed with bravery and wisdom to unite scattered tribes into flourishing kingdoms, and the complex forms of government they elaborated to hold heterogeneous tribes together.

Boas told his astonished audience, including Du Bois, that to understand "the possibilities of the African under the stimulus of a foreign culture," they should look at Sudan, south of the Sahara. The fourteenth-century reports of the Arab traveler Iben Batuta told the story of the Mohammedan conquest of old Negro kingdoms. First under the guidance of the Arabs and later acting on their own, Negro tribes in this area organized kingdoms able to survive for many centuries and founded flourishing towns whose history was recorded and kept in archives. All this was documented in the archives whose remains a white traveler discovered around 1850. Boas praised the great African markets, the judicial system developed early on in Africa, and the artistic skills of its native peoples. A walk through the museums of Paris, London, and Berlin revealed the fineness of African carving, copper decoration, and inimitable bronze castings. Without denying that African culture showed signs of the instability and weakness of other primitive cultures, Boas felt that such "thrifty people, full of energy, capable of forming large states," should inspire strength in his African-American audience, "for all the alleged faults of your race that you have to conquer here are certainly not prominent there." Africans were not indolent; they were thrifty, ingenious, industrious, and technically skilled. "If, therefore, it is claimed that your race is doomed to economic inferiority, you may confidently look to the home of your ancestors and say that you have set out to recover for the colored people the strength that was their own before they set foot on the shores of this continent," Boas exhorted his listeners. By reversing the current argument that slavery as an institution had the beneficial effect of turning savage Africans into disciplined laborers—an argument the great international fairs of the time popularized—Boas suggested a strategic counterargument: "To those who stoutly maintain a material inferiority of the Negro race you may confidently reply that the burden of proof rests with them, that the past history of your race does not sustain their statement, but rather gives you encouragement."

With these words Boas concluded the part of his speech in which, as a public intellectual, he manifested an explicit will to give African-American students a usable past with which to fight against racism in their country. As a scientist, Boas only touched on, in the second part of his speech, the question of "physical inferiority" of the Negro race by saying that it was "insignificant when compared to the wide range of individual variability in each race." Perhaps Du Bois would have liked to hear more evidence from the New York anthropologist who was the most experienced researcher in human differences in America. However, Boas simply remarked that there was no anatomical evidence available "that would sustain the view that the bulk of the Negro race could not become as useful citizens as the members of any other race." There might have been "slightly different hereditary traits," but it was arbitrary to infer, in Boas's view, "that those of the Negro, because perhaps slightly different, must be of an inferior type."[16]

Boas was more interested in going back to the role anthropology and history could play in developing intellectual weapons to dismantle racist views. He took the history of the Jews in Europe as the best example of a human group whose forced separation in the occupations and living conditions that had existed for hundreds of years generated a sense of difference and inequality in customs and ideals. Boas informed his black listeners that although the ancient barriers against the Jews had fallen in Europe, strong anti-Jewish feelings still persisted despite the slight difference in type between the European and the Jew, and that the reasons for those feelings no longer existed. Boas, who would spend the last part of his life mobilizing scientists against Nazi Germany, in 1906 offered to African Americans insights for a useful alliance between black and Jewish intellectuals in the common battle against racism and anti-Semitism. Years later, Du Bois recalled Boas's Atlanta speech and its strong impact on his own future research: "I was too astonished to speak. All of this I had never heard and I came then and afterwards to realize how the silence and neglect of science can let truth utterly disappear or even be unconsciously distorted."[17] If cosmopolitan Du Bois was astonished, the rest of the audience was certainly thrilled.

What Boas said at Atlanta in 1906 was already included in a 1904 article entitled "What the Negro Has Done in Africa." In Boas's view, current discussions of racial capacities confined to the American experience, where black people lived in absolute disadvantage with the oppressive heritage of slavery, were not leading very far. To give more sense to scientific investigation, African cultural achievement needed to be brought into discussion as a fundamental part of black heritage. Black Americans would appear under a favorable light when the achievements of their African ancestors were compared "with those of the tribes of the New World, and even with those of the tribes of northern Europe at a period before they had come under the influence of Mediterranean culture." Boas rejected claims scientists made of a presumed biological incapacity black people had in adjusting to the American environment by comparing the ease with which Mohammedans influenced Africans with the failure of white colonization. Whites sent the products of their manufacturing and a few representatives "into the Negro country," while the Mohammedans pursued amalgamation. Their success showed that African people were capable of assimilation, a fact that challenged current theories of black inferiority.

In his letter of invitation to attend the Atlanta University conference,

Du Bois asked Boas to present the latest findings on anthropometric research on black people. He foresaw the Atlanta conference as a "great opportunity . . . for physical measurement of the Negro," if Columbia University financed the project. Boas replied that he could not label any reference "particularly good on the physical anthropology of the Negro," but he would evaluate the possibility of Columbia financing an anthropometrical study of blacks. The reason why Boas chose to deliver a commencement address at Atlanta University in 1906 on African achievements instead of giving a paper on physical anthropology was perhaps his uneasiness in admitting his belief that races were not fully equal. This could be an expression of a conflict between science and ideology in Boas's thought that historian Vernon Williams has called the "Boasian paradox."[18] More than a paradox, however, this tension in Boas's thought was due to his two conflicting strategies to oppose false biological assumptions on racial differences. His thinking included a universalist-assimilationist perspective denying the importance of race as a category for understanding individual mental and emotional characteristics and predicting the progressive absorption of blacks and foreign immigrant groups into a uniform American culture. On the other hand, Boas's thinking also included a pluralist cultural approach that stressed the importance of understanding each culture in its own terms and emphasized the unique contribution of each culture to human civilization.[19] Boas was ready to admit that individual variations within each race were more important than a comparison of mental ability of different races. Yet because of the mark slavery had left on African Americans, Boas, like many other progressives of his time, including Du Bois, felt that as a group they were culturally undeveloped. Unlike the views of most social scientists of his time, Boas's egalitarian views made him stand for equality of opportunities for black people. What drove him in America was his early enthusiasm for the myth of American freedom and individualism. Boas was also driven by his search for an academic career, which he felt was hard for a Jew to pursue in Germany. Once established in New York, he kept his German sympathies and close ties to the New York Jewish-German community. A cosmopolitan intellectual, Boas did not accept the ultranationalism of American preparations for entering World War I and maintained a visibly pacifist position. His racial egalitarianism motivated him throughout his life until the very moment he died in 1942, at age eighty-five, at a Columbia Faculty Club luncheon: "Boas, with a comment on the need to press its exposure . . . fell over backwards in his chair, dead," his student and biographer Melville Herskovits recalled.[20] Boas's biographers agree that his attempt to theorize about race by integrating biology, social sciences, and linguistics occurred at a time in which there was no agreement among these disciplines. His interdisciplinary approach did not produce a systematic theory, yet, because of his egalitarian principles, Boas's views mobilized public opinion against racism.

To Boas, the egalitarian approach was a prerequisite of anthropological research. In his view the scientist needed to adapt his or her own mind to the people observed. Boas's new paradigm as summarized in *The Mind of Primitive Man* in 1911 was based on his evidence showing that "the organization of mind is practically identical among all races of man; that mental activity follows the same laws everywhere, but that its manifestations depend upon the character of individual experience that is subjected to the action of these laws." His first and most well known book followed the crucial research on "Changes in the Bodily Form of Descendants of Immigrants" he had begun in 1908 on behalf of the U.S. Immigration Commission. Boas proceeded to measure the skulls of first-generation Americans of Italian and Jewish descent and compared their cephalic index to the corresponding measurement of Italian and Jewish people living in their original countries. His conclusions showed that the difference between first- and second-generation Americans born to different ethnic groups was smaller than the difference between generations of the same groups living in Europe. These results undermined all previous assumptions of physical anthropology, which based its theories on physical stability of different races.[21]

Boas's findings did not match the goals of the Immigration Commission's project to investigate how new immigration caused the deterioration of the American stock. The voluminous reports of the Dillingham Commission published in 1911 became the basis of political propaganda for immigration restriction in the 1910s and 1920s. Boas's dissenting voice, temporarily suppressed by the winning of restrictive immigration policies, kept on stressing the primacy of nurture over nature in human development. Unlike Boas, other white social scientists offered their theoretical support to national reconciliation by speculating on the Negro problem at academic meetings.

Social Scientists and National Reconciliation

In December 1907, given his chronic lack of funds, W. E. B. Du Bois was unable to attend the annual meeting of the newly organized American Sociological Society (ASS) held in Madison, Wisconsin. Nevertheless, he sent his sharp comments to the conference called to discuss "Is Race Friction between Blacks and Whites in the United States Growing and Inevitable?" The society, of which Du Bois was a member since its founding in 1905, called on amateur sociologist Alfred Holt Stone, profes-

sionally a Mississippi planter, to give the introductory paper. A sophisticated southern gentleman, Stone had enchanted the North with his lectures on the Negro problem and the solution he saw in the continuing
natural extinction of the Negro race, and on his highly unsuccessful experiment of substituting southern Italians for black sharecroppers on
his plantation. He and Du Bois corresponded in 1906 over obtaining
funds from the Carnegie Foundation for their respective projects. Stone
proposed a broad investigation of the American race problem, and Du
Bois asked for funds for his successful Atlanta University conferences.
The planter convinced Du Bois to focus the twelfth Atlanta University
conference on "Economic Cooperation among Negro Americans."
When the Carnegie funding did not materialize, Du Bois realized that
Stone's gentle manners did not match his devious articles, in which the
planter belligerently asserted that intelligent Negroes existed only because of the white blood in their veins, and that white supremacy was
necessary to control Negro savagery.[22] When Du Bois sent his comments
on Stone's paper to the ASS meeting in Wisconsin, he knew the views
the amateur sociologist held on such racial matters as several recent racial riots, a wave of lynchings in the South, and the beginning of a mass
migration of black southerners to the urban North. Presumably Du
Bois's sharply worded paper arrived too late to be read at the conference, but it was included in the proceedings published in the May 1908
issue of the *American Journal of Sociology,* the ASS's official publication.

Stone's address was a well-sung hymn to white supremacy. At the first
official debate of the association, Stone argued that "race friction" was
based on "racial antipathy," that is, a "natural contrariety, repugnancy of
qualities, or incompatibilities between individuals or groups which are
sufficiently differentiated to constitute what, for want of a more exact
term, we call races." Although race was a term "not scientifically definite," he explained to his fellow sociologists that racial differences in
physical qualities, mental habits, social customs, and religious beliefs
were the cause of the "instinctive feeling of dislike" that Stone called racial antipathy. In the planter-sociologist's view, postbellum racial fric-
tions were the result of black Americans' claims after emancipation. Racial contacts no longer occurred with Negro individuals but with masses
of emancipated African Americans who were moving north and claiming social equality. Under these circumstances, Stone concluded, white
racial superiority and race separation had to be forcefully preserved to
avoid a degrading mongrelization of American society.[23]

Du Bois's response to Stone was as cautious as it was sharp. The Atlanta social scientist referred to the growing racial consciousness in the
protests of southern black people against lower wages, debasing per-

sonal treatment, inferior housing, and barriers to property holdings. This consciousness, in Du Bois's view, made unrealistic the hopes of those who linked peace and prosperity to the survival of "virtues" like ignorance or lack of aspiration that "we expect and cultivate in dogs but not in men." He dismissed Stone's notion of "racial antipathy" as a rhetorical variant of the social philosophy of Anglo-Saxon superiority. Racial friction was a "field of science rather than opinion," Du Bois argued. Although scientific knowledge on racial differences was still at an early stage, it already had produced evidence that most people of the world could be civilized, and that the world of races, like the world of individuals, "does not consist of a few aristocrats and chosen people and a mass of dark serfs and slaves." He also thanked anthropologist Franz Boas for having initiated the field of scientific study of racial differences and likenesses, believing that science could bring evidence that whites and blacks were not incompatible. Arguing against Stone's views, Du Bois made the point that forcing racial segregation in the modern world was unrealistic, as contacts of groups, nations, and races were constantly increasing: "People say very often with regard to the Negro that the Pilgrims of England found a place for liberty when they could not get it at home; why then does not the Negro do the same of his own motion and will? And then they explain it by a shrug and a reminder that one set of people were English and the other are Negroes. Flattering as this is to the sayers, yet this does not explain all. Today we have in the world growing race contact. The world is shrinking together; it is finding itself neighbor to itself in strange, almost magic degree."[24]

To the majority of social scientists, however, the growing racial contact was problematic at least, if not unacceptable. An article supporting the polygenist view had appeared in 1905 in the *American Journal of Sociology* asserting that "the absolute unity of human life in all parts of the globe, as well as the idea of the practical equality of human individuals . . . has been quite generally abandoned."[25] Social Darwinism was the theory the journal discussed most frequently in its early issues. English philosopher Herbert Spencer found that the notion of "survival of the fittest" in Charles Darwin's evolutionary theory matched his own view of evolution. In the 1870s Spencer suggested that governments and other institutions should not interfere with that principle. Nature took its course in society and established its social and economic hierarchies. Consequently, traditional forms of charity to the poor and the needy, the losers in the survival-of-the-fittest scheme, were useless and harmful to posterity. Spencer's books sold over three hundred thousand copies in the United States. Sociology departments at American universities were started at that time, and a Social Darwinian approach to race relations was the original American development of the theory. Blacks out of the beneficial influence of slavery could not sustain the survival-of-the-fittest dogma. Their destiny was extinction. Political and social reforms to improve their condition were useless intrusions into the evolutionary process. American social scientists offered a variety of versions of these beliefs.[26]

William Graham Sumner, professor of political and social science at Yale since 1872, insisted in his 1906 publication *Folkways* that legislation had a limited capacity to change any individual behavior that was physically and emotionally rooted. Sumner maintained that prior to the Civil War relations between black and white people in the South were based on legal rights, and there was peace and agreement among the races. He was convinced that the war was caused by a great divergence in the customs of the North and the South, and that in its aftermath both races were left to find a new ground for living together. This was a difficult undertaking, in Sumner's view, for there had not been any conversion from old customs, which he called "mores," to new ones. By using an argument that echoed the *Plessy v. Ferguson* decision, Sumner asserted that "legislation cannot make mores," that the two races were separated more than ever, and that any interference with this would be inevitably unsuccessful.[27]

The boundaries between those social scientists who read American society with the Social Darwinian lenses and those who thought government, legislators, and institutions should actively intervene to control social conflicts almost disappeared when racial relations were discussed. A common language of national reconciliation blurred existing theoretical differences. One powerful voice that spoke this language and agreed with Booker T. Washington's philosophy was that of John Roger Commons. In 1907 the Wisconsin sociologist gave the major paper at a meeting of the American Sociological Society entitled "Is Class Conflict in America Growing and Is It Inevitable?" Similarly phrased, Commons's paper and the proceedings of the conference appeared in the same issue of the *American Journal of Sociology* as the proceedings of Alfred Stone's conference on "race friction." An influential social theoretician, Commons became the political adviser of Wisconsin's progressive governor Robert M. La Follette and actively participated in several state and federal government committees on labor issues, including the U.S. Industrial Relations Commission, the American Bureau of Industrial Research, and the National Civic Federation. At the ASS meeting Commons suggested that class conflict could be turned into social cooperation and stability by putting industrial relations under the national control of experts working on government commissions.[28]

Commons dealt with racial relations in *Races and Immigrants in America* (1907), in which he asserted that "racial differences are established in the very blood and physical constitution," that they are the most difficult to eradicate, and that "they yield only to the slow processes of the centuries." An ardent believer in the application of science to social reforms, Commons hoped that assimilation of all races in America could eventually take place, for he was convinced that "a great nation need not to be of one blood, but it must be of one mind." Like most social scientists of his time, Commons gave to the term "race" a rather loose and spurious meaning. He was interested "only in those large and apparent divisions which have a direct bearing on the problem of assimilation"—that is, a cultural process able to unify minds and wills of different races in order to develop common thoughts and actions. The Wisconsin social scientist believed that racial inequality and inferiority were relevant only to the extent that they prevented mental and moral assimilation. Hence he encouraged plans for the "Americanization" of all races in the country in order to proceed toward "the more rapid movements of mental assimilation." Commons saw "Americanization" as the fulfillment of the promise for equal opportunities of democracy in America: "government for the people depends on government by the people, and this is difficult where the people cannot think and act together." In discussing the "Negro race," Commons did not fail to criticize the Fourteenth and Fifteenth Amendments, for he thought they were based on a wrong theory of the ballot. "Suffrage means self-government," he argued, "that means intelligence, self-control, and capacity of cooperation." Blacks and several groups of recent immigration lacked these qualities, Commons and the great majority of social scientists thought, and therefore did not qualify for suffrage. He did not approve of the way whites took the power back in the South, but he was glad for the end of Reconstruction. Blacks needed to be prepared for citizenship; this should be accomplished by beginning "at the bottom by educating the Negro for the ballot, instead of beginning at the top by giving him the ballot before he knows what it should do for him." The type of education required by blacks was a program like Booker T. Washington's Tuskegee Institute, which taught agricultural and industrial skills to southern blacks. Commons totally agreed with Washington's attempt to discourage black masses from leaving the rural South. If city life induced "dangerous effects" on foreign immigrants, Commons believed, then it created "degenerating effects" on blacks, who were accustomed to the southern country.[29]

The theory establishing that racial temperaments would instinctively keep the races apart found a major supporter in Robert Ezra Park. The sociologist who by 1920 had turned the Department of Sociology at the University of Chicago into the "Chicago school," and whose books were the most often read in college and graduate courses, spent seven years studying the Negro problem for Booker T. Washington. From 1905 to 1913, Park was actively involved with the Tuskegee principal by acting as his public relations man.

Like Alfred Stone, Park thought racial prejudice was an instinctive reaction to different racial temperaments. In 1919 he wrote: "The Negro is by natural disposition, neither an intellectual nor idealist like the Jew, nor a brooding introspective like the East Indian, nor a pioneer and frontiersman like the Anglo-Saxon. He is primarily an artist, loving life for its own sake. His metier is expression rather than action. The Negro is, so to speak, the lady among the races."

Two years later Park further qualified what he meant by "the lady among the races," without using that phrase. He defined as Negro "temperament" a few "elementary but distinctive characteristics, determined by physical organizations and transmitted biologically." This temperament consisted in "a genial, sunny, and social disposition, in an interest and attachment to external, physical things rather than subjective states and objects of introspection, in a disposition for expression rather than enterprise and action."[30]

Park's portrait of Negro temperament found its strongest critic years later in the African-American author Ralph Ellison. In writing a review of Gunnar Myrdal's *An American Dilemma* in 1944, which was not published until 1964, Ellison, the author of *Invisible Man*, held Robert Park "responsible for inflating Tuskegee into a national symbol." According to Ellison, Park's descriptive metaphor of the Negro as "the lady among the races" was so full of mixed feelings that it could bring only compromises and indecisions: "Imagine the effect such teachings have had upon Negro students alone! Thus what started as part of a democratic attitude, ends not only uncomfortably close to the preachings of [William Graham] Sumner, but to those of Dr. Goebbels as well."[31]

This is a quite understandable criticism at the time Ellison wrote, for Nazi Germany had recently made use of the language of biosocial science to justify the "final solution." Yet when Park wrote about Negro temperament, the intellectual context in which racial theories appeared was in flux. Park's definition showed a striking similarity to Du Bois's early idea of racial traits that he developed in his 1897 paper for the American Negro Academy. By 1919, however, Du Bois had already published *Morals and Manners among Negro Americans* (1914), *The Negro* (1915), and many articles in which any sign of biological definitions of race had disappeared. By then Du Bois favored culturally and historically relativistic notions leading to his retrieval of the African past as a source of racial pride, as is discussed later in this book.

Over the years, Du Bois explored several directions of the study of African past that Franz Boas pioneered in his Atlanta University lecture of 1906. The intellectual alliance between the two social scientists was based on the idea that science inspired by egalitarian values could be a weapon for the advancement of the human race. The alliance between Booker T. Washington and Robert Park was shaped by Washington's need to hire the sociologist's theoretical, writing, and organizational skills for his political machine.

When Robert Park Worked for Booker T. Washington

The alliance between the white sociologist from the Midwest and the Tuskegee Institute principal began at the Congo Reform Association, of which Booker T. Washington was a vice president and Robert Park the secretary. This association actively participated in the international campaign against King Leopold of Belgium's brutal exploitation of the Congo, which is the theme of Joseph Conrad's masterpiece *Heart of Darkness.*

Born in Pennsylvania, Park grew up in Minnesota, graduated from the University of Michigan, worked as a journalist on several newspapers in the Midwest and New York, and registered at Harvard for a master's degree in philosophy in 1898. Like Du Bois, Park studied with William James and went to Berlin. Unlike Du Bois, he obtained his Ph.D. from Heidelberg and received a one-year assistantship at Harvard from philosopher William James upon his return to the United States. In 1904 Park became secretary of the Congo Reform Association. He had become convinced that conditions in the Congo "were not the result of mere administrative abuses" but rather were the conditions "one was likely to meet wherever an European people invaded the territory of a more primitive folk in order to uplift, civilize and incidentally exploit them." To find out whether the colonization process could be made less painful, Park intended to travel to Africa, but before he could do so Booker T. Washington invited him to come to Alabama to see his Tuskegee industrial school. The black leader was more interested in someone as effective as the secretary of the Congo Reform Association organizing publicity campaigns for Tuskegee than in the welfare of Congo natives. Until Du Bois published his sharp and uncompromising criticism of the "Tuskegee Machine" in *The Souls of Black Folk* (1903), Washington had repeatedly offered the publicity position to the Atlanta scholar, but Du Bois always declined because he was afraid, for good reasons, to become Washington's ghostwriter. Park accepted Washington's job for several reasons. Besides being "sick and tired of the academic world" and feeling ready "to get back to the world of men," he was also under financial pressure.[32]

Park made his first trip to Tuskegee in February 1905 and found to his liking the relationship the institute had developed with the whole black community of the southern states. At Tuskegee, Park felt "at the very center of the Negro world." His first trip to the South was "a voyage of exploration and discovery" in which he examined how the lives of colored and white people "had been articulated if not integrated into a common pattern of life." He discovered to what extent the two groups lived in different worlds: "worlds that touched but never really interpenetrated." During that trip Park read all the local newspapers, talked to everyone he met, and was the most impressed with "the tragic insecurity" of colored people's lives. When he finally met Booker T. Washington at Tuskegee, Park was eager to tell him the tragic scenes he saw and the sad stories he heard. Washington listened patiently for quite some time, Park reported, and then said: "Well, that makes it all the more interesting, doesn't it?" That was the Tuskegee leader's only comment. "I never told Booker Washington any heart-breaking stories after that. I found that he was not interested," Park concluded.

Between 1905 and 1913, Park wrote articles for major magazines about the Tuskegee Institute to raise funds from northern philanthropists, traveled with Washington, ghosted two books for him, *The Story of the Negro* (1909) and *My Larger Education* (1911), and coauthored *The Man Farthest Down* (1912), which was the result of a trip to Europe they took together to look for people whose social conditions were worse than those of African Americans. What kept the interest of the social scientist alive during those years was "the Negro in the South and that curious and intricate system which had grown up to define his relation with white folk." Park believed that the study of the Negro in America could offer an understanding of "every type of man from the primitive barbarian to the latest and most finished product of civilization." To put it in other words, Park thought that the study of the Negro was the study of "the historic social process by which modern society has developed." Thus he looked at the Negro in the American environment as "a social laboratory."[33] The results this laboratory produced could be exported to Africa to uplift the natives through white-dominated industrial education.

Besides criticizing King Leopold II of Belgium, Washington's adventures to uplift Africans consisted in transplanting the Tuskegee Institute's principles of self-help to places like the German Togo, Anglo-Egyptian Sudan, the Union of South Africa, and Liberia. As a vice president of the Congo Reform Association, Washington could criticize

Belgian colonialism, but he carefully avoided expressing any negative judgment of the colonial policies of Germany in Togo, Morocco, and East Africa as part of Bismarck's *Mittelafrika* plan. A member of a German colonization committee asked Washington whether Tuskegee could provide the technical assistance of black Americans to train Togolese farmers in cotton production. Tuskegee black technicians would, of course, accept the colonial authority. Washington answered that there was no difficulty. His technicians were "all kindly disposed, respectful gentlemen" who would also be able to secure "the respect and confidence of the natives." Of the nine African-American men from Tuskegee who went to Togo between 1901 and 1909, four died, four left within two years, and only one stayed to train the natives in Washington's philosophy of racial success through self-help. The experiment was a failure.[34]

As a vice president of the Congo Reform Association, Washington received an invitation from King Leopold's agents to address an international congress on economic expansion to be held in Belgium. Park urged him to go, hoping that Washington would give a speech comparing the "enlightened" American colonial policies with the brutal European exploitation of native peoples. "The difference between our colonial system and others," Park wrote in a letter to Washington, was that "we are preparing the peoples we govern for citizenship, either in the United States or as independent states," whereas other countries were merely interested in a vague economic development of their possessions. Washington, however, did not accept King Leopold's invitation. Meanwhile he convinced Park to ghostwrite an article for *Outlook*, "Cruelty in the Congo Country." Washington and Park were convinced that Leopold's cruel exploitation of Congolese resources was responsible for reintroducing and reinforcing savagery, of which cannibalism was the worst practice, and that the natives were not the only victims of that system. Like Joseph Conrad's degenerated white characters in *Heart of Darkness*, they pointed out the effects that brutal and atrocious practices were having "upon the white men who are performing this degrading work." All reports showed that European men "almost invariably give themselves over to the worst vices." Wherever the white man put his foot in the Congo, "the black man has been degraded into a mere tool in the great business of getting rubber."[35]

In 1910 Park and Washington took a European tour to investigate "the man farthest down." Washington's purpose was to meet and describe in a book to the American public those European social classes whose opportunities, handicaps, and general living conditions were comparable with those of the Negro masses in America. "What Washing-

ton wanted to see abroad, and from the distance and point of view of
Europe, was America, and not America merely but the American Negro," Park later wrote. They visited London slums, the ghettos of Prague
and Cracow, the sulphur mines of Sicily, and Polish and Italian immigrants who had returned to their remote villages. Looking for "the man
farthest down," Washington wanted to understand this man's conditions not in racial terms but "with an optimism characteristic of other
self-made Americans." During that trip Park could grasp Washington's
will to believe that all men were predestined to rise, and those left behind were those who, like American Negroes, had started late but who
would soon be on their way thanks to special programs of industrial education and general economic betterment.[36]

Park left the Tuskegee Institute in 1912 to accept a teaching job at
the University of Chicago. In the fall of 1913 he addressed that university on "Racial Assimilation in Reference to the Negro" and in 1914
gave his first course in the Department of Sociology and Anthropology
entitled "The Negro in America."[37] The year Park left Tuskegee, 1912,
marked the beginning of the decline of Washington's political power.
His protector Theodore Roosevelt was defeated by Woodrow Wilson in
the president election that year. Although Roosevelt had appointed
fewer African Americans to federal positions than his predecessors,
Wilson's record would be much worse. But even more important to
Washington's losing ground was the growing opposition among African-
American intellectual activists to his interracial coalition of moderate
forces on which his Atlanta Compromise was built. By 1910 a growing
number of black Americans could realize that disfranchisement, lynching, discriminatory work practices, and the loss of Reconstruction civil
and political rights could not be stopped by the racial alliance of the Atlanta Compromise. The fight for civil and political rights could not be
left behind the goal of economic success. "The problem of the twentieth
century is the problem of the color-line, the relation of the darker to
the lighter races of men in Asia and Africa, in America and the islands
of the sea," Du Bois wrote in *The Souls of Black Folk* in 1903. This book, in
which Du Bois's high level of scholarship merged with his poetic genius,
included the sharpest criticism Washington had received so far: "Is it
possible, and probable, that nine millions of men can make effective
progress in economic lines if they are deprived of political rights, made
a servile caste, and allowed only the most meagre chance for developing
their exceptional men? If history and reason give any distinct answer to
these questions, it is an emphatic *No.*"[38]

Two years later Du Bois organized the first meeting of the Niagara
Movement with a group of his "Talented Tenth."[39] The following year

the group, doubled in number, openly met at Harpers Ferry, West Virginia, the scene of John Brown's raid. They sang "John Brown's Body" at the end of every meeting. To these men and women Du Bois submitted a five-point resolution asking for high-quality education, the enforcement of the Fourteenth Amendment provision establishing the reduction of representation in Congress for those states in which Negroes were legally or violently disfranchised, and the end of any job discrimination regardless of race and color.[40] These were radical requests requiring interracial alliances rather different from the moderate base of the Atlanta Compromise.

The New York National Negro Conference of 1909

In August 1908 a mob of frenzied whites, crying, "Abe Lincoln brought the niggers to Springfield, and we will drive them out," looted stores, shot innocent people, and mutilated and lynched two elderly black men. The cause of the riots in the Illinois state capital was the transfer of a black man, accused of having raped a white woman, to another jail. As it later turned out, the accuser confessed before committing suicide that the black man was innocent. All this and more the readers of the *Independent* magazine learned from William English Walling's description of the racial violence in Springfield. The young journalist made the country aware that lynching was not confined to the South. By the time he wrote about the rioting, Walling, a passionate reformer whose mother's family had been Kentucky slaveholders, had left the University of Chicago to become an Illinois factory inspector, a resident of New York's University Settlement, and a member of the American Socialist Party. As soon the riots broke out, he rushed with his wife to Springfield and reconstructed the events in a powerful article that called for the revival of the pre–Civil War abolitionist spirit. Walling's call inspired many white reformers, among them Mary White Ovington, and within two years led to the formation of the interracial National Association for the Advancement of Colored People.[41]

Walling argued that public opinion had too easily accepted the rationale that there were seriously provocative causes for complaints against black people in Springfield, Illinois—namely, the presence of an exceptionally criminal element among the black population encouraged by the bosses of both political parties. He blamed the local press for making improper connections between crime and racial problems and for maliciously suggesting to readers that the South knew how to deal effectively with them. Addressing northern public opinion, Walling stressed the fact that in the North people had closed their eyes "to the whole awful and menacing truth" that a large part of the white population of Lincoln's hometown, supported mainly by farmers and miners of neighboring towns, had initiated an ongoing warfare with the Negro race. What he found extremely disturbing was that racial violence could break out in a northern town where, unlike the South, black people did not make up more than one-tenth of the population and certainly did not endanger "white supremacy." Walling attacked northern public opinion for being so satisfied with the "mitigating circumstances" behind the "insane hatred of the Negro so clearly shown by the mob" that it could justify racial hatred. Before the Civil War, when northern abolitionism was at its height, such outrages would have inflamed the country, Walling contended. Now a whole town stood for the mob, convinced that a whole race was responsible for a handful of criminals. A leading minister, Walling reported, went as far as recommending the southern disfranchisement scheme as a remedy. Even more serious than the riot, in Walling's view, was the political and business boycott to drive all Negroes out of Springfield. If this pervasive attack was allowed to continue, Walling warned, whites would easily take over all black people's property, jobs, and economic activities and would reward, in so doing, the rioters. This would be a dangerous example that many other northern towns would be tempted to follow. Walling declared that "Either the spirit of the abolitionists, of Lincoln and of Lovejoy, must be revived and we must come to treat the Negro on a plane of absolute political and social equality," or racist southern spokesmen such as Vardaman and Tillman "will soon have transferred the race war to the North." How to fight against the widening persecution of African Americans was the question: "what large and powerful body of citizens is ready to come to their aid?"[42]

An immediate answer to Walling's call came from Mary White Ovington, the first New York reformer to devote herself to the betterment of the conditions of African Americans in the city. At the time of Walling's article, Ovington was living in a New York Negro tenement where her investigations and surroundings led her to share Walling's belief that "the spirit of the abolitionists must be revived." "Here was a white man," Ovington wrote in her autobiography, "who called upon both races, in the spirit of the abolitionist to come forward and right the nation's wrongs." She wrote to Walling, and the two decided to meet together with social worker Henry Moskowitz at Walling's apartment in New York the first week of 1909: "It was then that the National Association for the Advancement of Colored People was born. It was in a little room of a New York apartment," Mary Ovington recalled.[43] Southern Walling, Jewish Moskowitz, and descendant of old-time abolitionists Ovington constituted the backbone of a larger group of New York progressive reformers, including Lillian Wald of Henry Street Settlement, leading

American Zionist Rabbi Stephen Wise, and the *Evening Post* editor Oswald Garrison Villard. This group came up with the idea of a manifesto or "Call" for a national conference on the Negro question signed by people of national reputation and released to the public on Lincoln's birthday, 12 February, in 1909. It was Villard who drafted the Call and gave it wide publicity. In his appeal, the descendant of the great abolitionist William Lloyd Garrison pointed out the outrages African Americans were suffering in both the North and South that would dismay the Great Emancipator: "If Mr. Lincoln could revisit this country in the flesh, he would be disheartened and discouraged," for he would see Negroes disfranchised in most southern states, he would learn that the Supreme Court "had refused every opportunity to pass squarely upon this disfranchisement of millions," and he would discover, therefore, "that taxation without representation is the lot of millions of wealth-producing American citizens." Villard's Call was an emotional appeal meant to produce disgust and wrath in its readers: "In many states Lincoln would find justice enforced, if at all, by judges elected by one element in a community to pass upon the liberties and lives of another. He would see the black men and women, for whose freedom a hundred thousand of soldiers gave their lives, set apart in trains, in which they pay first-class fares for third-class service, and segregated in railway stations and in places of entertainment; he would observe that State after State declines to do its elementary duty in preparing the Negro through education for the best exercise of citizenship."

Signed by sixty prominent black and white people, the Call stressed the infamous disfranchisement of Negroes occurring with the silent or explicit complicity of the Supreme Court, which left millions of American taxpayers without representation. The Call also emphasized the revolting brutalities of the attacks upon Negroes that had occurred even in Springfield, Lincoln's town and burial site. "Silence under these conditions means tacit approval," warned Villard. The appeal ended by calling on the "believers in democracy" to actively put an end to the North's indifference, which made these attacks upon democracy itself possible, and urged them to join in a national conference.[44]

Although the Call did not receive any serious response in the New York press, including the Negro press, by March the little but growing group was still pursuing this project by meeting at the Liberal Club. By then it had grown in number to a total of fifteen, including three eminent African Americans—Bishop Alexander Walters, one of the organizers of the Pan-African Congress in London in 1900, the Reverend William Brooks, a friend of Ovington's, and Dr. William L. Bulkley, the only black school principal in New York City. Many of those New Yorkers who signed the Call helped the original group to organize a conference addressed to a representative group of scientists, academics, educators, journalists, and social workers, with one large public meeting at Cooper Union. Over one thousand people were invited, the Charity Organization Hall was secured, and on the evening of 30 May 1909 the National Negro Conference opened with an informal reception at the Henry Street Settlement given by Lillian Wald. The next morning two hundred men and one hundred women gathered at the auditorium of the Charity Organization Society and listened to the keynote speech of William Ward, the editor of the *Independent*. Ward said that the purpose of the conference was "to re-emphasize in word, and so far as possible, in act, the principle that equal justice should be done to man as man, and particularly to the Negro, without regard to race, color or previous condition of servitude." After the abolition of slavery and formal granting of suffrage and equal rights, interest in the Negro had vanished, Ward remarked. Evoking Frederick Douglass's theme, Ward observed that the new American generations had no memory of the Civil War, of the Proclamation of Emancipation, of the efforts made during Reconstruction to pass the Fourteenth and Fifteenth Amendments. Americans were too ready "to apologize for old wrongs" and "to pervert the history of the old struggle." The pervasive spirit of national reconciliation, the editor implied, had killed the abolitionist emotional fervor. Now the North showed a cool sympathy for the Negro, who was held in serfdom in the South. It was the common view, which the North and the South shared, of the Negro as inferior, not fully human, and incapable of civilization, that had made all that possible. It was therefore the major goal of the conference, Ward said, to make the final rebuttal of these assumptions on the mental and physical inferiority of the Negro, which were propagated in public speeches, editorials, books, popular novels, and plays, and supported by the authoritative language of science.[45]

During the two days of the conference, an interracial although largely white group of professional social workers, clergymen, journalists, affluent reformers, descendants of abolitionists, and academics discussed twenty-four papers ranging from Burt Wilder's on brain structure to sociologist W. E. B. Du Bois's on labor and prejudice to philosopher John Dewey's on education. These experts discussed detailed evidence available on human equality in front of a large public at Cooper Union on the morning of Memorial Day, 31 May 1909. The other sessions of the conference, which were closed to the public, examined the civil and political status of the Negro and discussed industrial and educational conditions, with participants arguing in favor of establishing a national interracial organization.

Franz Boas was not among the conference speakers, but his views appeared in ethnologist Livingston Farrand's speech, "Race Differentiation—Race Characteristics." A colleague of Boas's at Columbia University, Farrand declared that the word "race" was "in hopeless disrepute" among scientists. He informed the audience that recent investigations showed that there was no such phenomenon as racial purity, that races were not stable, immutable entities but changed according to environmental influences. The question whether civilized man represented a higher stage of mental evolution than the savage should be answered, Farrand said in Boasian terms, by remembering that "we are apt to form our judgements very largely upon differences of culture, and in so doing we are apt to confuse a perfectly obvious *cultural* evolution with a perfectly problematical *mental* evolution. The two terms are by no means synonymous." The Columbia ethnologist also made clear that there was no evidence establishing a positive correlation between mental capacity and brain development. Farrand argued, again in Boasian terms, that general mental processes like sense perception were identical in all human groups: "The acuteness of vision of the Englishman and the American Indian are perfectly comparable. The Indian or Australian may exhibit marvelous powers in following trails or in tracking game, but it has been shown that this skill is based not upon increased visual acuteness but upon training in perception of certain stimuli through a life of necessity." Similarly, the ability to inhibit impulses, which was commonly considered a mark of high mental development, whether individual or racial, was equal in different human groups: "You and I are taught from childhood to inhibit certain reactions and expressions and as we grow older such repression becomes habitual with us. The same is true for the savage." Drawing from his extensive experience with Native American cultures, Farrand could safely say that "the savage often exhibits self-control under conditions where you and I would be incapable of it." The capacity for resisting torture without moaning, or for engaging in starvation for religious reasons when there was plenty of food around, was rather common among the American Indians, the Inuits, the Australian aboriginals, the Africans, and other primitive groups. In Farrand's view, evolution and group conformity to ethical standards could be judged apart from the context in which any cultural group lived. In this perspective, "the strictness of conformity to ethical standards among savages is quite comparable to that which exists among civilized man."[46]

Other experts discussed Farrand's main points from different perspectives. Among the social scientists, John Dewey, who at that time taught philosophy at Columbia University, remarked that the latest research in biological science had clearly shown that "the characteristics which the individual acquired are not transmissible, or if they are transmissible, then in such a small degree as to be comparatively and relatively negligible." This doctrine of nontransmission of mental capacity was very encouraging, in Dewey's view, because it meant that individuals could have "a full, fair and free social opportunity." This doctrine indicated that each generation "biologically commences over again" and that there was no "inferior race." Individuals who belonged to what was called an inferior race should have "the same opportunities of social environment and personality as those of a more favored race." Dewey concluded that because recent research showed that race differences were comparatively slight and individual differences very great, it was "the responsibility of society as a whole, conceived from a strictly scientific standpoint leaving out all sentimental and all moral considerations . . . to see to it that the environment is provided which will utilize all of the individual capital that is being born into it."[47]

When it was W. E. B. Du Bois's turn to speak, the audience was engaged in a discussion of racial politics. The Atlanta University professor went through the history of disfranchising waves in the United States. From the early movement of the eighteenth century, when freedmen, Jews, and Catholics were deprived of voting rights, to the 1890s, when many southern states adopted educational, property, birth, and other qualifications to keep Negroes from voting and to eliminate an ignorant electorate, strong arguments were always made against disfranchisement laws. But in recent years a powerful counterargument had stopped any effective opposition to disfranchisement. It was argued that "the economic development of the Negro . . . demanded his exclusion from the right of suffrage at least for the present." Without mentioning the Tuskegee principal who successfully proposed this counterargument at the Atlanta Exposition in 1895, Du Bois pointed out its dangerous results: "the phrase 'take the Negro out of politics' has come to be regarded as synonymous with industrial training and property getting by black men." Du Bois indicated that the public had been misled to believe that Negroes were divided into two parties, "one asking no political rights but giving all attention to economic growth and the other wanting votes, higher education and all rights." Both groups wanted the ballot, Du Bois said. They just differed on how to gain it. Whereas one group favored open agitation, the other looked for "influence and diplomacy." Again, without mentioning Tuskegee, Du Bois said that the latter group had organized a political machine in the South that dictated the distribution of offices among black men and, sometimes, among whites. "But those of us who oppose this party," Du Bois explained, "hold that this kind of political development by secrecy and machine methods is both dangerous and unwholesome and is not leading toward real democracy." It was true, Du Bois conceded, that the most pressing problem of a group of people suddenly emancipated from slavery was getting work and property. However, this problem could not simply be reduced to a matter of manual dexterity that could be gained with vocational training. This led Du Bois back to the voting question. It was foolish to think that in a modern society two sets of workers could be trained "side by side in economic competition and make one set voters and deprive the other set of all participation in government." Such a practice would inexorably lead to conflict and oppression. "A nation cannot exist half slave and half free," Du Bois remarked. Taking race riots as an example, which usually involved white working-class mobs, Du Bois argued that these events clearly showed that public opinion stood on the side of the white working-class voters and forced employers to discharge the black working-class employees. It was a fact that judges and juries in the South were at the mercy of white voters, Du Bois said. Only rarely would a jury convict a white man for aggression against a black person. Excluded from public spaces like schools and parks, Negroes were taxed for what they could not enjoy. "I am taxed for the Carnegie Public Library of Atlanta where I cannot enter to draw my own books," Du Bois told the audience. Contrary to what most white social scientists of his time thought, Du Bois felt that the free exercise of the Negro vote would settle the Negro question. One of the recent political campaigns in Georgia, reported Du Bois, was openly "a campaign not against Negro crime and ignorance but against Negro intelligence and property owning and industrial competition."[48]

When Ida Wells-Barnett took the podium at the 1909 National Negro Conference, she discussed lynching as "our national crime." Many years had passed since her first article in the *New York Age* on lynching and her protest at the Chicago World's Fair. Wells-Barnett's anti-lynching campaign now involved a network of black women's clubs throughout the country. She gave the Negro Conference fresh data on lynching: from 1899 to 1908 the number of people lynched was 959, of which 857 were black. "No other nation, civilized or savage, burns its criminals; only under the Stars and Stripes is the human holocaust possible," Wells-Barnett remarked. After the recent mob riots and lynchings in Springfield, Illinois, she became convinced that agitation alone, although helpful, would not stop this crime. Since she started her anti-lynching campaign in 1892, year after year the statistics on lynching were made public, meetings were held, and resolutions were adopted, but the number of lynchings continued to grow. "The only certain remedy is an appeal to law," Wells-Barnett said. Federal protection of American citizenship was the remedy for lynching: "The strong arm of the government must reach across state lines whenever unbridled lawlessness defies state laws and must give to the individual citizen under the Stars and Stripes the same measure of protection which it gives to him when he travels in foreign land."[49]

Oswald Garrison Villard, the author of the "Call" for the national conference, stressed the need for a permanent organization to grow from the conference, which, the organizing committee decided, should become an annual event "for encouragement, for information, for inspiration" of those men and women who believed "that the welfare of the republic is bound up with fair play towards the Negro." Speaking on behalf of the organizers, Villard recommended the formation of a committee to take charge of the 1910 conference and carry out the project of forming a permanent organization. But what type of organization was needed? Villard was convinced that the time had come for the formation of a national committee or a board or a limited society that could do for the colored people what the Zionist committees did for the Jews, the Prussian Polish Committee for the Poles, and the Irish committees for their people. The most important undertaking of the political and civil rights bureau of this national organization would be to bring about the enforcement of the Fourteenth and Fifteenth Amendments and to call for court decisions upon disfranchising laws and other discriminatory legislation. To do so, the national organization should be able to raise large amounts of money. Villard also envisioned an educational department able to help Negro organizations raise their standards and to bring about more efficient methods of organization and an industrial bureau to deal with labor issues, housing, and migration of black people. The national association should provide education and training for exceptional Negroes and place them where they could best serve their race.

The final session of the conference was dedicated to the building process of this new national organization. Although all participants agreed on the need for forming such an organization, strong disagreements, suspicion, and hostility emerged among moderate and radical components and across the color line and political allegiances when it came to naming people who would take charge of its early stage. Resolutions were passed demanding equal civil, educational, and occupational rights, insisting on protection against violence and intimidation, and criticizing President Taft for his resistence to enforcing the Fifteenth Amendment. The editor of the *Boston Guardian,* William Monroe Trotter, who was also president of the National Independent Political

League, and the Reverend J. Milton Waldron, the president of the National Negro Political League of Washington, D.C., found it difficult to agree with the language of resolutions shaped in Villard's editorial terms. One of the most controversial issues, however, was whether to name Booker T. Washington to the Committee of Forty on Permanent Organization. The African-American component of the assembly was strongly anti-Washington. On the other hand, Villard and other white members of the nominating committee feared that without Washington's name the new association would run into serious difficulties in getting funds from white philanthropists. Finally the nominating committee reached an unsatisfying compromise. They omitted both Washington and his most severe critics—Trotter, Waldron, and Wells-Barnett.[50]

Thus the path leading to the formation of the NAACP was heavily marked, since the beginning, by the display of the rituals of political compromise common to many other organizations. Yet as it was the first attempt to build an interracial organization that was national in its scope, versions given by different voices on the contours of its initial political compromises, its relation to preexisting movements, and its problems of leadership are particularly enlightening for understanding the NAACP's potential for becoming a powerful weapon in the battle for racial and social equality.

The *New York Age,* controlled by Booker T. Washington, heavily criticized the National Negro Conference. As if attempting to break the already shaky alliance between black and white members of the new interracial organization in the making, the *Age* gave space to praising the ability of the distinguished white participants, the real friends of the Negro, but reserved only words of contempt for the black participants. The weekly ridiculed Du Bois for being involved in the Niagara Movement, which had failed, and for editing the two periodicals of the Niagara Movement, *The Moon* and *The Horizon,* which had likewise been unsuccessful; the paper also criticized other people like Trotter for having led disintegrating organizations. The *Age* predicted the certain failure of the new attempt because all the organizations and black individuals at the New York conference found themselves in paralyzing disagreements. It was worthy to remember, the weekly continued, that Negroes could solve their problems through work and thrift, by gathering together as doers, not as talkers.[51] Although the *Age* was correct in mentioning the previous failures of those black intellectuals who gathered in 1909 in New York, such a relevant public event in the history of the struggle for racial equality could not be dismissed. Its possible success, however, would have obscured Washington's political machine.

1. *Presentation of Colors to the Twentieth United States Colored Infantry, Colonel Bartram, at the Union League Clubhouse,* March 1864. Artist unknown. (Courtesy of the Photographs and Prints Division, Schomburg Center for Research in Black Culture, the New York Public Library, Astor, Lenox, and Tilden Foundations)

2. Cooper Union, 1861. From *Harper's Weekly,* 30 March 1861.

3. "Dixie" and "The Battle Hymn of the Republic." North and South united after the Spanish-American War, ca. 1899. (Library of Congress)

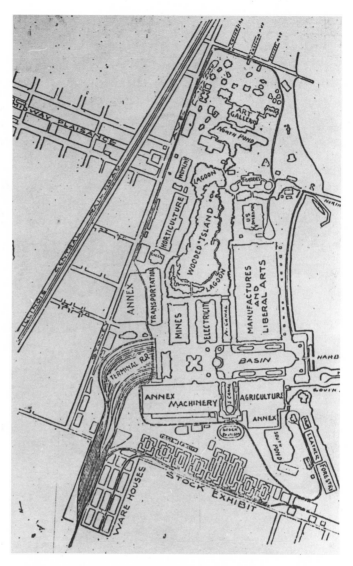

4. Map of the Chicago World's Fair exposition grounds. From the *New York Times,* 30 April 1893.

GRAND FINALE OF THE STUPENDOUS SPECTACULAR SUCCESS,
"UNCLE SAM'S SHOW."

UNCLE SAM.—
It's done, it's done! The show and fun
We've had for six months past;
I've made the world stare

At my wonderful Fair,
And swear that nothing could compare
With the beautiful, wonderful things seen there—
But the end has come, at last.

And now, it's over, we thank you all
For giving so hearty a curtain call;
And you all agree with me, I guess,
That it's been a howling, big success!

CHORUS OF ALL NATIONS.—
For he's a jolly good fellow,
For he's a jolly good fellow,
For he's a jolly good fellow,
Which nobody can deny!

5. "Uncle Sam's Show," Chicago World's Fair. (Prints and Photographs Division, Library of Congress)

6. Hudson-Fulton Celebration, 1909. From the *Saturday Evening Mail*. (Courtesy of the Museum of the City of New York)

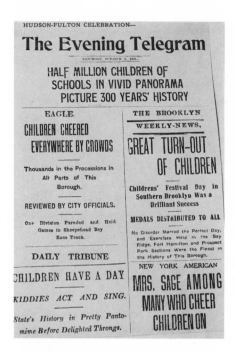

7. Press headlines, Hudson-Fulton Celebration, 1909. From *Playground* 3 (November 1909).

8. Drawing of the stage of Percy MacKaye's *Caliban*, 1916. From Percy MacKaye, *Caliban by the Yellow Sands* (Garden City NY: Doubleday, 1916).

9. Silent Parade from Harlem in which thousands marched down Fifth Avenue to protest the St. Louis Riot, July 1917. Photographer unknown. (Courtesy of the Photographs and Prints Division, Schomburg Center for Research in Black Culture, the New York Public Library, Astor, Lenox, and Tilden Foundations)

From the National Negro Conference to the NAACP

Rituals of Interracial Alliances

I am strongly of the opinion that you will want me to say something concerning my second marriage. I will tell you: My first wife, you see, was the color of my mother, and my second wife the color of my father; you see I wanted to be perfectly fair to both races.   FREDERICK DOUGLASS

Africa and Europe have been united in my family. There is nothing unusual about this interracial history. It has been duplicated thousands of times; but on the one hand, the white folk have bitterly resented even a hint of the facts of this intermingling; while black folk have recoiled in natural hesitation and affected disdain in admitting what they know.
W. E. B. DU BOIS

Raising the Curtain at the National Negro Conference

The "Call" to resolve the Negro question, the first National Negro Conference, and the building process of a national interracial organization changed the public definition of the Negro problem. In *The Souls of Black Folk* (1903), W. E. B. Du Bois had eloquently explored the subjective side of the question: "How does it feel to be a problem?" It was a strange experience, he felt, "peculiar even for one who has never been anything else, save perhaps in babyhood and in Europe." The African American always felt the "two-ness" of being "an American, a Negro; two souls, two thoughts, two unreconciled strivings; two warring ideals in one dark body, whose dogged strength alone keeps it from being torn asunder." If the history of the American Negro was the history of this strife, as Du Bois put it, the New York National Negro Conference made clear once and for all that the Negro problem was not and could not be kept separate from other American reform movements. White reformers engaged in the battle for women's rights, consumers' leagues, social settlements, and other humanitarian movements finally recognized the need for building a movement for racial equality. At the same time, those black intellectuals who had considered their own condition a world apart from other social problems and who had built their separate racial organizations became aware of the need for a broader interracial association. They realized that the struggle for racial equality was part of the struggle for democracy in America. The New York conference, in Du Bois's view, revealed the awakening of a consciousness of a new kind. Those social workers and other professionals who signed the Call were convinced that any problem related to progress and the uplifting of any group involved the condition of colored people. Those black intellectuals who responded to the Call had become aware that the so-called Negro problem was a universal problem of poverty, ignorance, suffrage, women's rights, distribution of wealth, and law and order among blacks and whites. Far from being a matter of "millionaires and almsgiving," it was a "human problem" demanding "human methods."[1]

By asserting that "the spirit of abolitionism must be revived," the authors of the Call meant to revive a spirit of building organizational alliances between the movements for women's rights and racial equality, which since the Civil War had grown apart. Although they knew it would be a long and difficult process, the beginning seemed promising. The fact that one-third of the signers of the Call were women and that most men at the conference advocated women's rights was an important step in that direction. The three hundred men and women signing the Call included affluent reformers, descendants of abolitionists, concerned academics, suffragettes, and a few labor organizers.[2]

Only two black women signed the Call: Ida Wells-Barnett of Chicago and Mary Church Terrell of Washington, D.C. They both moved north from Memphis, Tennessee, and had many common interests, yet they differed in their social backgrounds and ways of conceiving racial organizations. Wells-Barnett, the eldest of eight children, at age sixteen had to take charge of several siblings after her parents died of yellow fever, but Terrell was the daughter of a wealthy black man and received an interracial education at Ohio's Oberlin College and in Europe.[3] Both women married lawyers, but their husbands' careers followed different political affiliations. Whereas journalist lawyer Ferdinand Barnett extensively criticized Booker T. Washington's political compromises on

Negro rights from the pages of his Chicago paper, the *Conservator,* Robert Terrell received a federal appointment as municipal judge of the District of Columbia thanks to Washington's influence. Yet as race relations worsened in the country, Mary Church Terrell became very critical of Washington and accepted the invitation to sign the Call.[4]

White women signing the Call included Jane Addams, the founder of Hull House Settlement in Chicago and a nationally known reformer; Florence Kelley, the founder of the Consumer's League; Julia Lathrop, lecturer at the Chicago School of Civics and Philanthropy; social workers Sophonisba Breckinridge and Edith and Grace Abbott; New Yorkers Jane E. Robbins, a public health physician and director of New York's College Settlement, and Lillian Wald, the founder of the Henry Street Settlement. Unlike the white conference participants, who could take time off from their jobs and pay for their travel expenses to New York, most black participants found that time and money were not easily available. They held jobs as teachers, ministers, and journalists, and most black women did not have financial security even if they belonged to the middle class. Jane Addams raised funds to cover the travel expenses of Ida Wells-Barnett, the Chicago journalist and women's club organizer. Because it was more difficult for blacks to attend, the black presence at the conference was representative of the Northeast, with a strong component from the nearby New York area.

Ida Wells-Barnett's account of the stormy reaction at the National Negro Conference when Du Bois read aloud the list of names for the Committee of Forty on Permanent Organization emphasized personal differences between herself and the other leaders of the new association. She particularly resented the treatment she received "at the hands of the men of my own race" associated with the white founders. In the autobiography she wrote in the 1920s, Wells-Barnett minimized the role of the NAACP in the battle for racial equality by simply saying that the organization "had fallen short of the expectations of its founders." Her problem with the association began at the National Negro Conference of 1909. She had the uneasy feeling that Booker T. Washington and his theories, "which seemed for the moment to dominate the country, would prevail in the discussion as to what ought to be done." Oswald Garrison Villard was known as "an outspoken admirer of Mr. Washington, and the feeling seemed general that an endorsement of his industrial education would be the result," Wells-Barnett wrote. Although Washington did not appear at the conference, "this feeling, like Banquo's ghost, would not down." Wells-Barnett was among those who tried to lessen this feeling by asserting that "most of those present were believers in Dr. Du Bois's ideas." What made her solidly anti-Washington,

besides his compromise on Negro political and civil rights, was his superficial attitude toward lynching. "Mr. Washington says in substance,"
she wrote in 1904, "give me money to educate the Negro and when he
is taught how to work, he will not commit the crime for which lynching
is done." Yet Washington knew "that lynching is not invoked to punish
crime but color, and not even industrial education will change that."[5]

On the night of 1 June 1909, at the end of the last session of the conference, when Du Bois announced the Committee of Forty, which did
not include Wells-Barnett, "bedlam broke loose," she recalled. "I con-
fess I was surprised, but I put the best face possible on the matter and
turned to leave." When the organizers decided to close the conference
with the reading of the controversial list, "excitement bubbled over."
Some heated speeches against that decision were made by William Monroe Trotter, editor of the *Boston Guardian,* the Reverend R. C. Ransom,
pastor of the Bethel AME Church of New York City, Dr. J. W. Waldrom,
pastor of the large Baptist church in Washington, D.C., Dr. J. W. Mossell
of Philadelphia and his wife, Gertrude, T. Thomas Fortune, and others. These prominent African Americans were Wells-Barnett's personal
friends. After Du Bois read the list, she went around reassuring them
that "their fears were groundless," that she had seen the list before, and
that her name was on it together with other opponents of Washington.[6]

Wells-Barnett was determined to leave Cooper Union when John Millholland—a successful New York manufacturer, a warm defender of
civil liberties, a friend of Du Bois's and Ovington's, and "a warm friend
of the Negro"—approached her to let her know that when the list of
names left the hands of the nominating committee and was given to
Du Bois, her name led the rest. "It is unthinkable that you," Millholland
said, according to Wells-Barnett's memory, "who have fought the battle
against lynching for nearly twenty years single-handed and alone when
the rest of us were following our selfish pursuits, should be left off such a
committee." She replied that "it was very evident that someone did not
want my presence on it," but that she would continue her anti-lynching
campaign anyway. She was walking out of Cooper Union, when someone
called to her. As she was waiting on the sidewalk, Mary Ovington, "who
had taken active part in the deliberations, swept by me with an air of triumph and a very pleased look on her face." Wells-Barnett decided to return to the conference building where Millholland, William English
Walling, and other members of the nominating committee were waiting
for her. There was also W. E. B. Du Bois, the only African American on
the nominating commission for the Committee of Forty, who came to
her with a "lame apology" for crossing out her name. He apologized to
Wells-Barnett for thinking she would feel represented by the name of

Celia Parke Wooley, a black woman who worked at the Frederick Douglass Center of Chicago, and for replacing her with Dr. Charles Bentley, a loyal member of the Niagara Movement who also was from Chicago. Du Bois asked for her consent to reinstate her name on the list, but Wells-Barnett did not accept. She could not get over that Du Bois "had done this purposely." By the time she wrote her autobiography, she could admit that "of course, I did a foolish thing. . . . My anger at having been treated in such a fashion outweighed my judgement." Yet years later Wells-Barnett remained convinced that Du Bois and Mary Ovington were responsible for crossing out her name.[7] She believed that Ovington was jealous of her accomplishments and that Du Bois resented her outspokenness. It was true that Du Bois's large ego could have found the unrestrained frankness of Wells-Barnett's crusades hard to take. Furthermore, he ignored her work in all his autobiographical writings. In *Dusk of Dawn,* for example, Du Bois did not explain why Wells-Barnett, who had gained an international reputation for her anti-lynching campaign, did not participate on the executive committee of the NAACP, which was to become the most important anti-lynching organization in the United States. According to Du Bois's biographer David Lewis, however, it was Villard more than Du Bois who was to blame for erasing the name of Wells-Barnett and other radicals from the list for the Committee of Forty. Villard, the chair of the nominating commission, had made it clear that he did not want to include on the executive committee of the new organization any radical activists whose presence would be resented by Booker T. Washington's supporters. He believed that no civil rights organization could be strong and effective if run by radicals, and he had promised the Tuskegee leader that the new association was not going to be either a Washington or a Du Bois movement.

Wells-Barnett's resentment for how Du Bois behaved was understandable, but her judgment of Mary Ovington was unfair. In fact, Ovington was in favor of reintroducing Wells-Barnett's name on the list, "where it ought to be," the New York social worker wrote in her reminiscences. Ovington honestly thought Wells-Barnett was "a great fighter," but she also knew that the black journalist "had to play a lone hand." A generous organizer who never put her individual achievement first, Ovington was more concerned with keeping the new organization together than not hurting Wells-Barnett's feelings. She was convinced that "if you have too many players of lone hands in your organization, you soon have no game."[8] Whether it was a question of Wells-Barnett being a "lone hand" or whether there was something wrong with the rules of the game is open to interpretation.

Because of ambivalent racial perceptions, personal pride, and gender tensions, Ida Wells-Barnett did not join the NAACP. There is no doubt that she did not think very highly of Mary Ovington. She acknowledged that the NAACP represented a movement that "lasted longer than almost any other movement of its kind in our country." At the same time, Wells-Barnett thought that the association fell "far short of the expectations of its founders" and that the reason for this failure was highly visible: the movement kept Mary White Ovington as the chair of the executive committee. "Miss Ovington's heart is in this work," Wells-Barnett conceded, "but her experience has been confined solely to New York City and Brooklyn, and a few minor incidents along the color line." She was convinced that Ovington "has basked in the adoration of the few college-bred Negroes who have surrounded her, but has made little effort to know the soul of the black woman." Thus Ovington, in Wells-Barnett's view, fell "far short of helping a race which has suffered as no white woman has ever been called upon to suffer or to understand." Wells-Barnett, her pride still hurt many years after that night of 1 June 1909, concluded that had she not been so upset by the treatment she received "at the hands of the men of my own race and thus blinded to the realization that I should have taken the place which the white men of the committee felt I should have, the NAACP would now be a live, active force in the lives of our people all over this country."[9] It is a fact that by losing such a strong anti-lynching crusader and women's club organizer the new organization lost a great fighter, but pride led the radical Wells-Barnett to make the wrong decision. It is also a fact that her strong words against Ovington revealed ongoing racial and class tensions among women reformers.

Mary Ovington, whose determination and organizational work made the first National Negro Conference possible, believed that the conference's merit was bringing the two races together. Her reminiscences raise the curtain on the controversy about Booker T. Washington that pressured the organizers to extend an invitation that the leader would decline. "Could we ignore the man who was unquestionably the most influential and the most famous Negro living?" asked Ovington, reframing the question on which the stormy meeting leading to the formation of the Committee of Forty was held. A compromise was made: "If Washington's name was omitted, the radicals agreed to have a few conservative names on the committee and not to include Washington's bitterest enemies." Ovington's reconstruction of the events emphasized black members' distrust of a movement in which the majority of leaders were white people: "Were they going to be namby-pamby at last, as so many whites before them had been, and counsel halfway measures?" When around midnight resolutions were passed and the names of the new

Committee of Forty, of which William English Walling was made chair, were announced, there was "a little angry talk in the aisles when we disbanded," Ovington recalled. Because her father had recently died, when the conference was over she took her mother to their country house, where she learned by letter of the "thunderous recriminations" about the omission of some names from the famous list.[10]

If explicit recriminations came from the radicals excluded from the Committee of Forty, a covert operation of discredit and personal attacks on some of the promoters of the National Negro Conference had already been waged by Booker T. Washington's supporters. One of the early attempts to discredit his opponents was the role Washington had in misrepresenting a dinner Mary Ovington organized in 1908 for the Cosmopolitan Club at a restaurant in lower Manhattan. A founder of this liberal-radical-socialist club, Ovington gathered at a dinner party a relatively large interracial group of people to discuss addresses by Oswald Garrison Villard of the *Evening Post,* Hamilton Holt of the *Independent,* John Spargo of the Socialist Party, and two Negro speakers, William H. Ferris and the Reverend George Frazier Miller. As Mary Ovington described the crowd both in her reminiscences and autobiography, most black participants belonged to the established African-American middle class of Brooklyn. Except for a few socialists, the large majority of black participants believed that the best statement on individual rights was in Thomas Jefferson's Declaration of Independence, and they "would be satisfied if they could get as good a chance in America as the white man." White participants represented a large spectrum of ideas. There were those, like Villard, who came from the old abolitionist background, and there were some socialists, radicals, social workers, and several friends of the members of the club. "It was a sober gathering," Ovington reported. But the following day some New York papers maliciously reported that "colored and white had sat down together at a public restaurant," without giving any hint about the "almost religious" character of the speeches. The news became exciting reading in the South, where newspapers turned what had been a sober dinner into an orgy. "Those who wrote it up," Ovington said, "did not comment on the white man who sat next the Negro woman, but they poured their spleen on the white woman who sat next a colored man." According to the *Richmond Leader,* the interracial event illustrated that "degeneracy will seek its level." The *St. Louis Post Dispatch* declared it was a "miscegenation dinner" that was "loathsome enough to consign the whole fraternity of perverts who participated in it to undying infamy." Other southern papers gave even more picturesque descriptions of the participants at that dinner, such as a description of Ovington in the *Savannah News* as "the high priestess . . . whose father is rich and who affiliates five days every week with Negro men and dines with them at her home in Brooklyn, Sundays." Ovington was reported to have had "a hundred thousand Negroes at the Bacchanal feast" and to have taken "white girls into that den." Besides being horrified by the sight of "decadent women," the reporter of the *News* was amazed "to see editors of papers that hitherto have been considered decent"—the reference was obviously to Villard and Holt—"in that witches cauldron on that black night." Ovington had the most publicity: "My mail was very heavy . . . I was smothered in mud." That mail, entirely from the South, taught her an important lesson: "When I read of a lynching today, I think of those letters and know the men who engineered it."

Ovington thought that the president of the Cosmopolitan Club, André Tridon, "a Frenchman and delightful pagan," had invited reporters to publicize that unusual dinner of black and white people sitting at the same table. She also thought that the humiliating coverage by the white press in the South was the work of white negrophobes. Ovington was not aware of, or at least she did not mention, any other person behind the incident in her autobiographies or that enemies were not just on the white side. Booker T. Washington, via his New York ally Charles Anderson, had engineered the paper coverage of that "miscegenation dinner." Biographer Louis Harlan, by thoroughly looking at Washington's private papers, found that the Tuskegee leader and his partner Anderson "secretly arranged for the sensational press coverage of this dinner, and did so again in January 1911." According to Harlan's evidence, Washington and Anderson directed the discreditable attack to mock the little group of "racial liberals with a savagery that cannot be explained by Washington's social philosophy, racial policy or any other rational consideration."[11]

When in January 1911 the Cosmopolitan Club sponsored a banquet at the Cafe Boulevard in Manhattan, Washington and Anderson again tried for press coverage with lurid reports, but this time the *New York Times, Sun,* and *Herald* failed to mention the event. Anderson sent Washington a copy of the invitation on which he labeled speakers, discussants, and guests "a bunch of freaks" and mentioned that he would do his best to get "a full newspaper report." Washington suggested that Anderson should find the same reporter who did such a good job in 1908 and that the *New York Times* would work in harmony with him. Anderson could not find the same man who handled the matter in 1908, but he did find "a good friend." Although this time major New York papers did not cover the event, the *New York Press* carried the headline: "Three Races Sit at Banquet for Mixed Marriage." On 26 January 1911, the

Press reported that "white women, evidently of the cultured and wealthier classes, fashionably attired in low-cut gowns, leaned over the table to chat confidently with negro men of the true African type." By "true African type" the *Press* obviously meant men like W. E. B. Du Bois, one of the evening speakers, who was elegantly dressed in a tuxedo.

These attempts to discredit his political opponents showed that Washington was losing political power. Following the worst tradition of American political machines, he attacked the NAACP by using the African-American newspapers he still controlled, such as the *New York Age* and the *Washington Bee,* to launch a campaign against William English Walling. Those papers made public that the wealthy socialist had been sued by a Russian-Jewish woman for breaking an official marriage proposal in Paris. On 23 March 1911, the *Age* declared that "no colored man or woman will in the future disgrace our race by inviting Mr. Walling in their home or ask him to speak at any public meeting." These attacks on the NAACP leadership did not bring back the power Washington had already lost. They also showed that the Tuskegee leader failed to recognize the inner contradictions of the interracial NAACP, the differences between moderate liberals like Villard and the radical Democrats following Du Bois.[12]

It is sad that Washington's twilight as a great political leader coincided with a physical attack on him in the San Juan Hill district of Manhattan on the night of 19 March 1911. It is not clear what the Tuskegee leader was doing in that neighborhood. He had arrived in New York the day before, checked in at the first-class Manhattan Hotel, given talks at churches during the day, and returned to his hotel early in the evening. Then he took the subway and went up to West Sixty-third Street, at the edge of the disreputable Tenderloin district. He entered a building in front of a theater, inhabited by white lower-class people only. Washington rang one bell, received no answer, walked in and out the building several times, was passed by three white women, and finally was physically attacked by a huge and much younger German-American carpenter. Fifty-five-year-old Washington tried to defend himself and then ran out into the street, but the white man followed him and struck at the black man's head with a cane. Washington fell near a plainclothes police officer. At the station house the black leader was not believed when he declared his identity, and it appeared he would be charged with burglary or sexual harassment. One of the white women who passed by him while he was ringing the bell and who was a close friend of the German carpenter claimed that Washington was drunk and addressed her with "Hello, sweetheart." Finally Washington was able to convince the police officers of his identity, was taken to a hospital, and returned to his hotel with sixteen stitches on his head. The following morning the incident was sensationally reported in the New York papers. What was he doing in that neighborhood? Did he have an appointment with a white prostitute? Did he harass that woman as she claimed? On the advice of Seth Low, the president of Columbia University and former New York mayor, Washington gave detailed interviews to Villard's *Evening Post,* obtained public statements in his favor from President Taft and the industrialist Andrew Carnegie, and received a private message of solidarity from former president Roosevelt. Discrepancies in Washington's account of his night visit to that neighborhood concerned Villard: "If he should not be able to substantiate his story in court it would be a terrible thing, and I have been sick at heart over it because there are all sorts of stories already floating around among newspaper men that he really went to the place to meet a white woman, etc." If Villard had some doubts, Du Bois did not. "Most great men have had an occasional moral lapse," he told a friend many years later. "The only surprising thing is that [Washington] had only one to come to surface." Du Bois was convinced, according to his biographer Lewis, that it was not the first time Washington visited that neighborhood.

The new NAACP leaders handled the case admirably. It was not in their interest to speculate on Washington's possible interracial sexual activity, but it was profitable to the organization to act upon the truce that he needed. Du Bois was reluctant, but the organization passed a proposal from Villard asking Washington to make a public endorsement of the NAACP. The Tuskegee leader sent a telegram of official agreement to Villard. The affair ended with a successful fund-raising for the NAACP annual conference and a condescending resolution of "profound regret at the recent assault on Dr. Booker T. Washington in New York City," in which the association found "renewed evidence of racial discrimination and increased necessity for the awakening of the public conscience."[13]

Washington never fully recovered from that physical attack. His health was poor and worsened because of an incurable disease. He died in December 1915.

Public Exchanges on Controversial Matters

In 1903, when Mary White Ovington was spending her last year as a professional social worker at Greenpoint Settlement in Brooklyn, she went to a lecture Booker T. Washington gave at the Social Reform Club in Manhattan on Negro conditions in the urban North. "To my amazement," she confessed, " I learned that there was a Negro problem in my city. I had honestly never thought of it. . . . I went home with a new idea.

. . . Might not my next venture be among Negroes?" At that time Washington's autobiography, *Up from Slavery*, was being serialized in the *Outlook* magazine, whose editor, Charles Spahr, was the chair of the Social Reform Club of which Ovington was an active member. Spahr invited Washington to speak to the club on black poverty in the North. Washington's lecture was rather poor, and social worker Ovington was too radical to accept his philosophy. However, even though she would soon turn to Du Bois's opposite views on Negro education and civil and political rights, it was the Tuskegee principal who made Ovington aware of the Negro problem in the city where she lived: "It was a picture of ramshackle tenements, high infant mortality, and discrimination in employment that made it almost impossible for a Negro to secure work that paid a decent wage." On that day in 1903, thirty-eight-year-old Ovington made the most important decision of her social-reform career: she would become a new abolitionist. Just as her grandparents had worked to free the slaves, she would devote herself to Negro rights. Ovington kept that promise: she became the first professionally trained social worker in the United States to dedicate her career and money to the betterment of the conditions of African Americans, the author of *Half a Man* (1911), the first scientific study of Negro life in New York City, and one of the founders of the NAACP.

The daughter of a New York merchant, Mary White Ovington grew up in an exclusive section of Brooklyn and was sent to Radcliffe College to receive the typical education of a young woman of refinement. Her family came from New England, and her grandmother was a friend of William Lloyd Garrison. Ovington's parents were also abolitionists, and she grew up with no doubt about the right and wrong side of the Civil War, but she had no actual contacts with black people: "We did not have colored servants, and in no other way would I be likely in my home on Brooklyn Heights to speak to a colored person," Ovington recalled. She frankly admitted that in her youth she wanted to meet "the upper class of Negroes, the descendants, spiritually at least, of the fugitive slaves," to talk about her favorite books with them. "But I was as little likely to meet one of these people in my small world as to find Queen Victoria ringing my door bell." Although she did not meet any educated Negroes in her daily life, she heard Frederick Douglass speaking at her grandfather's church: "My first impression was of power, of dominating personality." W. E. B. Du Bois was at Harvard when she was at Radcliffe; they both had Albert Bushnell Hart as a history teacher, "but our paths did not cross." While a student at Radcliffe, tall, blond, blue-eyed Mary Ovington gave up the social life of a debutante to follow her interests in labor problems and socialism. She felt strongly motivated to become a professional social worker, so she registered at Pratt Institute in Brooklyn and started with other students the Greenpoint Settlement. During the period she spent at Greenpoint, from 1896 to 1903, she worked with foreign immigrant children, became aware of the nightmare of unemployment, and met unionists and factory girls. For the first two years of her social work career, "the Negro was non-existent." Then one afternoon Ovington went to Prospect Park with fifteen boys, the children of foreign immigrants representing eight nationalities. As they came closer to the park the car passed by a line of unimproved houses in front of which colored women sat and talked to each other. What happened made Ovington very angry. Suddenly, "as at a signal," every boy jumped on his seat and yelled, 'Nigger, Nigger, Nigger!'" The colored women did not pay any attention, "taking it as a part of life," but Ovington was furious and puzzled at the same time. She did not detect any sign of racial prejudice among the boys when the settlement employed a colored janitor. Those boys were fascinated by him and anxious to attract his attention. She concluded that their yelling at those black women on the streets "was a ritual they had learned," which did not imply any animosity.

Greenpoint Settlement, like most settlement houses, was mainly a woman's undertaking. The only men Ovington met during that period were those attending book discussions, theatrical events, and other cultural activities at the Social Reform Club. Although she enjoyed men's company, by the time she was thirty-five Ovington decided, like many other white women settlement workers of her generation, that she was not likely to marry.

At the beginning of the century, the Social Reform Club was a gathering place for New York intellectuals, professionals, and workers to discuss "practical and theoretical humanitarianism." They talked "socialism and single tax," read William Morris, sang the English socialist's hymn of the workers, and believed "that by sacrifice and hard work" Morris's dream might come true. Via the Social Reform Club, Ovington became a pragmatic parliamentary socialist who praised efficient reforms through legislation and the art of making the best compromise in order to pursue the strategic goals of a political organization—an art that she extensively practiced during the long-term major role she played in and the generous work she gave to the NAACP.[14]

In 1904, the year after Ovington heard Washington's speech at the Social Reform Club, Ovington left Greenpoint Settlement and became a fellow at Greenwich House, Manhattan, to carry out a survey of the Negro population in New York. The members of the Greenwich House Committee on Social Investigations, who gave Ovington a fellowship, were all on the faculty of Columbia University, including philosopher

John Dewey and anthropologists Livingston Farrand and Franz Boas. Ovington would later recruit these progressive academics to contribute to the NAACP's research activities. In a few years she became so knowledgeable about urban black economic and social conditions that W. E. B. Du Bois recommended Ovington's writings as indispensable readings on urban black economic and social conditions. Ovington's *Half a Man: The Status of the Negro in New York* (1911) was an important book. Franz Boas's foreword praised it as "a refutation of the claims that the Negro had equal opportunities with the whites, and that his failure to advance more rapidly than he has, is due to innate inability." Ovington took the title from a statement she once heard from a black college student: "My father comes north in the summer to be a man. No, (correcting himself), half a man."[15] Besides being the most relevant sociological study of New York's black community in the early twentieth century, *Half a Man* was Ovington's honest attempt to use social science as a weapon of change. The book seemed to contradict Wells-Barnett's assumption that Ovington did not show any interest in black women. In fact, *Half a Man* offered a thorough investigation of all aspects of life of the New York black population and fresh insights into the social conditions of working black women.

Ovington observed that the black girl in New York, more than the foreign immigrant, was subject to degrading temptations: the "good people" wanted her for her willingness to work long hours at a lower wage than the white woman; and the "bad people" offered her light labor and generous pay. That was particularly tempting for black girls, who more often than white girls lived away from their parental home. These young women who lived alone constituted the surplus of black women in the city. Some of them lived with their employers, but others lodged in already crowded tenements; usually the southern servant, unaccustomed to spending the night at her employer's, arranged to leave her mistress when her work was done. "In their hours of leisure," Ovington wrote, "the surplus women are known to play havoc with their neighbors' sons, even with their neighbors' husbands," as the lack of men made marriage impossible for about one-fifth of New York's young black women. According to Ovington, this led to additional social problems. "Surplus" black women, able to secure work, supported idle, ablebodied black men, such as "the lounger at the street corner, the dandy in the parlor thrumming on his banjo." It was easy for black men in New York to find young women who kept them in "polished boots, fashionable coats, and well-creased trousers."[16] The surplus of young black women increased steadily with the demand for black servants that attracted southern migrants.

From Reconstruction on, a few African-American women in the North and South organized settlements to provide services for black communities that the government and white social organizations failed to supply. One example was the work of the New York White Rose Mission, founded by Victoria Earle Matthews in 1897. The daughter of a courageous slave mother who managed to flee from Georgia with her children and to make her home in New York, Matthews believed in the importance of social work among black girls who had recently arrived in the city from the South seeking employment.[17] Settlement workers made arrangements to meet black immigrant girls at the steamships arriving from the South, where the agents who wanted to secure the girls for evil purposes usually operated. Accustomed to obeying white men's commands, the unsuspicious black girls believed the agents' promises of a safe and well-paid employment and fell into their hands. Ovington's findings showed that not all black women working in "questionable places and with questionable people" took the jobs by choice; some were sent without knowing the character of the house they entered. A system existed by which employment agencies were able to advance the traveling expenses of southern girls and keep them responsible for their debts until the cost of the journey had been repaid many times over.

Ovington's evidence showed that the young black woman frequently found domestic work in a small apartment with facilities such as a dumbwaiter, clothes dryer, and gas and electricity, which made housework less physically demanding. Work began early and lasted until dinner was cleared away. Then the young woman was released from further tasks; she could return to her tiny tenement room and put on a fresh dress. Her options for the evening included walking the streets, going to the theater, or attending a class or meeting at the church. Housework did not create much ambition, for just as the mistress moved, "flitting, in New York fashion, from one flat to another . . . the girl also flits among employers, changing with the whim of the moment." Racial prejudice confined black women to domestic service, a job that traditionally had particular connotations for them, for black men, and for the white women of the lower classes. Symbolically, domestic service was for blacks the social heritage of slavery; it re-created a continuity of the master-slave relationship in a different context.[18]

Ovington had already explored the important role of the black mother as a wage earner in an article she contributed to the 1905 special issue of *Charities* on the Negro in the urban North. Sometimes the woman of the household earned more money than the man. Domestic service took her away from home for eight to fourteen hours every day. Many mothers took in laundry instead in order not to leave their children alone and turned their homes into sweatshops. Husbands who worked on the railroads or on boats or as waiters in large hotels were absent from their families for long periods. The economic situation of black workers in New York often did not lead to a strengthening of the home life and the marriage tie. The economic independence of the woman and the frequent absence from home of the man led to desertions and separations. Some observers were impressed, however, that the morality of these black workers living in the Tenderloin district was relatively high. It seemed that these people were able "to live apart from the roughness about them, but close to their church and their children." Challenging racist assumptions about black women's sexual mores, Ovington's findings showed that "the loud colored woman who parades the streets counts for more in the minds of the most of us than a dozen of the quiet women of her race who pass by without our noticing them."[19]

Mary Ovington strongly believed in overcoming racial prejudice among the white women working in factories and department stores. The entrance of black women into the work force in stores and factories would give them "the discipline of regular hours, of steady training, of order and system" that they lacked in domestic service. According to Ovington, it was to the young black woman's advantage to become part of a strong labor group and share its working-class ideal and morality: "instead of looking into the mirror of her wealthy mistress, she needs to reflect the aspirations of the strong, earnest women who toil." Many black women did choose industrial employment when they were given a chance during World War I. It was an illusory progress, however, for most black women employed in industrial establishments were not machine operators or even semiskilled workers: instead, they swept factory floors, scrubbed equipment, and disposed of refuse. They could, however, aspire to leave those unskilled jobs and become nurses, teachers, charity workers, or theatrical performers. These were aspirations that black girls could entertain as possible alternatives to domestic service. Ovington found that in 1909 Lincoln Hospital graduated twenty-one black nurses, some of whom remained in New York and found satisfying employment. She also found that black women with intellectual abilities, particularly if they belonged to old New York families, could become kindergarten, primary, and grammar school teachers and make a good salary. Opportunities for intelligent black women were also available in the main charity organizations of the city for work among poor blacks. However, performing on stage was perhaps the most sought-after profession among young black women and men, who for the first time entered the world of musical comedy.[20] It was a new way for African

Americans to be in public and participate in the making of the new urban culture of early twentieth-century New York.

Ovington's deep social analysis of the conditions of black women workers shows that Wells-Barnett was unfair to accuse the social worker of scarce sensibility and exclusive interest in black intellectual men. It was true that Ovington highly admired Du Bois, who happened to be the most remarkable black intellectual of the time, but she related to him as a social scientist, a friend, and an efficient organizer of the NAACP in her attempt to overcome Du Bois's never-ending doubts about the association.

Ovington first met the black scholar in 1905 at Atlanta University after a period of intense correspondence in which she expressed her admiration. She let Du Bois know how his pioneering Atlanta Sociological Studies of black experience in the United States, for which she raised some funds, highly inspired her, and she asked his advice for her new social investigations in New York. Du Bois invited Ovington to attend the annual spring conference at Atlanta University. She was delighted to accept and finally meet the man "who had dared counter Booker T. Washington." When at dinner she found herself seated next to Du Bois, "his head like Shakespeare's done in bronze," she felt that her "cup of happiness was full." Du Bois talked nonsense throughout the meal just to show her that he was not "weeping all the time." This scene marked the beginning of a long-term friendship between the white social worker and the black scholar, in which Ovington acted as his invaluable ally and defender of his radical political stands and his gigantic ego among the white leaders of the NAACP. Du Bois, on his side, deeply respected Ovington's loyalty to the cause of black people and let her become his closest white friend.[21] This was probably what Ida Wells-Barnett found intolerable about Ovington's way of relating to black intellectual men. It was a question of style, class background, and temperament that negatively influenced Wells-Barnett's attitude toward Ovington.

Far from rejecting interracial sexual relations, Wells-Barnett was among the few who took a stand against the existence of laws forbidding interracial marriages in many states. She was one of the few black people who did not disapprove of Frederick Douglass's second marriage in 1884 to a white woman, Helen Pitts. "He, a colored man, and she, a white woman," Wells-Barnett wrote in her autobiography, "had loved each other and married so that they might live together in the holy bonds of matrimony rather than in the illicit relationship that was the cause of so many lynchings I had noted and protested against." Douglass thanked her for being the only colored woman who went to his house in Rochester as a guest and treated his wife, Helen, as a hostess. Wells-Barnett would have preferred, as did many of his other friends, that "Mr. Douglass had chosen one of the beautiful, charming, colored women of my race for his second wife. But he loved Helen Pitts, and married her and it was outrageous that they should be crucified by both white and black people for so doing." Many African Americans continued to criticize Douglass's second marriage even after his death in 1895. In 1906 Booker T. Washington published a book on the great black abolitionist in which he found fault with Douglass's choice for a second wife, "which caused something like a revulsion of feeling throughout the entire country." By marrying Helen Pitts, who had helped him in his work for many years and whom he admired enormously, Douglass "failed to take into consideration the offense his act might give to public feeling."[22] Wells-Barnett, who deeply respected Douglass, did not feel offended by a legally married interracial couple.

The former teacher from Mississippi had made Chicago her home after marrying journalist Ferdinand Lee Barnett in 1895. She became known nationwide for her articles in the *New York Age* of 1892, which marked the beginning of her international crusade against lynching. Wells-Barnett fought with the tools of a social investigator and the spirit of a crusader against lynching, the mob action raising the most explosive conflicts of race and gender at the turn of the century.

In May 1892 Ida Wells was traveling the Northeast when she found out via New York editor T. Thomas Fortune that the *Free Speech,* the paper she partially owned and worked for in Memphis, Tennessee, had been destroyed. A white mob, incensed by her documented article on the lynching of black men for the alleged rape of white women, attacked the premises in which the paper operated, but luckily the crowd could not find the journalist. Her detailed investigation was the result of one seminal event in her life: the lynching of three black men in Memphis on 9 March 1892. The men successfully operated the People's Company, a grocery business in a heavily populated black neighborhood, and thus challenged the monopoly of a white grocery store. Thomas Moss, Calvin McDowell, and Henry Stewart were close friends of Wells's. When their grocery store was attacked, these men were guilty only of resisting racist provocations of white businessmen trying to force them out of business; yet the black grocers were the ones to get arrested. They were taken from jail by a mob and lynched, and their store was destroyed. Then white mobs went around the town, shooting into groups of black people wherever they found them. Encouraged by Wells's editorials in the *Free Speech,* many black people left a town that could not protect their lives or property, and others resisted by boycotting stores and streetcars. Wells realized that the economic boycott, which nearly sent the streetcar company out of business, was a formidable weapon of protest.

Mob action against the *Free Speech* occurred when Wells presented the facts about the reasons African-American men and women were lynched throughout the South. It was the beginning of an explosive sociopolitical analysis of lynching that Wells carried out by using sophisticated sociological journalism and public speeches in national and international campaigns. She wrote in her autobiography that until the murder of her friends, she had thought lynching was the spontaneous response to the outrage generated among southern whites over the rape of white women by black men. But her friends were not accused of committing any rape. Their murder made her understand that lynching was "an excuse to get rid of Negroes who were acquiring wealth and property" and a political weapon to create an atmosphere of terror to "keep the nigger down." She decided to investigate other lynching episodes and reported the findings in the *Free Speech*. Wells's editorial, which appeared while she was traveling in the North, brought forth evidence on the real causes of recent lynchings and concluded that the victims, all black men accused of committing rape for which lynching was regarded as the appropriate punishment, were involved in consensual sexual affairs with white women. These men were lynched, she argued, to protect the reputation of the white women involved. Her editorial was an explicit accusation of the whole Memphis community: "Eight Negroes lynched since the last issue of the *Free Speech*. Three were charged with killing white men and five with raping white women. Nobody in this section believes the old thread-bare lie that Negro men assault white women. If Southern white men are not careful they will overreach themselves and a conclusion will be reached which will be very damaging to the moral reputation of their women."

Wells's final statement, a challenge to the southern belief in the purity of white womanhood, caused an immediate violent response. The lynchers "destroyed my paper," she wrote in her autobiography, "in which every dollar I had in the world was invested." They made her "an exile and threatened my life for hinting at the truth." She had exposed that illicit sexual relationships between white men and black women were commonly accepted in the South during slavery. During her investigations Wells found that "this rape of helpless Negro girls and women, which began in slavery days, still continued without hindrance, check or reproof from church, state, or press until there was created this race within a race—and all designated by the inclusive term 'colored.'" She accused white men of wearing the mask of hypocrisy: "They could and did fall in love with the pretty mulatto and quadroon girls as well as the

black ones, but they professed an inability to imagine white women doing the same thing with Negro and mulatto men." Whenever these trans-
gressive liaisons were discovered, "the cry of rape was raised, and the
lowest element of the white South was turned loose to wreak its fiendish
cruelty on those too weak to help themselves." But often white fear of
black economic competition caused mob action, as the lynching of her
friends clearly showed.[23] T. Thomas Fortune provided front-page coverage in the *New York Age* for the article based on Wells's investigations,
and as her return to Memphis was not advisable, he offered her a position as columnist and reporter for the black paper. The publishers of the
Age printed over ten thousand copies of the issue including Wells's investigations and statistics on lynchings. The young black journalist became
popularly known as "the princess of the press" and was invited to speak
in Philadelphia, New York City, Wilmington, and Brooklyn.

Wells-Barnett was most outspoken and ready to point out white wom-
en's contradictory and controversial attitudes on racial issues. Her analysis of lynching, which focused on manipulation of black sexuality by
current white morality, led her to a direct confrontation with several
white reformers. During her English anti-lynching campaign, she publicly attacked Frances Willard, the president of the Women's Christian
Temperance Union, for condoning lynching and for refusing to make a
public statement against that practice. Upon returning from a tour of
the South in 1890, Willard released an interview to the *New York Voice* in
which she affirmed that the colored race "multiplies like the locusts in
Egypt" and that "the safety of woman, of childhood, the home is men-
aced in a thousand localities at this moment, so that men dare not go
beyond the sight of their own roof-tree." In addressing the Women's
Christian Temperance Union in 1894, Willard condemned Wells's analysis of lynching for implying that white women encouraged sexual liaisons with black men. Willard strongly objected to Wells's imputation
"upon half the white race in this country." The leader of the temperance movement believed that the majority of people in the South had
good feelings toward black people and had the right to actively protect
themselves, and that the black vote was as wrong as the vote of "alien il-
literates" who, in her view, ruled American cities.[24]

In 1901 Ida Wells-Barnett had a public exchange with well-known
reformer Jane Addams of Hull House, whom she profoundly respected.
Wells-Barnett found herself in disagreement with Addams's view on
lynching as it was expressed in an article in the *Independent* of January
1901, entitled "Respect for Law." Wells-Barnett replied with an article
entitled "Lynching and the Excuse for It" in the May issue of that magazine.

Addams's settlement house in Chicago inspired similar efforts among black women who, like Victoria Earle Matthews of the White Rose Mission in New York, offered settlement services to black women and children. Wells-Barnett, like Addams, lived in Chicago. In 1899 she asked the help of the leader of Hull House to stop a series of articles in the *Chicago Herald* in favor of establishing a segregated public school system in the city. Addams promptly assembled representative white men and women, including some members of the board of education, whom Wells-Barnett addressed, and sent a delegation to the newspaper headquarters. The articles stopped, and no other attempt was made by the newspaper to support racial segregation. In February 1908, to celebrate the centennial of Lincoln's birth, the two women organized a mass meeting at the Orchestra Hall in Chicago, featuring W. E. B. Du Bois as the major speaker and calling for action against lynching, disfranchisement, and segregation. An early supporter of Du Bois's views and scholarship, Addams accepted the professor's invitation to participate that year at his Atlanta conference on "The Negro American Family."[25] A year later Addams and Wells-Barnett were among the signers of Villard's Call, which called for a national conference on the Negro question. The black journalist's reply to Addams's article in the *Independent* on lynching was therefore part of an ongoing professional relationship based on mutual respect and trust.

Addams wrote her article to condemn the growing lynching wave on the grounds that it endangered the whole idea of self-government. She also argued that such a horrendous practice reflected the false theory that criminality could be suppressed and prevented by terrorizing exhibitions of brutal punishment. Let us assume, Addams said, that southern citizens were honestly convinced that the southern Negro "in this present underdeveloped state must be frightened and subdued by terror." Lynching, accordingly, was given full publicity and gathered numerous spectators. Sometimes it was planned well in advance, and special trains would carry thousands of people to see the show. Under the assumption that the more terrifying the spectacle, the more likely that potential criminals would refrain from committing the very crime lynching was punishing, "the living victim is sometimes horribly mutilated and his body later exhibited." Addams wanted to give southern citizens the full benefit of being led by an honest belief for which they "set aside trial by jury and all processes of law." In other words, southerners had become convinced that "this brutal method of theirs is the most efficient method in dealing with a peculiar class of crime committed by one race against another." Addams gave historical examples of public punishment showing that this approach was taken by the classes in power in order to terrorize the so-called lower classes and keep them in their place. The message Addams wanted to send to "our fellow citizens of the South who are once more trying to suppress vice by violence" was that man's bestiality, "which leads him to pillage and rape," could never be controlled by public cruelty and dramatic punishment, "which too often cover fury and revenge." Furthermore, the risk was the brutalization of each spectator and the spreading, in so doing, of the seeds of violence. "Brutality begets brutality," Addams argued. Followers of the theory that "the Negro is undeveloped, and that therefore must be treated in this primitive fashion," forgot that "immatures pay little attention to statements, but quickly imitate what they see." To those southerners who justified these terrorizing acts in the name of chivalry to make the honor of white women safe, Addams suggested that "perhaps it is women themselves who can best reply that bloodshed and arson and ungoverned anger have never yet controlled lust." The honor of women, Addams believed, was only secure where law, order, and justice prevailed.[26] Addams ended her argument without questioning the issue of rape, for which many lynchings of black men were condoned.

In her reply, Wells-Barnett started from where Addams ended. She thanked the Hull House leader for such a forceful appeal that should be shared by "every preacher in every pulpit in the land." Yet she found that, although unintentionally, Addams's logical argument was built on an unfortunate presumption that injured "the memory of thousands of victims of mob law." It was Addams's assumption that southern citizens honestly believed that the lynching of Negroes was the only successful method of dealing with "a certain class of crime" that vitiated, in Wells-Barnett's view, whatever else Addams could add. It was the same assumption that influenced almost all the people who discussed this question—namely, that lynching was the desperate effort of southern people "to protect their women from black monsters." Because of this false assumption, the civilized world condoned "America's national crime." Wells-Barnett suggested looking at the compiled records of lynchings for the period 1896–1900, which the *Chicago Tribune* reported the first day of each year. From these records one could see whether southerners honestly believed that lynching was, as Addams implied, "the only successful method of dealing with a certain class of crimes." These records showed that hundreds of people, black in the majority of cases, were lynched for misdemeanors, mistaken identity, insult, bad reputation, unpopularity, violation of contracts, and other trivial offenses like "frightening child for shooting at rabbits." Thus a careful classification of the offenses leading to lynchings during those five years revealed that "race prejudice constitutes the real cause." If those lynchings were grouped under that cause, the records for the Negro victims during those five years indicate that 229 were killed for racial prejudice, 179 for murder, and 96 for rape. Thus out of a total of 504 victims, only a minority of 96 had been accused of that "particular class of crimes"— that is, assaults on white women. Wells-Barnett concluded her reply to Addams by arguing that no good result would come from any investigation refusing to consider this evidence.[27]

Mary Church Terrell, the other African-American woman who signed the Call, also dealt with lynching in an article she published in the *North American Review* in 1904, a year that by March had already witnessed the killing of thirty-one Negroes at the hand of the mob. "Those who are jealous of their country's fair name feel keenly the necessity of extirpating this lawlessness," Terrell declared. However, a means of prevention could not be devised until the cause of lynching was better understood. She thought that four mistakes were commonly made in defining the cause of lynching. The first mistake was to suppose that rape was the real cause of lynching in the South. Rape was the pretext, not the cause, as accurate statistics showed. Out of one hundred Negroes lynched, seventy-five to eighty-five were not even accused of the crime of rape. Yet men who would admit the accuracy of these figures would solemnly tell the country that lynching could never be suppressed until black men would stop committing the crime of rape. This was the alleged crime for which less than one-fourth of those murdered by mobs were charged. The second mistake made by the common interpretation of lynching was the assumption that Negroes' desire for social equality was related to the crime of rape. Eyewitness and newspaper reports showed that in general the Negro who was guilty of assault was an ignorant man, not someone who "had been taught he was the equal of white people or had even heard of social equality." Those Negroes who had received their education in northern institutions of learning with white men and women and who could learn the meaning of social equality as a rule did not assault white women or commit other crimes, Terrell argued. It was the South that coddled and caressed the illiterate Negroes, those who made up most of the criminal class. "There is no more connection between social equality and lynching to-day than there was between social equality and slavery before the war." The third mistake commonly made in judging the cause of lynching, according to Terrell, was the belief that the moral sensibilities of the best black people in the United States were so blunt and dull, and their standard of morality was so low, that they could not realize the enormity and atrocity of rape. This idea was the fruit of either ignorance or a will to misrepresent "thousands of reputable men and women of sympathizing with the rapists, either black or white, or of condoning their crime." Terrell argued that the fourth mistake in judging the cause of lynching was made by those who relied on newspaper descriptions of alleged crimes. Southern newspapers often distorted facts, as in the case of Sam Hose in Atlanta, a black laborer who murdered in self-defense the white planter for whom he worked after an argument over money.[28] Terrell reported that an influential newspaper offered a $500 reward for the capture of this black man who had dared to kill a white man and predicted a growing consensus in the community to burn him at the stake after torture. The local press also circulated the rumor that, after murdering his boss, Sam Hose assaulted his employer's wife. However, a Chicago detective who later investigated the case clearly established that Sam Hose did not commit any assault. The rumor was orchestrated by the press to make the burning of Sam Hose certain. The Sunday on which Sam Hose was killed and burned was treated as a holiday: "Special trains were made up to take the Christian people of Atlanta to the scene of burning, a short distance from the city. After the first train moved out with every inch of available space inside and out filled to overflowing, a second had to be made up, so as to accommodate those who had just come from church. After Sam Hose had been tortured and burned to death, the great concourse of Christians who had witnessed the tragedy scraped for hours among his ashes in the hope of finding a sufficient number of his bones to take to their friends as souvenirs."

Besides the lynching of Sam Hose—whose flesh and body parts Du Bois saw on display at a grocery store—Terrell offered other examples in which the press was responsible for building the inflammatory atmosphere leading to mob lynching. Local papers portrayed the victims as black desperados and rapists when they were people simply rebelling against injustice. By combining both Wells-Barnett's and Addams's conclusions, Terrell argued that the real causes of lynching were racial hatred and the lawlessness prevailing in the South, where nine-tenths of the lynchings occurred. "Lynching is the aftermath of slavery," she said. "The white men who shoot negroes to death and flay them alive, and the white women who apply flaming torches to their oil-soaked bodies to-day, are the sons and daughters of women who had but little, if any, compassion on the race when it was enslaved." Mobs were composed of the "best" citizens, "who quietly disperse to their homes as soon as they are certain that the negro is good and dead." For Terrell, it was impossible to understand the ferocity and barbarity of the lynching-bee without taking into account the debasing and brutalizing effects of slavery upon the southerners. By emphasizing the powerful role white womanhood played in southern societies, she appealed to white women: "But what a tremendous influence for law and order, and what a mighty foe to mob violence Southern white women might be, if they would arise in the purity and power of their womanhood to implore their fathers, husbands and sons no longer to stain their hands with the black man's blood!"

Terrell reminded southern white women that while their men were fighting a war to keep the Negroes in bondage, not a white woman was violated. She pointed out that in the year 1902 only one colored male out of every one hundred thousand was accused of assault on a white woman in the South, whereas in Chicago one male out of every twenty thousand was charged with rape. Thus boys and men were more addicted to rape in Chicago than were Negroes in the South. White men in the South were not punished or lynched for invading Negro homes and violating colored women. Taking a step further than Addams, Terrell concluded that the southern spirit of lawlessness was spreading throughout the United States, as recent lynchings in several cities of the North showed: "If the number of Americans who participate in this wild and diabolical carnival of blood does not diminish, nothing can prevent this country from becoming a byword and a reproach throughout the civilized world." The church was also to blame for not taking a firmer position against lynching. As many ministers did not support the abolitionist cause before the war, "so silence in the pulpit concerning the lynching of negroes to-day plunges many of the persecuted race into deep gloom and dark despair," Terrell observed. She finally suggested remedies, of which education and moral uplifting of the white southern masses were the most important. It was crucial that the southerners of any class learned to respect the rights of other human beings, disregarding the color of their skin. She also added, without mentioning Booker T. Washington's responsibility, that the South had insisted "so continuously and belligerently that it is the negro's best friend, that it understands him better than other people on the face of the earth and that it will brook interference from nobody in its method of dealing with him, that the North has been persuaded or intimidated into bowing to this decree."

Thus Terrell's was a powerful attack on national reconciliation at the expense of the Negroes, an argument with which Ida Wells-Barnett could easily agree. Yet it was made by someone married to an eminent Booker T. Washington man. Her article showed how independent Mary Church Terrell was from the Tuskegee machine, but it also explained why the *North American Review* did not want to publish anything else by her.[29]

Social Science as a Weapon to Mobilize
Interracial Alliances

At the end of the second National Negro Conference in May 1910, the name National Association for the Advancement of Colored People was chosen. "One could do almost anything under that title," Mary Ovington later observed. The word "colored" was meant to be inclusive of all dark people, although the association selectively chose to take a stand in some battles and not others. The early NAACP did not espouse the battle of the Filipinos or the East Indians but was directly involved in promoting pan-African conferences and the struggle for Haitian independence. W. E. B. Du Bois was put in charge of the research department of the new organization. The majority decided that the NAACP needed a media outlet of its own: the *Crisis* was born.[30]

In July 1910 Du Bois resigned from his professorship of economics and history at Atlanta University to accept the position of director of publicity and research for the new NAACP. William English Walling had urged Du Bois to take that risk, as the question of who was going to pay the scholar's salary, Villard said, was still open. When Du Bois accepted the position, the new organization was still debating whether it was going to be a white organization for the uplifting of the Negro race by extensive fund-raising or an interracial alliance able to challenge public opinion on civil, political, and social rights of racial minorities. That tension affected most members and caused suspicious practices and dangerous misunderstandings right from the start. It was true that the almost one thousand men and women who gathered at Cooper Union on 1 June 1909 had passed resolutions that attacked the position of the president of the United States on racial issues, demanded the strict enforcement of civil rights protected by the Fourteenth and Fifteenth Amendments, called for equal access to the ballot for African Americans (the issue of women's suffrage was not raised), and asked for equal educational opportunities for all American citizens.[31] Yet common agreement on these crucial questions was overshadowed by excruciating conflicts that arose over the organizational structure with the formation of the Committee of Forty.

When Du Bois received the offer to be in charge of the NAACP official magazine, he was quite pleased to leave Atlanta and move from the classroom to an office at the *Evening Post* building in downtown Manhattan. He felt the magazine could be the intellectual tool he needed to make social science an active weapon in the struggle for racial equality. The scholar was absolutely determined to undertake a national monthly magazine. Despite Villard's warning that it had not been decided who was going to pay his salary, Du Bois started the *Crisis: A Record of the Darker Races* as a personal challenge. By then he had come to realize that a problem like lynching could not be aggressively attacked in the classroom, but it could be thoroughly investigated and publicly exposed in the pages of a journal capable of reaching a large audience. It was a shift from "science to propaganda," as Du Bois's biographer Lewis has aptly put it. The fact that "racial distinction based on color" was the greatest thing in Du Bois's life, as he wrote in *Dusk of Dawn*, "and absolutely determined it" made Du Bois's shift from academic social science to propaganda almost inevitable. He made that decision in April 1899, after his shocking experience of seeing the body of a lynched man in Atlanta. The professor saw parts of Sam Hose's body on display at a grocery store after the black farmer had been lynched by a white mob of two thousand men, women, and children of the city. Du Bois saw some of these people fighting over the pieces of flesh from the man's burned body. The Atlanta professor was horrified and deeply affected: "I began to turn aside from my work." From then on, Du Bois's double-consciousness, his struggle between his American and Negro identities, became further complicated by his awareness that one "could not be a calm, cool and detached scientist while Negroes were lynched, murdered and starved."[32]

In 1910 Du Bois saw an opportunity to turn the impotence of social science into an active weapon of change by asserting the centrality of the Negro question to American democracy in the pages of the *Crisis*. The agenda of the militant journalism he envisioned appeared in his first editorial: to investigate and make public "those facts and arguments which show the danger of race prejudice." To put it another way, militant social science would show that racial inequality was not the product of inborn antipathy between white and dark races, as mainstream social scientists held, but the outcome of a social system of class and caste. The name of the magazine, inspired by an 1844 Russell Lowell poem, "The Present Crisis," reflected Du Bois's conviction that it was "a critical time in the history of the advancement of men." Such a critical time, which passively witnessed the lynching of hundreds of colored people, needed the formation of strong political interracial alliances beyond party lines to put an end to segregation in public spaces. In the first issue of the *Crisis*, Du Bois explicitly took a stand against racial separation in public schools by criticizing "some people," without mentioning them by either name or race, in many northern cities, including Chicago and Philadelphia, who were advertising the goodness of separate public schools for African-American children. Du Bois thought it was wrong: "Separate them by color and they grow up without learning the tremendous truth that it is impossible to judge the mind of a man by the color of his face. Is there any truth that America needs to learn more?"[33]

The second issue of the *Crisis* included Franz Boas's paper entitled "The Real Race Problem," which the anthropologist delivered at the second National Negro Conference in May 1910, the official beginning of the NAACP. Continuing to dismantle biosocial science's false assumptions on Negro inferiority, Boas dealt with the current claim that although the Negro child developed faster than other children, its development stopped at an earlier stage. Boas's counterargument pointed out that recent research showed that "the simple fact of an early completion of development does not by any means prove mental inferiority, because the better-situated element of our white population furnishes a disproportionately large number of capable and efficient individuals, as compared to the less favorably situated groups." Establishing the environmental causality of human differences, Boas repeated the argument he had developed in his Atlanta commencement address of 1906: "The existing differences are differences in kind, not in value." This implied that biological evidence did not sustain the common view "that the mental power of the one race is higher than that of the other, although their mental qualities show, presumably, differences analogous to the existing anatomical and psychological differences." Then, as he did in Atlanta, Boas went through the history of African peoples, from their discovery of the welding of iron to the contemporary peoples of Central Africa, "by far the most advanced" among primitive people of the world.

What was new in this paper presented at the National Negro Conference was Boas's explicit stand in favor of amalgamation of the Negro population. He rejected the argument of the assumed inferiority of mulattoes by identifying a contradiction in the theory that "the mulatto population is inferior to either pure race," or put in popular terms, the belief that mulattoes inherited "all the evil characteristics of both parental races, and none of the good qualities." Boas pointed out how contradictory this view was when those who held it had to justify a mulatto's exceptional abilities and moral strength with "the white strain in his blood." Far from being objective scientific observation, this common-sense view did not take into consideration the influence of social conditions on individual abilities. Boas reminded his audience that the original types of man "have not remained so, but extended migrations have been the rule since very early times." By focusing on Negro peoples in different parts of the world, Boas went through the history of these early migrations and gave many examples of successful mixing of the Negro type with other groups. He explained that in the olden times the area north of the Sahara was inhabited by people of lighter complexion, the descendants of an ancient group of Mediterranean people from whom the Egyptian civilization developed. After these people repeatedly made inroads into the Negro territory south of the Sahara, they established the empire of Sudan. Thus a mixed population developed in many of these regions "which has proved exceedingly capable, which has produced a great many men of great power, and which has succeeded in assimilating a considerable amount of Arab culture." Another example of successful mixing could be drawn from the history of East Africa, with its extended migrations that illustrated "the infusion of foreign blood into the African race without in any way modifying the cultural conditions of the continent, except so far as the introduction of new invention is concerned." Boas concluded that "biological analogy as well as historical evidence do not favor the assumption of any material inferiority of the mulatto."

Boas then examined the common misunderstanding of the intermixture between Negroes and whites in the United States. For those who feared that by this intermixture the whole mass of the white population might be infused with Negro blood, Boas reminded them that mulattoes were primarily the offspring of unions between white men and Negro women, that the total number of children depended upon the number of mothers, and that the number of children born to Negro or mulatto women "would be approximately the same, no matter whether the fathers are Negroes, mulattoes, or white men." As the mixture had been so far largely between white fathers and colored mothers, "the relative proportion of Negro blood in the following mixed generation becomes less, and that therefore a gradually increasing similarity of the two racial types might develop."

Unfortunately, Boas's conclusions revealed the pitfalls of the pro-amalgamation argument as the solution to the Negro problem. The anthropologist concluded, in fact, that "our race problems will become the less intense, the less the difference in type between the different groups of our people, and the less the isolation of certain social groups." Leaving cultural pluralism behind, Boas thought that one side of the solution was in the hands of the Negro himself: "The less Negro society represents a party with its own aims and its own interest distinct from those of the members of the white race, the more satisfactory will be the relation between the races." Inexorably, he thought, the most distinctive Negro type would gradually disappear, and "an unbiased examination of conditions as they exist at the present time points to the ultimate result of a levelling of a deep distinction between the two races and a more and more fruitful cooperation."[34] Thus Boas, the German-

Jewish scientist who always publicly spoke in favor of racial equality, showed a most pessimistic view of the possible ending of racial prejudice against Negroes—and also against the Jews.

Boas's thinking, however, was more complex than envisioning a mongrel society. The "father of modern anthropology" was also a cultural pluralist who taught his Columbia University students to value other civilizations different from the one in which they grew up. He reminded them that other societies had different traditions and were based on a different equilibrium of emotion and reason, that the general theory of valuation of human activities required a higher tolerance than the one now professed, and that "what we choose to call progress depends upon the standards chosen."[35]

Such higher tolerance based on mutual knowledge of different human groups was the declared goal of the Races Congress held in London in 1911, on which the *Crisis* extensively reported. Editor Du Bois went to the University of London, his expenses paid by New York industrialist John Millholland, to attend the congress. "When fifty races look each other in the eye, face to face, there rises a new conception of humanity and his problems," Du Bois informed the readers. Envisioned by Felix Adler, the secretary of the Ethical Culture Society, the Races Congress appeared to *Crisis* editor Du Bois as an example of social science as a weapon of racial equality by its enlisting of over 50 countries, presidents, or parliaments, 12 British governors, 8 British premiers, over 40 colonial bishops, some 130 professors of international law, leading anthropologists and sociologists, and many other distinguished and enlightened people. "To many people it seemed a visionary scheme," Du Bois admitted, but he thought the purpose of the congress of a thousand delegates representing fifty "races" would have a powerful impact on redefining the color line in the world. "The object of the Congress will be to discuss, in the light of science and the modern conscience, the general relations subsisting between the peoples of the West and those of the East, between so-called white and so-called colored peoples, with a view to encouraging between them a fuller understanding, the most friendly feelings, and a heartier cooperation." This was the initial statement in the introductory address of Lord Weardale, a representative of the intellectual aristocracy willing to make imperialism more humane without dropping the Kiplingesque white man's burden.

In that multiracial parliament, Du Bois noticed the "infiltration of Negro blood" among the delegates: "the two Egyptian Beys were evidently negroid, the Portuguese was without a doubt a mulatto, and the Persian was dark enough to have trouble in the South." Scholars, reformers, and members of parliaments and revolutionary movements

who highly impressed Du Bois included Rubasana, the only Negro
member of the Cape Colony Parliament; Hadji Mirza Yahya, the leader
of the Persian revolutionists; Native American scholar Charles Alexander Eastman; anarchist Russian prince Pyotr Kropotkin; Zionist novelist Israel Zangwill; and Annie Besant of the Theosophical Society, who
forcefully criticized the British Empire. Among the papers Du Bois
valued most was that of Dr. Felix von Luschan, a distinguished German
biologist, who asserted the "monogenetic origin of humanity," the impact of circumstances and environment in causing some human groups
to advance more rapidly than others, and the constant mingling of races
in human history in consequence of invasions, conquests, and commercial relations. Italian professor N. R. D'Alfonso asserted the same psychological possibilities for all human groups, whatever part of the globe
they inhabited; if there were psychological differences between races,
he said, these were the outcome of the particular history of various
peoples. On the ethical side, Professor J. S. Mackenzie from England
emphasized the role of moral education in leading to an appreciation
of "the essential likeness of the various races and classes, in spite of their
superficial differences." Educator J. Tengo Jabavu from South Africa,
speaking for the six million Bantu, criticized white colonization, including the good intentions of the Christian missions, for "attacking and destroying, instead of improving the organization of these reputed barbar-
ians." He thought the solution was to instruct these people in their
native language, initially concentrating on a small number who will af-
terward teach and lead the others. Social philosopher Felix Adler from
the United States discussed the ideal to be realized in international relations as the growing organization of these relations between peoples
and races. "The peace and progress of the world," he argued, "will depend on the formation of a cultivated class of all civilized peoples."
Summarizing the intentions of the conference, Adler concluded that
"civilized nations should treat backward races with more humanity and
intelligence," for the immediate benefit of those races and in the future
interest of humanity. He also suggested that colonial administrators
should make "a sympathetic study of the customs, manners, law and religion of the peoples to whom they are supposed to bring civilization."
Du Bois gave his readers a little taste of the congress's gorgeous recep-
tions, entertainments, official dinners, and the endless socials "given
quite regardless of the color line or racial lines." Yet Du Bois did not
point out, as Mary Ovington did in her reminiscences of that congress,
that the organizing committee, "with all its famous names, did not want
anything said in criticism of imperialism." Du Bois only mentioned Annie Besant's name without reporting that she was the only one to defy

the imposed restriction, but Ovington remembered that Besant "paced across the platform like a lioness" and said what she pleased.[36]

Du Bois had not yet completed his intellectual journey toward a full understanding of the roots and politics of imperialism. By the time World War I broke out, the analysis Du Bois offered in his "African Roots of the War" (1915) was the most comprehensive understanding of capitalistic expansionism, class, and race; his biographer Lewis rightly calls it "one of the analytical triumphs of the early twentieth century." The London Congress of 1911, as Du Bois saw it, was more an internationalization of his elitist notion of the "Talented Tenth" than an opportunity to organize the struggle of the "dark races" against imperialism. At the same time, he felt that a few congresses like that, regularly assembling every four years, would give history a new direction, for many of the great problems of the planet would be scrutinized by such a multiracial parliament: "World peace, world organization, conference and conciliation, the gradual breaking down of trade barriers, the spread of civilization to backward peoples, the emancipation of suppressed groups like the American Negro—seemed to me the natural, the inevitable path to progress."[37]

If the editor of the *Crisis* always found himself perfectly at ease in Europe's best intellectual circles and international events, his double American-Negro soul could not easily handle the battle for building an interracial organization. Du Bois, in fact, joined the NAACP with several reserves: "With some hesitation I was asked to come as Director of Publications and Research, with the idea that my research work was to go on and with the further idea that my activities would be so held in check that the Association would not develop as an organ of attack upon Tuskegee." He always frankly admitted that he was not an organization man and that, because of his personality, he was "no natural leader of man." He could not "slap people on the back and make friends of strangers"; he was reserved and had a "biting, critical tongue." Du Bois knew that the new position would be a difficult task for him, but he accepted it because he convinced himself that "it was a question of temperament and manner rather than subject." He saw his new task as an opportunity "to enter the lists in a desperate fight aimed straight at the real difficulty: the question as to how far educated Negro opinion in the United States was going to have the right and opportunity to guide the Negro group." Du Bois wanted to continue in New York his studies begun in Atlanta and to edit the *Crisis* as a periodical of "facts and agitation." Under Du Bois's leadership, the magazine became self-supporting within five years. "With this organ of propaganda and defense and with its legal bureau, lecturers and writers," Du Bois remarked, "the National Associa-

tion for the Advancement of Colored People was able to organize one
of the most effective assaults of liberalism upon prejudice and reaction
that the modern world has seen."[38]

Although the first issue of the *Crisis* in November 1910 sold only
1,000 copies, the number of copies the monthly magazine sold for the
year 1913 was 336,000. By 1 February 1914, the editorial board of the
Crisis had left the *Evening Post* building and occupied a suite of offices in
the Educational Building on Fifth Avenue near the executive offices of
the NAACP. During the first five years the *Crisis* sold 1,400,000 copies.
As the director of the Department of Publications and Research of the
NAACP, Du Bois could report its accomplishments for the first five
years: the establishment of a self-supporting magazine with a circulation
of 34,000 copies per month; research projects carried out on the condition of Negro graduates (1910), Negro common school education
(1911), the condition of Negro artisans and trade unions (1912),
manners and morals among American Negroes (1913), occupation statistics of the U.S. census (1914), African history (1913–15), lynchings
in the United States (1914–15); 314 lectures in thirty-one states and
three foreign countries before 137,017 auditors; a large number of
pamphlets, articles, and several books; and cooperation in promoting
the International Races Congress (1911), the New York National Emancipation Exposition (1913), the Child Welfare Exhibits (1914), and a
pageant called *The Star of Ethiopia* (Washington, D.C., 1915). All these
were successful undertakings despite a chronic lack of funds.[39] In his report Du Bois also announced that by January 1916, the NAACP "will no
longer be responsible for the salary of the Director of Publications and
Research, which will thereafter be paid by the *Crisis*." This final remark
stressed Du Bois's independence from the moderate leaders of the
NAACP, who feared the editor's bold and uncompromising positions
would alienate white philanthropic financial support.

Between radical Du Bois and moderate Villard an ongoing conflict
persisted, beginning with the early issues of the magazine, over authority and the editor's resentment of any interference in how the *Crisis*
would deal with powerful institutions, political leaders, and issues like
social equality and interracial sex. Du Bois resented Villard's paternal-
ism: "he is used to advising colored men and giving them orders and he
simply cannot bring himself to work with one as equal." Du Bois was correct in implying that Villard lacked the radical abolitionist ideology that
made his grandfather William Lloyd Garrison the ally of Frederick
Douglass until the latter left the field of apolitical abolitionism. Villard's
public commitment to racial equality did not match his paternalistic
relationship with black people. Because Mrs. Villard was from Georgia,

the Villards would not admit African-American or Jewish people to their New York home. Tensions between Du Bois and Villard exploded when Villard forced the editor to print "a list of Negro crimes" in addition to "the monthly record of lynchings." Du Bois declined "to receive orders from anyone but the board." Villard informed the board that he would no longer cooperate with Du Bois and resigned as the board chair. Jewish scholar and poet Joel E. Spingarn replaced Villard.[40]

The NAACP faced initial tensions, "common to all interracial effort in the United States," Du Bois remarked, because white members became dominant on an interracial executive committee. Given their superior training, influence, or wealth, the white members "take charge of the committee, guide it and use the colored membership as their helpers and executive workers in certain directions." Had the black membership attempted to dominate and lead the committee, the white members would feel dissatisfied and progressively withdraw. "In the NAACP," Du Bois observed, "it was our primary effort to achieve an equality of racial influence without allowing undue predominance to either group. I think we accomplished this for a time to an unusual degree."[41] Despite internal tensions, the early NAACP projected a public image of an effective organization, able to mobilize hundreds of people to fight for civil and political rights of the "dark races." One of the most strenuous battles of its early years was against *Birth of a Nation,* D. W. Griffith's pathbreaking movie from a technical point of view, the script of which was based on Thomas Dixon's negrophobic piece *The Clansman.*

Du Bois's magazine spread radical ideas on social equality, class conflicts, women's suffrage, and international politics. More than the radicalness of the ideas, what many white reformers found disturbing was its undeferential language toward established social, economic, and professional racial hierarchies. Du Bois was absolutely convinced that an article he wrote for the progressive *Survey* was rejected because it included an explicit call for the Negro's social rights: "His right to be treated as a gentleman, when he acts like one, to marry any sane, grown person who wants to marry him, and to eat and meet with his friends without being accused of undue assumption or unworthy ambition."[42] The idea that social equality was a human right as much as political and economic equality was too challenging even for great supporters of black people's rights such as Jane Addams. Among the NAACP's white leadership, Mary Ovington was the most convinced that racial, political, economic, and social equality belonged to the same battle. She tried to mediate between radical Du Bois and the moderate leaders of the association, as she was deeply convinced that the NAACP was a "work for colored and white people to do together."[43]

The early NAACP had the potential to build a powerful interracial coalition to continue Reconstruction's unfinished revolution. Yet its moderate leadership failed to see that the battle for civil and political rights of black people could not be separated from a broader battle for social equality. Like many other leaders of progressive movements, NAACP leaders chose national reconciliation over radical democracy.

5

From Stage to Street

Rituals of Color Consciousness

They could sing, and they did sing, with their voices, their bodies, their souls. They threw themselves into it because they enjoyed and felt what they were doing, and they gave a semblance of dignity to the tawdry music and inane words. PAUL DUNBAR

James Weldon Johnson and African-American
Musical Theater

James Weldon Johnson joined the NAACP in 1916 as a field secretary, despite Mary Ovington's opposition. She thought that the African-American former diplomat, versatile songwriter, poet, author of the anonymously written *The Autobiography of an Ex-Colored Man* (1912), and staff writer for the *New York Age* since 1914 was too compromised with black Republicans of Booker T. Washington's milieu, and that he held reactionary views on socialism and the labor movement. But by 1925 Ovington deeply admired him as "a man of much dignity, who never shows a sense of inferiority either by shrinking back or by pushing himself forward." If Johnson's records as educator, lawyer, diplomat, and NAACP officer were satisfactory, then his involvement in the world of the African-American commercial musical theater and the descriptions of that world in his fictional and autobiographical works were remarkable.

Eclectic genius Johnson was a participant observer of Manhattan's world of fiction writers, music composers, and actors of different sorts,

which powerfully affected American popular culture in the early dec-
ades of the century. This complex world, where racial uplifting also
meant business success, built a bridge between the old "black aristocracy," the nouveaux riches, black southern immigrants, black and white
liberal and radical politics, high and low culture, Du Boisian and Wash-
ingtonian fans, and New York's interracial commercial entertainments.
In this world of business and creativity, of amateurish and semiprofes-
sional performers, some fair-complexioned African Americans chose to
"pass" for whites either permanently or occasionally, convinced, like
Johnson's character in his *Autobiography of an Ex-Coloured Man,* that it
was the only means to gain equal opportunities. Color consciousness
had become a stronger feeling in the post-Reconstruction African-
American elite. According to E. Franklin Frazier, "a free and mulatto ancestry became the basis of important social distinctions," and even in
the Methodist and Baptist churches "there were separate church organizations based upon distinctions of colour and what were considered
standards of civilized behavior." Light skin was a requisite for gaining an
entry into the black elite, an asset that could be obtained by using special bleaches the African-American press constantly advertised. "Light-
en Your Dark Skin," an ad in the *New York Age* commanded. The ad portrayed a pretty "light" colored girl and read: "Race Men and Women
Protect Your Future by Using Black and White Ointment. By Mail 25¢.
See What it did for Viola Steele."[1]

Some African Americans crossed over the color line when they arrived in the anonymous city and passed to the white world. This form of
"passing" became a recurrent literary theme in black fictions that raised
all the ambivalences and conflicts of double-consciousness and group
identity, with which black Americans had always struggled.[2] James Weldon Johnson made his light-skinned protagonist of *The Autobiography of
an Ex-Coloured Man* reach the conclusion, after having struggled between loyalty to his race and the advantages of being capable of moving
freely across the color line, that "to forsake one's race to better one's
condition was no less worthy an action than to forsake one's country for
the same purpose." He finally makes up his mind:

> I would neither disclaim the black race nor claim the white race; but
> that I would change my name, raise a moustache, and let the world take
> me for what it would; that it was not necessary for me to go about with a
> label of inferiority pasted across my forehead. All the while I under-
> stood that it was not discouragement or fear or search for a larger field
> of action and opportunity that was driving me out of the Negro race. I
> knew that it was shame, unbearable shame. Shame at being identified

with a people that could with impunity be treated worse than animals.
For certainly the law would restrain and punish the malicious burning
alive of animals.[3]

Johnson published *The Autobiography of an Ex-Colored Man* anonymously. When the book came out, most reviewers "accepted it as a human document," Johnson wrote in his real autobiography. He admitted
that anonymity gave him a certain pleasure: "The authorship of the
book excited the curiosity of literate colored people, and there was
speculation among them as to who the writer might be—to every such
group some colored man who had married white, and so coincided with
the main point on which the story turned, is known." Johnson himself
met someone who tacitly passed in public as the author of the book.
The rumor that Johnson was the author soon spread. When the book
was reprinted, he put his name on it. He kept receiving letters from
readers inquiring about phases of his life as he portrayed them in that
fictional autobiography, which was probably one of the reasons why he
later wrote a real autobiography: he did not want to pass for an ex-colored man.[4]

Passing implied a series of ritualized actions that made the subject go
back and forth between black and white racial identities. Such passing
shows how racial identities, then as now, are social constructions.[5] Passing was the very denial of early twentieth-century scientific theories of
racial difference discussed earlier in this book. It represented Boas's ultimate vision of a completely amalgamated society in which physical differences were no longer racialized. Yet passing, as a gesture of rejection
of blackness, showed individual internalization of racial hierarchies.
This is why someone like Du Bois, despite his light skin and a high color-
consciousness, did not pass; he remained identified with the "oppressed
race" and chose to struggle with his split soul.[6]

In the realm of musical comedy, African-American ambiguities of
color consciousness, "two-ness," racial uplifting, and individual success
found the most creative outlet and shaped a complex interracial urban
culture. At the turn of the century, New York's youth showed the greatest interest in the "coon" song, one highlight of African-American
musical comedy. As historian Lewis Erenberg has shown, audiences
were ready to welcome the "impudent coon" to replace the "happy
darky" as the black stereotype in white minds.[7] African-American texts
of plays and songs popular in New York in the 1890s include such language as "All Coons Look Alike to Me," "Coon, Coon, Coon," "I Wish
My Color Would Fade," "You'll find no common second-class nigs / In
the gentlemen coons' parade," "Resolved, That Stealing Chickens Ain't

No Crime."[8] In these texts the coon's main characteristics were fighting, stealing, and ostentatious dress and speech. Coons were portrayed as lazy servants, porters, butlers, waiters; they shuffled in baggy pants and used ungrammatical language; they loved drinking and gambling and were permanently shiftless and carefree. A late nineteenth-century historian of American popular culture, Henry Collins Brown, pointed out that coon songs presented a "ribald school of 'babies,' 'honies,' mercenary wenches . . . and sundry 'no account niggers.'" James Weldon Johnson, who participated with his younger brother, Rosamond, and their friend Bob Cole in the production of these early musical shows, summarized the contents of coon songs in his autobiography: they were concerned with "jamborees of various sorts and the play of razors, with the gastronomical delights of chicken, pork chops and watermelon, and with the experience of red-hot 'mammas' and their never too faithful 'papas.'" These songs were for the most part crude, raucous, bawdy, and often obscene.[9] How did someone like Johnson, who was a fiction writer, a poet, a lawyer, a diplomat, and the secretary of the NAACP, feel about working on this ambiguous yet important form of popular culture?

The son of a freeborn headwaiter and a schoolteacher, James Weldon Johnson was born in Florida in 1871. His mother was a competent pianist and an inspiration to James and Rosamond, who learned piano at an early age. Johnson's self-educated father, a lay Baptist minister in later years, taught him the importance of the virtues of solid honesty, self-improvement, and racial uplifting through education. When Johnson attended Atlanta University in the late 1880s, the school's credo deepened those values, as he recalled in his autobiography:

> The conception of education then held there and at other Negro colleges belonged to an age that, probably, is passing never to return. The central idea embraced a term that is now almost a butt for laughter—"service." We were never allowed to entertain any thought of being educated as "go-getters." Most of us knew that we were being educated for life work as underpaid teachers. The ideal constantly held up to us was of education as a means of living, not of making a living. It was impressed upon us that taking a classical course would have an effect of making us better and nobler and of a higher value to those we should have to serve. An odd, old-fashioned, naive conception? Rather.[10]

If education was designed to make black students better servants to their race and if Johnson can be taken as a fair representative of the Atlanta University student body, then one can safely say that Franz Boas made the right decision to deliver a commencement address in 1906 that strongly emphasized the importance of African history as a usable past to an audience whose future would be education as "a means of living."

During his first year at the Atlanta University preparatory school, Johnson realized how valued oratory was on that campus. He joined a debating society and worked hard on public speaking, a skill he would master extremely well in later years. Johnson became fluent in Spanish and knowledgeable in Latin and Greek. He went to the Chicago World's Fair during his last year of college. Johnson was one of the visitors who heard Frederick Douglass speak, and he also met poet Paul Laurence Dunbar on Negro Day. When Johnson graduated in 1894, he delivered a commencement speech on "The Destiny of Human Race," an attempt "to break through the narrow and narrowing limitations of 'race,'" he explained. At graduation he had two options: a scholarship in medicine at Harvard or a position of principal at Stanton School in Jacksonville, Florida, his hometown. Johnson chose the latter, hoping to achieve major improvements in that school, but he was soon disappointed. He also wrote for the local newspaper and passed the state bar examination, a difficult achievement for a black in Florida. Johnson did not practice law for long, but he found his early legal training helpful for his future diplomatic career and his role in the NAACP.

In 1898, after the bar exam, eclectic James Weldon Johnson began to work with Rosamond, a music teacher, on some small musical projects for local audiences. This was the beginning of a fruitful collaboration between the two brothers, James the poet and Rosamond the composer, leading them in 1899 to New York City, which was heaven for the production of Negro musicals. Before leaving for New York, the Johnson brothers wrote a comic opera, *Tolsa, or the Royal Document,* which was a satire of the new American imperialism after the Spanish-American War. "The setting was an island kingdom in the Pacific," Johnson recalled, and the story concerned Tolsa, a beautiful princess; her prime minister, a handsome and heroic American lieutenant; and the annexation of the island. "Old stuff now," Johnson commented, "but not then," when the annexation of Hawaii occurred and when "nothing of the sort had yet been produced on the American stage." The praise the Johnson brothers received from both white and colored people in Jacksonville for their portrayal of well-intentioned American imperialism made them decide "to try our fate in New York." Early in 1899 they left for the metropolis, "to try for a place in the world of the light opera." The "glimpses of life" Johnson caught during his three weeks in New York showed him a new world, a "tempting world, a world of greatly lessened restraints, a world of fascinating perils; but, above all, a world of tremendous artistic potentialities." It was then that Johnson began to realize the importance of African American's cultural background, creative folk art, and to become aware of "the superstructure of conscious art that might be reared upon them." With Rosamond and their new friend, Bob Cole, James spent his last few days in New York attempting to write more refined texts for Negro songs to replace crude but popular "coon songs." The Johnson brothers and Bob Cole strenuously discussed "the manner and means of raising the status of the Negro as a writer, composer, and performer in the New York theater and world of music."[11]

The trio was hired by the Klaw-Earlanger organization, the most powerful production company of the day. They began by composing songs for white singers in productions made for the average white theatergoer at Broadway shows, as the musical market required. By 1910 the trio had written over 150 songs for more than a dozen shows for interracial and black-only audiences.[12] Johnson, however, felt ambivalent about writing commercial songs, in which racial stereotypes were often ostentatiously displayed to please the audiences. His creative self was more at ease and fulfilled when he worked on morally uplifting stanzas inspired by the noble ideal of education he had learned at Atlanta University.

In 1900 Johnson returned to his Jacksonville students, for whom he wrote the song "Lift Ev'ry Voice and Sing," which the NAACP would later adopt and which became known as the Negro National Anthem. Johnson recorded in his autobiography the inspired moments of writing that song for a chorus of five hundred schoolchildren celebrating Lincoln's birthday at Jacksonville. After he got the first line, "Lift ev'ry voice and sing," he worked around it and ended the first stanza with "Sing a song full of the faith that the dark past has taught us / Sing a song full of the hope that the present has brought us." At that point, he said, "the spirit of the poem had taken hold of me." In composing the other two stanzas he did not use pen and paper. While his brother worked on the musical arrangement, Johnson said he "paced back and forth on the front porch, repeating the lines over and over to myself, going through all of the agony and ecstasy of creating." When he wrote the last stanza, he could not control his tears: "I was experiencing the transports of the poet's ecstasy. Feverish ecstasy was followed by that contentment—that sense of serene joy—which makes artistic creation the most complete of all human experiences." He recognized a "Kiplingesque touch" in the last stanza where the American Negro was, "historically and spiritually, immanent." The last stanza of the Negro National Anthem reads as follows:

God of our weary years,
God of our silent tears,
Thou who hast brought us thus far on our way,

Thou who hast by Thy might
Let us into the light,
Keep us forever in the path, we pray;
Lest our feet stray from the places, our God, where we met Thee,
Lest, our hearts drunk with the wine of the world, we forget Thee.

Jacksonville schoolchildren kept singing that song after the celebration;
some brought the song to other schools; others became schoolteachers
and taught it to their pupils. In the next twenty years the song was sung
in schools and churches all over the country.[13]

Caught between the urge to create morally uplifting songs and the
economic success of his Broadway musicals—royalties for the first six
months of 1902 were almost $1,500, while Johnson's half-year salary at
Stanton was only $480—he did not object to his brother's request to
join him and Bob Cole in New York. During the first fall as full-time
songwriters, the trio sold four hundred thousand copies of "Under the
Bamboo Tree." The Johnson-Cole team achieved great popularity, and
by the second half of 1903 their royalties went up to $12,000. As the
only member of the threesome not performing on stage, Johnson
signed up for some classes at Columbia University, studying English literature and drama as a part-time student for three years. In 1905 the
Johnson brothers and Cole went to Europe and performed at London's
Palace Theatre. Their engagement in London was a triumph. In Paris
they had the pleasant surprise of hearing their songs "Under the Bamboo Tree" and "The Congo Love Song" performed at the Olympia
Theatre. Restless James, however, was growing tired of writing songs.
New York black politician Charles W. Anderson, Booker T. Washington's *longa manus* in the city, suggested that Johnson should apply for a
post in the U.S. Consular Service.

Johnson and Anderson had been friends for several years. Johnson
thought highly of the "recognized colored Republican leader of New
York," who in the summer of 1904, at the beginning of the campaign to
reelect Theodore Roosevelt, requested Johnson's help in running the
Colored Republican Club. Although Johnson was not eager to accept,
because he was busy writing songs and studying at Columbia and because he did not know anything about political organizations, he soon
became enthusiastic about the new job. Located on West Fifty-third
Street, the political club succeeded in attracting the "big guns" of the
campaign. The Johnson-Cole trio wrote a campaign song, "Teddy,"
which Roosevelt found a "bully good song."

During that period Johnson learned something about what he called
"the greatest American game"—namely, the workings of practical pol-

itics. He learned the meaning of political loyalty given primarily not to the party but to the boss, and how practical politicians controlled the political machine and made more than a living from politics. Johnson admired Anderson's political skills, his ability to manipulate people, his oratory, and his capacity to discuss English poetry, Irish patriots, and the members of the British Parliament. In Johnson's view, Anderson was a "cool, calculating player in the hard game of politics, but always playing the game rather on the grand scale for the higher stakes."[14] Perhaps Anderson's secret tactics to discredit Booker T. Washington's opponents can be better understood by including them in the heroic portrait Johnson left of his friend. As soon as Roosevelt was reelected, Anderson gained the appointment of collector for the Bureau of Internal Revenue for the New York district inclusive of Wall Street. The shrewd politician resigned from the presidency of the Colored Republican Club and had Johnson take that position.

Johnson was very keen on keeping the club alive, as "a power and an influence, socially as well as politically." He was less fond of the strenuous walks around Manhattan that Anderson forced him to take to discuss club matters. It was during one of these walks that Anderson told Johnson to consider a possible appointment to the U.S. Consular Service. As a Booker T. Washington man, Anderson was sure that President Roosevelt would be willing to appoint someone with Johnson's qualifications. Although Johnson initially dismissed Anderson's suggestion, he found the idea appealing.

James Weldon Johnson was at a point in his musical career where he felt it was time to move on. He strongly opposed Rosamond and Bob Cole's idea to start their own theatrical company. Now that they were independent and free from the responsibilities and concerns that a theatrical company would have, they played in the best houses of the biggest cities and had time for composition; should they pursue the project of their own company, Johnson felt they would play, like all colored companies, in second-class houses for just one night. Furthermore, he could not picture himself in the role of business manager of that company. Johnson's point was based on a real understanding of the main trends in musical theater.

Among commercial entertainments, minstrelsy and vaudeville were the most profitable business. In the first decade of the century, white investors were rewarded for supporting black theater business. White support continued, to some extent, into the second decade. When white businessmen realized that white patrons were losing interest in a certain black show, they would put it on a touring circuit of second-class theaters. Black musical entertainer S. H. Dudley declared that he would rather retire from the production of big shows than offer "first class entertainment in second class theaters"; he maintained that it was untrue that colored show business was a financial failure, and stated that it was simply "prejudice on the part of the syndicates that are in power and control the theatrical situation in the United States." Prejudice may have been a factor in the decline of the touring theatrical companies, but other causes of this decline may have been the growing popularity of the movies after 1910 and the increasing interest of black companies in producing shows for Harlem theaters.[15]

Rosamond Johnson and Bob Cole put aside the idea of starting their own musical company for a few months. Cole saw their engagement at the Palace Theatre in London as a great farewell to vaudeville and the beginning of their own show upon their return to New York. The threesome worked on a new musical comedy on the outbreak of the Spanish-American War, with scenes representing a Negro industrial school in the South and the Philippine Islands. "The Shoo-Fly Regiment" was the last piece the trio would do together. Once the work was finished, James Johnson made up his mind to pursue a career in the Consular Service. He passed the exam and received Roosevelt's appointment as U.S. consul at Puerto Cabello, Venezuela, in May 1906.

Fluent in Spanish, Johnson really enjoyed the period he spent in Venezuela. He had plenty of time for his writings. He contributed poems to the *Century Magazine* and the *Independent* and worked on his novel, *The Autobiography of an Ex-Coloured Man,* while studying international law and sending official reports to Washington, D.C. There was no racial consciousness in Venezuela, he found; he could join the social club of the leading men of Puerto Cabello and participate in all sorts of social events. In 1909 he was appointed to Corinto, Nicaragua, although he had hoped to be moved to France. He found Corinto a shantytown, with unpaved streets and no electricity. The consulate was shabby, but he managed to turn it into a comfortable and presentable place by the time he married and brought his wife, a Brooklyn colored "aristocrat," to live there in 1910.[16]

Johnson resigned from the Consular Service in 1913, not because he disliked the work, but because the victory of Woodrow Wilson in the 1912 presidential election made his chances of being appointed to a better post very slim. Loyal Democrats were rewarded at that point, and he could only hope to keep his post in Nicaragua. Johnson returned for a short period to Jacksonville and then moved back to New York, where he had no job. However, in a few weeks Fred R. Moore, the owner and publisher of the *New York Age,* offered him an editorial position at the paper. That marked the beginning of an almost nine-year collaboration of Johnson with the *Age,* a collaboration that definitively improved the paper's style. Similarly to what Du Bois thought the *Crisis* should be, Johnson saw African-American weekly papers like the *Age* as organs of "propaganda," whose chief business was to provide their readers intellectual stimulation about issues vital to them. Johnson's editorials, among other things, urged his readers to look at the Harlem branch of the New York Public Library as a resource of learning and deplored examples of rowdyism in what was progressively becoming black Harlem. Upon his return to the city, he found New York "more changed than ever." His wife's parents had followed the tide of respectable colored people flowing uptown and moved to Harlem. By the time he and his wife settled in Harlem, thousands of stable middle-class colored families resided on the numbered streets in the mid 130s between Fifth and Seventh Avenues, thanks to the entrepreneurial efforts of African-American realtor Philip A. Payton Jr. Behind Payton's undertaking was the richest African-American man in New York, James C. Thomas, whose fortune was the outcome of a lucky sale of property on Seventh Avenue for $103,000 cash to the Pennsylvania Railroad. Thomas, a former waiter and mortician, was brought into Payton's real estate speculation in Harlem by investing a quarter of a million dollars in apartment buildings. By 1910, Eighth Avenue separated black from white buildings. On the east side of the avenue, between 130th and 145th Streets, was black Harlem.[17]

The sixty thousand African Americans who in the 1890s lived in midtown Manhattan in the overcrowded Tenderloin and San Juan Hill districts were a nonwhite aggregation forerunning the idea of black Harlem. The Tenderloin, from West Twentieth to Fifty-third Streets, had been the home of nonwhites since the early nineteenth century. By the 1890s, African Americans were moving above Fifty-third Street to the already congested area of San Juan Hill. The continuing migration of southern black people to this area of Manhattan created tensions with the Irish neighborhoods, leading to the riots of 1900. Tenderloin cabarets, which launched the best popular music in New York, moved to Harlem. The most important cabaret was Jimmie Marshall's hotel on Fifty-third Street, the cradle of talented black musicians like the Johnson brothers and Bob Cole. In *Black Manhattan* (1930) Johnson described New York's "black Bohemia," the artistic life of "Negro talent," of which the Marshall Hotel represented a new phase. It became a gathering place for actors, musicians, composers, writers, and the better-paid vaudevillians. White actors and musicians—sometimes including Broadway stars—jockeys, prizefighters, and racially mixed theater fans also met at the Marshall. "To be a visitor there, without at the same time being a rank outsider, was a distinction."[18]

The music brought to Harlem had already conquered the city. The white urban middle class was breaking away from Victorianism at the time when blacks were moving in great number to northern cities. This double movement reflected both young white Americans' separation from Victorian culture, which nineteenth-century New England had sponsored, and American blacks' recovery of their own heritage from hegemonic white culture. New York became the cultural capital of the world and the center of black and white "collaborative energy," as historian Ann Douglas calls it.[19]

Exoticism and Racial Uplifting in African-American Musical Theater

The world of commercial entertainment stimulated interracial contacts. Everybody in New York seemed to be dancing the new steps from black musical comedies. "Far from being 'new,'" a *Sun* editorial charged, "these dances are a reversion to the grossest practices of savage man." Indeed, the editorial continued, they "are based on the primitive motive of orgies enjoyed by aboriginal inhabitants of every uncivilized land." According to social worker Belle Israels, New York was invaded by a real "dance madness." In 1911 in the over five hundred dance halls, academies, and amusement resorts of the city "where dancing may be indulged in the year around," the average yearly attendance was roughly four or five million young people between the ages of fifteen and thirty. Observers described this dance madness as an infection striking New York's youth. They found that "vulgar dancing," which caused "sexual excitement," existed everywhere. Unlike the Victorians' favorite dance, the waltz, the patterns of new dances were not regular movements of feet, but rather the movement of the entire body.[20]

Comedian George Walker wrote that in 1902 and 1903 his friend Bert Williams and he "had all New York and London doing the cakewalk." This dance, originating among slaves on southern plantations when they dressed in their masters' and mistresses' discarded finery and competed for a prize, usually a cake, soon penetrated even New York high society. It was a natural shuffle walk-step, in which partners moved about shuffling their feet as if walking and which put greater emphasis on body movement than patterned feet movement. In 1892 the first annual Cakewalk Jubilee was established at Madison Square Garden. This was a three-night contest presenting a variety of acts and a national cakewalk competition among dancers who had won small-town contests all over the country.[21] In his fictional *Autobiography of an Ex-Colored Man*, James Weldon Johnson gave a vivid picture of a cakewalk contest:

A half-dozen guests from some of the hotels took seats on the stage to act as judges, and twelve or fourteen couples began to walk for a sure enough, highly decorated cake, which was in plain evidence. The spectators crowded about the space reserved for the contestants and watched them with interest and excitement. The couples did not walk round in a circle, but in a square, with the men on the inside. . . . The men walked with stately and soldierly step, and the women with considerable grace. The judges arrived at their decision by a process of elimination. . . . In this way the contest was finally narrowed down to three or four couples. Then the excitement became intense. . . . This was the cake-walk in its original form, and it is what the coloured performers on the theatrical stage developed into the prancing movements now known all over the world, and which some Parisian critics pronounced the acme of poetic motion.[22]

Urban whites turned with ever-increasing frequency to the more primitive steps of black dances. The "Texas tommy," "turkey trot," "foxtrot," "Charleston," and "black bottom" originated either in black community ballrooms or in red-light districts. Ragtime, the music for the new dances, also came from black urban culture. Officially introduced at Tony Pastor's Music Hall in 1896, ragtime started when southern blacks began moving in increasing numbers into the city and came into contact with each other, with minstrel show music, and with the formal written composition of European training. Ragtime was the first appropriation of white piano techniques by black musicians; it was a fusion of older musical traditions that black migrants brought with them to the city and the "new learning"—namely, "the adjustment to the conflicts and strangeness of the city." This music originally allowed black musicians to laugh at white culture and behavior through the "ragging of the host culture's cherished melodies and sentiments."[23] Emphasizing rhythm and beat, this complex music encouraged spontaneous movements and undercut the formal conventions about moving the body that had prevailed in social dancing. The simplicity of the shuffle walk and the accented musical rhythms encouraged dancers to interpret the beat in a variety of ways.[24] "They marched, in ragtime, onward," historian David L. Lewis aptly puts it. All the nation danced the cakewalk when it wanted to dance, and when it wanted to sing it sang "All Coons Look Alike to Me" and "Under the Bamboo Tree."[25]

Manhattan streets numbered in the upper twenties and lower thirties were the business and social center for most black people engaged in professional sports and minstrel shows. They were mostly men, who earned and spent large sums of money and who dominated what Johnson called "a flourishing black Bohemia";[26] but black women were entering the world of musical comedy, too. Matilda Sissieretta Jones, for example, was one of the first black women to gain stage popularity. In the spring of 1892 her gorgeous voice dominated the Jubilee Spectacle at Madison Square Garden; in the fall Jones was invited to sing at the White House.[27] But in 1893 she refused to sing on Negro Day at the Chicago World's Fair.

The movement from minstrel show to musical comedy, from the cheapest form of buffoonery to attractive farce, and even to good comedy, was accomplished by a number of black comedians.[28] Black burlesque circuit manager Sam T. Jack arranged *The Creole Show* along minstrel lines but with the innovation of a chorus of sixteen black girls. The show opened in Boston in 1891 and later moved to Chicago for the World's Fair.

Black minstrelsy reached its peak in the summer of 1895, when a plantation literally came to Brooklyn. A black village, with real log cabins, hen yards, hay wagons, mules, chickens, and cotton balls, was built in Ambrose Park and populated with five hundred "genuinely southern negroes" from Virginia and the Carolinas. The manager stressed the authenticity and naturalness of what the audience, invited to wander among the cabins, was seeing. It was a pageant of plantation life. According to Toll's depiction of the event, what was called the "realistic" representation of plantation life fit the stereotype of what whites thought plantations were like. Choruses sang "Kentucky Home," "Roll, Jordan, Roll," "Carry Me Back to Old Virginia," and "Old Black Joe." When a watermelon cart entered the arena, the entire cast jumped on the melons and devoured them with visible pleasure. Then, a cakewalk followed, in which the audience was to decide the winner. Matching the caricatures of black dancers, black people danced a frenzied series of contortions. Other features followed, including the marching of a Negro regiment on leave and another dance contest that lasted until dancers collapsed from exhaustion.[29]

The two racial stereotypes of blackface minstrelsy were the plantation "darky" and the city "coon." The former was the happy, funny, shuffling, lazy, childish, and irresponsible but loyal and contented singing and dancing slave; the latter was the freed Negro, the flashily dressed, shifty, smart-talking dandy of the streets, with a gold watch chain and patent leather shoes. This powerful form of popular entertainment changed dramatically after Reconstruction. Blackface white actors progressively dismissed their personification of black caricatures and took over the ethnic cultures of recently arrived immigrants. At that point black grotesque caricatures were performed by real black actors who for the first

time could find an access to the American stage. By the 1900s the
African-American weekly *New York Age* noted more than twenty troupes
of black vaudeville actors touring in the larger cities of the North and
the West. Yet, black minstrelsy was much more than the history of
troupes, the struggle for ownership, and the careers of stars. It was also
the story of thousands of black people who became minstrels but never
stars, and thousands of others who cheered for them. In 1894, when a
New York theatrical manager advertised for forty black minstrels, approximately two thousand blacks showed up at his office and more than
one thousand left their names. This new profession was rather appealing to young black persons, Mary Ovington pointed out in *Half a Man:*
black comedians "were far better off than their more sober brothers
who stick to their elevators or their porters' jobs."[30] Although minstrelsy
was, on the whole, a caricature of African-American life and fixed on
stage the stereotype of the happy-go-lucky, wide-grinning, loud-laugh-
ing, shuffling, banjo-playing Negro, it nevertheless provided stage training and theatrical experience for a large number of black people. The
sooty, burnt-cork makeup, the exaggeratedly wide lips, the gold teeth,
the gaudy clothing, the loud jokes, the fantastic dialect, the watermelon
and razor props, and the dice were established features of popular commercial theater in the United States. Black performers initially could
succeed only by imitating these blackface whites.[31] Sometimes they even
made their skin much darker than their actual hue and spoke a dialect
that they had never heard except from white performers.

Many of these people, as white minstrelsy waned, passed to what
James Weldon Johnson called the "second phase" or "middle period" of
black theater in America. It was at this point that black American art
and folkways began to exert a visible influence on mainstream urban
culture: the blues were making their way up the Mississippi River, jazz
was stirring New Orleans, and ragtime was electrifying the New York
scene. Theatrical activities flourished among black New Yorkers.
Worth's Museum, at Sixth Avenue and Thirteenth Street, housed a
black stock company spearheaded by the Johnson brothers' friend Bob
Cole, who was, according to contemporary records, a good singer, a
good dancer, and an excellent actor. He wrote a show with an operatic
finale for Matilda Sissieretta Jones that played for many years in New
York and in many northern cities. In 1898 Cole wrote, directed, and
produced *A Trip to Coontown*, a musical with a plot that completely broke
with the minstrel tradition. Initially boycotted by theater managers who
did not support the idea of autonomous black companies, the show successfully toured Canada. As soon as the show opened in Manhattan in
1899, the *New York Dramatic Mirror* wrote that most of its songs had al-

ready become popular and "were applauded vigorously."[32] An innovative feature of *A Trip to Coontown,* besides an all-black cast, was the presence of women performers. In 1900 a Boston reviewer of the show
pointed out this innovation, but unable to accept any change in black
theatrical features, the reviewer described the alteration in the popular
racist terms of the time:

> The Freeman sisters abandoned the grace and joy of their native danc-
> ing, and formed a style mixed with the idiotic acrobatic of white
> dancers and contortionists; thus doth civilization ruin the blithe free-
> dom of them that it absorbs. The first act ended with the most astonish-
> ing demonstration of the facility with which the African face can be
> made to represent other dark-skinned races. It was an elaborate ballet.
> Four misses looked and acted more like Japanese girls than most white
> chorus girls in comic opera. A group of men made perfect Arabs. Three
> more girls were vivid Egyptians, with sinuous suggestion. Two men rep-
> resented Chinamen. One group was of Spanish girls. All of these were
> remarkable in their way, and interesting food for reflection. The cos-
> tuming was rich and tasteful, and the dancing pretty and vivacious in a
> manner not specially recalling the usual ragtime steps.[33]

To this unknown reviewer, writing shortly after the Spanish-American
War, it was clear what would be proper "native dancing" for black
women, meaning perhaps the sort of African tribal dances of the Dahomans at the Chicago World's Fair. At the same time, the reviewer made
the point that the "African face" could represent all the dark races of
the world, as the new imperialist mood required.

In 1899 musician Will Marion Cook wrote *Clorindy, or the Origin of the
Cakewalk* with poet Paul Laurence Dunbar. Cook, the son of college-ed-
ucated parents, was able to study violin in Berlin with the famous Hungarian violinist Joseph Joachim thanks to a benefit concert the elderly
Frederick Douglass organized in Washington, D.C., to raise money to
send the young musician to Europe. Cook spent three years in Germany
studying violin, piano, harmony, and counterpoint; back in the United
States, he continued his studies at the National Conservatory in New
York. His idea, as he wrote in an unpublished autobiography, was to pursue a concert and orchestral career in the States. Facing discrimination
at every step, Cook took the path of popular music. He lived at the Marshall Hotel in New York and often stopped by at the Johnson brothers'
room to take part in heated discussions on "the manner and means of
raising the status of the Negro as a writer, composer and performer in
New York theater and the world of music." The only real clashes were
those between Cook and Cole. "Seldom did they meet and part without

a clash," Johnson recalled. Johnson thought Will Marion Cook was the most original genius of Negro musicians, able to throw all European standards over. Cook believed that the Negro in music and on stage had to be "a Negro, a genuine Negro," and was convinced that "white" patterns should be shunned and not be employed in an attempt to do what the white artist could do, and usually better. Hot-tempered and eccentric, Cook "never hesitated to make belittling comments on Cole's limitations in musical and general education; he would even sneer at him on a fault in pronunciation," Johnson observed.[34]

Cook's *Clorindy* was his first success. He himself described the great finale of the performance at the Casino Theatre Roof Garden in Manhattan by a group of only twenty-six people: "My chorus sang like Russians, dancing meanwhile like Negroes, and cakewalking like angels, black angels! When the last note was sounded, the audience stood and cheered for at least ten minutes." George Lederer, in Johnson's view the most skillful producer of musical plays at that time, learned new things from *Clorindy:* "He judged correctly that the practice of the Negro chorus, to dance strenuously and sing at the same time, if adapted to the white stage would be a profitable novelty; so he departed considerably from the model of the easy, leisurely movements of the English light opera chorus. He also judged that some injection of Negro syncopated music would produce a like result."[35] This was just one example of the innovative role black musicians had in the development of American popular culture at the turn of the century. Cook played that role for the next fifteen years, writing the music for many other all-black shows, including assisting the popular team of Williams and Walker in their successful shows *In Dahomey* (1902), *Abyssinia* (1906), and *Bandanna Land* (1907).

Bert Williams and George Walker were the pioneers of what Johnson called the "middle period" of black theater. Their lives and careers are examples of the cultural ambivalences and ambiguities of many black performers. A British West Indian and a westerner, respectively, Williams and Walker met in San Francisco, where they played in burnt-cork comedies billed as the "real coons." They thought, in so doing, that they made a radical departure from the "darky" style of singing and dancing of the old minstrel show. Williams and Walker moved to New York and rented an apartment on Fifty-third Street that soon became the headquarters of all aspiring black performers. George Walker, who on stage played the strutting, city-slicker, overdressed Negro, would sadly admit off stage that "the white man won't let us be serious!"

When Bert Williams began his career in 1892, he found he had to conform to a theatrical convention that in many ways crippled his talent and limited his achievement. A pioneer of black musical performance, he was forced into a blackface role he detested, but in the theater the warmth of his comic genius was visible behind the make up.[36] George Walker recalled his experience:

> All that was expected of a colored performer was singing and dancing and a little story telling, but as for acting, no one credited a black person with the ability to act. Blackfaced white comedians used to make themselves look as ridiculous as they could when portraying a "darky" character. In their make-up they always had tremendously big red lips, and their costumes were frightfully exaggerated. The one fatal result of this to the colored performers was that they imitated the white performers in their make-up as "darkies." Nothing seemed more absurd than to see a colored man making himself ridiculous in order to portray himself.[37]

In 1893 a black male performer starting a career in popular entertainment faced only one choice: if he wanted audiences to watch him, he had to assume the "nigger" characterization. Although Bert Williams was a West Indian, his main role was to portray "the shiftless darky to the fullest extent; his fun, his philosophy. There is nothing about this fellow I don't know. I must study his movements. I have to. . . . He is not in me. The way he walks; the way he crosses his legs; the way he leans up against a wall, one foot forward. I find much material by knocking around in out of the way places and just listening. Eavesdropping on human nature is one of the most important parts of a comedian's work."[38] Bert Williams was proud that he had never considered himself a close relative of anyone from the South, but he had learned that for the general public there was only one kind of "darky," and anyone whose skin was colored was a target of race prejudice.

Although all this was true, there was also a different type of black theater when Williams and Walker chose to employ their talents in the "Ethiopian business" of burnt-cork caricature. By the 1890s the Jubilee Singers, a student group from Fisk and Hampton Universities that since the 1870s held concerts of spirituals around the country, including a performance on Negro Day at the Chicago World's Fair, had established the value of black music to the extent that Anton Dvorak, then the director of the National Conservatory of Music in New York, said, "In the Negro melodies of America I discover all that is needed for a great and noble school of music."[39] Yet to Williams and Walker, exoticism paved the way for racial uplifting.

On 18 February 1903, after a tour of several months in the country, the New York Theater at Broadway and Forty-fourth Street staged the first black musical comedy, *In Dahomey*, by Williams and Walker, who headed a cast of fifty people. The play included contemporary popular music, and its plot evolved around two funny rascals (Williams and Walker) who become involved in a plan to take possession of the fortune of some African colonizers and their rich leader. After all sorts of adventures and tricks, and the election of one of the two characters as governor of Dahomey, they return to America with a colonial court.

The *New York Times* gave a good review to this musical comedy and concluded it was "well up to the not very exalted average in this kind of show." The reviewer praised the text as "well above the average" and "an admirably conceived satire on racial foibles that gave scope to no little fun in the picturing of character types." Two months later, *In Dahomey* went to London. Besides regular performances in a London theater, the whole cast entertained the royal family at Buckingham Palace for the birthday party of the Prince of Wales. Williams and Walker mastered the skill of stirring the exotic chord of British imagination. A London reviewer detected in the show "the strangeness of the colored race blended with the strangeness of certain American things."[40]

The two comedians proceeded with their elaboration of the exotic side of the African colonization theme in *Abyssinia,* a better financed show than *In Dahomey* and employing almost the same cast. More lighting effects, gorgeous costumes for a cast of one hundred, waterfalls, and wild animals were brought on stage for a plot that told the story of two rascals from Kansas who returned to Abyssinia, the land of their forefathers, together with many female cousins, an Asian cook, and a Baptist minister. In 1908 the Williams and Walker company tried another adventure with *Bandanna Land.* A larger cast and the new unpublished songs by Will Marion Cook made the musical a success. Less exotic than Bert Williams and George Walker's previous comedies, the plot evolved around the world of Manhattan real estate business: a minstrel show performer (Williams) inherits a large sum and gets involved in a land sale to a railroad company. Meanwhile, with his partner (Walker), the clever performer plans the building of an amusement park, Bandanna Land, in the same black neighborhood to force the railroad company to pay the highest price for the land.[41]

Less famous black musicians in Manhattan found jobs in those Broadway cabarets and restaurants from which they were excluded as customers. By 1910 many black entertainers had turned to vaudeville and specialized in impersonation, acrobatics, body contortion, dancing, singing, or comical acts. Yet access to the stage did not defeat racial discrimination in the performing arts. Although whites to a degree could accept black musical comedies because of the stereotypical images of blacks, they were reluctant to accept serious black music and acting.

"The public gives the colored man no opportunity as a tragedian, demanding that his comedy shall border always on the farcical," Mary Ovington observed.[42]

Matilda Sissieretta Jones, the "Black Patti," was an example of this distortion. A talented soprano trained at the New England Conservatory, she was the black version of the European soprano Adelina Patti. Her splendid voice and her dignified look could not hide her beautiful Negroid features and dark skin, which were not considered valuable qualities for a mainstream career in classical music at the beginning of the century. Jones, like other classically trained black performers, had no choice but to stay in recognizable Negro music and style. Like Will Marion Cook, who gave up his high-level European training in classical music to write "Negro music," Jones formed a variety show company, the Black Patti Troubadours, which toured the United States with musicals consisting of a melange of popular opera arias and ragtime. Her superior singing was what made her shows successful.[43]

In 1910 the Troubadours produced *A Trip to Africa.* In the second act of this musical, Madame Jones appeared in gorgeous raiment in the jungles of Africa and was acclaimed princess. With a sextet in the following act she played selections from *Lucia di Lammermoor. A Boston Transcript* reviewer of the company's 1911 performance in that city found the story of colored characters in a jungle, "where they become as royal folk, ruling over their own kind," and their ragtime ditties and dances exceedingly comical. The overall effect of the show, the reviewer wrote, was "the boisterous humor that colored companies carry off much better than do their white rivals."[44]

Thus, to succeed, black performers had to wear an exotic mask. Access to drama was precluded because the pervasive racial stereotypes embodied in black images were the reverse of what American public culture found worthy of emulation and recognition. As Gilbert Osofsky points out, "the Negro was conceived as lazy in an ambitious culture; improvident and sensuous in a moralistic society; happy in a sober world; poor in a nation that offered riches to all who cared to take them; childlike in a country of men."[45]

At the same time, these un-American characteristics found a receptive public among those urban whites who were willing to break with the traditional white American culture. There were places in New York where "both white and coloured people of certain classes" went to listen to ragtime and to meet famous prizefighters, jockeys, and noted minstrels, as James Weldon Johnson vividly described. In places such as the Club, "a centre of coloured Bohemians and sports," the walls "were literally covered with photographs or lithographs of every coloured man

in America who had ever 'done anything.'" Pictures of Frederick Douglass were placed together with those of stage celebrities and prizefighters. Here one could see a minstrel who, whenever asked to do
something, "never essayed anything below a reading from Shakespeare." This was an example, Johnson commented, of a man "who
made many people laugh at the size of his mouth, while he carried in
his heart a burning ambition to be a tragedian." One could also see,
among the white patrons who came to the Club in cabs, "variety performers and others who delineated 'darky characters,'" who went there
to get their imitations from the black entertainers they saw at the Club.[46]

In 1907 an article in *Variety*, the New York leading magazine of theatrical reviews, commented on the boundaries delimiting the roles of
black entertainers: "The American public refuses to take the colored
race seriously as entertainers," the commentator declared. The American public, he continued, wanted them "with a dash of comedy and con-
sistently refuses to accept them in any guise than the jester's motley."
This commentator reviewed the performance of a vaudeville act by a
group called the Four Georgia Belles, who made the mistake, in his
view, of taking themselves too seriously by clinging to sentimental songs.
They had good costumes, their voices were pleasant, and the harmony
was well arranged, "but they would do better did they make a conces-
sion in favor of popular prejudice and confine themselves more to plantation songs and native melodies." The reporter admitted, however, that
there was an element of novelty in the idea of such a type of colored
quartet, and he was interested to know what the public's verdict would
be. A form of communication between white and black lower-class cultures, the minstrel show constantly changed its contents. It is true, as
Robert Toll has pointed out, that black actors adjusted to the stereotypes inherited from white minstrelsy and that, in so doing, they added
credibility to black caricatures. This adjustment, however, implied a further elaboration of those ludicrous caricatures in order to be distinguished from blackface actors. At the beginning, black actors imitated
white minstrels offering even more grotesque caricatures, but in a following phase they introduced themselves to the public as "real Negroes"
and dismissed burnt cork.[47]

In 1895 Ernest Hogan, a member of the Black Patti Troubadours, had
starred in his own show and composed "All Coons Look Alike to Me,"
which became the most popular "coon" song. In *Black Manhattan* James
Weldon Johnson portrayed Kentuckian Hogan as "a veteran minstrel
and a very funny, natural-blackface comedian," whose comic effects "did
not depend upon the caricature created by the use of cork and a mouth
exaggerated by paint," but on his mobile face "capable of laughter-pro-

voking expressions that were irresistible, notwithstanding the fact that he was a very good looking man." Hogan, who described himself as "the Unbleached American," was chosen by Will Marion Cook to train and appear with the dancers in *Clorindy, or the Origin of the Cakewalk* and soon became the highest-paid individual colored vaudeville performer.[48]

It was a fact, Johnson remarked, that when black performers attempted to gain recognition for themselves as true artists, not buffoons, they were unable to convince theater managers that the production would be profitable; "every show had to be studied carefully, for anything that might offend white prejudices." Consequently Johnson's friend Bert Williams made a point of including in his comedies "only certain conceptions about Negro life that his audience was willing to accept and ready to enjoy."[49]

Many educated African Americans, however, could not see in black minstrelsy any positive aspect for the improvement of black conditions and seriously objected to these ludicrous characterizations of black life. In 1907 the *New York Age* angrily denounced "plays which burlesque the character of a people and tend to degrade them in the estimation of their fellow citizens." It proposed that they "be prohibited." But since black urban masses enjoyed such characterizations, comedian Bert Williams believed that his job was "to make them laugh."[50]

Several African-American authors have pointed out that in order to survive, blacks developed masks and facades that allowed whites to indulge their racial fantasies, while blacks created their real identity in a separate cultural world. Ralph Ellison's depiction of the atmosphere at a black college during the visit of its white benefactors is particularly telling:

> Around me the students move with faces frozen in solemn masks, and I seem to hear already the voices mechanically raised in the songs the visitors loved. Loved? Demanded. Sung? An ultimatum accepted and ritualized, an allegiance recited for the peace it imparted, and for that perhaps loved. Loved as the defeated come to love the symbols of their conquerors. . . . Here upon this stage the black rite of Horatio Alger was performed to God's own acting script, with millionaires come down to portray themselves; not merely acting out the myth of their goodness, and wealth and success and power and benevolence and authority in cardboard masks, but themselves, these virtues concretely![51]

Poet Paul Laurence Dunbar, who like James Weldon Johnson knew the world of New York black musical comedies intimately and had a similar ambivalence about writing lyrics for that world, caught the meaning of the mask in an 1895 poem:

We wear the mask that grins and lies,
It hides our cheeks and shades our eyes—
This debt we pay to human guile;
With torn and bleeding hearts we smile,
And mouth with myriad subtleties.

Why should the world be over-wise,
In counting all our tears and sighs?
Nay, let them only see us, while
   We wear the mask.[52]

The act of wearing the mask was often seen as a survival technique. It was a form of self-defense born out of slavery and a response to the permanent possibility of conflict in black-white relations. Crossing black class lines, the mask was a part of growing up black. Hiding real feelings could be a part of the experience of "being a problem," as W. E. B. Du Bois put it, or a part of learning "the weight of white people in the world," in James Baldwin's words, or a response to the discovery that the adversary is everywhere, "on the street, on the job, in the school," as Richard Wright observed. Furthermore, the mask could help leave the white world out of one's life in order to protect one's self. The distrust, suspicion, and contempt of whites in general made the mask a permanent shield in black experience, a protection from racism but also an impenetrable wall for those whites who truly wanted to eradicate any form of prejudice and discrimination from human experience. Wearing the mask was also a means of social mobility for many black performers. By presenting audiences with their own racial caricatures and making them laugh, these black performers gained economic success. Northern urban society wanted to believe that blacks were contented to be servants; black minstrels put a face mask on and made whites believe so, while laughing at themselves. A 1900 *New York Times* editorial said: "Let the Negro learn to clean stables, care for horses, feed and harness and drive them, run lawn mowers, make and keep gardens, and also keep engagements." In the words of W. E. B. Du Bois, this was what America at the turn of the century expected from black people: "Be content to be servants, and nothing more; what need of higher culture for half-men."[53]

From Stage to Street: "A Nigger Chase" in Manhattan

On the night of 15 August 1900, James and Rosamond Johnson were at their rooms on West Fifty-third Street. Rosamond played the songs for the coming season of Bob Cole's company with Billy Johnson, Cole's

theatrical partner. The rehearsal took longer than expected, and Rosamond could not keep a previous engagement with a friend, Barry
Carter, and two women to attend some sort of entertainment. They
stopped the rehearsal around ten-thirty; then the two brothers walked
Billy to the corner of Eighth Avenue to take a streetcar to go down Thir-
tieth Street, where he lived. The three men waited for an hour, and no
car passed in either direction. It was strange, they thought. Finally Billy
stopped a hansom, and the two brothers went back home. They had just
gone to bed when the doorbell rang, and a young white man asked
them if they knew Barry Carter. He told the brothers that Carter had
been beaten up and brought to the Jefferson Market jail. The Johnson
brothers were eager to go to see their friend, but "the young man impressed on us that we shouldn't even try to go; that a mob was raging up
and down Eighth Avenue and the adjacent side blocks from 27th to
42nd Streets attacking Negroes wherever they were found, and that it
was not safe for any colored person to go through that section." The two
brothers followed the advice and the next morning read in the newspapers the story of "a great race riot." They found Carter "in a sad condition." He had kept the appointment the previous evening and was
walking with the two women "when a crowd of young hoodlums ran up
from behind and began beating him over the head with pieces of lead
pipe." Carter struggled, ran away, and reached a squad of policemen,
"but they met him with more clubbing." His scalp was cut in several
places, his arms were terribly swollen from the attempt to protect his
head from the blows. "It was a beating from which he never fully recovered," James Weldon Johnson sadly recalled. That riot "had more than
local significance," Johnson wrote, as it was "only a single indication of
the national spirit of the times toward the Negro."[54] The New York riot
of 1900, in fact, was the first of a number of ugly negrophobic explosions in urban America during the Progressive Era.

In the summer of 1900, Bert Williams and George Walker appeared
at the Proctor Theater on Fifty-eighth Street in a new vaudeville sketch
that, according to the *Dramatic Mirror*, showed the two comedians were
"endeavoring to get as far away as possible from the conventional Sixth
Avenue coon type." Their new act closed with an exotic "moonlit African jungle scene, as Walker, dressed in a negligee costume of a dusky female savage, and his partner, attired after the fashion of a male warrior,
hop around the stage in a realistic aboriginal manner." The night of 15
August Williams and Walker ended their daily appearance at the Proctor Theater unaware that the worst race riot following those of 1863 was
occurring in the Tenderloin district. The following day the *New York
Herald* reported that "for hours last night hundreds of policemen . . .

battled with a frenzied mood. In the heart of New York a race war was on between whites and blacks—as fierce if not as fatal as those that have taken place in the South."[55]

The Tenderloin district, the area where many black immigrants from the South were settling, was the stage for a riot whose racial stereotypes reflected the ambiguous characters of a minstrel show. The inciting episode was the murder of a white policeman by a young black man. On the night of 13 August, twenty-two-year-old Arthur J. Harris left his room located on Forty-first Street to buy some cigars and stopped at the local saloon. He was born in Virginia in an unstable black family and had migrated North in 1899. In Jersey City he had worked at odd jobs— as a cook, baker, carpenter, and poolroom attendant—and met a young black woman with whom he moved to New York early in August and rented the room on Forty-first Street. That night the young woman was waiting for him near a saloon when policeman Robert J. Thorpe, wearing plain clothes, approached her and charged her with "soliciting." Harris saw Thorpe grabbing his woman and fought with him; the policeman clubbed him, and Harris pulled out a knife. Thorpe was injured and died the next day.[56]

Had Harris been a foreign immigrant to New York, his case would have ended with a trial and a severe sentence. But he was a black southerner, recently migrated, and his crime set fire to the racial tensions of the Tenderloin. Together with San Juan Hill, the Tenderloin was the most densely populated black area in the 1890s. Between 1890 and 1900 the city's black population expanded by twenty-five thousand people. Blacks filled the places of those immigrants who could afford to leave the area, which had the worst reputation and housed Manhattan's red-light district and underworld characters. As far as prostitution was concerned, the owners of disorderly houses paid a regular fee, and streetwalkers negotiated their use of public space with the policemen who protected them. Was Thorpe connected to the graft system when he charged the young black woman standing on a street corner with soliciting? Did he think she was invading someone else's space, for which a fee had already been paid? Or did he simply follow the common racist assumption that all black women were potential prostitutes?[57]

Another fight occurred near Thorpe's house the night before the burial, and that was the signal for a mob attack: "If there had been a carefully arranged plot and this had been the agreed signal, the outbreak could not have been more spontaneous. . . . Men and women poured by the hundreds from the neighborhood tenements. Negroes were set upon wherever they could be found and brutally beaten."[58]

The word spread that a "nigger chase" was on. A crowd of five hundred white men and women congregated at Seventh Avenue and Thirty-fifth Street at one o'clock in the morning. Black riders who were returning home, unaware of the events, were pulled off their bicycles and beaten. The crowd moved down Thirty-fifth Street crying, "Down with the Negroes!" The white mob beat and chased John Williams, a black vaudeville actor, when he got off a streetcar. The next victim of the growing crowd was George Walker's friend Ernest Hogan, who advertised himself in the *Dramatic Mirror* as the "Creative Comedian and Great Unbleached American." Hogan, who was playing the leading role in *Clorindy,* was flashily dressed and leisurely riding down Broadway on an open streetcar to meet Walker. He was stopped and beaten, while Walker was able to escape and hide in a cellar. Black comedians were the only colored individuals the mob recognized. According to James Weldon Johnson, during the height of the riot the cry went out to get Ernest Hogan, Williams and Walker, and Cole and Johnson, as they seemed to be "the only individual names the crowd was familiar with."[59]

On the night of 15 August, many other innocent black people were assaulted by the mob. Early the following evening a large crowd gathered on Eighth Avenue. By nine o'clock the avenue was packed with people who had come to see "the fun," but nothing major happened. Black people did not show up: "every one who went to see crowds of hoodlums chasing negroes was bitterly disappointed. But it was a free show, and nobody was angry because it didn't quite come up to expectations." The crowd was left with the meager satisfaction of complaining that blacks had too many privileges in the city, that they had abused these privileges, and that the time had come "to teach them a lesson." According to the *Herald,* the white women of the area took a prominent part in the riot: "they shrieked vengeance against the negroes." At the funeral of police officer Robert Thorpe, the younger women seemed most anxious "that the rioting of the preceding night should be resumed and that it should be more effective in the way of bloodshed." It seemed that "girls scarcely out of their teens became loud mouthed advocates of murder." Yet there were also white women who helped the black men who were chased and beaten. A Mrs. Davenport, for example, refused to turn over to the police the black men she sheltered in her home on the night of 15 August. The policemen replied, "What kind of woman are you to be harboring niggers?"[60]

The New York press unanimously agreed that the race riots were fomented by the police. Witnesses reported having heard policemen in the crowd advocating violence. A white observer remarked that "a squad of police marched up the street, and made a demonstration against every negro in sight." Other observers accused the police of clubbing and kicking innocent blacks: when a black woman asked a police officer to protect her from the mob he replied, "Go to h——, d——n you"; a black man appealed to a policeman for help and "received a smash over the head with a nightstick in reply." Whenever the crowd collected to chase some unfortunate black fellow who happened to be in the street, the police followed, formed a wedge, dispersed the surrounding crowd, and used their clubs "on the unoffending negro and if they could find any excuse hurried him to the police station." The rioting extended from Thirty-third Street up to Forty-fourth Street on both Seventh and Eighth Avenues. More than sixty colored people were injured, and a dozen white men received gunshot wounds.[61]

African Americans felt they were in danger, having realized the unwillingness of the city authorities to punish their assailants and to protect them in the future. A "well dressed negro" told a reporter for the *Herald* that he did not know what to do: "Many of the best friends I have made in this city are white men, but I know that in an emergency like this the fact that my skin is black places me in serious danger."[62]

In the aftermath of the riots, African Americans organized the Citizens' Protective League under the leadership of the Reverend William Henry Brooks of St. Mark's Methodist-Episcopal Church. Brooks wrote an appeal to Mayor Robert A. Van Wyck in which he condemned "in unqualified terms lawlessness among our people" and the crime of Arthur Harris. At the same time, Brook made the point that Harris's crime, "as black as it may be," could not justify the New York policemen in their "savage and indiscriminate attack upon innocent and helpless people." He therefore appealed to the mayor, as the chief magistrate of the city, for the conviction and removal from the police force of those officers "whom we are able to prove guilty." Brooks concluded his appeal by saying that the color of a man's skin "must not be made the index of his character or ability." He informed the mayor that the "many ugly threatening letters" he had received indicated that his own life was not safe, but that he was unwilling "to purchase it by silence at the expense of my unfortunate race." During the day of the funeral there were rumors of coming troubles. "Several officers told an informant of mine," wrote Frank Moss, the lawyer for the Citizens' Protective League and the report compiler, "that they were going to punish the Negroes that night." Those colored people who had illicit dealings with the police, like keepers of gambling and disorderly houses, saw signs of coming trouble; they closed their places and kept off the streets. "There are numerous gangs of rowdies in the district who are hostile to Negroes and friendly with the unofficial powers that are now potent in police affairs," Moss remarked. On that night there was an understanding between those gangs and some police forces that resulted in the holding of the streets for hours by crowds who raced up and down Broadway between Seventh and Eighth Avenues and the side streets from Thirty-fourth to Forty-second Streets, hunting Negroes indiscriminately, and who were not attacked by the police. Mobs could have been broken up and dispersed with no difficulty, newspaper reports and witnesses unanimously said. "In many instances of brutality by the mob policemen stood by and made no effort to protect the Negroes who were assailed. They ran with the crowds in pursuit of their prey; they took defenseless men who ran to them for protection and threw them to the rioters, and in many cases they beat and clubbed men and women more brutally than the mob did. They were absolutely unrestrained by their superior officers." Taken to court, policemen made many false charges against Negroes; although some blacks were discharged, others were convicted on false accusation. The Citizens' Protective League, together with the Society for the Prevention of Crime and the City Vigilance League, wrote the mayor urging him to hold an investigation. The mayor answered that the whole matter was in the hands of the Board of Police. A number of injured Negroes brought suits against the city for damages inflicted on them by the mob.[63]

On 12 September 1900, a large meeting attended by thirty-five hundred people was held at Carnegie Hall to protest against the police brutality and the failure of the city authorities to act. The addresses were given by the Reverend R. S. MacArthur, the Reverend D. W. Cook, the Reverend C. T. Walker, the Reverend W. H. Brooks, the Reverend Bishop W. B. Derrick, Miss M. R. Lyons, and the Honorable D. M. Webster. At that meeting an amount of money was collected, and measures were taken to make the Citizens' Protective League a permanent organization. "The League and its representatives are using every possible lawful measure to secure justice to its people, and to vindicate their right to live in peace," promised lawyer Frank Moss, who legally represented the associations, despite the difficult task of getting a hearing. They had several cases, but because of the "solid and lusty swearing lot of policemen," they could not show "the crime in its mass" and could not reveal "the responsibility of the higher officials for the outbreak and for the failure to discover and punish the guilty policemen and their commanders." Furthermore, in spite of the fact that the mayor had authority to intervene in this matter, "he has washed his hands of it, and the Police Board has not hesitated to write another page of its damning history." Moss advised the Citizens' Protective League to publish witness affidavits, sworn in front of New York county notaries, so that they could be read and considered by the public in relation to each other. This was an attempt to present "the great wrong that the Negroes have suffered," to gather "the sympathy and support of the good people of New York to secure a vindication, and to prevent a recurrence of the outbreak." Moss ended his introduction by remarking that "the dissolute Negroes who are so often seen lounging about the 'Tenderloin' and its neighborhood are not to be found among the witnesses. They are the friends of the police, contributing very largely to their comfort and happiness, and it is quite clear that they had their warning and kept out of the way."[64] In fact, all witnesses were "respectable" people, caught unprepared by the brutality of the mob. They all had become aware that the "anti-Negro ways" were spreading northward.

Most of the injured people who were attacked by the mob under the eyes of the police and beaten at the police headquarters experienced the dreadful feeling of being chased just because of the color of their skin. On those August nights they were simply returning home from work or walking on the street, minding their own business. They experienced the fear of being hunted for no reason except the dark color of their skin. "Kill the nigger, lynch the nigger," were the shouts most of them heard from their persecutors. No one was lynched in the southern fashion. No one was accused of raping or molesting white women. Most of them were badly beaten and could not go back to work for several days. A few were permanently injured. In many cases they were beaten by the very police officers whom they had asked for protection.

William J. Elliott gave the most detailed testimony. At the time of the riot he lived on West Thirty-fifth Street. He was twenty-six and had been employed at the Imperial Hotel for almost two years. He moved to New York from Florida, where he attended the state college but could not finish because he had to work in a drug firm as an apprentice. Within a year he was made a prescriptionist. He moved to New York in 1899 and worked in a drug firm, and in a short time he became responsible for two drug stores in Atlantic City, New Jersey. When the stores were sold by the owner, Elliott had to move back to New York. "My intention has been to accumulate enough money to take a pharmaceutical course," he said. Meanwhile, he found work at the Imperial Hotel. The story of what happened on the night of 15 August 1900, seen through Elliott's eyes, started with a colored man at the hotel informing him that there was no way of getting home because of the riots in the street. Elliott managed to avoid the mob attacks and arrive home safely on the first night. The real nightmare began the following morning when he tried to go back to work. Wherever Elliott went, he was chased by gangs of white boys and men. He felt the danger, constantly followed by a mob shouting, "Kill the nigger," "Catch the nigger," "Take the nigger off the car." He was given a small gun by a neighbor to protect himself if necessary. Determined to go to work, Elliott ran up Ninth Avenue, chased by a mob, and found refuge in a pawnbroker's shop. From the window he saw some police officers standing at the corner of Thirty-sixth Street. He left the shop, walked toward the police, and asked them if they could take him up Forty-second Street. But after a few steps in their direction, Elliott was grabbed by a man in civilian clothes whom he later learned was a police officer. The man asked him where he was going and what he was doing at the pawnbroker's shop. Before he could explain, the plainclothes policeman searched him, found the small gun in his pocket, and accused him of having bought it at the pawnbroker's shop. Meanwhile, four police officers came around him, and the mob was yelling, "Kill the nigger!" "Lynch the nigger," getting closer and closer with sticks and stones. The officers kept the mob away and took him to the station house on Thirty-seventh Street. There he was accused of carrying a concealed weapon bought at the pawnbroker's shop. Elliott denied the accusation and started to tell the accusing officer "about my reputation and not being a rioter, and that I was trying to get to my work." The answer was that they had no time to look up his reputation, and Elliott was put in jail. While following the jailer, he passed a policeman leaning against a door. "As I passed him he threw out his foot and tripped me. I stumbled out but did not fall," Elliott remembered. As he looked around, another officer struck him on the jaw with his fist, and then another hit Elliott's head with his club, "and all the policemen in the muster room jumped up and jumped on me, yelling 'Kill him!' 'Kill the nigger!'" Elliott begged for mercy, fell down under the strikes, and felt the policemen "kicking and beating me about." He heard a Captain Cooney rush in and tell the officers not to kill him because journalists were around. Elliott had to pay three dollars for carrying a concealed weapon before being released. Because of the wounds he was unable to work for days.

Other witnesses reported similar stories of gratuitous brutality by the police and of being attacked by the mob on account of their skin color. Fifteen-year-old Harry Reed was returning home with four companions on an open Eighth Avenue streetcar on the night of 15 August when a mob at the corner of Thirty-seventh Street attacked them. One of his companions, a nineteen-year-old white boy, was not touched, and another companion, a light-complexioned colored boy, was also saved. But Reed and another dark-skinned boy had to jump off the car and run away, chased by the mob. While he was running up Thirty-eighth Street, Reed saw a few police officers. He asked for protection, but they beat him up.[65]

No place was safe for dark-skinned people during those days. Those who had the misfortune of riding on Eighth Avenue streetcars were attacked by white men jumping on them. "The next I knew," Isaiah O. Ferguson reported, "a number of men jumped on the car, some coming through the windows, and commenced beating me, and continued to beat me until I was insensible." William Hamer, a musician, was riding a Seventh Avenue horsecar with his wife, also a musician, when the car was stopped, and they both were dragged from the car by a crowd of men and boys with sticks and stones. Hamer was hit by a stone in his stomach and taken away from his wife. She was struck in the mouth with a brick.

That policemen were willing to humiliate and abuse colored people clearly emerged from the testimony of John Hains, a longshoreman. Still in bed, he was awakened at two o'clock in the morning by six police officers who broke into his room. They asked him if he had a revolver. Hains said he did not, but he was not believed. They clubbed him and searched his house, but the only weapon they found was a broken toy revolver. They dragged him out of his house in his undershirt only. He begged them to be allowed to wear his trousers and shoes. They only sneered, and one officer said that he should consider himself lucky if he could get to the station house alive. The officer beating and abusing Hains charged him with firing a pistol through the window. Hains, brought in his undershirt before the magistrate, tried to explain he was asleep and did not fire any pistol, but the magistrate did not listen and sentenced him to the penitentiary for six months. He was released after ten days.

That the whole aim of the riot was catching, abusing, and humiliating colored people as a group was clear to two white witnesses, Paul Leitenberger and Alfred E. Borman. They heard a crowd yelling, "Give us a coon and we'll lynch him," while chasing a colored man, watched a Negro be pulled off a streetcar and beaten, and saw that the police made no efforts to disperse the crowds and actually ran along with the crowd. These two witnesses made up their minds about the rioters' aim. Later they talked to one of the leaders of the young gangsters: "He said he had been a leader in the riots and would do it again—that the 'niggers' must be treated the same as down South."[66]

Mayors of southern cities discussed how the New York riots differed from similar mob actions in the South. They established that whereas northern mobs directed their "vengeance" against the whole Negro race, southern mobs "punished" only "guilty" Negroes. A southern paper, by comparing the New York and the recent New Orleans riots, sarcastically remarked that in the South, "when a nigger goes a-niggering, he generally does the thing at first hand, in an original, niggerly way, while the Northerner nigger tries to emulate the Northern tough and is merely an imitator." The paper added that people in the South were having "lots of fun" with New York newspapers:

> The tall towers of the *World* and *Tribune* must have shaken their sides with glee as the surging, shrieking mass of blacks, pursued by the shooting Four Hundred in dress suits. . . . What a pity that Mr. Hearst was in Chicago! Happily, however, the Sun was there to shine and the Times to shed its sad moon-beams upon the scene. The HERALD, however, had much the best of it. Being situated uptown in the heart of the Beau Quartier, it was able to get snap shots at the leaders of the Eastern morality and fashion as they dashed out of adjacent clubs and hotels, each holding a gun in one hand and a nigger in the other.[67]

By giving such a grotesque image of the riots, the southern paper implied the end of the northern antebellum alliance between wealthy abolitionists and blacks. Now that southern blacks were moving north as free laborers and were "a-niggering," "those to whom the world looks for examples of piety and manners, whose lives are at best but a melancholy round of plenty and ennui," were not there "to help run down the fleeing blacks in their automobiles and otherwise to add to the gaiety of an affair that, perchance, may not happen again in a twelve-month!" The paper concluded its anti-North and anti-Republican attack by saying that what the New York papers did not understand was that "we . . . the progeny of the Anglo-Saxon and Scotch-Irish pioneers who settled the country, are the most homogeneous people on the face of the globe." By mocking New York's cosmopolitan intellectuals, the paper reestablished its own rhetoric of reconciliation:

> It is next to impossible—particularly after dinner—to tell the difference between the gentlemen who make merry with the world at one another at the Algonquin Club, in Boston, and the Palmetto Club, in Charleston. The poor provincial, who has never been either to Boston or Charleston, cannot realize the close kinship between the two; and the writers for the New York newspapers, being merely provincial literary men—untravelled except in Europe and untaught except out of text books—knowing least of all about America, however versed in the ways of London and Paris, Berlin and Vienna, naturally take a narrow and jaundiced, ill-conditioned view of American affairs.[68]

Ironically, this was one of the winning arguments made to reject New York's application to Congress to be chosen as the site of the Columbian Exposition of 1893.

A few days before the vitriolic attack by the southern paper, an editorial writer for the *New York Times* had firmly given a negative answer to the question whether the riot and the reaction to it were a sign of intensified racial friction in the city. According to the *Times,* there was no "settled race hatred" in the city: "There are no signs that the citizen of African descent is distrusted or disliked. . . . His crude melodies and childlike antics are more than tolerated in the music halls of the best class."[69] This self-inflicted tolerance—the price, one could say, the city had to pay for the sake of reconciliation—was not enough, however, to nurture a peaceful multiracial and multiethnic community in a period in which New York was becoming the first and final destination in the United States for thousands of southern and central European immigrants.

The riots of 1900 had a profound effect on black comedian Bert Williams. In an attempt to escape from what he thought was a hopeless situation, Williams tried to reduce his opportunities to face intolerance and discrimination. After the riots, Williams's public life and private life became separate. On stage, he presented himself "as another person" who could express a comic personality under the mask of blackface. In his private life, he removed himself emotionally from his black identity. In later years, Williams became more and more convinced "that each member of the race must take it upon himself to solve the Negro question." He came to believe that "the Negro is bound to get on top eventually, but it will be by pursuing a conservative policy."[70]

In 1905 Williams and his partner George Walker were the main entertainers at the annual meeting of the National Negro Business League held in New York. By that time, Williams had embraced the conservative racial policies of Booker T. Washington, and the Tuskegee leader thought highly of the comedian because he had not ever "heard him whine or cry about his color, or about racial discrimination."[71]

If the riots of 1900 taught Bert Williams the lesson of individual success and conservative policy, then for other black Americans who did not believe in the myth of a color-blind market but who did have high standards of intellectual and social achievement, events like the New York riots of 1900 or the Atlanta riot of 1906 meant that they had to embrace more radical politics. These tensions profoundly affected the black educated elite and the meaning of racial uplifting.

6

Myths of Economic Success

Rituals of Race Uplifting

> The myth of the Negro business is fed by the false notions and values
> that are current in the isolated social world of the Negro, a world domi-
> nated by the views and mental outlook of the black bourgeoisie.
>
> E. FRANKLIN FRAZIER

The Social Rituals of the African-American Middle Class

In 1901 W. E. B. Du Bois published a study on the African-American community in New York at the turn of the century. According to his findings, there were probably fewer than ten blacks owning more than $50,000 worth of property, and the total value of property held by blacks could be roughly estimated at between three and four million dollars.[1] Yet, the fact that a small group of relatively wealthy blacks did exist affected the whole community. This small group of self-made people were there to show to other African Americans that it was possible for black individuals to succeed in American society if they believed in its values and behaved accordingly. Furthermore, the presence of a small wealthy black aristocracy and a growing number of nouveaux riches became a strong point of reference for the black middle class, who could dream about imitating their success. In order to do so, it was necessary to develop a strong class consciousness and a lifestyle based on an effective differentiation between the lower and upper classes of the black community. Unlike in the antebellum period, "uplifting the race" became less of a moral goal and more a material one. In a period of rapid social change, blacks, as well as other marginal groups, picked up material symbols of social status and shaped their lives around these symbols. Yet, public behavior was still considered the source of respectability. Nevertheless, both concepts of "public" and "respectability" came to have different meanings for different groups of the African-American community.

In examining the New York African-American press from the 1870s to the early 1900s, one is struck by the mushrooming of social activities whose goals were more secular than in the period preceding the Civil War. What appears is an ongoing process of cultural remaking of a distinctive New York African-American community in which economic and political goals are redefined, however, within the changes of the general American society.[2] Furthermore, what could be called the secularization of the African-American press paralleled a class and gender redefinition of public behavior. The rituals of respectable social gatherings of associations, clubs, and Masonic lodges advertised in the African-American press showed the existence of a class differentiation and a marked gender difference within the black community.

In the first half of the 1880s, the *New York Globe* published the announcements of many celebrations of Masonic lodges. From this source one learns about the extraordinary capacity Masonic parades had to attract crowds for their ostentatious display of exotic masquerades. For example, in 1883 the Terry Lodge held its anniversary celebration with a "grand march of the Patriarchs" preceded by a festive gathering at Wendell's Assembly Rooms, on West Forty-fourth Street, where eight hundred people participated. The representatives of the *Globe* found "a bewildering phantasmagoria of feminine beauty and grace, and masculine gallantry," with strains of sweet music that "assailed the ear intoxicatingly," American flags "in endless profusion," and wine that "flowed like water."

A few weeks later the paper gave a description of a festival of the Edmonia Social Club, held at Tammany Hall, which demonstrated the widespread popularity of this association, as nearly one thousand people attended. There was a "Kaleidoscopic procession" under the leadership of the president of the club, who escorted his "fair lady." The attires of the ladies, in silks and satins ornamented with diamonds and precious stones, were "rich and rare and would have done credit to the Parisian King of fashion." Everyone was happy, according to the reporter, and the scene was "one of beauty and splendor." Among the many familiar faces who apparently never missed a reception were young ladies under parental care, society men "who stand above par in our social world," club men, sporting men, and "lovers of a good time in general." During the same period the Hamilton Lodge also held a masquerade reception with two grand parades. This lodge was the most conspicuous in grandiosity and exoticism. In fact, when the carriages arrived at Wendell's Hall "bearing with them masked visages that excited the admiration and wonderment of the onlookers at the door for their diversified character, no two being alike," it was clear that it was going to be "one of the best masked balls ever given in this city." And when the procession took place, it brought to mind the recent Mardi Gras festival at New Orleans. The following year the festival overshadowed "any and all attempts in this particular direction ever made by any organized body among us," the *Globe* reported. The presence of eighteen hundred people in the ballroom reminded one "of some Eastern tale or almost forgotten dream of the Arabian Night": "Silks, satin, jewels, spangles, glittered and glistened at every turn; long dresses and short dresses, Indians, counts, cavaliers, judges, priests, devils, queens, witches mingled in graceful confusion. Friars hobnobbed with goblins; cowboys were on familiar terms with the meekest of Quakers; queens smiled complacently upon peasant girls; Irishmen and English lords felt glad of each other's company; his Satanic majesty led an angel in the waltz."[3]

These carnivalesque scenes, far from being examples of saturnalia, symbolized the prestige and high social status of the participants. When placed within the universe of a segregated group, those scenes of "world turned upside-down" and status reversal, which those masked balls seemed to show, became a symbolic appropriation of themes of European high culture and folklore. At the same time, the carnivalesque themes of plentiness and excess ruling these festivals celebrated the recent gain of material wealth for a small number of blacks, who could feel part of the American myth of the "self-made man" that Booker T. Washington, with a different style, later represented.

In 1883, a few days before the Hamilton Lodge festival, a meeting of the Bethel Literary and Historical Society was held at the Bethel Church to discuss a subject that seemed to anticipate the Washington–Du Bois controversy: "Resolved, We Need Wealth More Than We Do Education." According to the *Globe*, both sides of the subject were so well argued that the president concluded that wealth and education "went hand in hand" and that "our people should strive to acquire both."[4] This thin evidence reveals that different concerns existed within the New York black community. There were those who gave emphasis to economic and educational improvement, and those who gave priority to the acquisition of material wealth over the battle for civil rights. At the turn of the century, these issues became extremely complicated because of the cultural fracture that the coming of European immigrants and southern blacks caused in the process of remaking the New York African-American community.

Scholarship on northern black communities in early twentieth-century cities has shown that the changing class structure of the urban North was related to the new pattern in race relations fostered in a re-unified country, a turning inward of black communities as the hopes of the Civil War generation had faded away, and the increasing flow of southern black migrants to cities. The inwardness of urban black communities at the turn of the century was the outcome of a race consciousness that white racism nurtured. Concern with color became a force of race solidarity.[5]

The center of these communities was still the church, although its influence in the North was less than in the South. Churchgoing was a class matter among African Americans. In New York, the older families of free blacks, who constituted the community's aristocracy and who could boast an "unspotted family life for two centuries," gathered at St. Philip's Episcopal Church, on Twenty-fifth Street. The mass of middle-class blacks, whose parents were New Yorkers, worshiped at Mother Zion, at Tenth and Bleecker Streets. The newer immigrants from Georgia and Virginia went to the large Mount Olive Baptist Church on West Fifty-third Street or to the Union Baptist Church, which had a Virginian pastor and congregation, educational facilities for children, weekly socials, fairs like those in Virginia, and big revivals during the first two months of every year in which up to a hundred converts were made.[6] By 1910 many churches had followed their congregations and moved from the Tenderloin district to Harlem after selling their property for fortunes. In 1909 the St. Philip's Episcopal Church sold its property on West 55th Street for $140,000 and built a new building in Gothic style on West 134th Street. The same church was also able to purchase apartment buildings for $640,000. A few years later an African Methodist Episcopal congregation, following this example, purchased in the area the Church of the Redeemer and renamed it Mother Zion. The Abyssinian Baptist Church sold its property for a fortune and moved to Harlem, as did several other old black churches.[7]

In the 1880s African-American churches tried to reestablish the primacy of spiritual values in their communities over the mounting materialistic culture of economic success that was growing in America. In 1883 a minister of New York's Bethel Church said during a Sunday sermon: "A gentleman is born, not manufactured; he is the noblest work of God. Neatly fitting garments, flashy jewelry, and lofty carriage cannot make a gentleman: his nature must be instinct with the elements of an honest manhood. So with women, they too are born. Rustling silks, sparkling diamonds, assumed modesty—these cannot make a lady."[8]

The African-American press, in commenting on these issues, still spoke the nineteenth-century moral language of "uplifting the race" and respectability. It was observed that blacks put too much stress upon the amount and quality of clothes and looked too much at the appearance and not enough at the character of a person. It was complained that respectability was frequently "victimized" by men and women who composed the "flashy" and "impudent" element of the black community. According to one editor, "this element, unfortunately, is a large one, and does us more solid injury than any other agency of evil." This group was described as "loud" in dress and "loud" in speech. On the streetcars, in the streets, or in the drawing room, "their vulgarity mortifies quiet colored people and scandalizes the race."

Public behavior was still a crucial element of class differentiation among African Americans. There was a general agreement that "in every community the colored man is on trial for good behavior, and the heavy hand of uncharitable criticism falls upon him from all sides." It was also observed that both poverty and wealth were "contagious" and affected all races alike. Poverty bred "viciousness and mendacity in all classes it attacks," whereas wealth tended "to refine the disposition and energize the mental faculties of its possessor." Unfortunately blacks had the disadvantage of sharing poverty with the other races but not wealth, although the number of blacks who were becoming moderately rich was increasing.[9]

By the 1920s class lines of the black urban community followed those of the white class structure, but it is rather difficult to define these lines in the 1890s. According to occupational criteria, class structure of northern urban black communities at the turn of the century was dominated by domestics and service workers. At the top was a small, well-educated, economically independent, and experienced elite, while at the very bottom there was an even smaller group of black outcasts. The largest part of the social structure—eighty to ninety percent—was made up of people in the middle. Students have named these people the "respectables" and have given various meanings to this value-laden term.[10] "Respectability" has been defined as the tacit acknowledgment that a person was doing the best that could be done under all sorts of social and individual difficulties. To the majority of the community it meant the mere earning of a living in an acceptable and rather steady manner, and with an appropriate lifestyle and public behavior.[11]

According to Willard Gatewood, the social behavior of the "aristocrats of color" toward those who were socially inferior was distant and

exclusive. Old and well-established black families perceived the social
pretensions of ambitious middle-class blacks as the triumph of vulgarity
and the public behavior of the lower classes as a major source of racial
prejudice. To black aristocrats, respectability meant refinement, education, culture, cleverness, and belonging to exclusive circles of people.
They valued marital stability, good manners, and conservative tastes,
and they despised black dialect and any "vulgar" display of wealth, over-
dressing, and craving for amusements. Thus, respectability meant the
possession of moral character and virtue, and the black aristocrats expressed a need to present themselves as a different group of people in
opposition to racial beliefs that made all black people alike.

After the Civil War, the "mulatto elite" was composed of old families
tied by blood and culture to the white social world, and this elite func-
tioned as the carrier of white high culture into the black community.[12]
Occupying a "distinct world of their own," black aristocrats would never
parade on Fifth Avenue or try to get into popular theaters. Since they
were unwelcome in New York's best restaurants, such as Delmonico's,
they spent their money organizing tasteful entertainments at their own
places. Although their social life was home-centered, belonging to socially exclusive and sexually segregated clubs was a mark of their distance from other blacks in terms of lifestyle, emphasis on education,
pride in family heritage and traditions, and adherence to a rigid moral
code. Some "aristocrats of color" alternated a view of "uplifting" the
lower classes with one of distancing themselves from the "vulgar
masses." Others pointed out that any attempt to distance themselves
from the black masses was bound to fail because the race could "be
saved [only] through the salvation of the masses." They held that the el-
evation of the masses was the responsibility of those who had experience
and education. They were aware that placing a distance between themselves and the lower classes would create a strong resentment among
the latter. As a New York black citizen complained, the black aristocracy
seemed to be "more hurtful than helpful, because it stands with frown-
ing face and open sneers at the threshold and sends shivers down the
spine of the working middle class." Besides ridiculing the lower classes'
lack of social etiquette, the aristocrats of color also made them feel "that
labor, except of a certain sort," was a "badge of shame."[13]

All this supports Kevin Gaines's argument on the limits of racial uplift ideology as a force against white prejudice. If E. Franklin Frazier's
analysis overemphasized the black bourgeoisie's materialism and status
symbols by reducing them to a mere mimicking of white behavior, then
Gaines's reasoning gives a broader meaning to the values of self-help,
racial solidarity, temperance, thrift, chastity, social purity, patriarchal au-

thority, and the pursuit of wealth constituting the ideology of racial up-lifting. These values cannot be seen simply as the expression of the ed-ucated blacks' will to be white, for they also reveal a deep search for a positive black identity. In a pervasively racist society there was nothing wrong with African Americans' desire for human dignity, economic se-curity, and social mobility. The problem was, as Gaines puts it, "the con-struction of class differences through racial and cultural hierarchies," and the fact that black elites "believed they were replacing the racist no-tion of fixed biological racial differences with an evolutionary view of cultural assimilation," and that "uplift ideology's argument for black hu-manity was not an argument for equality."[14]

In the 1880s New York's African-American press reported on many meetings of exclusive clubs of black gentlemen, such as the Lyric Swan Club. The editor of the *Globe* was invited to a reception given by this club, at which he congratulated its members that "everything bears the impress of taste, culture, and refinement." A select school of music at-tached to the club used music arranged and written expressly for them. The editor observed that it was a club with a proud membership, for he was told that it was "almost impossible for any one to become a member of it." There were handsome pictures on the walls, piles of valuable and instructive books on the tables, and fine classical music, showing that "the man who gains admission to the club must possess good traits of character, a fair education, and a taste for the beautiful; and above all, he must be a favorite of the entire club, for it is whom the club wants and not who wants to enter it."[15]

The Society of the Sons of New York was perhaps the most exclusive club in the metropolis. Becoming a member was the ambition of every respectable black man in the city. Started in the 1880s by a few wealthy black New Yorkers, by 1892 the society was recognized as "the most wor-thy association of colored people in the State of New York, or, it might be said, in the United States." Snobbery was not recognized as a sign of distinction by this organization, but before a man could become one of its members he must have given evidence of being "a respectable mem-ber of society and a citizen in good standing in the United States." Orig-inally, when the society was organized in June 1884, its main goal was the promotion of "social intercourse among the influential colored ele-ment of the city," and birth in the state of New York was one of the req-uisites for membership. In 1890 an amendment was added that pro-vided for associate members whose native state was not New York, giving them all privileges of the regular members except the vote. In the re-vised constitution of the society, its social and philanthropic objectives were clearly stated. The society provided for the burial of its deceased members, and it drew together, made known to each other, and united "in closer fraternal and business relations" the sons of the Empire State, whose motto was "Excelsior": "the wonder of the world, the pride of the continent, the heart from whose pulsation throbs through many arteries the great financial and commercial enterprise of this vast confederation of States." When the Sons of New York reached three hundred members, the association decided to purchase a comfortable clubhouse. However, the committee appointed for this purpose met with the sneers and insulting language of many white property owners who bluntly informed them that "as they were colored they could not transact business with them."[16] The committee finally succeeded in buying a three-story stone facade house on West Fifty-third Street from a Scottish man for $20,000. The building was refurbished in the fashion of the best all-male clubhouses of the city, such as the Union League Club, to contain the following: dining room, kitchen, and the steward's apartments in the basement; reception rooms, library, and reading and writing rooms on the first floor; buffet, billiard, and card rooms on the second floor; and one large lecture hall on the third floor that could comfortably hold 250 people.

This episode in the life of this exclusive club clearly shows that racial prejudice affected all blacks, in spite of their social status. It is therefore rather understandable that aristocrats of color were the most acutely sensitive to racial discrimination. However, at the turn of the century, their responses to the growing racial prejudice were by no means identical. Some, like the Sons of New York, isolated themselves in their own safe world of their peers, whereas others became the vanguard of civil rights movements.[17]

Those who responded to white racism by isolating themselves in their socially exclusive world usually made black southern immigrants the scapegoats of their frustrations. The African-American press partially helped foster nativistic feelings. In 1883 the *New York Globe* denounced the "swaggering, bumptious" southern black for bringing discredit to the race.[18] Several African-American spokespersons attributed the increase in black criminality and antisocial behavior to the southern newcomer. In 1889 at a meeting of colored people at Cooper Union, the audience responded with "great applause" to a southern black clergyman's speech that criticized those undesirable individuals migrating North: "You don't even see the representative negro in New York. We get the nigger up here with a cigar in his mouth, with a gold-headed cane and a high silk hat, and it's doubtful if he's got enough money in his pocket to pay his room rent."[19]

In 1900 Booker T. Washington's friend T. Thomas Fortune, the editor of the *New York Age,* went so far as to argue that the many southern residents of New York City represented a threat to law and order. In 1891 the *Age* had counseled southern blacks to "shun" New York City unless they had "plenty of money or a position secured before coming here." In 1907 the same paper saw only the "loud of mouth, flashy of clothes, obtrusive and uppish southern negro" streaming into the city. Many Negroes who went to New York from the South were "undesirable persons" as well as "criminally inclined" before they left the South, wrote the *Age.* By their disorderly behavior, the "few undesirables" brought down upon the entire black community the contempt of the whites. The editors of the *Age* were also hostile to southern and eastern European immigrants whose odd languages, alien ideas, and strange customs were perceived as a threat to American democracy. In the 1900s, the paper wrote, the "Puritan civilization of New England and the cavalier civilization of the South, which laid the foundations of the Republic . . . are being replaced by a new citizenship," which was giving up the tradition of the Christian Sabbath "for that of European license and the clamor for innovation of all sorts in the character and administration of the Government."[20]

The fact that after the draft riots of 1863 the most affluent blacks had left Manhattan and settled in Brooklyn led to the development of a rivalry between what became known as the "Manhattan set" and the "Brooklyn set."[21] This rivalry was easily recognizable by James Weldon Johnson, musician, poet, novelist, and future leader of the NAACP. In his experience, whereas the active social life of Manhattan's black elite offered a variety of public events like concerts, dances, and picnics attended by anyone who could afford the price of admission, the most highly cultivated blacks went to Brooklyn, where a "real society among colored people" did exist, and its social intercourse was confined "more or less to the people one knows or knows about." Their exclusive entertainments were "largely a private matter," resembling the social gatherings Johnson had attended among the black elite of Jacksonville after he graduated from Atlanta University in 1894. The fact that he belonged to Jacksonville's black upper class made him easily accepted in the Brooklyn best set.[22]

At the turn of the century, the black elite did not have a monolithic position on racial politics. Around 1900 there were many complaints that Booker T. Washington's ideology of racial solidarity, self-help, and group economy that shaped black business did not receive sufficient support from the black elite. It could be argued that the black middle and lower classes were more inclined to the philosophy of race enterprise than were professional people. There is evidence that in the North there was a correlation between membership in the older upper class and opposition to Washington. Between 1890 and 1920, particularly in those cities where immigration from the South was substantial, the forces of racial segregation and discrimination indirectly helped create a new black bourgeoisie of business and professional men who depended on black masses for their existence. This group was gradually assuming upper-class status and either merged with or replaced in status the older upper class, whose leading members were often business and professional men serving the white community. Having placed their economic roots among the newly urbanized blacks, the self-made men of the new black bourgeoisie found the philosophy of self-help and racial solidarity of Washington a perfect expression of their experience and interests. The first platform of the National Negro Business League, whose early meetings are discussed later in this chapter, expressed the point of view of this group. However, the lifestyle of these nouveaux riches, who made an ostentatious public display of their newly acquired wealth, often met the disapproval of the old upper class. Many aristocrats of color easily identified with W. E. B. Du Bois's "Talented Tenth" and with the black leader himself in terms of his Harvard education and elitist leadership and agreed with him on the necessity of observing class distinctions. As elitist Du Bois put it, "a rising race must be aristocratic; the good cannot consort with the bad—not even the best with the less good." Generally, black aristocrats were neither traitors to their race nor mere imitators of middle-class whites; they can be seen as culturally and often racially composite people who were capable of blending black culture with the white high culture they knew and praised.[23]

In 1895, the year of Booker T. Washington's Atlanta speech, the *New York Times* published a report entitled "Wealthy Negro Citizens," which examined blacks in New York and Brooklyn who were "prominent in many walks of life." Giving a good example of the white perception of the "progress of the race" according to the liberal values of American individualism, the paper addressed those who still imagined that the black population of the city was composed of "peddlers, whitewashers, and bootblacks" and invited them to observe "the real progress which the race has made in New York, as indicated by the prosperity of its representative men and women." A certain number of black men and a few black women owned and occupied brownstone dwellings in fashionable neighborhoods, employed white servants, and rode in their own carriages "behind horses driven by liveried coachmen."

In the words of one "representative man," the Negro race was "still progressing, in spite of most discouraging obstacles. . . . it is anxious to make its own way in the world." This representative man said that young black men wanted a chance to learn a business; trades were closed to them and unions were against them. Because of existing prejudice, they could not obtain situations or apprenticeships at the ordinary trades; consequently, instead of becoming trained carpenters and mechanics at the best age to learn such trades, they were shut out and had to take menial occupations to make their living. In this way, "the growth and development of the entire race is retarded."[24]

Most wealthy blacks lived in Brooklyn, where they could find more economical and satisfactory investments for their fortunes. William H. Smith, for example, who held a responsible position in the Bank of the State of New York, was said to be worth $100,000; he occupied a handsome house on Brooklyn's Lafayette Avenue and had several servants. Mrs. Daniel Brooks was a widow who was counted among the wealthiest women of the Eastern district of Brooklyn; she lived in a beautifully furnished house and had white servants. Theodore Vandeveer, one of the leading tailors in the city, employed many workers, most of whom were white, and owned property on the upper west side of the city. Mr. Peter Freeman controlled a large carpet-cleaning establishment that employed white men. A druggist on Sixth Avenue and Twenty-eighth Street, Dr. John W. Thompson, was a wealthy black man who had been minister to Haiti during Grover Cleveland's first administration. The Reverend Daniel W. Wisher was the pastor of Mount Olive Baptist Church, on West Fifty-third Street; he lived in Jersey City, owned several valuable houses in Harlem, had a large family, and employed a number of Swedish servants; his carriages and livery were among "the most stylish" in Jersey City. In selecting servants, wealthy blacks preferred Swedes and Poles, although some hired southern blacks; they thought Swedish and Polish women were "more tractable" than others.

Flushing, Long Island, also had a number of black elite families among its residents: the Reverend Dr. Derrick, secretary of the Mission Board of the African Methodist Episcopal Church, lived in Flushing, where he owned several houses; Ella Day Spencer, an art teacher at Cooper Union, was a black woman living in that neighborhood. On De Kalb Avenue, one of the most fashionable quarters of Brooklyn at that time, lived Dr. Susan McKinney, the first black woman to graduate from the Long Island College Hospital. Charles H. Lansing held a responsible position in the Brooklyn Department of City Works and was the owner of considerable real estate on West Tenth and Bleecker Streets in Manhattan. It was also reported that many black women who acquired property had earned their money as trained nurses and dressmakers; others had inherited their money.

Many prominent African Americans felt it was humiliating "to be regarded as a curiosity." They felt that colored people were an enigma to most white people, who could not understand that "a colored person is endowed with the same human nature as themselves," and who imagined that "anything is good enough for a negro." The point these elite blacks made was that "all negroes are not alike. There are various grades of colored people, just as there are various grades of white people." It was observed that "the lowest grades of whites and blacks are about on a par," and "no respectable negro would want to associate with either."

The *Times* also reported cases of black businessmen who employed only black workers in their firms. There was an office building in downtown Manhattan run by a crew of black men. James R. Braxton was the janitor, and all the elevator men and porters were black; the engineering departments were likewise run by black men. Another case was that of chief engineer Thomas W. Bohannah, who had studied engineering in Virginia before moving to New York, where he became an expert electrician; he was connected with the Edison General Electric Company and was in charge of the first isolated electric plant started by that company. That plant was one of the largest in any of the office buildings in the city, and Mr. Bohannah was proud that he did not require the assistance of white men to run it.[25] It was successful self-made black businesspeople like these who inspired Booker T. Washington in the organization of the National Negro Business League in 1900.

The Early Meetings of the National Negro Business League

The National Negro Business League was one of Booker T. Washington's most interesting attempts to bring together "the leading and most successful colored men and women throughout the country who are engaged in business," as he declared at the founding meeting in Boston on 23 August 1900. The white press reacted enthusiastically. The *Boston Transcript*, by the pen of Henry J. Barrymore, reported that the meeting was a great event "that answers race antipathy with commercial success." The almighty dollar was "thoroughly color blind," the reporter wrote in harmony with Washington's principles, and the Negro businessman was finally getting "the public notice he so genuinely deserves." The reporter confessed he went to that meeting at Parker Memorial "with ill-stifled chuckles of expectant amusement." As soon as he entered, however, he was impressed by "the gravity of the colored audience, and something wonderfully earnest about the big banner at the back of the stage." He also confessed that he was looking for "the tall silk hat and the flashy suit of clothes" but could not see them among the delegates. "The silly, uneducated, shiftless Negro puts his pay on his back; the business Negro puts his pay in the bank," the reporter observed. He found himself among people who had penetrated "the real secret of success," men who had clear in their mind that the only sure basis of progress was economic, "men who would sacrifice to-day's indulgence for to-morrow's independence, men who cared so much for social and educational advancement that they had come to despise the puerile strut and brag of the Negro dandy." The reporter felt these men were right in expecting that the word "Negro" should be written with a capital N. The reporter had thought that he could classify Negroes by types—"the cake-walk Negro," "the old-Confederate-colonel Negro," and "the well-to-do-merchant Negro." However, he could not recognize the "round-faced, shavey-headed, black as a coal scuttle, clad in rainbow-tinted cheap finery" Negro dandy among the delegates, nor the "gray mustache and imperial, gold-bowed spectacles and sombre dress" of the old respectable Negro from the South. Even the merchant Negro was hard to recognize because some delegates had whiter skin than the reporter's. Not only was it difficult to tell who was white and who was "colored," but even the idioms of the delegates and their perfect grammar and pronunciation did not sound to the reporter's ear like Negro slang at all.[26]

The National Negro Business League (NNBL) held annual meetings in Chicago (1901), Richmond, Virginia (1902), Nashville (1903), Indianapolis (1904), New York City (1905), and Atlanta (1906). Several of those eminent and socially concerned white intellectuals who in 1909 organized the first National Negro Conference, which led to the formation of the NAACP, participated at the NNBL annual meeting in New York in 1905. It was the league's largest convention thus far; around forty different kinds of Negro business were represented, and the entire press of New York sent reporters to give extensive coverage. The annual address of the president of the NNBL, Booker T. Washington, appeared in almost every important paper of the country. After his keynote speech, the stage was taken by prominent New Yorkers, including William Lloyd Garrison's grandson Oswald Garrison Villard, who was the editor of the *New York Evening Post,* and industrialist John Millholland, two key figures in the founding of the NAACP. A relevant feature of the NNBL's New York meeting was the presence of the popular black comedians George Walker and Bert Williams, who performed selections from their repertoire entitled "Comrades in Arms" and "Nobody." President Theodore Roosevelt sent a congratulatory message in which he wished success to the NNBL, an organization he defined as "absolutely out of politics," although most people knew how Booker T. Washington was politically dependent on the Republican leader and still remembered the two men lunching together at the White House in 1901. Roosevelt praised the NNBL for stimulating the business mentality among black people and for increasing their efficiency in the industrial world. "It is as true of a race as of an individual," Roosevelt continued, "that while outsiders can help to a certain degree, yet the real help must come in the shape of self-help."[27]

Abolitionist descendant Oswald Garrison Villard walked to the podium amid a "thundering applause" to read a lengthy paper on the problem of colored servants. His approach seemed to be influenced by his southern wife, for he framed the problem around the good and fond memories wealthy southerners he knew had of their Negro mammies. Villard told the audience his experience as the guest of a millionaire southern banker who sincerely thought that "the Negro never could or never ought to be anything else than a servant or a laborer." But with tears in his eyes, Villard's host remembered "the wonderful tact and ability and skill of his old Negro mammy who had nursed or served five generations of his family before dying near the century mark." When she died, "he and his children and grand-children wept over her as over a member of his own exclusive family" and struggled to have her buried in the best white-only cemetery in town. The editor of the *Evening Post* and future founder of the NAACP believed that the colored race had the duty to produce "thousands of mammies like this." Because he thought such a servant was the best intermediary between the races, he felt that if "a well-trained and respectful colored servant" like that would be put in every southern home, "the relation of the races would change overnight." Of course, Garrison's grandson did not think that colored people should be made perfect servants only. With training, they could get broader opportunities as hotel keepers, he thought. Could the daughters of those famous mammies become "the innkeepers of America"? Villard wondered. They needed to be properly trained in the skills of cooking and housework in technical schools. The North had the same problem. It was extremely hard for people like himself to find good servants in those days. Negroes in the cities preferred to live "in their dilapidated Negro quarters until driven to work by necessity." They were "dirty, slovenly, often impudent, habitually lazy and dishonest and unwilling to work steadily," Garrison's grandson complained. The Irish, the Germans, the Swedes, and other foreign immigrants had monopolized domestic service in the North. Yet since eighty percent of colored women, and a high percentage of men, were presently engaged in household service of one kind or another, Villard urged his audience of colored businesspeople to convince their race "to see in this service one of its greatest opportunities of the present time."

Colored women needed that training for their own families as well, he argued. Everybody knew that nothing could lower family life more quickly than to have "the home-mother a shiftless slattern, too ignorant to place well cooked food on the table and too spend-thrift to make every dollar of the house-hold count."[28]

Justice of the Peace Robert H. Terrell, Mary Church Terrell's husband, found Villard's address absolutely "splendid." Having a direct experience with the "servant problem," Terrell agreed with Villard's points. The judge told the audience the story of his own uplifting: he started as a hotel boy, struggled for his own education, and became a headwaiter, but he had serious problems in dealing with the waiters under his care because they did not do their job well. He was therefore a perfect example of a colored self-made man, who started from the bottom, struggled hard, did every menial job he took at his best, got his own education, and eventually became a justice (thanks to Booker T. Washington's political power). Even T. Thomas Fortune, the editor of the *New York Age* and the chair of the Executive Committee of the NNBL, discussed the problem of "how can we get good servants," but he felt that the term "house people" was more suitable than the word "servants." He raised the issue, which other delegates discussed, that "black folks don't want to work for black folks in the domestic service." Thus, those Negroes in New York who could afford to hire housepeople had to rely on the Irish, Germans, and Swedes. Fortune concluded that domestic occupations "are valuable to us," and that the establishment of domestic science schools, operating in all large cities, should be pursued for "lifting up the masses of our race from their present condition to industrial independence."[29]

President Booker T. Washington's annual address was filled with his usual self-help philosophy: "We can do more in a day to advance our cause than legislation can do in a year. More and more we must turn our faces toward the rising sun of constructive, creative and progressive effort and away from the setting sun of whining and complaining." He urged his people not to blame other people for their lack of decent homes or work and to turn instead "to the policy of going to the fundamental sources of all occupations; that is, create out of the soil, out of wood, mineral, water, the products the world wants." This policy, in Washington's view, "will make us creators of jobs and not mere seekers after jobs." Progress in business and commerce, he recommended, should be mainly in the South, because "the ten million members of our race, the great masses are in the South, and there, in my opinion, they will remain."[30]

Washington felt very optimistic about his racial strategy when he decided to hold the seventh annual meeting of the NNBL in Atlanta in August 1906. The place decided, he wrote to the general manager who controlled the railroad terminal, a white friend of his, to see if something could be done during the days of the NNBL meeting to modify "the rule now existing in the new depot which requires colored people to enter and leave the depot at a side door." Washington told the manager that many colored businesspeople would come from northern states where public transportation was integrated, and they could find it difficult to adjust to Atlanta's segregation rules. The terminal general manager refused to make any change. To him, "White Entrance" and "Negro Entrance" were perfectly clear signs that even a northerner could understand. Unwillingness to suspend the "separate but equal" social rule, even for a few days, did not affect the conference's opening rituals enhancing progress in racial cooperation. The mayor welcomed the delegates on behalf of the city of Atlanta, and the president of the Chamber of Commerce brought his greetings. Mayor J. C. Harwell, a businessman himself, said that "busy men don't commit crimes," followed by a great applause, for "they haven't got time for that." Crimes were committed by the idler, by the man "who wants no business." Samuel D. Jones, the president of the Chamber of Commerce, cheerfully addressed the delegates and reminded them that "there are more people of your race in our state, than in any other same-sized piece of territory on the face of earth outside of Africa." They all laughed and applauded.[31]

At the evening session of 29 August, Booker T. Washington gave his enthusiastic presidential address. He declared that it was good that the NNBL held its annual meeting in the heart of the South, "where the great body of our people live and where their salvation is to be worked out." He reminded the audience, interrupted by its hearty applause, that the policy of the organization was "to hold up before the race its advantages rather than its disadvantages . . . its successes rather than its failures . . . to call the attention of the world to the efforts of our friends rather than to those of our enemies." The world might pity a crying, whining race, Washington said, but it would show no respect. The NNBL, "while not overlooking or justifying injustice or wrong or failing to recognize the value of other methods seeking to reach the same ends, feels that the race can make progress and secure the greatest protection by its efforts in progressive, constructive directions, by constantly presenting to the world tangible and visible evidences of our worth as a race." He strongly believed "that the influence of one great success, in really accomplishing something that the world respects, will go furthest in promoting our interests." He knew of no other section of the country where his people were making more progress and where the future was so full of promise than in the South.

There was a duty, however, that the leaders of the race had to accomplish—that is, getting rid of the criminal Negro whenever possible. "I have no hesitation in saying," Washington gravely continued, "that one of the elements in our present situation that gives me most concern is the large number of crimes that are being committed by members of our race." He emphasized, however, that the crime of lynching should be condemned. Followed by a long and continued applause, Washington's words turned into an explicit condemnation of the lynching mob and its supporters: "Our Southland today has no greater enemy to business progress than lynchers, and those who provoke lynching." For Washington, the real issue was lawlessness: "every man, white or black, who takes the law into his hands to lynch or burn or shoot human beings supposed to be, or guilty of crime is insulting the executive, judicial and law-making bodies of the state in which he resides." He devoted the last part of his speech to the Negro criminal classes—namely, "the loafers, the drunkards and gamblers, men for the main part without a permanent employment, who own no homes, who have no bank account, who glide from one community to another without interest in any one spot." The efforts of the members of organizations like the NNBL and of the black religious leaders had to be directed toward getting hold "of the floating class of our people and see to it that their lives are so changed as to make them cease to disgrace our race and disturb our civilization." He finally recommended the cultivation of "a spirit of racial pride" to learn to be as proud as the French, the German, the Japanese, or the Italian people were of their own "race." By giving to "race," "people," and "nation" an identical meaning, as many social scientists did, Washington concluded that "the race that has faith and pride in itself will eventually win the respect, the confidence and co-operation of the rest of the world."[32]

Although Washington had given the Atlanta newspapers copies of his annual address in advance and had personally spoken to all newspaper editors, his speech was badly misreported. The friendly *Atlanta Constitution* wrote that the keynote of Washington's address was that the worst enemies of the Negro race were those Negroes who committed crimes "which are followed by lynching," and that the South was the best place for those black people who were willing to work. There was no mention of Washington's words on injustice and his familiar theme that the race could make progress by constantly presenting to the world visible evidence of its worth, which was the real keynote of his speech. The *Constitution* did not acknowledge that in his speech black criminals and white lynchers were equally condemned. The atmosphere in the city that in 1895 celebrated Washington's "compromise" on racial coopera- tion had dramatically changed. As discussed in the last section of this chapter, a complex interaction of political alliances and mounting ne- grophobia exploded in a bloody riot on 22 September 1906.

How did the idea of "Negro business" emerging from the meetings of the NNBL relate to the social rituals of the black middle class and the tension between integration and segregation that those rituals ex- pressed? Booker T. Washington "stole" the idea of "Negro business" from W. E. B. Du Bois. In May 1899 the social science professor had dedicated the fourth Conference for the Study of the Negro Problems, held at Atlanta University, to "The Negro in Business." In explaining the results of his investigation on the type of colored people undertaking business ventures after emancipation, Du Bois elaborated a definition of the term "business man" itself, drawn from the census data of 1890. According to his study, the term included "all with stocks of goods to sell, and also all other persons who have at least $500 of capital in- vested." Although, for example, an ordinary barber was classified as an artisan, the owner of a barber shop worth $500 or more, with several hired assistants, was classified as "business man." In 1899, around five thousand colored people in the country could be included in that def- inition. Du Bois's study classified them by occupation and disaggregated census data concerning their activities in major cities all over the coun- try. Although physical emancipation came in 1863, "economic emanci- pation is still far off," Du Bois remarked, as the great majority of Ne- groes "are still serfs bound to the soil or house servants."

Du Bois's conference, in which 1,900 colored businesspeople partic- ipated, as "pioneers in a great movement," adopted resolutions that in large part were in agreement with the philosophy of the NNBL when it was founded the following year. One resolution concerned the necessity for Negroes to enter into business life in increasing numbers to over- come the existing unfortunate disproportion in the distribution of Ne- groes in various occupations, with Negroes heavily concentrated in do- mestic service, catering, and other services. It was argued that "the growth of a class of merchants among us would be a far-sighted measure of self-defense, and would make for wealth and mutual cooperation." Another resolution, the content of which Washington's NNBL would not have accepted, read that highly trained young people were needed for business undertakings, and a college preparation for a broad busi- ness life was therefore indispensable. Still another resolution rec- ommended that the mass of Negroes "must learn to patronize business enterprises conducted by their own race, even at some slight disadvantage." Cooperation was a requirement of success: "Ten million people who join in intelligent self-help can never be long ignored or mistreated." In order to stimulate cooperation, churches, schools, and newspapers were called on to stress the necessity of business careers to young people, and habits of saving and thrift needed to be encouraged so that the young would have capital at their disposal. Finally, it was recommended that the organization of a Negro Business Men's League take place in every town and hamlet and that a federal organization process occur at state and national levels.[33] This was precisely what Washington's NNBL became.

If their goals were so close, why did Washington not collaborate with Du Bois? The Atlanta University conference was not a "radical" meeting, with Allan D. Candler, the governor of Georgia and also the oldest member of the Coca-Cola clan, giving the opening address. The governor defined the recent Civil War as "one of the most unnecessary wars that ever devastated the face of earth," which resulted in the freeing of the colored race. The members of this race, "like the young child which has not long had an opportunity to be taught," had a new world opened to them, but they were like "a child that is transported in a day from the scenes of his birth to other scenes, entirely different, if you please, on another continent." With his friendly and patronizing metaphors, the governor told the Negro businessmen and academics in his audience that he was in "full sympathy" with them, and that he represented the ninety percent of the people of his race in Georgia. Booker T. Washington could have participated in and applauded that conference.

Yet, Washington's biographer Louis Harlan points out, and Du Bois's biographer David Lewis confirms, that the Tuskegee leader preferred to exploit Du Bois's idea on his own, at a stage in which the scholar's economic thinking was still within the boundaries of conventional laissez-faire philosophy. When in the summer of 1900 Washington called the first organizational meeting of the NNBL in Boston, Du Bois and his friends in several northern cities accused him of stealing the idea of the Negro Business League. Washington ignored this and insisted that this idea was the outcome of his traveling around the country, where he met many isolated black businessmen. He believed in these self-made people who, like himself, had emerged from slavery and had reached the status of middle class after Reconstruction. Du Bois's background was complex enough, but it did not include slavery. The scholar activist identified himself with the free people of color in antebellum New England, with those black abolitionists who never had physical contact with their slave brethren and yet felt affected by their plague. These free people of color generally praised education over money making.[34] By the end of the century, however, the values and style of the colored middle class profoundly changed. The old black elite in northern cities was visibly losing its superior position to a middle class in terms of job stability and income security due to the transformation of the urban social structure.

"A Litany of Atlanta"

In August 1906 Mary Ovington went back to Atlanta, where in 1905 she had met Du Bois at one of his Atlanta University conferences. This time the New York social worker went to the South as the correspondent for Villard's *Evening Post* to cover the annual meeting of the National Negro Business League. In her reminiscences, *Black and White Sat Down Together,* she remembered that Philip Payton, the New York real estate agent, was in the audience. "I went down the church aisle and talked with him, but, though we were in a colored church, I could see that I made him uneasy," Ovington wrote. Because of recurring episodes of lynching in Atlanta, she thought Payton was perhaps right in thinking that "my cordial greeting might endanger him."[35] In her reports for the *New York Evening Post,* Ovington wrote about the meetings of the NNBL but also gave her northern readers a taste of that pervasive negrophobia that within a few weeks would explode into the bloodiest race riot in the history of the symbolic capital of the New South; she showed the dark side of its bright external image of modernity and progressive future.

On the night of 22 September 1906, ten thousand white people, most of them under twenty, attacked every black person they met on the streets of Atlanta. White mobs pillaged the post office, the train station, and any white business where they felt there were black employees. They also violently removed colored passengers from the electric trolleys. The *Atlanta Constitution* reported that in some streets "the sidewalks ran red with the blood of dead and dying negroes." The immediate cause of the riot or, more correctly, the massacre, as Leon Litwack remarks, was rumors local newspapers spread of alleged assaults on white women by black men. The riot was also the result of an eighteen-month campaign for disfranchisement—as Georgia was the only southern state not to have legal restrictions on the Negro vote. The campaign for the gubernatorial race between negrophobe Hoke Smith, former interior secretary in the Cleveland administration and supported by populist Tom Watson, and the editor of the *Atlanta Constitution,* Clark Howell, who was backed by the state Democratic party, destroyed whatever had remained of the alliance between moderate forces backing Booker T. Washington's speech in 1895. For many months the *Atlanta News* filled its columns with sensational headlines of fabricated rapes and other crimes committed by blacks. Its circulation rose, and the paper went as far as offering a reward of $1,000 for every lynching of blacks and calling for the revival of the Ku Klux Klan.[36]

Accounts of the horrible days of "nigger rule" during Reconstruction were offered to readers too young to remember, and they could also see at a local theater a play based on Thomas Dixon's *The Clansman*, a negrophobic glorification of the old South and the KKK that in a few years would become D. W. Griffith's film *The Birth of a Nation*. An editorial in the *Atlanta Journal*, supporting Smith's campaign of disfranchisement, read: "Political equality being preached to the negro in the ring papers and on the stump, what wonder that he makes no distinction between political and social equality? He grows more bumptious on the street, more impudent in his dealings with white men, and then, when he cannot achieve social equality as he wishes, with the instinct of the barbarian to destroy what he cannot attain to, he lies in wait . . . and assaults the fair young girlhood of the south."[37]

Hoke Smith won the Democratic primary. This inflammatory atmosphere exploded during the night of 22 September 1906. On a street in the "vice district" of the city, a white man on a dry goods box, raising his hand with the latest edition of an Atlanta paper, screamed that a third assault by a black man on a white woman had occurred and that white men could no longer tolerate the insult. "Save our women!" "Kill the niggers!" was the answer of the crowd he gathered. The inflamed crowd turned into a mob and spread in nearby areas, assaulting any black person in its way. By eleven o'clock more than ten thousand white men, many with guns, were roaming the city looking for blacks. The police tried to block them off but had no success. The mob destroyed stores run by black people and assaulted, or sometimes killed, those unlucky black men or women who were inside. One black man was tortured to death, his fingers and toes cut off as souvenirs. The bodies of some black people were piled at the base of the statue of Henry Grady, the publisher of the *Atlanta Constitution*, as a symbolic gesture that no racial alliance would ever be possible. The Atlanta Compromise of 1895 ended with the riot of 1906. Around twenty-five black people and one white person were killed, and a large number were wounded.[38]

"It is impossible for one who has not been brought up among Southern conditions to stay in Atlanta and not be deeply impressed with the separation between the two peoples who make up its population, the white and the colored," New Yorker Mary Ovington had written a few weeks before the riot broke out. She was struck to see that on streetcars whites and blacks never sat side by side, that white and black children went to racially separated schools and never met in their leisure time, and that the only black persons white people knew where those they saw in domestic service. In her articles from Atlanta, Ovington also discussed the effects of Negro disfranchisement: more than forty percent of the city's population had no part in the framing of the city's laws or in the choice of its officials. The two peoples were separate but not equal, Ovington's report showed. She informed the readers of the *New York Evening Post* that the most explicit discrimination occurred in the public school system. In 1903 Atlanta's white children had two high schools, sixteen grammar and primary schools, and one night school. The only schools the city provided for colored children were five grammar and primary schools. Ovington also found the most open discrimination in the judiciary system. "In my visit to an Atlanta court," she reported, "the white man was always called a gentleman and the colored man a 'nigger.'" When a black man had a case against another black man, the verdict was usually impartial; "but if he is on trial on a charge made by a white man, his position is not enviable." Ovington also remarked on the absurdity of the discriminatory practices of the Atlanta Public Library, a splendid gift from Andrew Carnegie to the city. "It is not a public library," Ovington asserted, as only sixty percent of the city population— that is, its white part—was given access.[39]

W. E. B. Du Bois, the Atlanta University professor who, like all other blacks in town, could not use the "public" library, heard about the riot while he was in Alabama doing research for the U.S. Bureau of the Census. He rushed back to the city to protect his wife and daughter. In the segregated passenger car on the way to Atlanta, he wrote a prose poem, "A Litany of Atlanta":

> O Silent God. . . . Listen to us, Thy children: our faces dark with doubt, are made a mockery in Thy sanctuary. . . . Is this Thy justice, O Father, that guile be easier than innocence, and the innocent crucified for the guilt of the untouched guilty? . . . Is not the God of the fathers dead? . . . Thou are not dead, but flown afar. . . . Sit no longer blind, Lord God, deaf to our prayer and dumb to our dumb suffering. Surely Thou too art not white, O Lord, a pale, bloodless, heartless thing? . . . Forgive the thought! Forgive these wild, blasphemous words. Thou art still the God of our black fathers, and in Thy soul's soul sit some soft darkenings of the evening, some shadowings of the velvet night.[40]

By the time he reached his Atlanta home, Du Bois's "Litany" had turned into practical considerations on how to protect his family from a possible mob attack. Although he thought he could not imagine himself "killing a human being," he bought a "Winchester double-barred shotgun and two dozen rounds of shells filled with buckshot." He was ready to shoot any white who would come next to his front porch. Fortunately no one came.[41]

While Du Bois was mourning the riot with his poem, Booker T. Washington, in the aftermath of the riot, renewed his optimism about race relations in the New South. But Washington's compact, which he metaphorically signed in 1895 at the Atlanta Cotton Exposition, no longer held. The Tuskegee leader was in New York City at the time of the Atlanta outbreak. From the front page of the *New York Age* he begged that "the best white people and the best colored people come together in council and use their united efforts to stop the present disorder." He particularly urged colored people in Atlanta and elsewhere to abstain from making any fatal attempt at retaliating, to exercise self-control, and to rely on the efforts of "the proper authorities to bring order and security out of confusion." Washington kept saying that he always found "the leading colored people as much opposed to crime as the leading white people," and that he would do his best to guarantee their cooperation. He thought the Atlanta riot, far from discouraging colored people, "should teach a lesson from which all can profit." Without explaining what this lesson would be, he finally reminded readers that "while there is disorder in one community there is peace and harmony in thousands of others," and he expressed his personal feeling "of very deep grief" for the death of many innocent men "of both races because of the deeds of a few despicable criminals."[42] Washington did not mention Hoke Smith's disfranchisement campaign or the racial passions stirred by several reports of assaults on white women orchestrated by the *Atlanta News*.

"Dr. Washington hurries to succor his afflicted people," ran the headline in the *New York Age,* as it printed a letter from Washington to the editor of the weekly. Washington said he had left New York "on the fast Southern express for the scene of the atrocious riots." He reported his consultation with the leading people of the African-American community in Atlanta and praised their actions at a time that was the "most trying which our race has experienced in a good many years." Washington found that the "self-control, patience, courage and patriotic spirit exhibited by the people here have been almost beyond description." He felt optimistic: he had spent much time the night before and during the day "in getting the temper of both races and the facts." He could confidently say that those outbreaks would not occur in Atlanta again for a long time. Washington found it most encouraging that ten "of the strongest white men" were appointed during a mass meeting to meet in the afternoon with "a committee of twenty of the same class of colored men for a conference, where it is proposed to have a frank discussion of the situation, and to bring about harmonious relations and friendly co-operation for the future." He believed that all were "thoroughly in earnest and good will result," and that state and city authorities would end any disturbance "with an iron hand if need be."[43]

Following Washington's lead, the *Age* concluded that it was "white trash" that needed to be subdued by the Atlanta aristocrats, including in the trash the *Atlanta News* "for its diabolical work in inciting a race war." In a few days the Fulton County Grand Jury adopted a resolution establishing that "the creation of the spirit animating the mob" was largely influenced by the "sensational manner" with which the Atlanta newspapers had described recent criminal acts. The resolution expressed the most severe condemnation of the "editorial utterances of the *Atlanta News*," calculated to create "a disregard for the proper administration of the law, and to promote the organization of citizens to act outside of the law in the punishment of crime." According to the *Age* correspondent from Atlanta, it was the "white aristocracy" of the South, the descendants of former slaveholders, who came "to rescue the Afro-Americans from the murderous assaults of the poor white class." Atlanta was a "poor white trash" town. Although the aristocrats were in a great minority, their influence was powerful and effective in adopting successful measures "to crash back the maddened poor whites, who correspond to the Jew-baiters of Russia." The parallel came easily to the reporter, for the major newspapers at the time ran editorials on murders of Jews in Russia because of their "race." The *Age* unquestionably accepted that the African Americans' "best friends" among the white people of Atlanta were those "most prominent for wealth and position."[44]

This peculiar alliance seemed a southern version of the one between the aristocracy of the Union League Club and the African-American community in the aftermath of the New York riots of 1863. The Atlanta elite aroused public sentiment by pressing for the prosecution of guilty mob leaders and by opening public subscriptions for the families of the victims. "A woman of social distinction," the *Age* reporter wrote, "hearing that a family, formerly slaves of her father, were in danger, went bravely to their cottage and carried them off to safety." This was an acceptable revival of the old feudal spirit of slaveholding days, "when the lord of the plantation was both master and protector." Mrs. Warren Boyd, "one of Atlanta's most able and thoughtful white women," in an interview with the *New York World,* expressed her strong condemnation of the "mob spirit" and without hesitation declared that "riots are invariably originated and led by white men of the lowest class," whose "mark of supremacy is a white skin." The Atlanta City Council, besides appropriating a fund of $1,000 for the victims of the massacre, offered a $200 reward for the arrest and conviction of any person participating in the killing of African Americans on the streets on the day of the riot.[45]

The echoes of the Atlanta riot reached African-American communities in every part of the country. In Rochester, New York, on 3 October, at a mass meeting held at the city hall, an African American refugee from Atlanta, whose sister had been killed in his presence, gave a firsthand account of the massacre. Resolutions were adopted that congratulated the African American race in the North and South for the wonderful progress made since the Civil War; thanked God for having intelligent leaders like Booker T. Washington; and condemned Hoke Smith, the Democratic candidate for governor "who succeeded in getting that nomination by creating the bitterest race feeling against Afro-American citizens," and most of the Atlanta press for its advocacy of a revival of the Ku Klux Klan, Thomas Dixon's play *The Clansman,* and any form of crime.[46]

To those who could not separate black economic achievement from civil and political rights and social equality, the Atlanta riot confirmed that whatever success the men and women of the National Negro Business League might have, it would not make them American citizens. Ida Wells-Barnett's early socioeconomic analysis of lynching could have easily included the Atlanta race riot.

Race riots north and south were the dark side of national reconciliation. Yet the rhetoric of Progressive America enhanced its brightest sides with magnificent pageants of democracy celebrating an ethnically inclusive but racially exclusive country.

Pageants of American Racial Democracy

Rituals of Civil Society

Between 1909 and 1918, six events, representing "rituals of race" of different kinds, occurred in the theater of New York City's public culture: the Hudson-Fulton Festival (1909) that celebrated the tercentennial of Henry Hudson's voyage of discovery and the centennial of Robert Fulton's inauguration of steam navigation on the Hudson River; the staging of W. E. B. Du Bois's pageant of African-American history, *The Star of Ethiopia*, for the fiftieth anniversary of Emancipation (1913); the first public showing of D. W. Griffith's epic movie, *The Birth of a Nation* (1915); the staging of Percy MacKaye's masque, *Caliban of the Yellow Sands*, for the tercentennial commemoration of Shakespeare's birth (1916); the "Silent Parade" (1917) by which African-American New Yorkers responded to the massacre of black people in East St. Louis, Illinois; and the parade of the 367th Infantry, the colored "Buffalo soldiers," receiving the colors from the Union League Club "to fight for the cause of humanity" in World War I (1918).

These public events expressed different versions of the reconciliation theme of how to unify a multiethnic and multiracial country. By combining recreation, patriotism, and community pride, the magnificent Hudson-Fulton Festival celebrated historical knowledge as a source of tradition and, consequently, Americanization. Du Bois's pageant made the ambitious attempt to give history to the people of African descent and placed the African-American experience at the center of U.S. history, but Griffith's movie had the powerful and ambivalent appeal of mass culture conveying through a modern and urban medium the most conservative and racist values of the South. MacKaye's pageant of 1916 was a northern progressive celebration of democratic art inspired by the theory of stages of human civilization, whereas the African-American Silent Parade was a utopian response to racist crimes of that time. The colored soldiers' parade of the following year brought into public culture the spirit of the "warriors-entertainers," the singing 367th Infantry, by uniting African-American musical legends with the pervasive patriotism of "making the world safe for democracy."

The Hudson-Fulton Festival of 1909

From 25 September to 11 October 1909, the multiethnic population of Manhattan, Brooklyn, the Bronx, and the Hudson Valley participated in and witnessed magnificent pageants, naval parades, commemorative exercises, and exhibitions to honor Henry Hudson's voyage of discovery in 1609 and the successful inauguration of steam navigation upon the Hudson River by Robert Fulton in 1807. The rich calendar of events included the naval parade on 25 September, with replicas of Hudson's vessel, the *Half Moon,* and Fulton's steamship, the *Clermont,* sailing from Manhattan to Brooklyn; a concert by Irish citizens at Carnegie Hall and one by the United German Singers at the Hippodrome on the 26th; music festivals continued in New York boroughs on the 27th; and on the 28th, the great Historical Parade, forming at Central Park West and 110th Street, proceeding down to 59th Street, to 5th Avenue, and down to Washington Square, was one of the major events. On 29 September, general commemorative exercises were performed at universities, colleges, schools, museums, and learned and patriotic societies throughout the state; in New York City, under the auspices of the Board of Education, special exercises were held in every elementary school; the dedication of monuments, tablets, parks, and other memorials occurred throughout the state.

The Manhattan Military Parade was the major event on 30 September. Federal troops from the Department of the East, the National Guard of the state of New York, the U.S. Navy and Marine Corps, and the Naval Reserve, members of veteran organizations, and sailors from foreign warships marched following the same route of the Historical Parade on the 28th. On Saturday, 2 October, the Children's Festival crowded public parks in greater New York, where historical plays, folk dances, and other forms of playground amusements were performed. In the evening of that day, the great Carnival Parade in the borough of Manhattan followed the same route as the Historical Parade and the Military Parade of the previous days. During the week religious ceremonies and civic parades occurred in Yonkers, Poughkeepsie, Kingston,

Catskill, Hudson, and Albany. In New York City free exhibitions were ar-
ranged with the direct cooperation of the Hudson-Fulton Celebration
Commission at a number of institutions: the American Geographical
Society showed books and maps relating to Henry Hudson and Robert
Fulton; the American Museum of Natural History had special ethnolog-
ical exhibits dedicated to the Native American tribes of the New York
City area and the Iroquois of New York State; the American Society of
Mechanical Engineers showed material related to Fulton and steam nav-
igation; the Brooklyn Institute of Arts and Sciences had a special exhibi-
tion of the past and present life of the Native American tribes of Long
Island; the City History Club of New York showed pictures, maps, and
drawings illustrating the early history of New York; documents of similar
nature were exhibited at the College of the City of New York, while the
Fraunces' Tavern showed an exhibition prepared by the Sons of the
Revolution featuring portraits, historical relics, and other objects related to the period of the American Revolution; the Metropolitan Museum of Art showed a loaned exhibition of paintings by Dutch artists
who were contemporaries of Hudson; the New York Historical Society
exhibited portraits, miniatures, manuscripts, and relics relating to Robert Fulton; and the Lenox branch of the New York Public Library exhibited drawings, prints, maps, books, and manuscripts concerning the
Hudson River, the river valley, and early steam navigation of the river.[1]
According to the local press, this grandiose celebration attracted between two and three million people.

The Hudson-Fulton Celebration Commission, including the mayors
of forty-six cities of New York State and the presidents of thirty-eight
villages along the Hudson River, was a large body ranging from 212
members appointed by the state governor in 1902, when the idea of the
celebration took form, to 805 at the time of the festival. The commission, together with 3,000 citizens of the New York boroughs appointed
by the mayor, was the festival's organizational machine.[2] This growing
organizational body planned the parades as early as 1905.

The Historical Parade of 28 September 1909 in Manhattan had the
goal of illustrating by moving tableaux "memorable scenes in the history of the City and the State for public education and entertainment,"
as the commission's report read. A group of artists under the direction
of Captain of Pageantry A. H. Stoddard, the former master of Mardi
Gras pageants in New Orleans, constructed the historical floats after the
colored designs had received the final approval of the Historical Committee chaired by Samuel V. Hoffman, the president of the New York
Historical Society. The civic parade's didactical aim was linked to the social goal of uniting in the procession "the representatives of as many as

possible of the nationalities composing the cosmopolitan population of the State, so as to make them feel that the heritage of the State's history belonged to them as well as to those more distinctively American." The long list of nationalities represented in the marching bodies included seventy "real Iroquois Indians . . . secured from the Indian reservations," who played native characters performing ceremonial dances while dressed in exotic costumes on floats representing the "Indian period." Ironically, citizens of African descent were enlisted among the twenty nationalities of foreign immigrant groups.

Arranged in four divisions, the historical floats presented a sequence of fifty-four scenes illustrating the progress of the state from the Indian period to the present time. Each division, led by ethnic bands, included significant examples of this historical reconstruction. There were floats entitled "The Empire State," "Indian Period," "Legend of Hiawatha," "The Five Nations," and "The First Sachem" in the first division, led by Thomas Kelly, grand marshal of all Irish societies, and accompanied by Italian, Bohemian, Polish, Hungarian, and Norwegian bands and societies. The second division, led by bands of Italian and Irish societies, included floats entitled "Fate of Henry Hudson," "First Vessel Built on Manhattan Island," "The Purchase of Manhattan Island," and "Reception of Stuyvesant." A band of Irish societies led the third division covering colonial and revolutionary periods and including floats entitled "Colonial Period," "The Stamp Act," "Publishing the Constitution," "Hamilton's Harangue," "Washington Taking Oath of Office," and "Legend of Rip Van Winkle." The fourth division showed floats entitled "United States Period," "Fulton's Ferry," "Reception of Lafayette," "Erie Canal Boat," "Old Broadway Sleigh," "Garibaldi's Home, Staten Island," and "Bartholdi's Statue of Liberty," accompanied by the colored and Syrian bands.[3]

Local press compared the huge crowd watching the parade to "the audience at the interesting point of a show." Children seemed to be especially interested in those graphical illustrations of what they had learned in their history classes, and "parents had their hands full explaining things to them." The instructive nature of the pageant "was one of the chief features, not only for the little folks but for the grownups as well," the *New York Sun* remarked. An immigrant father explained to his daughter that all the world was represented there: "From one end of the world to the other we came, together, to build this country." The daughter later recalled that the floats made a profound impression on her: "Much of it we didn't understand, but what wonderful bits of Americana these were for the newcomers around the turn of the century."[4] The members of the Hudson-Fulton Celebration Commission believed the whole immigrant family, exposed to the disintegrating effects of city life, could be unified by this celebration of American history.

The floats were "Americana" at its best. We can imagine what these immigrants felt when they saw a float like "The Empire State" representing the state of New York "from the day of the canoe to the modern skyscraper." They saw a seated female figure that symbolized the state. The figure had an open book in her lap representing history. On the back of her throne, our foreign immigrants could see a perched owl, symbolizing wisdom, while behind her a wigwam and a skyscraper represented progress in architecture. Immigrant spectators were certainly taken by the "Legend of Hiawatha," the float telling the story of the formation of the League of the Iroquois. The canoe in which Hiawatha arrived in the land of the Iroquois with his beautiful daughter was at the front. At the prow of the canoe stood Hiawatha. Lying upon a rock was his daughter, in the clutches of a huge eagle. Behind the two stood a group of Native Americans. From the float presentation the spectators perhaps could not grasp the full meaning of the legend—with Hiawatha, after mourning his daughter for three days, rising to form the League of the Iroquois—but certainly they enjoyed it. Immigrant spectators probably laughed and thought the natives quite credulous when they saw the float "Purchase of Manhattan Island." Here a group of natives under a tree was approached by a group of Dutchmen, just landed, offering them $24 and European wares in barter. Contemporary observers reported that many foreign and American spectators raised their hats respectfully at the arrival of the float "Washington Taking Oath of Office," which represented the balcony of Federal Hall upon which stood George Washington and some members of Congress. Perhaps foreign immigrants did not understand the meaning of the float dedicated to the "Legend of Rip Van Winkle," the celebrated legend of the Hudson River valley written by Washington Irving and dealing with the good but intemperate Dutchman who slept for twenty years after drinking with Henry Hudson's ghostly crew. Italian immigrants certainly cheered the float "Garibaldi's Home, Staten Island" representing the Italian hero living in a cottage in Clifton, Staten Island, after the failure of the European revolution of 1848 and making candles together with Meucci, the inventor of the telephone.[5]

On Saturday, 2 October, the Manhattan Carnival Parade followed the same marching route as the Historical Parade, moving down Central Park West, across Columbus Circle, and then down Fifth Avenue. The Historical and Carnival Parades Committee, under whose direction the Carnival Parade took place, was chaired by Herman Ridder, who had received hearty support from the several large German societies in New

York City acquainted with pageantry in their fatherland. The committee made it clear that the meaning of "carnival" conveyed by this parade was "in the derivative, not the primary sense of the term"—namely, a "general public festivity" with no connections to the original Roman and modern European carnivals. In other words, the Carnival Parade did not mean merrymaking, for it was designed to teach the sense of universality of poetry, myth, legend, and allegory by giving a vision of human nature in which the traditions of the Enlightenment and Romanticism were combined. Although the legends and allegories represented were not indigenous to America, the organizers conceived of them as "a real part of our culture, inherited, like the cumulative facts which constitute our progressive civilization, from the past." It was observed that American civilization "young as it is, has advanced to the stage where it appreciates its intellectual heritage from the Old World, and nowhere in this country is that heritage more highly prized than in New York City and State."

All these myths and legends were overwhelmingly northern European. There was a float entitled "Lohengrin" that showed Elsa, Duchess of Brabant, unjustly accused by her guardian of the murder of her brother and defended by a knight, Lohengrin, who appeared on a boat drawn by a swan. Another float, named "Lorelei," represented a siren, a favorite theme in German songs and poetry. There was also a float entitled "Death of Fafner," showing the giant taking the form of a dragon to guard the Rheingold, and Siegfried appointed to kill him and recover the golden glimmer of the Rhine. The float "Götterdämmerung" showed Siegfried wresting the magic ring from Brunhilda, the Rhine daughters regaining the ring, and the burning of Valhalla. Another popular Wagnerian theme was introduced by the float "Meistersinger," in which Walter, a young knight in love with Eva, wins her hand by singing in a tournament. Northern myths and legends were portrayed in the float "Walküre," showing the warrior maidens riding through the air, and "Tannhäuser," narrating the myth in which one of the best harpers and singers of Thuringia is attracted to Venus's mortal cave. Other floats represented the valley of "Father Rhine" and two Swiss legends, "Wilhelm Tell" and "God of the Alps." About 12,500 people of both sexes participated in the Carnival Pageant illustrating "that great body of Old World folklore which has inspired so much of the beautiful imagery of the poetry, song, and drama of all civilized nations," the commission's report read.[6]

Saturday, 2 October, had also been designated the children's day under the direction of the Children's Festival Committee. On that day, approximately five hundred thousand children from public, parochial, and private schools and public institutions in the city filled the parks in Manhattan, Brooklyn, the Bronx, and Staten Island to join the general celebration by performing particular ceremonies and exercises. According to contemporary observers, the result was "a memorable demonstration, surpassing anything of its kind in the history of New York."[7] It was the most telling of all celebrations.

By 1909 social scientists had discovered childhood and adolescence and defined them as the most susceptible stages in life for being molded by external stimuli. In Progressive America, psychologists and sociologists joined social workers and other reformers in putting immigrant children at the center of their theories and programs.[8] The thousands of children participating in the Hudson-Fulton Festival, coming from the schools of the Lower East Side and from Sunday schools, missions, and settlements, were taught a play tradition on "the background of American history, with emphasis on prominent personalities and events," as described by the *Playground*, the official journal of the recently formed Playground Association of America. The effort was extraordinary and required a high level of preparation and mobilization of civil society; well in advance, many pastors of churches, superintendents of Sunday schools, playground teachers, presidents of clubs, societies, settlements, and other organizations were contacted and asked to cooperate in the training of children for participation in the pageants. The city was divided into fifty pageant districts, and each district was to give its contribution to the general organization. This effort was conceived as a community-building process and was highly rationalized in terms of tasks and general organization. People in charge of children in the various sections of the city "were encouraged to produce some civic phases of life, such as Congress of Nations, as shown by a representation of life and processes at Ellis Island in the management of immigrants."[9]

The spectacle was extraordinary. In greater New York about five hundred thousand children of all nationalities were involved in the festival. Children were organized into forty divisions, throughout the city parks and avenues, and all did the same exercises, sang the same songs, gave the same salutes, took the same oath of allegiance to the flag, and produced their dance tableaux, which told the story of different periods of New York history since Henry Hudson sailed up the river. The same festival scheme was followed throughout the city; parades formed at public schools, churches, clubrooms, and private schools.

Mulberry Bend, in downtown Manhattan, was the gathering place of thousands of children from the schools of the Lower East Side. Primarily Jewish and Italian, they pledged their loyalty to the American flag with impressive ceremonies. In Central Park thousands of children waving Hudson-Fulton flags marched in at the eastern gate at Seventy-second Street. Boys and girls of the Bohemian Free School dressed in red, white, and blue gymnasium suits to form an enormous American flag.[10] The rendezvous of one of the largest parades, including pupils from six public schools together with children of various settlements and church associations, was at the Court of Honor on Fifth Avenue, between Fortieth and Forty-second Streets. Boys and girls of church schools danced an Indian snake dance dressed up in native costumes and then performed a Dutch dance and a minuet in colonial costumes. Many other dances were performed, including a Hungarian peace dance by little girls in Hungarian costumes and a Japanese dance by black girls of the Abyssinian Baptist Church Sunday school.

One wonders why black children were not trained to perform an African dance to include their African-American heritage in a festival that was meant to highlight the traditions of all immigrant groups living in the city. The fact that black girls were trained to perform a Japanese dance was an example of how decontextualized the teaching of folk dancing on American playgrounds could be. By the beginning of the century, the educational value of folk dancing was commonly accepted among playground educators. Folk dancing was seen as a potential antidote to counteract the "dance madness" that was capturing the city. Unlike the sexually explicit dances of commercial dance halls, folk dancing could be taught and supervised in a public place, by giving emphasis to rhythmic movements as a chain of steps to be learned. By teaching folk dances out of their original context, however, the rich symbolic context of their movements and gestures was lost.[11]

In the formal context of the playground, immigrant children were taught folk dances with time and space under strict control. Hence dancing became an organized game among many others. Children were admitted to folk-dancing classes only "through faithfulness in the performance of some of the less attractive exercises set down in the playground program."[12] That black girls were trained to perform a Japanese dance instead of an African or an American dance depended on the meaning educators gave to the Americanization of immigrant children. These children, it was thought, needed to be exposed to the influence of "the best" of human civilization and to be protected from those cultural traditions that could undermine what were commonly considered the highest levels of human achievement. Consequently, in order to grow up according to a feminine American identity, black girls were symbolically asked to dismiss their African heritage—which had already profoundly influenced the world of urban entertainment—and learn a decontextualized exotic dance.

The New York African-American press extensively reported on the Hudson-Fulton Festival and linked this event to the presence of Matthew Henson, the Negro explorer on the team that discovered the North Pole, as the principal guest of the celebration. The *New York Age* fully described the Historical Parade, the floats, and other aspects of this great festival of Americanization. Nearly three hundred African-American citizens, preceded by the New Amsterdam band, took part in the Historical Parade, the paper proudly reported. Favorable comments were also made about the whole program of celebrations. A few days later, however, the headlines of the *Age* reported the open discrimination against Negro sailors who were not allowed to take part in the big naval parade: "In last Thursday's parade the Negroes were made conspicuous by their absence. . . . Many remarked that it was strange that while there are several hundred Negro sailors with the American fleet, not one was seen in the parade." Instead of parading, "Negro sailors were assigned to duty on the battle ships on the day of the parade, and that such a course is pursued by the officers whenever there is a parade." It was also reported that Filipino sailors paraded with the other sailors, and other instances of discrimination against black sailors were described.[13] According to the *Age,* this exclusion aroused a storm of criticism from African-American residents in greater New York and a general condemnation. Why were black sailors excluded from the public ceremonial space during a festival that was meant to celebrate the progress of American civilization as the unity of all ethnic groups?

Native American history was given great space in the Historical Parade of 1909; those seventy "real" Indians from the reservations were there to represent a glorious past that could conceal what was commonly perceived as their inglorious present and hopeless future. In the Hudson-Fulton Festival, Native Americans were to tell their legends, myths, and history. They were given only the past of a "dying race" whose culture, however, enchanted early twentieth-century anthropologists.

White women were fully present on the floats of the Historical and Carnival Parades of 1909. Young women presented themselves as real subjects, dressed up in the colorful costumes of their immigrant mothers.[14] Their official entrance into the public ceremonial space represented the relevant presence of young white women in the work space of factories and department stores. Middle-class women were among the organizers of the festival and had already given life to the tens of committees, clubs, Sunday schools, settlements, and other organizations populating New York's civil society at the beginning of the century.

In the Hudson-Fulton Festival the three hundred African-American participants were meant to represent an immigrant group among many others. Black children, like all other immigrant children, skillfully performed their tableaux and drills. In the ideal society designed by the festival, all were given the same right to fully enjoy American citizenship. Yet the exclusion of black sailors from the aquatic parade brought all participants back to the ugly reality of racial discrimination that the "separate but equal" formula had sanctioned. There was no conflict between the reality of this formula and the need of the United States to become a "mental community" as social engineer John R. Commons stated: "To be great a nation needs to be not of one blood, it must be of one mind."[15]

In New York City the groups of city reformers constituting the Hudson-Fulton Celebration Commission staged a gigantic celebration in which the history of the American republic was taught to and performed by the new immigrants, white and black alike. The commission's main goal was "to promote the assimilation of our adopted population," as was stated in the group's report. The celebration, accordingly, had to be "educational, not commercial," and "everything should be as educative as possible and . . . the greatest number of people possible should freely see the public spectacles."[16] History was the core of this project: "Knowledge of the history of a city, or a state, or a nation," it was observed, "is conducive to love of country, civic pride and loyalty to established institutions." It was believed that this knowledge was able "to bind a people together, make it more homogeneous and give it stability." Furthermore, this knowledge made "the inhabitants better citizens by holding up to their eyes lofty traditions to enlist their affections and inspire their imitation."

Reformers in New York City seemed to be very aware of the value of traditions. The festival was conceived, in fact, as the celebration of the past of the American republic within a linear progression of the development of American civilization. As the power of tradition, the commission's report read, "has been one of the most fundamental and conservative forces of all people of all times," a people "naturally tends to follow the impulses of the past and to adhere to tradition unless turned therefrom by other influences." Therefore the ingrained history of a nation, broadly called tradition, was "a balance wheel, tending to restrain sudden and spasmodic departures from the normal mode of progress." This one-million-dollar celebration of "historical culture" to commemorate Henry Hudson's and Robert Fulton's undertakings was conceived as "a rational festival of patriotic sentiment."[17] Traditions to be passed on to immigrants were selectively chosen and included in intellectually convincing and emotionally compelling pageants.

Pageantry was an art that Americans learned from the British and re-interpreted for the multicultural society they envisioned. The pageant movement in the United States assumed proportions and directions that went far beyond the British pageants that inspired it: pageantry made history vivid while promoting community solidarity through mass participation. Pageantry's colorful invitation to mass participation would make one community, it was believed, out of people divided by race or ethnicity, class, and interests. City reformers hoped that pageantry could help a composite people to envision "the community" and feel loyal to it. In 1910 the *Century* remarked that the new celebrations were of deep sociological value "in giving cohesiveness to our community life, which, as it becomes more complicated, is exposed to many centrifugal forces."[18]

The typical pageant form before World War I emphasized historical continuities between past and present generations. Traditions invented in the early republic were reinvented within the dramatic industrial and urban changes that altered the idea of a cohesive community. Between 1908 and 1917, more than three hundred pageants were performed whose contents included fairy tales, classical themes, the Bible, and medieval and Renaissance legends. History into ritual, as cultural historian David Glassberg argues, was the belief of progressivism that "history could be made into a dramatic public ritual through which the residents of a town, by acting out the right version of their past, could bring about some kind of future social and political transformation."[19]

William Langdon, one of the creators of the new art, believed that pageantry was a way to emphasize the "underlying public spirit" beneath differences of class, race, and ethnicity. He devised a celebration plan for the Fourth of July that could be used both in small towns, where a sense of community could be easily stirred, and in big cities, where many communities could be unified on that day. Included in Langdon's plan were "Between the Lines during the Civil War," on the background of the notes of the southern and northern hymns, and a procession of "The Reunion of the Blue and the Gray." Langdon recommended that pageant organizers study and dramatize "the public question" in a "fair, human, impartial spirit" and present both sides: "The essential is that the episode shall hold, in the midst of a picture of actual present struggle, the confident hope that will put vigor into action, that will extend the soldier's good hand of understanding to the other side and that will in the end bring about the high solidarity of a united nation. This is the great human essential. This is what will bring about the Triumph of Freedom." The final act of Langdon's outline of a pageant for the celebration of Independence Day was a symbolic representation of "America." It portrayed Liberty, Democracy, Industry, Health, and Patriotism coming from the woods, and all groups of people taking part in the pageant, from slaves to foreign immigrants. The last tableau of the act showed all these groups building a throne, "white and of classical design," and inviting Liberty to ascend the steps to the throne.[20]

The imagery of a cohesive community that civic celebrations offered was educational, for it indicated the criteria for membership in that community and the nature of the bond that should exist among its members. Pageants based their appeal to community solidarity not only upon its residents' belief in the "principles of the past" embodied in the dramatic depiction of local history but also on their common partic-ipation in the pageant experience itself.

The Beginning of African-American Pageantry

Pageantry as an art form could offer rival versions of historical mem-ories supporting the "separate but equal" formula. This was what W. E. B. Du Bois had in mind, among many other things, when in 1911 he wrote the first draft of *The Star of Ethiopia,* the first pageant in the United States whose subject was the history of the "Negro race." Besides being convinced of the great educational value of pageantry to colored people, Du Bois also thought the staging of a pageant could be a source of financial support for the NAACP. However, the association's officers hesitated to endorse Du Bois's high-cost plan (more than one thousand local black people were needed to perform the pageant), which even-tually materialized, thanks to external sponsorship, in New York City at the National Emancipation Exposition (October 1913), in Washington, D.C., for the celebration of the fiftieth anniversary of the Thirteenth Amendment abolishing slavery (October 1915), and in Philadelphia for the centennial celebration of the General Conference of the African Methodist Episcopal Church (May 1916).[21]

The first staging of *The Star of Ethiopia* occurred in New York City in October 1913, as the main event in the celebration of the fiftieth anni-versary of the Emancipation Proclamation. The enthusiastic response of a very large crowd repaid Du Bois for "an avalanche of altogether unme-rited and absurd attacks" that made him classify the Emancipation Ex-position as "the worst of all my experiences." The more than 350 black schoolchildren, teachers, and amateur dancers and actors who vol-unteered to take part in four performances kept the attention of a cu-mulative audience of over fourteen thousand. The Twelfth Regiment Armory at Sixty-second Street and Columbus Avenue was jammed every evening the pageant was shown: "Literally thousands besieged our doors and the sight of the thing continually made the tears arise." The *New York Times* made short but highly favorable remarks about Du Bois's historical pageant and its capacity for reenacting the history of colored people, "of their rise from ignorant, wild men and slaves to their present state."[22]

The National Emancipation Exposition, held in New York City on 22–31 October 1913, became a rather controversial event among African-American spokespersons. The *New York Age*, which followed Booker T. Washington's lead, heavily criticized the organization of the exposition. The strong surveillance of the NAACP officers in general and of Du Bois in particular that Washington expected from his people in New York perhaps explains the negative reports on the exposition in the *Age*. The African-American paper complained that the exhibition was not ready when the doors were opened, that exhibitors who had been urged to take part found, when looking for space for their products, that they would be charged $30–55 for the privilege, that some of the booths were not lighted until the last day, that pictures of prominent Negroes were indiscriminately arranged, and that many guests invited to the official banquet were unable to find it. These and many other similar grievances made the event, according to the *Age*, a poor celebration of the progress African Americans had made in industry and agriculture during their first fifty years of freedom. It was rather clear that the Washington–Du Bois controversy was behind these negative comments. The *Age*, in fact, heavily criticized the opening remarks of the chair of the organization committee, Robert N. Wood, the African-American printer and head of the branch of Tammany in Harlem, who had put Du Bois on the Emancipation Celebration Committee. According to the *Age*, Wood "devoted his time to diatribes against THE NEW YORK AGE and its editor." What the paper called "coarse and out of place remarks" and "vituperative outbreak" paralleled the "inconspicuous position" given to Booker T. Washington's picture hung on a "lower row," and the prominence given to "the ancient history of the Negro," while "very little is shown as to what is actually doing to-day."[23]

Du Bois was certainly not an easygoing fellow, and it is conceivable that he tended to feel rather stressed for the catastrophic deficit (around $8,000) accumulated by that all-Negro event. But after seeing the large enthusiastic audience gathered at the armory, an excited Du Bois exclaimed: "The Pageant is the thing. This is what people want and long for. This is the gown and paraphernalia in which the message of education and reasonable race pride can deck itself." Du Bois's dream was coming true: "It seemed to me that it might be possible with such a demonstration to get people interested in this development of Negro drama to teach on the one hand the colored people themselves the meaning of their history and their rich, emotional life through a new theatre, and on the other, to reveal the Negro to the white world as a human, feeling thing."[24]

Central to the 1913 production of *The Star of Ethiopia*, which the *New York Times* called "a scenic production of the history of the black race," was the idea of "gifts" of the Negro race to the world as a crucial component of African-American identity. As early as 1897, Du Bois had made it clear that this racial identity was neither "African" nor "American." In "The Conservation of Races," the paper he gave to the American Negro Academy, he clearly stated his notion of black people's "double identity": "We are Americans, not only by birth and citizenship, but by our political ideals, our language, our religion. Further than that, our Americanism does not go." By constructing the history of Americans of African descent in *The Star of Ethiopia*, Du Bois combined this Americanism with the aesthetic of a Negro ancient past and anticipated, in so doing, one of the major literary themes of the Harlem Renaissance. In his 1897 paper, Negroes were members of "a vast historic race that from the very dawn of creation has slept, but half awakening in the dark forests of its African fatherland."[25]

By the time he wrote the first draft of *The Star of Ethiopia*, however, Du Bois had retrieved the full awakening of the Negro race by using the symbolic allegories of American pageantry, his Harvard and European cultural backgrounds, and his own reinterpretation of current scientific racial theories. A pragmatic historian, Du Bois aimed for the retrieval of the African-American past to defeat contemporary white supremacist misrepresentations that the "separate but equal" doctrine had strengthened. According to Du Bois, his pageant succeeded. Almost twenty years after the first performance of *The Star of Ethiopia* in New York, he recalled that every night the pageant "simply jammed the armory where we were, and received considerable notice."[26] We can try to imagine what those crowds saw and felt by looking at the sketchy drafts of Du Bois's pageant.

The Star of Ethiopia portrayed five scenes of African and African-American history divided into several episodes covering a period of ten thousand years.[27] It began with prehistoric times and proceeded with the tale of the discovery of the art of working metals by "the Eldest and Strongest of the Races of men whose faces be Black," as the herald announced. This was, in fact, the first gift they gave to humanity: the Gift of Welding Iron. Ethiopia, the Mother of Men, was a tall veiled woman in splendid garment, with Fire in her right hand and Iron in her left. As she slowly proceeded on stage, the rhythmic roll of tom-toms began, the arts blos-

somed, wild animals were brought in, and the whole picture created a
general atmosphere of merry feasting and dancing. The second gift of
black people to the world was the Gift of Civilization of the valley of the
Nile. The episode portrayed how the civilization of ancient Egypt came
about. One hundred Negroes dressed like savages filled the scene together with fifty veiled figures, the Sphinx, the Pyramid, the Obelisk,
and the empty throne of the Pharaoh. The Egyptians unveiled and displayed Negroes and mulattoes magnificently dressed. One of the Cush-
itic chiefs was crowned Pharaoh, and the Queen of Sheba and other African rulers paid a visit. The culture of Egypt spread to Central Africa,
where empires flourished from the sixth to the sixteenth centuries.
Slowly, at the sound of music, all people left the stage except fifty savages, who stayed to examine their gifts. When the lights grew dim as the
Egyptian culture died, the fifty savages fell asleep.

Then the light returned to herald the third gift of black people to the
world: the Gift of Faith. The episode depicted how the Negro race
spread the faith of Muhammad. But with Muhammadanism came numerous religious wars that weakened and divided black people and
made them an easy prey to the slave trader. The next scene dramatically
showed Ethiopia blotted out by fire and pillaged by slave hunters. During this pillage two monks representing the Christian world looked on
in silent acquiescence. The Muhammadans forced their slaves forward
as European traders entered the stage and took gold in barter. The Negro race learned to suffer and hence gave the fourth gift to humanity:
the Gift of Humiliation to teach that human beings can bear even slavery and still live. The following scene showed the Negro race trans-
planted in the Americas. Hordes of slaves filed in. As the chorus sang
spirituals, black people faced the lash, and over the prostrate and bend-
ing forms of the slaves the ghosts of slavery danced in and out. A group
of Native Americans danced, too; as they left the stage they vainly urged
the slaves to follow them to the forests. Then the slaves' toil was interrupted by a lively Creole dance announcing the fifth gift of the black
people to the world: the Gift of Struggle toward Freedom. The following scenes depicted the actions of Toussaint L'Ouverture, David Walker,
Nat Turner, Denmark Vesey, Sojourner Truth, Frederick Douglass, William Lloyd Garrison, Harriet Beecher Stowe, and John Brown. Ethiopia
awakened when Shango, the Thunder God, called her to duty. She rose
with the glistening sword in one hand and the brightly shining "Star of
Freedom" in the other. As black Union soldiers entered the stage, the
chorus sang "Marching through Georgia." The last scene portrayed
African-American history since the Civil War. Groups of black people
were shown at work in various trades. Groups of businessmen, athletes,

ministers, physicians, teachers, trained nurses, and others acted as they
were quietly enjoying freedom in their own ways. Suddenly they were viciously attacked by the "furies" of race prejudice, envy, gambling, idle-
ness, intemperance, and the KKK. At first some of the groups gave in,
but others stood up. The furies tried to seize the Star, but the freedmen
appealed to Ethiopia, the mother of all human beings. She called forth
her sons and daughters all over the earth to come and build a "Tower of
Light" upon which she set the Star of Freedom so high that it would be
forever safe. The last gifts of black people to the world were the Gift of
Laughter and the Gift of Hope.

Du Bois conceived of pageantry as a form of black drama and included in each scene either traditional "sorrow songs" or original music
by black composers dominating the world of New York's commercial
theaters, such as Samuel Coleridge-Taylor, Bob Cole, J. Rosamond Johnson, and Du Bois's army friend Charles Young.[28] A cosmopolitan intellectual, Du Bois also selected two pieces from Verdi's *Aida* for the Egyptian scene in *The Star of Ethiopia.* Du Bois's pageant, like most historical
pageants staged during the Progressive Era, emphasized continuities between past and present in order to make history intelligible to contemporary audiences. In *The Star of Ethiopia* Du Bois created an illusion of a
structured African past construed around the literary idea of "gift" that
made African-American history coherently develop into an allegorical
uplifting of a racial group.

Although *The Star of Ethiopia* cannot be considered one of Du Bois's
major creative works, his biographers have failed to place its staging
within the broader pageant movement of the Progressive Era. It is true
that Du Bois wrote the pageant with pan-Africanism in mind and shortly after he had become the editor of the *Crisis,* the official organ of
the NAACP, which he viewed as a voice for the civil rights of colored
people in America and "a valuable source of Pan-African ideas."[29] Consequently, *The Star of Ethiopia* can appear as a minor episode in Du Bois's
"glorification" of African ancestors. Without dismissing the presence of
this aspect in Du Bois's pageant, it should be kept in mind, however,
that the invention of a glorious American past, the creation of particular versions of group history, and the selection of traditions to be transmitted to the new generations were fundamental characteristics of progressive pageantry. As the Hudson-Fulton Festival showed, in this form
of educational theater a complex notion of participatory democracy
and cultural pluralism, to which recently arrived immigrant groups
from central and southern Europe should be educated, was at play in
mobilizing civil society.

According to David Levering Lewis's authoritative biography of the

first half of Du Bois's life, *The Star of Ethiopia* "was the most patent, ex-
pansive use yet made by Du Bois of an ideology of black supremacy in
order to confound one of white supremacy"; in this work Du Bois elaborated "the basics of an Afrocentric aesthetics and historiography."[30]
But at a closer reading the central theme of this pageant appears to be
the idea of "gifts" of the Negro race to the world as a crucial component
of African-American identity.

Du Bois gave race a substantially cultural meaning that went far beyond skin color. His pageant, in fact, visually depicted a wide range of
colored people whose unity and conflicts were mostly cultural and
created an educational "usable past" for African Americans, who were
generally excluded from mainstream pageants and historical parades.
The exclusion of black sailors from the naval parade during the Hudson-Fulton Festival was an example. Du Bois remarked that "the American Pageant Association has been silent, if not actually contemptuous,
of efforts to use pageantry as a black folk drama." This seems to undermine the whole idea of historical pageantry, which was an inextricable
part of the pluralistic culture of the Progressive Era. In most pageants
produced during the period 1905–17, African, Native, and Asian Americans were either absent or asked to play exotic characters.[31]

Du Bois wrote *The Star of Ethiopia* at the time in which Progressive social rhetoric articulated a language of reform that was both ethnically
inclusive and racially exclusive. In Progressive America, the language of
efficiency, rationalization, and social engineering of white academics
like sociologist John R. Commons coexisted with the antiracist cultural
theories of anthropologist Franz Boas and the humanitarian language
of Jane Addams and the other liberal intellectuals who joined the
NAACP. Du Bois's pageant came to light the year after the Progressive
convention, held in Chicago in August 1912, in which "disquieting rumors arose concerning Negro delegates," reported Jane Addams in the
Crisis while commenting on the exclusion of the colored delegates from
Mississippi.[32]

As an art form, pageantry certainly appealed to Du Bois. He wrote
The Star of Ethiopia a year after the founding meeting of the NAACP and
the year of the Universal Races Congress held in London in July 1911.
In his view, the Negro race's unique gift to the world "has been and will
be a gift of art, of appreciation and realization of beauty." This aesthetic
gift, however, could not be delivered to a world where "the problem of
the twentieth century is the problem of the colour line," as Du Bois had
declared in London in 1900 at the first congress of black people of African descent. With the publication of *The Negro* in 1915, he made it clear

that historical scholarship could become collective memory by means of aesthetic stimulus. Without essentializing Africa as a monolithic entity but spending instead more than half of the book demonstrating the complexities of the different parts of the continent and its diverse peoples, Du Bois's history of the African diaspora was a scholarly version of *The Star of Ethiopia.* Like the pageant, *The Negro* was an attempt to give Africa a historical past at a time in which the world powers were scrambling to colonize the land and resources of that continent.[33]

Appearing at the same time as *The Negro* was Du Bois's more effective article, "The African Roots of the War," in the May 1915 issue of the *Atlantic Monthly,* anticipating Lenin's *Imperialism as the Highest Stage of Capitalism* (1917). By reviewing the history of European hegemony over the continent based on technological superiority and by citing Franz Boas's argument that iron was first smelted in Africa and that agriculture and commerce flourished there when Europe was still a wilderness, Du Bois looked at the economic motives that led to the present conflict to achieve domination over tropical Africa: "Africa is a prime cause of this terrible overturning of civilization." In a striking parallel to Lenin, Du Bois wrote of the "white workingman" who was asked to share "the spoil of exploiting 'chinks' and 'niggers'" as a force united to capitalists: "it is the nation; a new democratic nation composed of united capital and labor." Welfare concessions on the one side and the threat of competition of colored labor on the other made the Western white working class potentially available to share the spoils of the darker nations of the world: "It is increased wealth, power and luxury for all classes on a scale the world never saw before." These words enlighten the profound relationship between domestic racism and imperialistic views binding together different groups of a mass democracy. This cement was made of mainstream scientific views, preconceptions, and racial stereotypes based on deep and archaic fears, which by 1915 found a powerful channel of popularization in a mass media like the movies. It was in 1915, in fact, that D. W. Griffith's film *The Birth of a Nation* made soundly visible and appealing to the general public a profoundly racist version of the history of the Civil War and Reconstruction by merging melodrama, stirring actions, and the close-up technique with the use of pageantry's abstract symbolism, allegorical themes, and historical *tableaux vivants.* The battle against the screening of *The Birth of a Nation* in which Du Bois and the NAACP became deeply involved lasted many years. This fight mobilized thousands of black and white people all over the country, but at the same time, as Du Bois admitted, the battle "probably succeeded in advertising it even beyond its admittedly notable merits."[34]

The Birth of a Nation *and the NAACP's*
Fight against It

D. W. Griffith's *The Birth of a Nation,* the most controversial film in the
early history of the movies, was released under the title *The Clansman,*
the popular novel by Thomas Dixon on which it was based. It opened in
Los Angeles at the Clune's Auditorium on 15 February 1915. The New
York premiere of *The Clansman* at the Liberty Theatre on 3 March 1915
received more than favorable reviews from the drama critics of daily
papers. The premiere audience included many prominent men and
women of "filmdom" and of the best "literary and society circles," commented the reporter for the *Moving Picture World.* The stage of the Liberty Theatre was undecorated, for film director Griffith wanted to eliminate any distraction: the stage was merely a black background in front
of which the screen was placed. An orchestra played the music, and a
chorus sang popular melodies. To create an ambiance, there were men
in the uniforms of Union and Confederate soldiers, and the ushers
were young women dressed in the fashions of the South at the time of
the Civil War.[35]

This version of the film, consisting of thirteen reels and lasting three
hours, was given the definitive title *The Birth of a Nation.*[36] Such an imposing title was to symbolize the historical beginning of a new country
from the ashes of Reconstruction. It was President Woodrow Wilson
who emphasized the historical meaning of the movie, the first to be
shown at the White House, when he remarked that "it is like writing history with lightning." In many ways, Griffith's *Birth* resembled the structure of a pageant with its allegoric end, abstract symbolism, and *tableaux
vivants* of historical scenes. Welcomed by critics as a pathbreaking masterpiece, *The Birth of a Nation* immediately raised the controversial issue
of censorship and suppression of works of art and profoundly divided
American public opinion. The recently founded NAACP organized an
intense campaign against the movie, including public demonstrations
in major cities and informative articles in the *Crisis.* Within four days of
the opening of *Birth* in New York, the NAACP made a public announcement of its intention to apply local laws governing the new movie industry in order to either ban or censor the film.[37] However, the exploding
controversy made the film even more appealing and an immediate commercial and critical success, with tickets sold for two dollars apiece on
Broadway, where it stayed for forty-four weeks. Editor W. E. B. Du Bois
actively participated in the NAACP's campaign against Griffith's movie
and made the staging of his *Star of Ethiopia* in Washington, D.C., in

1915, performed in honor of the fiftieth anniversary of the Thirteenth Amendment, a specific response to *Birth*'s racist epic.

Why was Griffith's masterpiece so powerful? A biographer described Griffith's *Birth* as "a film of emotional excess with the immediacy of the close-up." By making a remarkable use of filmic storytelling and realistic battle scenes, Griffith "played on the fears of his white audience, appealed to their prejudices," and above all showed that "an audience would accept fiction as reality." The controversial *Birth* awakened the nation to the social importance of motion pictures, and the film's damaging effect on racial relations in the country persisted for a long time.[38]

What kind of history did Griffith write in his successful three-hour film that during the first week was viewed by more than 18,000 New Yorkers and that in less than a year secured 6,266 showings for over 825,000 people in the New York area alone?[39] It was the history of the Civil War and Reconstruction written "with lightning," or from the perspective of the values of the antebellum South, which presented the social relationship of slavery as the source of the best life for the kind master and the loyal and happy slave. From Thomas Dixon's popular novel *The Clansman*, D. W. Griffith, a Kentuckian, reproduced the atmosphere of the antebellum South as a world of warm feelings opposed to the cold and mechanical inhumanity of the North.[40] Griffith's movie told the story of the war's disruption of the perfect harmony of the plantation society and of its further destruction by Radical Republicans and freed blacks during Reconstruction.

The movie portrayed the story of the Old South, the Civil War, Reconstruction, and the rise of the KKK by following the epic of the Camerons, a respectable South Carolina family. The first part of the movie showed the ideal life the family lived before the war: Dr. Cameron and his sons were gentle and benevolent masters to their childlike slaves, who were happy to pick cotton, dance, and sing for their masters. The Big House was the realm of perfect harmony. Mammy happily went about her chores, and everybody knew his or her place. This social order broke down with the Civil War when the South underwent at the hand of Negro raiders "ruin, devastation, rapine, and pillage," as read an intertitle in the movie. War scenes followed, with the most elaborated effects and accompanied by appropriate music: Grieg's "In the Hall of the Mountain King" from the *Peer Gynt* suite accompanied the pictures of the burning of Atlanta; "Marching through Georgia" set the pace for General Sherman's march; and Wagnerian arias were the musical background for cannonades and infantry charges at Petersburg. The scene of Lincoln's assassination immediately followed "Hail to the

Chief" and preceded the overture from Bellini's *Norma*. "The Star-Spangled Banner" marked the victory of the North, and the strains of "America" accompanied the reunion of North and South with Grant and Lee shaking hands at Appomattox. Then came the horrors of Reconstruction. Northern carpetbaggers and blacks came down to the South, exploited and corrupted former slaves, and turned loyal "good old darkies" into renegades. *Birth* showed scenes of former slaves quitting work for dancing, roaming the streets, and insulting whites. When they got the vote, they managed to disfranchise whites, and they celebrated a black political victory with an orgiastic street festival. Then there was a scene with lusty, ignorant, and arrogant black legislators eating fried chicken and drinking whiskey from the bottle, bare feet on their desks, while trying to pass bills to legalize intermarriage. The viewer's disgust reached its apex when "renegade" Gus—a former slave of the Camerons who appeared in the uniform of the Union Army—tried to rape Flora, the younger Cameron daughter. Rather than submit to Gus's advances, she jumped off a cliff to her death. Just when everything seemed lost for the good people of the Old South, the "Invisible Empire" upsurged and directly confronted black rebels to put them back in their place. In an impressive scene, the riding knights of the KKK, led by "Little Colonel" Cameron—who in a previous scene got the inspiration for the Klan's white hood by watching silly black children running away in fear at the sight of white children masked like ghosts—to the sound of Wagner's *Die Walküre*, defeated black rebels and restored the Old South's glory by defending white womanhood and supremacy. These were the values on which a new nation was born: the North and the South united in a common defense of the white race. In a pageant-like fashion, the final version of the epilogue sequence of *Birth* showed the marriages of the Stoneman (the North) and Cameron (the South) children on the riverbanks, and the god of war dissolved into Christ, the Prince of Peace. (The original epilogue showed Negroes being transported back to Africa).[41] These were the values that stirred *Birth*'s audiences to cheer white heroes and curse black felons. From an audience's perspective, the characters made a predictable impact: the "renegade" Gus, venal and lusty mulatto Silas Lynch, heroic "Little Colonel" Cameron, frail and pure Elsie and Flora, and dark and sinister half-breed Lydia.

Especially in the South, the epic meaning of the movie provoked a visceral impact on the viewers. Ward Greene of the *Atlanta Journal* reported that Griffith's film swept the audience at the Atlanta Theater "like a tidal wave" of collective hysteria: a youth in the gallery "leaped to his feet and yelled and yelled," a little boy downstairs "pounded the man's back in front of him and shrieked," a young lady kept "dabbing and dabbing at her eyes," and an old lady "just sat and let the tears stream down her face unchecked." The reporter followed the progression of feelings stirred by the movie: "Loathing, disgust, hate envelope you, hot blood cries for vengeance." When the riders of the Ku Klux Klan arrived, the ecstatic crowd, in a release of emotions, yelled: "They are coming, they are coming!" Ned McIntosh of the *Atlanta Constitution* went as far as making a hazardous comparison between Homer of ancient Greece and D. W. Griffith of modern America. He explained to his readers that the emotional reaction of the Atlanta audience became "altogether unrestrained" because Griffith "awakens the memories of childhood; warms the heart with romance; quickens the pulse with patriotism; forces the exultant cheer from the lips in the midst of great battles; turns the heart sick with scenes of bloodshed; dims the eyes with tears for woman's sufferings." Not only southerners but also drama critics across the country gave enthusiastic reports. In both the North and South, many reviewers did not seem to find the film's extremely racist portraits particularly disturbing. That every single Negro character was a caricature was considered either irrelevant or a minor flaw in an otherwise magnificent spectacle. According to Mark Vance of the *New York Variety*, "the bigness and greatness of the entire film production itself completely crowds out any little defects." In 1953 African-American author Ralph Ellison observed that one had to accept that the release of *The Birth of a Nation* in 1915 "resulted in controversy, riots, heavy profits and the growth of the Klan."[42]

As the most controversial film of its era, *The Birth of a Nation* made contemporary critics aware of the powerful impact of motion pictures. In 1916 Harvard psychologist Hugo Münsterberg wrote an important study of the movies in which he analyzed the powerful influence on the audience. He observed that "the intensity with which the plays take hold of the audience cannot remain without strong social effects." As sensory hallucinations and illusions creep in, according to Münsterberg, "neurasthenic persons are especially inclined to experience touch or temperature or smell or sound impressions from what they see on the screen." Various aspects of motion pictures, such as depth and movement, depended on the illusion created by particular techniques. Both depth and movement "come to us in the moving picture world, not as hard facts, but as a mixture of fact and symbol." For example, the "close-up" technique, of which Griffith was the first to make extensive use, by objectifying "in our world of perception our mental act of attention," had given art "a means that transcends the power of any theater stage." Similarly, the technique of "cutting" allowed the shaping of the objective world by the interests of the mind: "Events which are far distant from one another so that we could not be physically present at all of them at the same time are fusing in our field of vision, just as they are brought together in our consciousness." All these techniques gave the movies a great power of suggestion. Although the sources of danger could not be overlooked, as the movies could induce imitation and other motor responses to the sight of crime and vice, at the same time, since millions were daily affected by the screen, "any wholesome influence emanating from the photoplay must have an incomparable power for remolding and upbuilding the national soul."[43]

In 1913 an anonymous author explained in an article in the *American Magazine* the meaning the movies had to their audience: "It is art democratic. . . . It is in a way a new universal language, even more elemental than music, for it is the telling of a story in a simple way the children are taught—through pictures. . . . There is no bar of language for the alien or the ignorant." Motion pictures were in fact a great attraction among recent Italian immigrants, who would check billboards every day to see which new pictures were available because they were anxious to see what they thought were examples of "*really* American life."[44]

There is no doubt that by 1915 a large part of the city audience was composed of non-English-speaking immigrants. The silent film was the perfect entertainment for people who faced language barriers daily. Immigrant neighborhoods were the expanding market for the new media. In New York small theaters—where admittance cost one nickel—increased from fifty in 1900 to more than four hundred by 1908 and served a daily crowd of over two hundred thousand. Everyone went to the movies: moviegoing became an urban ritual capable of uniting generations in a common experience of what was believed to be the real American culture. Families and friends went together, as a form of socializing. One observer commented: "Visit a motion picture show on a Saturday night below 14th Street when the house is full and you will soon be convinced of the real hold this new amusement has on its audience." The *Jewish Daily Forward* described the growing popularity of the movies among women and children who were the patrons of early shows. Abraham Cahan, the editor of the Jewish paper, in 1906 noticed how music halls had shut down, Yiddish theaters were "badly hurt," and candy stores had lost their customers, whereas nickelodeons were booming: "Hundreds of people wait in line. A year ago there were about ten Jewish music halls in New York and Brooklyn. Now there are only two." There were about a hundred movie houses in the city, many of them on the Lower East Side. The movies did not suffer from the depression, "for people must be entertained and five cents is little to pay." Movies generally lasted half an hour, could be seen several times in a row, and opened in the afternoon; their customers could "eat fruits and have a good time." Some years later, the *Forward* remarked: "Everybody loves the movies. Our Jews feel very much at home with the detectives, oceans, horses, dogs, and cars that run about on the screen." When owners of small theaters gathered to protest against a city ordinance to close the movies in 1908, the *New York Tribune* reported with surprise that the majority of the movie protestors were Jewish Americans; there were also some Italians, Greeks, and Hungarians and a few Germans. It is not by chance that by 1915 some members of the Board of Censors who were behind the closing of small movie theaters run by ethnic groups began praising the work of D. W. Griffith. The most powerful vice crusader in New York City, the Reverend Charles Parkhurst, for example, held that from Griffith's films "a boy can learn more pure history and get more atmosphere of the period . . . than by weeks and months of study in the classrooms." Griffith's career was an example of the merging of politics, vice crusading, and films.[45]

Even before *Birth*'s opening in New York City, the NAACP had tried to prevent its premiere in Los Angeles. After five weeks of pressure by opponents in New York City, Griffith agreed to eliminate the most offensive scenes from the movie, such as those dealing with white girls viciously attacked by wild black men, and the original epilogue showing a letter from Lincoln in which the president declared he did not believe in racial equality and suggested the deportation of Negroes to Africa as the final solution to racial problems in America. Griffith also added in the epilogue a sequence shot at the Hampton Institute, the Negro industrial school in Virginia from which Booker T. Washington graduated, showing contemporary "progress" of the Negro race. The filmmaker had explored the possibility of shooting this sequence at Tuskegee, but Washington, approached by Philip Allston, a representative of the National Negro Business League, turned the offer down. The Tuskegee leader's answer was very clear: he thought *Birth* was a "hurtful, vicious play," he did not believe Tuskegee would be helped in relating to it, he felt the film was "stirring up a lot of useless race prejudice wherever it has gone," and he strongly wished "that the play might be stopped." But Washington died the same year *Birth* was out. According to the *New York Age*, Hampton representatives had made a great mistake in accepting the inclusion of the institute in Griffith's epilogue, as it could "only injure Hampton and not improve the picture."[46] Against *Birth*, at least, the NAACP found an ally in Washington's "Tuskegee Machine," as Du Bois called it.

In the May 1915 *Crisis*, Du Bois explained to his thirty-five thousand readers the grounds on which the NAACP's campaign against the screening of *Birth* was carried out, without denying that the first half of the movie contained "marvelously good war pictures." The second part, however, viciously misrepresented the Negro "either as an ignorant fool, a vicious rapist, a venal or unscrupulous politician or a faithful but doddering idiot." Furthermore, he stated that the film distorted the figure of abolitionist Thaddeus Stevens by suggesting in highly emotional scenes that he "was induced to give the Negroes the right to vote and secretly rejoiced in Lincoln's death because of his infatuation for a mulatto mistress."[47] This highly sophisticated film was viciously racist propaganda at a time in which the lynching of black men for the alleged excuse of attacks on white women was all too common, racial segregation of residential areas proliferated, and antiblack feelings were the core of a "reconciled" America.

Du Bois reminded his readers that only a few years had passed since Thomas Dixon had turned his novel into a "sordid and lurid melodrama," and several cities prohibited the performance of this play "because of its indecency or incitement to riot." But when that vicious play was made into a motion picture, continued Du Bois, it received the preliminary approval of the National Board of Censorship, located at that time in New York. Du Bois and other NAACP officers rushed to the Board of Censorship when announcement of the showing of the movie in New York appeared in the local press. But the majority of the board did not find anything objectionable in the movie to reverse their positive judgment. With the exception of a few insignificant scenes, on 15 March the board passed the movie over the protests of a minority of nine members, including its chair, Frederick C. Howe. During the second half of March, the NAACP had the owner and the producer of the film summoned to the Police Court on the grounds that they were "maintaining a public nuisance and endangering the public peace." Jane Addams and Lillian D. Wald, as original members of the NAACP, saw the movie on behalf of the association and condemned it. Addams gave an exclusive interview to the *Evening Post,* the only paper in New York refusing to advertise *Birth.* On 19 March the NAACP wrote New York mayor John Mitchell requesting that he exert his authority to suppress the film as "an offense against public decency and as endangering public morals." On 27 March the NAACP was denied permission to organize a parade in front of the mayor's office. The police department notified the NAACP that it would not issue the permit "for the reason that the streets can only be used for processions on holidays and Saturdays."[48] On 30 March the mayor agreed to receive an NAACP delegation. Two Tuskegee men—shrewd politician Charles Anderson and Fred Moore, the editor of the *New York Age*—anticipated the NAACP

delegation, which included W. E. B. Du Bois, Mary Ovington, Joel Spingarn, and Oswald Garrison Villard, and reached city hall first, appearing to head the delegation. Before the mayor stood an interracial group
of five hundred people composed of ministers, editors, educators, and
representatives of civil rights organizations.[49] According to editor Fred
Moore, this group of clergy, businesspeople, and professionals "deeply
interested in the progress of their race were on hand, and their neat
personal appearance was in itself a strong denial to the slurs made
against the Negro in 'The Birth of a Nation.'" Frederick C. Howe, commissioner of immigration and chair of the National Board of Censorship, of which he represented the minority willing to stop the movie, together with other eminent reformers, participated as a simple citizen to
protest against *Birth.* Moore discussed some data on the number of
practicing colored physicians and lawyers in greater New York, the
amount of real estate owned by black New Yorkers, and the large sums
of money they had on deposit at local banks. The editor of the *Age*
wanted to make the point that there was no question that black people
were "other than beastly."[50]

The mayor said he had seen the movie and agreed that it might incite
viewers to disturb the public peace, and that he had already advised the
management of the theater and the owner of the film; he told the delegation that the latter had consented to cut off the most objectionable
scenes. The NAACP officers decided they would discontinue the legal
case if the promised changes were made in the film. However, on 1 April the delegation saw the revised version and realized that only unim-
portant changes had been made: a quote from Lincoln opposing racial
equality had disappeared (although the president actually said those
words), Lincoln's solution concerning the deportation of black people
to Africa had also been removed, and some scenes of black sexual assaults on white women and Gus's castration at the hands of the KKK no
longer were part of Griffith's masterpiece.

The NAACP appealed to the mayor again, joined by New York activists
for women's suffrage, who also were protesting the showing of the movie.
Yet *Birth* continued to be shown in New York, Boston, Los Angeles, and
San Francisco.[51] In New York, the management of the Liberty Theatre,
fearing violence, excluded from the audience as many black people as
possible. Only light-skinned African Americans, those who could pass for
whites, were admitted to the show. Toward the end of March, the movie
was still extensively advertised in greater New York and presented as "the
wonderful attraction at the Liberty Theatre," the *Age* reported.[52]

Paradoxically, in a way *The Birth of a Nation* and the NAACP helped
each other in getting public attention. Du Bois keenly observed that the

battle against the film probably "succeeded in advertising it even beyond its admittedly notable merits." Yet the fight against *Birth* made
thousands of respectable black people mobilize across the country by
developing various forms of protest, such as picketing theaters, march-
es, and legal banning of the film. Against the injurious *Birth,* former enemies such as the Tuskegee machine became the NAACP's temporary
allies, and many white religious and urban organizations joined in the
battle. The fact that censorship was, and still is, a very controversial issue
for the liberal community was partly responsible for causing the failure
of the NAACP's campaign against *Birth.* A few leaders of the association
opposed censorship on the grounds of the First Amendment and stood
for the right of the individual viewer to judge, but at the same time they
advocated forms of protest able to raise popular consciousness without
suppressing the movie. Other eminent white supporters of the NAACP,
such as social worker Lillian Wald, were strongly in favor of a legal campaign for censorship. According to Du Bois, who favored censorship but
was fully aware of the danger of limiting expression, it was a "miserable
dilemma": without some limitations "civilization could not endure."[53]
Because *Birth* was such a powerful work of propaganda carried out by a
new medium, the NAACP feared its racist message would be inexpungi-
ble, and therefore the organization continued the fight against the film
for years.[54] In spring 1915, however, there were long lines of people in
New York waiting for tickets.

At that time no one seemed to pay attention to the fact that Griffith's
main characters were not performed by black actors but by "blackface"
white actors who took the role of both blacks and whites. The same actors appeared in one scene with the Klan sheet and in the next wore
blackface makeup to portray the most revolting and clownish black
characters of the movie. Although black actors were not given major
roles in silent movies, Griffith employed hundreds of them as extras in
his film. He was following the tradition of pre–Civil War blackface minstrelsy in which white blackface male actors portrayed grotesque Negro
characters. What was new in Griffith's use of blackface dramatization
was its target: a large multiethnic audience that no theatrical blackface
show could reach. Griffith's purpose, as he candidly admitted, "was to
create a feeling of abhorrence in white people, especially white women
against colored men." Nevertheless, his southern identity could make
him candidly declare his love for Negroes: "I grew up with negroes. I was
nursed by a negro mammy."[55]

In a candid response to a powerful editorial in the *New York Globe* that
stressed *Birth*'s "cruel distortion of history" by portraying members of
the Negro race "as women-chasers and foul fiends," Griffith stated he

had simply contrasted "the bad with the good." He claimed to have followed "the formula of the best dramas in the world" by which "we estab-
lish our ideals by revealing the victory of right over wrong." Griffith felt
he had not been unfair to the Negroes, for his film paid particular attention "to those faithful negroes who stayed with their former masters and
were ready to give up their lives to protect their white friends." He
therefore found the *Globe*'s editorial "an insult to the intelligence and
human kindness" of the nearly one hundred thousand "of the best
people in New York City" who looked at and praised the picture from an
artistic point of view only. Griffith was convinced that the strenuous organized attacks of those who opposed the film focused upon one of its
features they deemed might have a negative influence on intermarriage
of blacks and whites: "The organizing opponents are white leaders of
the National Association for the Advancement of Colored People, including Oswald Garrison Villard and J. E. Spingarn, who hold official
positions in this prointermarriage organization." He had hard words for
the *Crisis,* which he found an incendiary publication fighting against
"anti-intermarriage legislation."[56]

By the first week of April 1915, Boston had become the center of the
fight over *The Birth of a Nation.* It was in Boston that the new feature in
the epilogue filmed at Hampton Institute in Virginia was added to show
"the advance of Negro life." Young blacks learning industrial discipline,
the film suggested, were the "good Negroes" of today, the new socially
segregated working class of the South. Conversely, those intellectuals
like W. E. B. Du Bois, James Weldon Johnson, and other black activists
of the NAACP were the "bad Negroes," who fought for equality and political rights.[57]

The *Boston Journal* reported Griffith's position against the introduction of a bill in the Massachusetts legislature by Representative Lewis R.
Sullivan that would make it a criminal offense to produce any show or
entertainment that excited racial or religious prejudice or that broke
the public peace. According to the film director, the bill had been
rushed to criminalize *Birth.* He argued that the supporters of the bill
were so narrow-minded that they did not realize "universal dramatic art
is practically impossible without the excitation of some degree of race or
religious feelings." Race and religion, in Griffith's view, could not be
dragged into the realm of censorship: "It is unwritten law that neither of
these matters belong to legislative regulation, but are reserved within
the clause of the Constitution that grants freedom of speech." If legislation should deal with these issues, Griffith's argument continued,
then the Jews would find themselves object of prejudice in Shakespeare's *Merchant of Venice* and the Irish in Bernard Shaw's *John Bull and*

His Other Island, and other representatives of various groups would be given an opportunity for "petty persecution and spite against the theatrical producers and managers."[58]

In the spring of 1916, Griffith published a lengthy pamphlet, *The Rise and Fall of Free Speech in America,* in which he articulated a still astonished response to the nationwide controversy his movie had created, and he strongly expressed his conviction that movies should enjoy the same constitutional freedom as the printed page. The first page of Griffith's pamphlet, which defined film censorship as the first serious attack on freedom of expression in the United States since colonial times, shows a dark, animal-like figure putting on the mask of reform. According to the author, hiding under the disguise of virtue, "the malignant pygmy has matured into a *caliban.*"[59]

Caliban of the Yellow Sands: *A Metaphor of Human Progress*

Ironically, *Caliban* was the community masque written by Percy MacKaye and presented by some fifteen hundred players that became the culmination of the numerous celebrations for the tercentenary commemoration of Shakespeare in New York. Staged almost at the same time as Du Bois's *Star of Ethiopia* was shown in Philadelphia, *Caliban* was performed ten times from 24 May to 5 June 1916 at the City College Stadium; it cost $110,000 to produce and took months of work by people of genius.[60]

"It's like a tempest full of stars," poet Edwin Markham told Percy MacKaye after the latter had read his prologue of the community masque to the hundreds of people working for the Shakespearian celebration who had gathered for the occasion in the foyer of the Metropolitan Opera on 10 January 1916. MacKaye's prologue explained the meaning of the masque, which was freely based on Shakespeare's *Tempest* and portrayed the characters of Prospero, Ariel, Caliban, and Miranda. In the course of MacKaye's presentation, the walls of the Opera House were shaken at intervals by dynamite explosions in the excavations for the new Broadway subway. This created a suitable background, quite similar to the thunders of a tempest.[61]

The original idea of staging the masque in Central Park met the strong opposition of park lovers afraid of a potential invasion of thousands of people stepping on well-kept meadows. Those opposing the park location won, as did Central Park's friends when New York lost the battle for the World's Columbian Exposition of 1893. This time it was decided to hold the performances at the City College Stadium, and architects were consulted to enlarge its semicircular structure. Thanks to the patronage of philanthropists like Andrew Carnegie, Joseph P. Morgan, Jacob H. Schiff, William K. Vanderbilt, Daniel Guggenheim, and several other representative names of New York's large fortunes, a complex organizational machine for perfecting the masque and for turning the stadium into a large open-air theater was made possible.[62] The "philanthropic" help was a good step toward the financial success of MacKaye's pageant, something on which Du Bois's *Star of Ethiopia* could not count.

Major roles in *Caliban of the Yellow Sands* were given to professional actors, including dancer Isadora Duncan, who performed without remuneration.[63] Rehearsals began in April at city schools, where MacKaye explained the general plot of *Caliban of the Yellow Sands* to the hundreds of men, women, and children recruited for the various scenes of the masque. In his view, a community masque meant democratization of poetry as it found its inspiration and theme in the "unlabored and untrammeled resources of our national life." But a masque, he warned, "stands for the democracy of excellence, not the democracy of mediocrity." What is art, he continued, "but self-government and harmonizing of the elements of the mind." MacKaye believed there could be no art without discipline or a high standard of excellence.[64]

The theme of the pageant for the New York Shakespeare festival, as MacKaye conceived it, was Caliban seeking to learn the art of Prospero. Symbolically it meant "the slow education of mankind through the influence of cooperative art, that is, of the art of the theatre in its full social scope." MacKaye viewed Caliban as "that passionate child-curious part of us all . . . grovelling . . . yet groping . . . toward that serener plan of pity and love, reason and disciplined will, where Miranda and Prospero commune with Ariel and his Spirits."[65] MacKaye's masque delivered a message of social cohesiveness and hope when it was feared the war in Europe would cause original allegiances to resurface among immigrant groups in America.

It was not by chance that the theme of *The Tempest* inspired MacKaye's masque. Shakespeare's play can be approached as an extraordinary tale about the creation of a new society in America, in which the English expansion becomes, in Ronald Takaki's words, "a defining moment in the making of an English-American identity based on race." Just as the theatergoers of Shakespeare's time saw in blackface Caliban the representation of the instinctual forces of human nature that had to be repressed to reach a higher place on the scale of development of human civilization, the multiethnic New York crowd saw in MacKaye's blackface Caliban the representation of those internal forces that could disintegrate the American community. Caliban was a New World inhabitant, and his racial identity was ambiguous: "Freckled," dark-complected, a "thing of darkness," Caliban was the son of a witch who had lived in Africa. Similar to the blackface characters of Griffith's *Birth,* Caliban was half-human, half-beast. For MacKaye, however, Caliban could be regenerated; in fact, in perfect agreement with psychologist G. Stanley Hall's fusion of Darwinism, neo-Lamarckianism, geneticism, and primitivism of his "recapitulation theory," establishing a curious analogy between stages of individual development and stages of the progress of the species, the masque ended with Caliban rising from his stooping vision to his height and sailing to the spirit of Shakespeare for "More visions—visions, Master!"[66]

Before taking charge of the gigantic masque for the Shakespeare celebration in New York, MacKaye had also elaborated pageant schemes against the "insanity and death" of the Fourth of July in many cities. According to MacKaye, this was the result of the fact that America "has ignored the function of art as the salvation of our civilization." The art of pageantry was perfectly functional to the creation of a tamed theatrical space that would turn popular barbarism into "popular expression." Pageantry, as MacKaye conceived it, was "the art of audiences . . . a kind of dream in which the people are not merely spectators but participators." This popular expression was directed by "constructive leaders" who were creative artists "imbued with the insight, desire and capacity to lead communities to express themselves in forms of civic art." MacKaye devised a two-year plan for pageant masters to revive customs that could become "national traditions" to be celebrated by American communities on the Fourth of July. The suggested features included street participants wearing vivid costumes in various sections of a city; ballad and carol singers chosen among schoolboys; street vendors selling articles of arts and crafts made in public schools; a children's parade in four divisions, with a color scheme representing the four seasons; pantomime artists; athletic competitions and awarding of prizes; the historical military parade as a vivid spectacle of all former American troops and armies, accompanied by cheering crowds; and the folk pageant symbolizing the fusion of many nationalities in the American nation, in their national costumes, singing their national anthems, and led by their national heroes.[67]

The most important theorist of American historical pageantry, New Yorker Percy MacKaye, like New Englander W. E. B. Du Bois, studied at Harvard but majored in the classics and drama. Upon his return to New York, MacKaye became friends with the circle of radicals surrounding Mabel Dodge, including the younger John Reed, whom he had met at the Harvard Dramatic Club. Unlike Du Bois, who pragmatically supported Woodrow Wilson in 1912 as the lesser evil for African Americans and whose subsequent disgust for Wilson's racial politics progressively led him to Marxism, MacKaye supported the socialist candidate in 1912 but then became an ardent follower of Woodrow Wilson. MacKaye obtained his greatest achievement in 1914 with the Pageant and Masque of St. Louis, in which seventy-five hundred people performed the history of America to an audience estimated at half a million. Yet in reconstructing the city's multiethnic history, the St. Louis Pageant Drama Association decided not to make use of real Native Americans and had, instead, copper-colored local residents dressed up as "Indians" and performing as Native-American characters. The association also forgot to include in the pageant the city's large black population but invited all recently arrived immigrant groups, even those whose number was insignificant, to play in the pageant.[68]

However, when MacKaye discussed his experience in St. Louis while working on *Caliban* in New York, he enthusiastically portrayed it as the most successful for the cause of democratic art. He said that he read his St. Louis masque before assemblies of ministers, in Negro high schools, before clubs of advertising businessmen, at meetings of the Industrial Workers of the World, "before men of all conditions of life and shades of opinion." Like Langdon's pageant for the celebration of the Fourth of July, MacKaye's was an instrument of pacification, Americanization, and patriotic indoctrination of foreign immigrants. In 1915, the year of Du Bois's *Negro* and Griffith's *Birth of a Nation*, MacKaye made this function of pageantry explicit by writing *The New Citizenship: A Civic Ritual Devised for Places of Public Meeting in America,* a pageant designed to accompany the naturalization ceremony and to underline through mass movement, song, and dance the transformation of the foreigner into a patriotic American citizen. The pageant ended with a stirring proclamation about the joys of labor during which a symbolic figure of Liberty unfurled the American flag above the nationalized immigrants' heads.[69]

Finally, on 24 May 1916, came the great opening of the "biggest dramatic entertainment in history of New York." Fifteen thousand people coming from every corner of the city filled the open-air theater on the Heights and attended the "sumptuous pageant." It was a real New York audience that saw the first performance of the masque, an audience that represented the city's makeup, from the Lower East Side to Riverside Drive, the *New York Times* observed. In this sense, "it was more nearly a community affair, perhaps, than any dramatic performance that has ever been held here."[70] People from shops and factories arrived as early as 5:30 p.m., bringing their suppers. From that time on, limousines, taxicabs, trolleys, Fifth Avenue buses, and the subway were packed with people coming to see *Caliban*. These people were welcomed by more than one hundred Boy Scouts acting as messengers, guides, and information clerks, ready to help. "The spirit of the Masque was caught quickly, and an outburst of applause followed the prologue," the *New York Times* reported. President Wilson sent a letter saying how sorry he was not to be able to attend the event and enjoy "pleasures of that sort" because the pressure of Europe at war kept him on duty in Washington, D.C. Similarly, Mayor Mitchell could not come but was represented by his secretary, Theodore Roosevelt.

Was a community dramatic entertainment feasible in a city of millions like New York? Garnet Holmes, the director of the pageant, did not have any doubt. To Holmes, because the community drama was the very essence of democracy, the cast of the pageant was "the most cosmopolitan group imaginable."[71] The director said that thanks to the mediation of Arturo Giovannitti, the Italian socialist poet, thirty members of the Italian club offered to act as Roman soldiers in the pageant; twelve Greek little boys were sent by the Hebrew Orphan Asylum to act as Roman fauns; there were actors from the Carnegie Hall studios, students from the Harlem Evening High School, singers from every choral society in the city, men and boys from the YMCA, volunteers from social settlements, girls from the National Cloak and Suit Company, who went to rehearsals after working hours.

The *Times* and all the New York press reacted enthusiastically. The *Evening Post* reported fifteen thousand people gathered to see "the largest dramatic representation ever given in this city." The stadium of the City College of New York in the Heights was filled four hours before the pageant began with crowds who poured from the subway and buses and drove up in automobiles. They came from all parts of the city, and some even traveled from Boston and Philadelphia. "Slowly the white of the Stadium and the gleam of the scaffolding disappeared as black figures took their places, until the amphitheater was filled with a huge crowd, expectant, motionless." The *Brooklyn Eagle* commented, "nothing quite so magnificent has ever been shown in this city or in the country." It was a New York poet with his fellow artists, but mainly "the men, women, and children of this big and busy city," who conceived and visualized for fifteen thousand people a pageant that could "revolutionize the theater and dramatic art in many of its aspects." The *New York World* focused on the impressive attendance and proposed to enlarge the City College Stadium for similar community uses in the future. The *Morning Telegraph* enthusiastically appreciated the "magical effects" and the multitudes whose participation "broadened it into a carnival fete"; it was an epical drama "in which antiquity and modernity joined hands and danced

upon the 'yellow sands' of now, within the outward circle of eternity."
For the *New York American,* it was the realization of the democratic ideal
because art was made not only "for the people, but also by the people,
and all the people will cooperate to make the common life more beautiful until the communal life itself shall become a living work of art."[72]

Theater reformer Louise Burleigh shared a similar enthusiastic reaction. In a chapter of her *Community Theatre in Theory and Practice* dedicated to MacKaye's *Caliban of the Yellow Sands,* she argued that the pageant was more ambitious than any previous civic attempt, as New York
was the most complex, the most varied in population, and the most vol-
atile of cities. But the introduction of the new art form to the great city
"was a strategical masterstroke." Its central message, in Burleigh's view,
was profoundly effective: "Caliban, from howling brutishly on his belly,
had been raised to the dignity of wearing the trappings of art, through
the teaching of his master." In other words, the whole fundamental idea
of *Caliban,* like the basic concept of community theater, was the value
given to directed education and growth, in feeling and doing. *Caliban*
was a metaphor of the progress of the human race: "mankind, stirred by
imagination through the inspiration of a seer, acts, and so learns."[73]

Burleigh was particularly interested in the reaction of the fifteen to
eighteen thousand people who gathered at the stadium of the City College of New York for the first performance. She felt a "friendly neighborliness" about the entire gathering, as if those thousands had a genuine interest: "the friendly flock on the Broadway car which carried me
northward might have been migrating toward the circus on an annual
outing." At the end of the spectacle, the bus she took was filled with
people talking about *Caliban.* Some of them were pleased, others un-
moved, and one was puzzled. Although it was not clear for them what it
was all about, they were all eager to discuss what they had seen. Burleigh
therefore concluded that the faults of that great community festival
were less important than its promise "of progress to better and greater
achievement." As capitalistic and commercial organizations tended "to
separate individuals into classes rather than unite all classes into a unified community," community theater could become a national institution for "constructive leisure" and therefore an antidote to counteract
immoral urban culture.[74]

Yet there were some dissenting voices. If pageantry was a representation of a selective past aiming at the creation of a common culture as a
utopian vision of the future, this could not succeed in a city like New
York, drama critic John Collier observed. The founder of the National
Board of Censorship and the director of a training school for community workers, Collier remarked that MacKaye's giant pageant was, in-

deed, a magnificent production, with a powerfully conceived dramatic figure of Caliban, the dim and chilling awe of the Roman mimes, the music, the thrilling Egyptian interlude, the march of Isadora Duncan down the rejoicing beam of light. In the view of Collier and other critics, however, the whole project was "amorphous." The main problem, Collier claimed, was the pageant's failure to stimulate community participation, for "Greater New York is not a community, but at best a slowly-forming aggregate of nascent communities." As Collier saw it, the pageant did not do justice to the depth and wealth of folklife in New York. Furthermore, when measured against "those common problems and confused but unmistakable tendencies which are going to make a community out of this crossroads of the worlds and the ages," the Shakespeare pageant was not a communal product and did not significantly influence community life in an immediate way: "to gather up New York City as one is like gathering up the world as one."[75]

This was the impression that New York City left on contemporary visitors. Everyone wondered how representative of the nation it was. Whatever symbolic meaning different observers may have attached to life in Manhattan, they all seemed to see the same life. Rush, scramble, frantic pace, movement, noise, and excitement were thought to be New York's unique attributes. From contemporary visitors' impressionistic descriptions of the city, one can see a mass of mobile and cosmopolitan humanity in which each individual seems recognizable in terms of class, race, ethnicity, and gender. English novelist, poet, and social critic G. K. Chesterton observed:

> New York is a cosmopolitan city; but it is not a city of cosmopolitans. Most of the masses in New York have a nation, whether or not it be the nation to which New York belongs. Those who are Americanised are American, and very patriotically American. Those who are not thus nationalised are not in the least internationalised. They simply continued to be themselves; the Irish are Irish; the Jews are Jewish; and all sorts of other tribes carry on the traditions of remote European valleys almost untouched. In short, there is a sort of slender bridge between their old country and their new, which they either cross or do not cross, but which they seldom simply occupy. They are exiles or they are citizens; there is no moment when they are cosmopolitans.[76]

There were black New Yorkers, however, who were neither exiles or full citizens. They were a highly differentiated community. A few belonged to an old "aristocracy of color," with their exclusive social clubs, literary societies, and churches. Others constituted a growing group of self-made people, owned small business undertakings, and loved to show off their recently achieved social status. The majority were servants, porters, butlers, waiters, and in other lower-working-class jobs. How did this culturally, politically, and socially differentiated group of people respond in a period in which the press reported almost daily on discriminations and atrocities committed against blacks in the South and other parts of the country? In an act of empowerment they all came together in a "Silent Parade" on 28 July 1917.

The New York Silent Parade of July 1917

Racial violence culminated in East St. Louis, Illinois, on 2 July 1917 when 125 black men, women, and children were tortured and killed, and nearly 6,000 were driven from their burning homes by mobs of white strikers. The NAACP sent Martha Gruening and W. E. B. Du Bois to East St. Louis as special investigators to discover what had driven mobs of white men, women, and children to burn and destroy at least $400,000 worth of property belonging to the city's white and black population, invade the homes of 6,000 black people, and willingly shoot, hang, torture, and injure 200 African Americans living there.

In a stirring editorial in the *Crisis,* Du Bois described the East St. Louis massacre as "the shame of American democracy," the pogrom that Samuel Gompers and his trade unions had engineered to stop the flow of black labor into the North. Du Bois warned that black workers would continue to go North to work for higher wages than the slave South ever paid, "despite the Trade Unions and the murderers whom they cover and defend." Du Bois saw the shadow of the notorious Bastille that a furious and desperate populace destroyed on 14 July 1789 in Paris—and whose key was brought to America by Lafayette and given to George Washington—over the path of American democracy. It was the "Black Bastille of Prejudice," America's curse, that fell over East St. Louis in July 1917. James Weldon Johnson, in recalling that event in his autobiography, observed that it "was the more bitterly ironical" because it happened when black citizens, as all others, were urged to do their part to "make the world safe for democracy."[77] Many agreed that what happened in East St. Louis was the most criminal outrage ever perpetrated in the country. The reaction was widespread.

Congress called for an investigation. At the hearings, witnesses reported that members of the Illinois militia and East St. Louis police shot black people; mobs went to the homes of black people, nailed boards over the doors and windows, and then set the homes afire; and little black children were taken out of their mother's arms and thrown into fire. At a meeting of the executive committee of the Harlem branch of the NAACP, Johnson suggested the staging in New York City of "a silent protest parade." It was agreed that the parade should not be made merely an affair of the NAACP and its Harlem branch but should involve all colored citizens of greater New York. Again, in a "reconciled" and unified country, New York was to play the symbolic role of moral witness of the nation's Bastille of prejudice. For the NAACP, the Silent Parade was the second remarkable organizational effort after the campaign against *Birth of a Nation* and made the interracial association representing black people's civil rights a credible and effective instrument of mobilization.

A large committee, including the pastors of the leading churches and other eminent men and women, was formed to make preparations for the parade. On Saturday, 28 July 1917, nine to ten thousand black women, men, and children marched down Fifth Avenue. The community that Du Bois in 1901 described as "a world of itself, closed in from the outer world and almost unknown to it . . . with its own social distinctions, amusements and ambitions," entered the public space as a whole with a parade the local press defined as a "sober, dignified protest against the wrongs": "Virtually every Negro church, Sunday school and society in New York was represented," the *New York Tribune* reported. Children dressed in white marched first, some of them not older than six. They were followed by the women, also dressed in white. Then the men marched in dark clothes behind the flags of the United States, Great Britain, and the Negro nations, Liberia and Haiti. Both marchers and watchers kept silence. Twenty thousand black people lined Fifth Avenue and gave their silent approval to the demonstration. "Among the watchers were those with tears in their eyes," James Weldon Johnson recalled.[78]

Author Toni Morrison has placed two characters in her novel *Jazz,* Alice and her little niece Dorcas, in this crowd of parade spectators. The girl has just lost both her parents in the East St. Louis riots, and Alice reflects on her fears:

> It was July in 1917 and the beautiful faces were cold and quiet; moving slowly into the space the drums were building for them. . . . The drums and the freezing faces hurt her, but hurt was better than fear and Alice had been frightened for a long time—first she was frightened of Illinois, then of Springfield, Massachusetts, then Eleventh Avenue, Third Avenue, Park Avenue. Recently she had begun to feel safe nowhere south of 110th Street, and Fifth Avenue was for her the most fearful of all. That was where whitemen leaned out of motor cars with folded dollar bills peeping from their palms. It was where salesmen touched her and only her as though she were part of the goods they had condescended

to sell her; it was the tissue required if the management was generous
enough to let you try on a blouse (but no hat) in a store. It was where
she, a woman of fifty and independent means, had no surname. Where
women who spoke English said, "Don't sit there, honey, you never know
what they have." And women who knew no English at all and would
never own a pair of silk stockings moved away from her if she sat next to
them on a trolley. Now, down Fifth Avenue from curb to curb, came a
tide of cold black faces, speechless and unblinking because what they
meant to say but did not trust themselves to say the drums said for
them. . . . The hurt hurt her, but the fear was gone at last. Fifth Avenue
was put into focus now and so was her protection of the newly orphaned
girl in her charge.[79]

Although many white spectators witnessed the Silent Parade, the
public ceremonial space belonged to the whole black community.
Women and children carried banners, some of which read: "Mother, do
lynchers go to Heaven?" "Give me a chance to live," "Treat us so that we
may love our country," "Mr. President, why not make America safe for
democracy?" The streets of New York had witnessed many strange
sights, but "never one stranger than this," Johnson recalled in his autobiography. The parade moved in silence and was watched in silence.[80]
Black Boy Scouts distributed to those lined along the sidewalks printed
circulars that stated some of the reasons for the demonstration in tones
as varied as the composite black community. One could read: "We
march because by the Grace of God and the force of truth, the dangerous, hampering walls of prejudice and inhuman injustices must fall," or
in a similar vein, "It is time that the Spirit of Christ should be manifested
in the making and execution of laws," or with a more secular emphasis,
"We march because we want our children to live in a better land and enjoy fairer conditions than have fallen to our lot."[81] The people on the
sidewalks could also read more radical and political comments: "We
march in memory of our butchered dead, the massacre of honest toilers
who were removing the reproach of laziness and thriftlessness hurled at
the entire race. They died to prove our worthiness to live." Spectators
were also reminded that "We have fought for the liberty of white Americans in 6 wars; our reward is East St. Louis," and that unions discrimi-
nated against black workers: "We are maligned as lazy and murdered
when we work," "We are excluded from the unions, and condemned for
not joining them," "Repelled by the unions we are condemned as
scabs." Finally, spectators could read statements on the influence of
African-American culture: "Our music is the only American music."[82]
The September *Crisis* included an extraordinary report on the events

leading to the East St. Louis massacre. In June, editor Du Bois and social worker Martha Gruening spent a full week of extensive investigation with the help of some hired researchers and many volunteers. In a twenty-four-page article the sociology professor and the social worker offered their readers firsthand detailed information of the socioeconomic aspects of the riot and concluded that it was primarily caused by "a combination of the jealousy of white labor unions and prejudice." Thousands of readers—that particular issue of the *Crisis* sold fifty thousand copies—found a "gruesome reading" of firsthand descriptions of horrifying episodes of violence perpetrated against black citizens. Readers were informed that East St. Louis, a great industrial center, had huge packing and manufacturing houses and was one of the biggest markets in the country for imported unskilled labor. With the beginning of war in Europe, the scarcity of white foreign immigrant workers had brought about an influx of black laborers who were leaving the South because of their desperate conditions. In the summer of 1916, when 4,500 white workers were on strike in the packing plants, black laborers were called in as strikebreakers. When the strike was over, the owners kept the black workers and refused to reemploy the white men. Union leaders realized that the supply of black workers from the South was practically inexhaustible, and consequently the effectiveness of any possible strike had decreased.[83]

Angry workers started small but indicative riots in May 1917 "to restore these white Americans their privileges." The fact that black workers were also Americans meant nothing to the unions, the NAACP investigators concluded. Du Bois and Gruening also mentioned how capitalists manipulated black workers to break the unions, but their main point was to denounce organized labor's racism. They informed the readers of the *Crisis* about a letter that Edward F. Mason, the secretary of the Central Trades and Labor Union, wrote on 23 May 1917 to the delegates of his union, in which he did not hesitate to suggest that some unspecified action should be taken to retard the growing threat of undesirable Negroes pouring into "our community" to the "detriment of our white citizens." Du Bois and Gruening did not want to give their readers the impression that the East St. Louis massacre of black citizens in a town largely made up of foreign immigrants was a direct result of the meeting called for in Mason's letter to the union delegates. Yet they strongly believed the massacre was the outcome of the attitude revealed in the letter. At that meeting, held on 28 May, some union leaders warned members that if the authorities took no action to prevent the importation of black laborers into town, they should resort to mob law.

Hence Gruening and Du Bois concluded that the East St. Louis outrage was "deliberately planned and executed." They then gave detailed descriptions from eyewitnesses they had interviewed who had seen and survived the reign of the mob law on 2 July. The accounts revealed the fury of white men, women, boys, and girls who enjoyed "butchering" black men and women of any age. Nevertheless, all the black people they interviewed agreed they would never return to the South, no matter what might happen in East St. Louis. However, after the riot, the city's white citizens seemed unrepentant.

The two investigators reported some statements released by the best citizens, newspaper editors, and people of property who resentfully thought too many "niggers" were going North, and felt offended that black men could exercise their voting rights, ride on streetcars next to white women, and pretend to have their way on a sidewalk.[84] Thomas Dixon or some other racist southerner could have said these words, but they reflected a pathetic attitude that was rather popular in the substantially "reconciled" North. This is why on 28 July thousands of African Americans marched in the streets of Manhattan in silent protest.

The Silent Parade that marched from Fifth Avenue down Fifty-seventh Street to Madison Square was also against Jim Crow cars, segregation, disfranchisement, and any form of brutality. The black clothes of men and the white dresses of women were the only choreographed details of a parade in which "all social lines were obliterated and the question of morals temporarily put aside," the *New York Age* remarked. The coming together of all classes of blacks—American born, West Indian, and Haitian—in a large procession was seen as an encouraging sign for the future. It was meant "to bridge over the gap of comprehension that exists between the better thinking members of both races." "There was no holiday air about this parade." In fact, it was its silence and simple style that struck observers: "Nobody tried to appear bigger than the rest. . . . The glitter of gold braid and riot of gay colors, the play of inspiring melodies and the martial mien of the participants—usual features of the Negro parade—were noticeably absent. . . . The spirit of hilarity, supposed to be a racial trait, for once was missing."[85]

There was no music other than the beat of muffled drums, and the banners served as reminders of not only black people's suffering but also their accomplishments in the United States. What struck observers was the absolute lack of visual effects in the parade: there were no marshal of the day, no regalia, and no other ostentatious ornaments, the effect being completely dependent upon the spiritual atmosphere that the parade was able to stir in participants and spectators as well. It was the march of a whole community in the public space. From the pages of the *Age*, James Weldon Johnson communicated his feelings to the whole African-American community:

> When the head of the procession paused at 30th Street I looked back and saw the long line of women in white still mounting the crest of Murray Hill, the men's column not yet in sight; and a great sob came up in my throat and in my heart a great yearning for all these people, my people, from the helpless little children just at my hand back to the strong men bringing up the rear, whom I could not even see. I turned to Dr. Du Bois at my side and said, "Look!" He looked, and neither of us could tell the other what he felt. It was a great day. An unforgettable day in the history of the race and in the history of New York City.[86]

The message of the Silent Parade was delivered in the language of utopia. Those dehumanizing, grotesque caricatures of *The Birth of a Nation* were symbolically defeated by the silent pride of the white garments black women wore to affirm their womanhood and to purify a racially segregated society based on white supremacy. The parade was a response within what Cornel West has called the African-American "humanistic tradition": a tradition that accepts the African-American culture for what it is, "the expression of an oppressed human community imposing its distinctive form of order on an existential chaos, explaining its political predicament, preserving its self-respect, and projecting its own special hopes for the future." The silent protest was staged in the most multiethnic of American cities, where nevertheless examples of racial discrimination were daily routine. Black people were hardly represented in municipal employment, experienced difficulties in getting access to public accommodations, and were excluded from the best restaurants, theaters, and movie houses of the city, or when given service, they were asked to pay higher prices than white customers. Recently arrived foreign immigrants could easily see that there was always a group of second-class American citizens whose subordinate status could be taken for granted, as the Americanizing epic story of *The Birth of a Nation* showed. To foreign immigrants, blackface masquerades made visible the meaning of race in the continuing creation of American identity.[87]

The fact that President Wilson welcomed *The Birth of a Nation* as "history with lightning" was not a surprise given the president's stand on racial matters. The Wilson administration treated African-American protests for civil and political rights with contempt and greatly increased the segregation in federal offices, where white women, according to Wilson's secretary of treasury, had been "forced to sit at desks with colored men."[88] By 1915 Wilson had changed his originally negative view of foreign immigrants and no longer saw in them a threat to America's Teutonic identity. Immigrants were becoming "Americanized," in the view of Wilson and other progressive politicians; they had given up their inherited traditions and allegiances in order to embrace American ideals. Griffith's Klan was taken as the symbol of this regenerate national identity. Thanks to the Knights of the KKK, southern civilization and the purity of white women were redeemed from shame. By making a political appeal to its large inter-ethnic audiences, *Birth* overcame class, ethnic, and sectional lines, and in so doing, it replaced the opposition of North versus South and American-born citizens versus foreign immigrants with the antagonism between black and white. The new Klan, organized in 1915 in response to *Birth*'s popularity, showed the film as the main attraction at its rallies and built the largest membership in its history, numbering in the millions. Quite commonly, however, at Klan rallies speakers charged that Catholics controlled New York City and other northern cities, and that "immoral" Jews ran the motion picture industry. As a Klan member flatly put it, "I want to put all the Catholics, Jews, and Negroes on a raft in the middle of the ocean and then sink the raft."[89] Thus, although *Birth* presented the Klan to large multiethnic audiences as the symbol of national unity, in reality the new Klan was the expression of the most provincial, patriarchal, anti-urban America.[90]

President Wilson, by welcoming Griffith's film as "history with lightning," hailed the South's revenge for Reconstruction and, as a scholar, shared the views of scientific racism held by those who argued that no political order could survive in the South unless based on racial inequality. It was an attack on the "New Negro," the generation of African Americans who had come of age in the South by the time of World War I, for whom the Civil War and slavery were only childhood tales. It was a generation of African Americans who distanced themselves from what southern whites had always defined as the "Negro place" that the "grand old darky" had deferentially kept. It was this new generation of African Americans who experienced the most systematic practices of disfranchisement, racial segregation, and lynching. Many of them went North to look for a better future. Some became successful performers of the new black comedies whose music and dances appealed to multiethnic urban youth.

The songs of the permanently shiftless and carefree "impudent coon" became popular together with the new dances encouraging spontaneous movements and breaking formal conventions in social dancing. From black theater also came ragtime, the music for the new dances. In the segregated city space, black musicians found jobs in those Broadway cabarets and restaurants from which they were excluded as customers. Their access to the stage was limited to black musical comedies.

In the eyes of many white and some black educators, this fragment of urban culture, together with the movies and ethnic pastimes, was crude, vulgar, and commercially exploited.[91] Consequently, they saw in the art of pageantry a potential redeemer. Ethnic groups were urged, as it happened in *Caliban of the Yellow Sands,* to participate in pageants and to incorporate those old traditions and customs that could be blended and reshaped in one big American society. Pageantry made history vivid while promoting community solidarity through mass participation.[92] Pageantry's colorful invitation to mass participation would make one community, it was believed, out of people divided by race or ethnicity, class, and interests. To most pageant masters, however, community solidarity meant a stable, cohesive hierarchy of local groups, not equality or homogeneity. In mainstream pageants, with the exception of John Reed's *Paterson Pageant,* workers always found joy in their work in perfect harmony with their bosses. A similar harmony was found in the relationship between masters and slaves in those few pageants dealing with such a subject of historical disunion.

In general, social conflicts were concealed. Enslaved blacks were represented as contented and loyal workers who never tried to escape, as William Langdon portrayed them in his plan for celebrating the Fourth of July. Foreign immigrants were shown performing colorful dances, well accepted in their new country but placed at its margins. Nearly every pageant included a scene in which white colonizers peacefully purchased native land as if it was the price of inevitable progress and not an expression of white conquest. Hence Du Bois's ambitious attempt to offer an oppositional definition of pageantry by including it within the black folk drama tradition. His *Star of Ethiopia* gave history and memory to the people of African descent in America and placed their experience at the center of the country's history.

Massive historical demonstrations used the power of the multitude to strengthen the appeal of the past. Percy MacKaye's self-description as a "dramatic engineer" and expert in "crowd psychology," in an age in which the principle of efficiency and expertise passed from mechanical to human engineering, showed an expert's confidence in his capacity to manipulate the emotions of large audiences. In a sense, as a representation of the idea of progress and a metaphor of the human race, his *Caliban* was an attempt to turn the city's class, race, and ethnic differences into a source of ideological and social unity. MacKaye's pageant may have failed to "gather up New York City as one," as John Collier put it, but the parade of the colored 367th Infantry leaving for the French front in 1918 succeeded.

Warriors and Entertainers: The "Buffalo" Soldiers Parade

On 23 March 1918, New York "capitulated to the 367th Infantry," the *Age* commented on the parade and the following musical performance of the colored "Buffalo soldiers." Two records were established, according to the black paper. As warriors, the colored soldiers showed their soldierly appearance in the parade on Saturday. As entertainers, they gave the most unique performance at the Manhattan Opera House on Sunday. "It was a complete and unconditional surrender."[93]

The Buffaloes received a stand of color from the Union League Club. In the official report of the still exclusive all-male club, a continuity was established between this event and the parading of the U.S. Twentieth Colored Troops of 1864. Portrayed as an example of the Union League Club's stand for "equal justice," the parade of the 367th Colored Regiment, the Buffalo soldiers, was presented in 1918 by the members as the natural evolvement of the club's campaign for raising colored regiments during the Civil War. On 23 March 1918, New York City "informally declared a holiday and marked time" while the Union League Club, "still hewing straight to the line of equal justice," presented a stand of colors to the regiment of black soldiers organized in November 1917.[94] Hundreds of thousands of white people lined both sides of aristocratic Fifth Avenue to cheer the march of the three thousand colored soldiers. The "Buffaloes"—as the Native Americans who fought against them in the days of the western frontier called this regiment—arrived in the metropolitan area, and the Union League proudly declared that it was "undoubtedly one of the biggest things that has ever been done for the Negro race." Although the field officers, the regimental adjutant, the regimental supply officer, the regimental surgeon, and the commanding officer of the headquarters company were white, the regiment included eighty-seven black company officers, six black medical officers, three black dental surgeons, and one black chaplain.

It was "a triumphal procession" of young men whose "martial appearance . . . and the precise, rhythmic way in which they swept along," after only four months of training, stunned the great white crowds who saw them from their motorcars or mansions on Fifth Avenue or the black crowds that cheered them from Harlem's sidewalks with an uproar. The main purpose of the event was taking the regiment to the city to show the 150,000 blacks living in greater New York "what Uncle Sam had done for them, what an efficient fighting man the colored soldier could make," and to show the whole New York population "what the National Army had done for the Negro." Colonel James A. Moss, the commander of the regiment, invited Governor Charles S. Whitman to review the parade in front of the Union League Club's house at Thirty-ninth Street and Fifth Avenue.

The ceremony of presentation of colors by Governor Whitman "was notably impressive and witnessed [by] an enormous throng." This time no "Loyal Ladies" were included in the ceremonial space, which was dominated by masculine military values. The governor addressed the gentlemen of the Union League—who had recently voted in majority against women's suffrage—on whose behalf he delivered the American flag to Colonel Moss, the officers, and the men of the 367th Infantry: "I charge you by all that is sacred to defend this banner with all the strength and power that God has given you. . . . Your country will trust you to be true to yourselves, true to the land of your birth, true to the record of those other soldiers of your race whose valorous deeds have brought glory to these Stars and Stripes. Go forth and fight for the cause of humanity as those other colored patriots have done."

In accepting the stand of colors, Colonel Moss praised "the generous, patriotic impulse that prompted their donation. . . . another expression of the patriotism of the Club . . . the historic friendship of the Union League Club for the colored man—a friendship based on the spirit of the 'square deal' for all men." The colonel, who had served eighteen years with colored troops, promised that upon the regiment's return from France, the very same stand of colors would be presented in a new ceremony. After the regimental buglers sounded patriotic hymns, the regiment's march was resumed up Fifth Avenue. The aristocratic avenue had already applauded and admired the march of white soldiers, but this time "it was no less lavish with its plaudits than were Lenox and Seventh avenues," the main thoroughfares of Harlem, "New York's colored district," as the regiment "swung along in perfect alignment."

The Union League Club's official version of this public celebration—without mentioning events like the East St. Louis massacre, the general dreadful wave of racism pervading the country, or the North's indifference to rampageous lynching and Jim Crowism—interpreted this parade as a sign of racial harmony that marked the African-American right to equal citizenship: "Every man in line looked like a soldier and wore a distinguishable expression of pride . . . Harlem has never seen such crowds as those that turned out to welcome the 'Buffaloes.' What it thought it would see and what it did really behold have made some very important history for the colored race. Harlem went mad . . . with delight and amazement at the showing made by the 'Buffaloes'—Their Own!" It seemed that Governor Whitman, by observing the regiment from a special grandstand on 137th Street, was honoring that neighborhood. Yet it was also a way of separating neighborhoods, of marking Harlem as a black ghetto under the "separate but equal" formula.

The Union League Club's report emphasized aspects of the event, stressing "what an efficient fighting man the colored soldier could make," and that as the rich man's club, loyal to the principles of constitutional government of moderate Republicans, the club actively participated in national preparedness for World War I. A March 1917 report of the Special Committee on Immediate Defense and National Service of the Union League Club defined participation in WWI as "a contest for freedom, for justice, for civilization, in which we are as much interested as the allies themselves." It was the American mission for liberty and justice, requiring entrance into the war. Club member and former president Theodore Roosevelt reminded his audience that when the club was founded during the Civil War, "manhood of this nation showed its practical realization of the fact that only those are fit to live who are not afraid to die." As in 1864, when the club fought against the Peace Democrats at a time when there was no peace, "we have not now the choice between peace and war," Roosevelt warned. To him, loyalty meant that "the American who loves Germany more than he loves America is not a good American. . . . The American who hates England more than he loves America is not a good American." Loyalism and patriotism so defined, in April 1917, while voting for their strong involvement in national preparedness, the members of the club voted on women's suffrage, with anti-suffragists winning 141 to 45 votes.[95] The Buffaloes' march and the presentation of colors were also conceived as the Union League Club's patriotic contribution to the American manhood the warriors represented.

The *New York Age*'s coverage of the event gave large space to the other side of the warrior-entertainer Buffaloes. It was "colored America's versatility," the *Age* stressed in reporting on the regiment's Sunday show at the Manhattan Opera House. The Buffaloes sang and danced like professionals and showed that the Negro was "an unusual person who, if given an opportunity, can do many things above the level of mediocrity." The regimental chorus sang "Roll, Jordan, Roll," "Mister Zip, Zip, Zop," and "Old Black Joe" as only Negroes can, the *Age* reported. Corporal Thaddeus Drayton, a talented vaudeville performer until he entered the regiment, did "some fancy dance steps" to syncopated music; Corporal Walter B. Williams, from Harlem, was the principal soloist, and his tenor voice was still as sweet as it was before he wore the uniform of Uncle Sam, perhaps even better; Corporal Lester Miller, another young man from Harlem, played his one-stringed instrument remarkably well; and Barney Clark, who before becoming a recruit was a female imper-

sonator on the stage, played that role at the Manhattan Opera House.[96]
As the African-American paper portrayed the event, there was no conflict between the warriors and the entertainers. Both sides of the Buffaloes conquered the city space and American public culture.

"We return. We return from fighting, we return fighting," stated Du
Bois's conclusion to his *Crisis* article on the returning colored soldiers.[97]
The value of participating as "Americans" in WWI was in African-American hopes for inclusion in what America stood for. The battle for racial
equality was suspended for national preparedness. What Du Bois had
called the "two-ness" of the African-American soul gave way to America
first. By showing patriotism and manhood in freeing the world for democracy, in Wilsonian terms, black soldiers would demonstrate, once
again, their virtuous citizenship, their capability of uplifting their entire
race. The unsolved question was the design of the American democracy
they helped to frame, by becoming integrated in its institutions.

Today the U.S. Army is the most integrated institution, and the warriors-
entertainers of World War I contributed significantly to its integration.
Yet the question is, how much have African Americans and other minorities, women included, changed the army hierarchies, discipline, and
normative goals? The question is broader, however. What does group
battling for integration in a society mean? Does it mean they simply
share with other integrated groups whatever the society has and whatever its purpose, or does the group force the society's acceptance of a
group difference, an acceptance that would challenge the common definition of that society? On the other hand, the issue of group separation, if it does not challenge the common values of the society from
which the group is claiming separation, creates a "society within society"
that differs only in size but not in quality. What rituals of race from the
Civil War to WWI show is that there was always a tension between integration in and separation from American public culture. This tension
was expressed by radical minorities whose broad perception of the
limits of this group integration-separation alternative designed a different notion of American democracy.

To stand for peace during the Civil War was different than being a
pacifist during WWI. The so-called Peace Democrats were mainly pro-
Confederates and rejected the war in the name of their economic and
political interests in keeping slavery alive, whereas pacifist positions during WWI had a different meaning. The slogan "to make the world safe
for democracy," as mobilizing as it could be, was the expression of a universalist principle coinciding with the new imperialism. Pacifist voices in

the United States included Jane Addams, Mary Ovington, and Franz
Boas. The NAACP's leadership was divided over war, with Oswald Garrison Villard taking a stand against the war, J. E. Spingarn actively involved in war efforts, and William English Walling breaking his allegiance to the Socialists because of the party's position against the war, a
position that Ovington, on the other hand, supported. "I felt for a moment as the war progressed that I could be without reservation a patriotic American," W. E. B. Du Bois later admitted in his *Autobiography*.[98]
Although Du Bois shared Spingarn's enthusiasm for a segregated camp
for colored officers in Iowa and with regret distanced himself from Eu-
gene V. Debs's Socialist Party for its stand against war, anthropologist
Franz Boas took an opposite stand. By connecting the "aggressive imperialism" of 1898, which opposed the fundamental ideas of what was
right held by the American people and made America "a young giant,
eager to grow at the expense of others, and dominated by the same desire of aggrandizement that sways the narrowly confined European
states," in 1916 the German-American scientist protested against "the
popular demand for preparedness." In 1918 Boas publicly demanded
the repeal of the Federal Espionage Act, which had caused the end of
civil liberties, and declared his vote for the Socialist Party. What Boas objected to most was a general inclination to consider American standards
of thought and action as "absolute standards" and the will to impose or
"raise" everyone else to these standards. Americans claimed that their
government was the best not only for themselves but for the rest of the
world as well. Boas believed that Americans had no right to impose their
"ideals upon other nations," no matter how slow these nations might be
in utilizing their resources. As a German-born American who had lived
in the United States more than thirty years, Boas spoke of "our intol-
erant attitude," highly pronounced when Americans talked of "our free
institutions," on which modern democracy was founded. What he found
disturbing was an easy identification of "the particular machinery of
democratic government" with "democratic institutions." He held that
democratic control of government had found different solutions in
other countries. "To claim as we often do, that our solution is the only
democratic and the ideal one is a one-sided exaggeration of Americanism."[99] Du Bois's language was more vivid than Boas's. He eloquently
phrased the conflict African Americans faced, between submitting to
school segregation and segregated military camps as the lesser evil and
not having education at all or having no black man in position of
authority, as the "perpetual dilemma." Yet Boas lucidly foresaw the
dangers of imposing American standards of democracy in the name of

"free institutions," which clearly emerged with the Spanish-American War. It was a danger undermining American democracy itself, as a disillusioned Du Bois concluded in his later years, leaving the country for Ghana. Although American democracy included a radical definition emerging throughout its history by means of the voices of political minorities, powerful socioeconomic processes always kept radical values at the margin. Yet these conflictual values are those making democracy broader and inclusive.

Notes

CHAPTER 1. Parades in New York City

1. Benjamin Quarles, *The Negro in the Civil War* (New York: Russell & Russell, 1953), 190–91; and Will Irwin, Earl Chapin May, and Joseph Hotchkiss, *A History of the Union League Club of New York City* (New York: Dodd, Mead, 1952), 33–36.

2. *New York Tribune,* 7 March 1864.

3. Ibid.; *New York Times,* 6 March 1864; and Union League Club of New York, *Report of the Committee on Volunteering* (New York: Club House Printers, 1864), 22; Quarles, *Negro in the Civil War,* 191.

4. Union League, *Report of the Committee on Volunteering,* 24; and Irwin, May, and Hotchkiss, *History of the Union League Club,* 35.

5. On the visibility of women in public and its contemporary perceptions, see Mary Ryan, *Women in Public: Between Banners and Ballot, 1825–1880* (Baltimore: Johns Hopkins Univ. Press, 1990). Ryan observes that the Whig tradition introduced women into politics as passive and respectable representatives of femininity (136).

6. Union League, *Report of the Committee on Volunteering,* 25, 26; and *New York Tribune,* 7 March 1864.

7. Quoted in Irwin, May, and Hotchkiss, *History of the Union League Club,* 34.

8. Mary Ryan, "The American Parade: Representations of the Nineteenth-Century Social Order," in Lynn Hunt, ed., *The New Cultural History* (Berkeley: Univ. of California Press, 1989), 131–53; and Ryan, *Women in Public.*

9. *New York Times,* 6 March 1864.

258

NOTES TO CHAPTER 1

10. George M. Fredrickson, "The Doctrine of Loyalty," in *The Inner Civil War: Northern Intellectuals and the Crisis of the Union* (New York: Harper & Row, 1965), 130–50; and David W. Blight, *Frederick Douglass' Civil War: Keeping Faith in Jubilee* (Baton Rouge: Louisiana State Univ. Press, 1989), 155.

11. *Douglass' Monthly,* April 1863, 819, 828.

12. James M. McPherson, *The Negro's Civil War* (New York: Vintage Books, 1967), 180, 181.

13. Quarles, *Negro in the Civil War,* 183–89.

14. *Douglass' Monthly,* June 1863, 839, and Aug. 1863, 849.

15. Joel Schor, *Henry Highland Garnet* (Westport CT: Greenwood Press, 1977), 20–21.

16. *Douglass' Monthly,* June 1863, 838; Blight, *Frederick Douglass' Civil War,* 164; and Quarles, *Negro in the Civil War,* 185.

17. Henry W. Bellows, *Historical Sketch of the Union League of New York: Its Origin, Organization and Work, 1863–1879* (New York: Club House Printers, 1879), 54, 5–7, 9.

18. New York Common Council, *Documents of the Board of Aldermen,* 1861, reprinted in Howard B. Furer, comp. and ed., *New York: A Chronological and Documentary History* (New York: Oceania, 1974), 84–85.

19. Bellows, *Historical Sketch of the Union League,* 11.

20. Frederick Law Olmsted to Oliver Wolcott Gibbs, New York, 5 Nov. 1862, in Jane Turner Censer, ed., *The Papers of Frederick Law Olmsted,* vol. 4, *Defending the Union: The Civil War and the U.S. Sanitary Commission, 1861–63* (Baltimore: Johns Hopkins Univ. Press, 1986), 466–67, 469; and Thomas Bender, *New York Intellect: A History of Intellectual Life in New York City, from 1750 to the Beginnings of Our Own Time* (Baltimore: Johns Hopkins Univ. Press), 172–74.

21. Eric Foner, *Free Soil, Free Labor, Free Men* (New York: Oxford Univ. Press, 1970), 42–43. On landscape architect Olmsted, see Roy Rosenzweig and Elizabeth Blackmar, *The Park and the People: A History of Central Park* (New York: Holt, 1994); and Bender, *New York Intellect,* 175.

22. Bellows, *Historical Sketch of the Union League,* 80.

23. Ibid., 55.

24. Irwin, May, and Hotchkiss, *History of the Union League Club,* 31.

25. Union League, *Report of the Committee on Volunteering,* 6–7.

26. Ibid., 8–13. The Committee on Volunteering established that colored recruits would receive the state bounty of $75 and the local bounty paid to other volunteers at the place of enlistment, relief for their families, and pay of $10 per month, although there was a common belief that Congress would increase the pay of all soldiers, blacks and whites, and this did occur in 1864.

27. The 262 black men mustered in New York City received only $80 each, and the $22 per man the county had paid "went into the hands of someone other than the recruits." Ibid., 14–15.

28. *New York Times*, 6 March 1864; and Union League, *Report of the Committee on Volunteering*, 44.

29. Iver C. Bernstein, *The New York City Draft Riots* (New York: Oxford Univ. Press, 1990), 67–68.

30. A similar alliance occurred with the Federalists for the emancipation law of 1799 and for the state constitution of 1821.

31. Union League, *Report of the Committee on Volunteering*, 18.

32. Bellows, *Historical Sketch of the Union League*, 58.

33. By the end of the war, the freedmen's aid movement had sent to the South more than one thousand teachers, who taught two hundred thousand black pupils, and hundreds of thousands of dollars. See Robert H. Bremner, *The Public Good: Philanthropy and Welfare in the Civil War Era* (New York: Knopf, 1980), 37–54.

34. *New York Herald*, 9 March 1864.

35. Union League, *Report of the Committee on Volunteering*, 48–50; and Irwin, May, and Hotchkiss, *History of the Union League Club*, 116.

36. See Bernstein, *New York City Draft Riots*.

37. Eric Foner, *Reconstruction: America's Unfinished Revolution, 1863–1877* (New York: Harper & Row, 1988).

38. *New York Tribune*, 7 March 1865; *New York Times*, 7 March 1865; *National Celebration of Union Victory: Grand Military and Civic Processions; Mass Meeting at Union Square, New York, March 6th, 1865* (New York: George Nesbitt, 1865), 6, 11, 15–16; and *New York Times*, 7 March 1865.

39. *National Celebration*, 16–19.

40. On the volunteer firemen as popular heroes of Jacksonian New York and their distinctive male group culture and republicanism, see Sean Wilentz, "The Republic of the Bowery," in *Chants Democratic: New York City and the Rise of the American Working Class, 1788–1850* (New York: Oxford Univ. Press, 1984).

41. *New York Times*, 7 March 1865.

42. *National Celebration*, 22.

43. Ibid., 28–29, 31, 55, 57–58, 59.

44. Ibid., 69–70, 71–72.

45. Ibid., 3. Promoters included Moses H. Grinnell, Moses Taylor, Samuel Sloan, Chas. A. Heckscher, Henry Clews, and R. H. McCurdy.

46. Altogether, such Union economic policies as the creation of national paper currency, a growing national debt, a national bank system, tariffs and the imposition of new taxes, and the Homestead Act and the Land-Grant College Act, which offered public lands to settlers and gave assistance to the states in establishing agricultural and technical colleges, respectively, constituted an extraordinary impulse and shaped change in the postwar society. See Foner, *Reconstruction*, 21.

47. Ibid., 460–511.

48. Union League Club of New York, *Address of the President, June 23,*

1866 (New York: Union League Club, 1866), 55–56, 60; and Foner, *Reconstruction*, 190, 192.

49. Bender, *New York Intellect*, 113–16. Abraham Lincoln launched his presidential campaign in the city with a speech at Cooper Union on 27 February 1860.

50. Foner, *Reconstruction*, 248.

51. *Mass Meeting of the Citizens of New York Held at Cooper Institute, February 22, 1866, to Approve the Principles Announced in the Messages of Andrew Johnson, President of the United States* (New York: George Nesbitt, 1866), 4.

52. Ibid., 4–6, 9, 10, 15, 23–24, 29, 33.

53. Johnson quoted in Foner, *Reconstruction*, 250.

54. James C. Mohr, *The Radical Republicans and Reform in New York during Reconstruction* (Ithaca: Cornell Univ. Press, 1973).

55. In 1869 the *New York Times* published an investigation of the conditions of the colored population in New York that estimated 12,250 individuals thus distributed: Mulberry, Crosby, Chrystie, Delancy, and Baxter Streets, 1,500; the Five Points Mission district, 250; Twenty-Seventh, Twenty-Eighth, Twenty-Ninth, and Thirteenth Streets, extending from Fifth Avenue to the North River, 4,500; Thompson, Laurens, York, Wooster, and Sullivan Streets, between Bleecker and Canal Streets, and from Bleecker to Eighteenth Street, 4,500; and some 1,500 scattered indiscriminately over the city. Colored men were employed mainly as coachmen for private families, waiters in hotels and dining saloons, barbers, whitewashers, and bricklayers; many were teamsters and longshoremen, and a few were artisans. The principal occupations of colored women were washing, ironing, dressmaking, and hairdressing. *New York Times,* 2 March 1869.

56. *New York Times,* 9 April 1870.

57. *New York Times,* 8 April 1870.

58. For the list of the associations in New York's colored community, see *New York Times,* 2 March 1869. For a study of the class and gender differences in these associations, black leaders' discussions of their aims, and their forms of public celebration in antebellum New York, see Alessandra Lorini, "Public Rituals, Race Ideology and the Transformation of Urban Culture: The Making of the New York African-American Community, 1825–1918" (Ph.D. diss., Columbia University, 1991), 52–107.

59. *New York Times,* 8 April 1870.

60. *Workingmen's Advocate,* 9 April 1870, reprinted in Philip S. Foner and Ronald L. Lewis, eds., *The Black Worker: A Documentary History from Colonial Times to the Present,* vol. 2, *The Era of the National Labor Union* (Philadelphia: Temple Univ. Press, 1980), 274.

61. Douglass quoted in Foner, *Reconstruction*, 75.

62. Ibid., 221–35, 471. Also see Eric Foner, *Politics and Ideology in the Age of the Civil War* (New York: Oxford Univ. Press, 1980); Mohr, *Radical Repub-*

licans and Reform; and Phyllis Frances Field, *The Politics of Race in New York* (Ithaca: Cornell Univ. Press, 1982).

63. Ingersoll quoted in Morton Keller, *Affairs of State: Public Life in Late Nineteenth-Century America* (Cambridge: Harvard Univ. Press, 1977), 143.

64. Greeley quoted in Seth M. Scheiner, *Negro Mecca* (New York: New York Univ. Press, 1965), 53–54.

65. Leslie H. Fishel Jr., "Repercussions of Reconstruction: The Northern Negro," *Civil War History* 14 (Dec. 1968): 340–41; and Foner, *Reconstruction*, 446.

66. Ellen Carol Du Bois, *Feminism and Suffrage: The Emergence of an Independent Women's Movement* (Ithaca: Cornell Univ. Press, 1978), 69; Paula Giddings, *When and Where I Enter: The Impact of Black Women on Race and Sex in America* (New York: Bantam Books, 1984), 65–68; and Angela Y. Davis, *Women, Race and Class* (New York: Vintage Books, 1981), 83–85.

67. John W. Blassingame and John R. McKivigan, eds., *The Frederick Douglass Papers*, series one, *Speeches, Debates, and Interviews*, vol. 4, 1864–80 (New Haven: Yale Univ. Press, 1991), 216.

68. *Revolution*, 1 Oct. 1868, reprinted in Philip S. Foner and Ronald L. Lewis, eds., *The Black Worker: A Documentary History from Colonial Times to the Present*, vol. 1, *From Colonial Times to 1869* (Philadelphia: Temple Univ. Press, 1979), 411.

69. Michael Kammen, *Mystic Chords of Memory: The Transformation of Tradition in American Culture* (New York: Vintage Books, 1993), 104, 106; and *New York Times*, 26 May 1888.

70. Frederick Douglass, *The Life and Times of Frederick Douglass: Written by Himself* (1881; reprint, New York: Collier Books, 1962), 449.

71. Frederick Douglass, "There Was a Right Side in the Late War: An Address Delivered in New York on May 30, 1878," in Blassingame and McKivigan, *Frederick Douglass Papers*, 4:480–92.

72. *New York Times*, 31 May 1888.

73. *New York Times*, 23 Feb. 1888.

74. Philip S. Foner, "Black Participation in the Centennial of 1876," *Negro History Bulletin* 39 (Feb. 1976): 533–38.

75. Frederick Douglass, "Celebrating the Past, Anticipating the Future: An Address Delivered in Philadelphia, Pennsylvania, on April 24, 1875," in Blassingame and McKivigan, *Frederick Douglass Papers*, 4:409, 413.

76. *New York Times*, 25 July 1877.

77. On labor unrest in this period, see David Montgomery, *Beyond Equality* (New York: Knopf, 1967); Herbert Gutman, "The Tompkins Square Riot in New York City on January 13, 1874: A Re-examination of Its Causes and Its Aftermath," *Labor History* 6 (winter 1965): 44–70; and Leon Fink, *Workingmen's Democracy* (Champaign: Univ. of Illinois Press, 1983).

CHAPTER 2. International Expositions
in Chicago and Atlanta

1. In the United States between 1865 and 1890, truck extension, or miles of public roads, went from 35,000 to 200,000 miles; west of the Mississippi public roads went from 3,300 to 72,000 miles; total miles of railroad tracks in the South went up to 25,000. See Alfred D. Chandler, ed., *Railroads: The Nation's First Big Business* (New York: Arno Press, 1965).

2. For a general history of international fairs, see Kenneth W. Luckhurst, *The Story of Exhibitions* (London: Studio Vista, 1951); John Allwood, *The Great Exhibitions* (London: Studio Vista, 1977); and Robert W. Rydell, *All the World's a Fair: Visions of Empire at American International Expositions, 1876–1916* (Chicago: Univ. of Chicago Press, 1984), an excellent study.

3. William Dean Howells, "Letters of an Altrurian Traveller," *Cosmopolitan* 16 (1893): 219–32, quoted in Rydell, *All the World's a Fair,* 40.

4. *Chicago Tribune,* 5 July 1893; and Walter Besant, "A First Impression," *Cosmopolitan* 15 (1893): 536–37, quoted in Rydell, *All the World's a Fair,* 48.

5. Bessie Louise Pierce, *A History of Chicago,* vol. 3, *The Rise of a Modern City, 1871–1893* (Chicago: Univ. of Chicago Press, 1957), 501. By the summer of 1889, Chicago had a committee of three hundred people, composed of prominent citizens appointed by Mayor Cregier and working under the auspices of the Chicago City Council. They issued $5 million worth of stock at $10 per share, which was completely sold by April 1890.

6. See Robert D. Parmet, "Competition for the World's Columbian Exposition: The New York Campaign," *Journal of the Illinois State Historical Society* 45 (1972): 365–81; "The World's Fair of 1892," *Harper's Weekly* 33 (1889): 614; Astor quoted in Parmet, "Competition for the World's Columbian Exposition," 369.

7. "New York and the Fair," *Harper's Weekly* 33 (1889): 1011; and *New York Times,* 19 Sept. 1889.

8. Parmet, "Competition for the World's Columbian Exposition," 373, 375.

9. Ibid., 379.

10. See Annie Randall White, *The Story of Columbus and the World's Columbian Exposition . . . Designed for Young Folks* (Chicago: Monarch Books, 1892), 288, 355–56; and Rydell, *All the World's a Fair,* 46.

11. *New York Times,* 6 Sept. 1901.

12. *Harper's Weekly* 37 (4 Nov. 1893): 1059.

13. *Oriental and Occidental* quoted in Rydell, *All the World's a Fair,* 53; *New York Times,* 19 June 1893; Sickles quoted in Rydell, *All the World's a Fair,* 63.

14. See Curtis M. Hinsley, "Zunis and Brahmins: Cultural Ambivalence in the Gilded Age," in George W. Stocking Jr., ed., *Romantic Motives: Essays on Anthropological Sensibility* (Madison: Univ. of Wisconsin Press, 1989), 170.

15. Denton J. Snider, *World's Fair Studies* (Chicago: Sigma, 1895), 255–57; *New York Times,* 30 April 1893; and Frederick Starr, "Anthropology at the World's Fair," *Popular Science Monthly* 43 (Sept. 1893): 619.

16. Edward B. McDowell, "The World's Fair Cosmopolis," *Frank Leslie's Popular Monthly* 36 (Oct. 1893): 415.

17. *Harper's Weekly* 37 (19 Aug. 1893): 797.

18. *New York Times,* 30 April 1893.

19. On the importance of associating Turner's thesis with the Chicago World's Fair, see Rydell, *All the World's a Fair,* 47; and Alan Trachtenberg, *The Incorporation of America: Culture and Society in the Gilded Age* (New York: Hill & Wang, 1982), 11.

20. Otis T. Mason, "Ethnological Exhibit of the Smithsonian Institution," in C. Staniland Wake, ed., *Memoirs of the International Congress of Anthropology* (Chicago: Schute, 1894), 210, 211–12.

21. Frederick Douglass, introduction to Ida Wells, *The Reason Why the Colored American Is Not in the World's Columbian Exposition,* in Trudier Harris, ed., *Selected Works of Ida B. Wells-Barnett* (New York: Oxford Univ. Press, 1991), 58; and Ida Wells-Barnett, *Crusade for Justice: The Autobiography of Ida B. Wells,* ed. by Alfreda M. Duster (Chicago: Univ. of Chicago Press, 1970), 116, 117.

22. Elliott M. Rudwick and August Meier, "Black Man in the 'White City': Negroes and the Columbian Exposition, 1893," *Phylon* 26 (winter 1965): 356.

23. Douglass, introduction to Wells, *Reason Why,* 54, 57, 58.

24. Wells, *Reason Why,* 62, 63, 65–66.

25. Ibid.; extract from the *Memphis Commercial,* 84, 76. *Chicago Tribune* (Jan. 1892) data of the victims' alleged crimes for the period 1882–91: 269 for rape of white women, 253 for murder, 44 for robbery, 37 for incendiarism, 4 for burglary, 27 for "race prejudice," 13 for quarreling with white men, 10 for making threats, 7 for rioting, 5 for miscegenation, and 32 for no reason. Wells's comments are taken from Wells, *Reason Why,* 74, 75, 79.

26. Wells, *Reason Why,* 119, 122, 123, 128, 129, 135, 136.

27. See Gerda Lerner, ed., *Black Women in White America: A Documentary History* (New York: Pantheon Books, 1972), 165; and Giddings, *When and Where I Enter,* 86.

28. Frances E. W. Harper, "Woman's Political Future," speech given at the World's Congress of Representative Women at the Columbian Exposition, reprinted in Henry Louis Gates Jr. and Nellie Y. McKay, eds., *The Norton Anthology of African American Literature* (New York: Norton, 1997), 436–39.

29. Rudwick and Meier, "Black Man in the 'White City,'" 360; and Wells-Barnett, *Crusade for Justice,* 119.

30. *Indianapolis Freeman,* 2 Sept. 1893.

31. Louis R. Harlan and Raymond W. Smock, eds., *Booker T. Washington Papers,* vol. 3, 1894–95 (Champaign: Univ. of Illinois Press, 1974), 364–65.

32. *New York Times,* 2 Nov. 1895.

33. *New York Times,* 19 Sept. 1895.

34. Booker T. Washington, *Up from Slavery: An Autobiography* (1900; reprint, New York: Dodd, Mead, 1965), 141. Also see the comprehensive biography of Washington by Louis R. Harlan, *Booker T. Washington: The Making of a Black Leader, 1856–1901* (New York: Oxford Univ. Press, 1972), 218. For an analysis of Washington's racial thought compared to the views of other black leaders of his day, see August Meier, *Negro Thought in America, 1880– 1915* (Ann Arbor: Univ. of Michigan Press, 1972); for an insightful and detailed account of the social and political spheres of a rigidly racially segregated society in the post-Reconstruction South and how its articulated structure of oppression affected black people's daily life and hopes for the future, see Leon F. Litwack, *Trouble in Mind: Black Southerners in the Age of Jim Crow* (New York: Knopf, 1998).

35. See Edward L. Ayers, *The Promise of the New South: Life after Reconstruction* (New York: Oxford Univ. Press, 1992), 7. According to Ayers, this era begins in the mid to late 1870s, when biracial Republican Reconstruction ended and the white Democrats won power in the southern states. For facts and figures about the Atlanta Exposition, see Rydell, *All the World's a Fair,* 73–85, 102.

36. Henry Grady, *The New South: Writings and Speeches of Henry Grady* (Savannah: Beehive Press, 1971), 11–12, quoted in Ayers, *Promise of the New South,* 21; on Grady and Atlanta, also see Harold E. Davis, *Henry Grady's New South: Atlanta, a Brave and Beautiful City* (Tuscaloosa: Univ. of Alabama Press, 1990). See also Harlan, *Booker T. Washington,* 228.

37. Circular quoted in Rydell, *All the World's a Fair,* 76.

38. On the New South's business community and how it supported the Atlanta Exposition, see Ayers, *Promise of the New South,* 64–66, 322.

39. Harlan and Smock, *Booker T. Washington Papers,* 3:364–66; and Washington, *Up from Slavery,* 130, 131.

40. Rydell, *All the World's a Fair,* 83; and Washington, *Up from Slavery,* 131, 132.

41. I. Garland Penn to B. T. Washington, 12 August 1895, cited in Harlan, *Booker T. Washington,* 209; and Washington, *Up from Slavery,* 134.

42. Washington, *Up from Slavery,* 134–37.

43. Ibid., 139–42. The best critic of Washington's speech is still Rayford W. Logan, "The Atlanta Compromise," in Hugh Hawkins, ed., *Booker T. Washington and His Critics: The Problem of Negro Leadership* (Boston: Heath, 1962), 21.

44. *Atlanta Constitution,* 19 Sept. 1895.

45. *New York World,* 19 Sept. 1895.

46. Washington, *Up from Slavery,* 144–45.

47. Du Bois quoted in Harlan, *Booker T. Washington,* 225.

48. Washington, *Up from Slavery,* 149; and Thomas Holt, "The Lonely

Warrior: Ida Wells-Barnett and the Struggle for Black Leadership," in John Hope Franklin and August Meier, eds., *Black Leaders in the Twentieth Century* (Champaign: Univ. of Illinois Press, 1982), 44.

49. The tower's height was 73 feet; the building covered 25,000 square feet, was 276 feet long, and was 112 feet wide. The total cost of the building was $10,000. See Ruth M. Winton, "Negro Participation in Southern Expositions, 1881–1915, *Journal of Negro Education* 16 (1947): 37–38.

50. *New York Times*, 2 Nov. 1895, 19 Sept. 1895, 22 Oct. 1895.

51. *Atlanta Constitution*, 22 Oct. 1895.

52. *New York Times*, 8 June 1895; *Atlanta Constitution*, 13 Jan. 1895; Alice M. Beacon, *The Negro at the Atlanta Exposition* (Baltimore: J. F. Slater Fund, 1896), 19, quoted in Rydell, *All the World's a Fair,* 84–85; *People's Advocate* quoted in "The Negro at the Atlanta Exposition," *Literary Digest* 22 (Nov. 1895): 6.

53. *Atlanta Constitution*, 22 Nov. 1895.

54. *New York Sun*, 15 Dec. 1895; on the conflictual alliance between Fortune and Washington, see Emma Lou Thornbrough, *T. Thomas Fortune: Militant Journalist* (Chicago: Univ. of Chicago Press, 1972), 186–87.

55. Speer quoted in Rydell, *All the World's a Fair,* 88.

56. Ibid., 5; and Trachtenberg, *Incorporation of America,* 213.

57. McDowell, "World's Fair Cosmopolis," 416.

58. Rydell, *All the World's a Fair,* 95.

59. Quetelet produced data on human physiognomy by examining Belgian soldiers, convicts, and Cambridge University students. See John S. Haller Jr., *Outcast from Evolution: Scientific Attitudes of Racial Inferiority* (Champaign: Univ. of Illinois Press, 1971), 18, 21.

60. Benjamin A. Gould, *Investigations in the Military and Anthropological Statistics of American Soldiers* (1869), 14, 218–27, quoted in Haller, *Outcast from Evolution,* 22, 26–29.

61. Sanford B. Hunt, "The Negro as a Soldier," *Anthropological Review* 7 (Jan. 1869): 42–43, quoted in ibid., 31–32.

62. Ibid., 55–57; Nathaniel S. Shaler, "An Ex-Southerner in South Carolina," *Atlantic Monthly* 26 (July 1870): 57; "Science and the African Problem," *Atlantic Monthly* 64 (July 1890): 41, quoted in Haller, *Outcast from Evolution,* 180–81.

63. See George W. Stocking Jr., ed., *A Franz Boas Reader: The Shaping of American Anthropology, 1883–1911* (Chicago: Univ. of Chicago Press, 1974).

64. *New York Sun*, 30 May 1909; Charles W. Eliot, "The Anglo-Saxon Solvent," editorial, *Boston Evening Transcript*, 9 March 1909.

65. On *Plessy v. Ferguson* and relative quotes, see Richard Hofstadter, ed., *Great Issues in American History: From Reconstruction to the Present Day, 1864–1969* (New York: Vintage Books, 1969), 55–58; Charles A. Lofgren, *The Plessy Case: A Legal-Historical Interpretation* (New York: Oxford Univ. Press, 1987), 196–208; and Donald G. Nieman, *Promises to Keep: African-*

Americans and the Constitutional Order, 1776 to the Present (New York: Oxford Univ. Press, 1991), 110–11.

66. Willard B. Gatewood Jr., *Black Americans and the White Man's Burden, 1898–1903* (Champaign: Univ. of Illinois Press, 1975), 7.

67. Ibid., 24, 34.

68. Willard B. Gatewood Jr., ed., *"Smoked Yankees" and the Struggle for Empire: Letters from the Negro Soldiers, 1898–1902* (Champaign: Univ. of Illinois Press, 1971), 159–60.

69. *Atlanta Constitution*, 11 and 12 June 1898, quoted in Gatewood, *Black Americans,* 52–55.

70. Edward A. Johnson, *History of Negro Soldiers in the Spanish-American War and Other Items of Interest* (Raleigh NC: Capital Printing, 1899), 85, 43; and Theodore Roosevelt, *The Works of Theodore Roosevelt*, vol. 11, *The Rough Riders and Men of Action* (New York: Scribner's Sons, 1925), 109–10. See also Johnson, *History of the Negro Soldiers,* 40–46, for eyewitness reports.

71. For a treatment of Roosevelt's racial views, see Thomas G. Dyer, *Theodore Roosevelt and the Idea of Race* (Baton Rouge: Louisiana State Univ. Press, 1980); Roosevelt quoted in William A. Williams, *The Tragedy of American Diplomacy* (New York: Dell, 1962), 72; McKinley quoted in R. Hal Williams, *Years of Decision: American Politics in the 1890s* (New York: Wiley, 1978), 146.

72. Roosevelt quoted in George M. Fredrickson, *The Black Image in the White Mind: The Debate on Afro-American Character and Destiny, 1817–1914* (New York: Harper & Row, 1971), 308.

73. McKinley quoted in Howard Zinn, *A People's History of the United States* (New York: Harper Collins, 1980), 305–6; for black Americans debating Philippine annexation, see Gatewood, *Black Americans,* 182–97; senator quoted in Ayers, *Promise of the New South,* 333.

74. "Platform of the American Anti-Imperialist League, October 17, 1899," in Hofstadter, *Great Issues in American History,* 202.

75. From the *Report of the Pan-African Conference, Held on the 23rd, 24th, and 25th July, 1900 at Westminster Townhall, Westminster S [London],* reprinted in Herbert Aptheker, ed., *Writings by W. E. B. Du Bois in Non-Periodical Literature Edited by Others,* Complete Published Works of W. E. B. Du Bois (Millwood NY: Kraus-Thomson Organization, 1982), 11. On Du Bois and the Pan-African Conference, see David Levering Lewis, *W. E. B. Du Bois: Biography of a Race, 1868–1919* (New York: Holt, 1993), 246–51.

CHAPTER 3. Social Science as Public Culture

1. Booker T. Washington, *Black Belt Diamonds: Gems from the Speeches, Addresses and Talks to the Students,* selected and arranged by Victoria Early Matthews, introduced by T. Thomas Fortune (1898; reprint, New York: Negro Univ. Press, 1969), 9, 14.

2. See Alfred A. Moss Jr., *The American Negro Academy: Voice of the Talented Tenth* (Baton Rouge: Louisiana State Univ. Press, 1981), 38–39, 263.

3. W. E. B. Du Bois, "The Conservation of Races," *American Negro Academy Occasional Papers,* no. 2 (Washington DC: American Negro Academy, 1897); reprinted in Herbert Aptheker, ed., *Pamphlets and Leaflets by W. E. B. Du Bois,* Complete Published Works of W. E. B. Du Bois (White Plains NY: Kraus-Thomson Organization, 1986), 2, 3–4, 5.

4. Douglass quoted in August Meier, *Negro Thought in America, 1880–1915: Racial Ideologies in the Age of Booker T. Washington* (Ann Arbor: Univ. of Michigan Press, 1966), 77; Du Bois quoted in Aptheker, ed., *Pamphlets and Leaflets by Du Bois,* 5, 6, 7.

5. Wilson J. Moses, *Alexander Crummell: A Study of Civilizations and Discontent* (New York: Oxford Univ. Press, 1989), 264–65; Moss, *American Negro Academy,* 50–51.

6. W. E. B. Du Bois, *Dusk of Dawn: An Essay toward an Autobiography of a Race Concept* (1940; reprint, Millwood NY: Kraus-Thomson Organization, 1975), 100, 98, 99, 101–2.

7. Stocking, ed., *Franz Boas Reader,* 220; on Clark University and faculty disagreement with President G. Stanley Hall, see Stocking, ed., *Franz Boas Reader,* 58; on Boas's problems and dissatisfaction with his role at the Chicago World's Columbian Exposition, see Douglas Cole, *Captured Heritage: The Scramble for Northwest Coast Artifacts* (Seattle: Univ. of Washington Press, 1985), 133, 126. Boas's dissatisfaction with the role of a "circus impresario" referred to the problems he had in displaying a group of fifteen Kwakiutl adults and children.

8. W. E. B. Du Bois, "The Study of the Negro Problems," *Annals of the American Academy of Political and Social Science* 11 (Jan. 1898), reprinted in Herbert Aptheker, ed., *Writings by W. E. B. Du Bois in Periodicals Edited by Others,* Complete Published Works of W. E. B. Du Bois (Millwood NY: Kraus-Thomson Organization, 1982), 1:52; Du Bois reported on his speech in W. E. B. Du Bois, *The Autobiography of W. E. B. Du Bois: A Soliloquy on Viewing My Life from the Last Decade of Its First Century* (New York: International, 1968), 200.

9. Du Bois, *Autobiography,* 206.

10. W. E. B. Du Bois, *The Philadelphia Negro: A Social Study* (1899; reprint, New York: Schocken Books, 1967); Du Bois quoted in Lewis, *W. E. B. Du Bois,* 209.

11. Du Bois, *Autobiography,* 148; on the review of Du Bois's book and its methodological innovations, see Lewis, *W. E. B. Du Bois,* 200–208; on the influence of William James on Du Bois, see Cornel West, *The American Evasion of Philosophy: A Genealogy of Pragmatism* (Madison: Univ. of Wisconsin Press, 1989), 138–49.

12. Frederick L. Hoffman, *Race Traits and Tendencies of the American Negro* (New York: Macmillan, 1896), 1, 37, 99, 148, 206–7.

13. W. E. B. Du Bois, review of *Race Traits and Tendencies of the American Negro* by Frederick L. Hoffman, *Annals of the American Society of Political and Social Science* 10 (Jan. 1897): 128, 132.

14. W. E. B. Du Bois, *Autobiography,* 197.

15. For extensive information on the Atlanta conferences, see Lewis, *W. E. B. Du Bois,* 214–21, 343–52.

16. Franz U. Boas, "Commencement Address at Atlanta University, May 31, 1906," *Atlanta University Leaflet,* no. 19, reprinted in Stocking, ed., *Franz Boas Reader,* 310, 311, 312, 313–14.

17. On the history of this crucial and difficult alliance between blacks and Jews, see Jack Salzman and Cornel West, *Struggles in the Promised Land: Toward a History of Black-Jewish Relations in the United States* (New York: Oxford Univ. Press, 1997). See also W. E. B. Du Bois, *Black Folk: Then and Now* (1939; reprint, Millwood NY: Kraus-Thomson Organization, 1975), vii.

18. W. E. B. Du Bois to Franz Boas, 11 October 1905, and Franz Boas to W. E. B. Du Bois, 14 October 1905, in *Franz U. Boas Papers,* quoted in Vernon Williams Jr., *Rethinking Race: Franz Boas and His Contemporaries* (Lexington: Univ. Press of Kentucky, 1996), 41. The "Boasian paradox" refers to the contradiction between Boas's philosophical egalitarianism and his reformed use of European and American physical anthropology.

19. This tension clearly emerged among Boas's students: whereas Ruth Benedict's work was inspired by the universalist approach, Melville Herskovits's early assimilationist views gave way, after the Harlem Renaissance, to a strong emphasis on African traits in black American culture. See Walter Jackson, "Melville Herskovits and the Search for Afro-American Culture," in George W. Stocking Jr., ed., *Malinowski, Rivers, Benedict, and Others: Essays on Culture and Personality,* vol. 4 in History of Anthropology series (Madison: Univ. of Wisconsin Press, 1986), 95–126.

20. George W. Stocking Jr., *Race, Culture and Evolution: Essays in the History of Anthropology* (New York: Free Press, 1968), 139; also see Marshall Hyatt, *Franz Boas, Social Activist: The Dynamics of Ethnicity* (New York: Greenwood Press, 1990); on Boas's death, see Melville Herskovits, *Franz Boas: The Science of Man in the Making* (New York: Scribner's, 1953), 120–21.

21. Franz U. Boas, *The Mind of Primitive Man* (1911; reprint, New York: Macmillan, 1938), 281; Franz U. Boas, *Changes in the Bodily Form of Descendants of Immigrants,* 61st Congress, 2d sess., 1911, S. Doc. 208; see Boas's letters to Jeremy W. Jenks, a Cornell University economist and member of the Commission of Immigration, 23 March 1908, 3 Sept. 1908, 11 March 1909, and 31 Dec. 1909, printed in Stocking, ed., *Franz Boas Reader,* 202–14.

22. On Stone's ability to deceive both Du Bois and Washington on his racial ideas, see Lewis, *W. E. B. Du Bois,* 367–69.

23. Alfred H. Stone, "Is Race Friction between Blacks and Whites in the United States Growing and Inevitable?" *American Journal of Sociology* 13 (March 1908): 677, 680–82.

24. W. E. B. Du Bois, "Discussion of the Paper by Alfred Stone: Is Race Friction between Blacks and Whites in the United States Growing and Inevitable?" *American Journal of Sociology* 13 (May 1908): 838, 836–37.

25. Paul S. Reinsch, "The Negro and European Civilization," *American Journal of Sociology* 11 (Sept. 1905): 148. Until the 1850s the most common views on the so-called typological theory of race differences came from Samuel G. Morton's *Crania Americana* (1839) and J. C. Nott and G. R. Glidden's *Types of Mankind* (1859). This theory was based on three fundamental beliefs: individual variations in constitution and behavior were the expression of differences between underlying types of a relatively permanent kind, each of which was suitable for a particular continent; natural categories produced social categories, and the latter reflected and aligned in the long run with the former; and individuals belonging to a particular racial type displayed an innate antagonism toward individuals of other racial types. See Ernst Mayr, *The Growth of Biological Thought* (Cambridge: Harvard Univ. Press, 1982), 487–88.

26. See Carl Degler, *In Search of Human Nature: The Decline and Revival of Darwinism in American Social Thought* (New York: Oxford Univ. Press, 1991), 3–55; William H. Tucker, *The Science and Politics of Racial Research* (Champaign: Univ. of Illinois Press, 1994), 9–36.

27. William Graham Sumner, *Folkways: A Study of the Sociological Importance in Usages, Manners, Customs, Mores, and Morals* (Boston: Ginn, 1906), 81–82.

28. John R. Commons, "Is Class Conflict in America Growing and Is It Inevitable?" *American Journal of Sociology* 13 (May 1908): 759.

29. John R. Commons, *Races and Immigrants in America* (1907; reprint, New York: Augustus M. Kelley, 1967), 7, 13, 209, 20–21, 42, 45, 49, 172.

30. Robert E. Park, "Education and Its Relation to the Conflict and Fusion of Cultures with Special Reference to the Negro," *Journal of Negro History* 4 (April 1919): 129–30; Robert E. Park and Ernest W. Burgess, *Introduction to the Science of Sociology* (Chicago: Univ. of Chicago Press, 1921).

31. Ralph Ellison, "*An American Dilemma*: A Review," in *Shadow and Act* (New York: Vintage Books, 1964), 307–8.

32. On Washington's offer to Du Bois, see Du Bois, *Dusk of Dawn*, 78–80; and Lewis, *W. E. B. Du Bois*, 228–34; on Park's acceptance, see Winifred Raushenbush, *Robert Park: Biography of a Sociologist* (Raleigh NC: Duke Univ. Press, 1979), 39–41. When Washington made the offer, Park had a large family and three precarious jobs: assistant at Harvard, secretary of the Congo Reform Association, and director of the Sunday edition of a Boston paper.

33. Park quoted in Raushenbush, *Robert Park*, 40, 42, 57, 50.

34. Washington quoted in Woodruff D. Smith, *The Ideological Origins of Nazi Imperialism* (New York: Oxford Univ. Press, 1986), 34. German importers did not purchase the varieties of staple-length cotton produced by

Tuskegee-trained Togolese, and an increase in cotton production caused a fall in price and the ruin of small producers like Togo (77).

35. Park quoted in Louis R. Harlan, *Booker T. Washington* (New York: Oxford Univ. Press, 1972), 271; and Booker T. Washington, "Cruelty in the Congo Country," *Outlook* 78 (Oct. 1904): 376–77.

36. Robert E. Park, *Race and Culture* (Glencoe IL: Free Press, 1950), 166–67.

37. Raushenbush, *Robert Park,* 77. By the 1920s Park had developed at the University of Chicago the most important social studies department in the United States.

38. W. E. B. Du Bois, *The Souls of the Black Folk* (1903), reprinted in Gates, ed., *Norton Anthology of African American Literature,* 620, 638.

39. On the Niagara Movement, see documents reprinted in Aptheker, ed., *Pamphlets and Leaflets by Du Bois,* 53–65, 69–81. In 1903 Du Bois defined the "Talented Tenth" as follows: "The Negro race, like all races, is going to be saved by its exceptional men. The problem of education, then, among Negroes must first of all deal with the Talented Tenth; it is the problem of developing the Best of this race that they may guide the Mass away from the contamination and death of the Worst, in their own and other races." See W. E. B. Du Bois, "The Talented Tenth," reprinted in Aptheker, ed., *Writings by Du Bois in Non-Periodical Literature Edited by Others,* 17–29.

40. Du Bois, *Autobiography,* 249–51; and Lewis, *W. E. B. Du Bois,* 330.

41. See Mary White Ovington, "William English Walling," *Crisis* 43 (Nov. 1936): 335.

42. William English Walling, "The Race War in the North," *Independent* 65 (3 Sept. 1908): 530, 534.

43. Mary White Ovington, *The Walls Came Tumbling Down* (1947; reprint, New York: Schocken Books, 1970), 102; and Mary White Ovington, "How the National Association for the Advancement of Colored People Began," *Crisis* 4 (Aug. 1914): 184.

44. Ovington, "How the National Association for the Advancement of Colored People Began," 184–85. Among the tens of people who signed the Call besides the promoters were Jane Addams, Chicago; Ida Wells-Barnett, Chicago; Prof. John Dewey, New York; Dr. W. E. B. Du Bois, Atlanta; writer William Dean Howells, New York; Lincoln Steffens, Boston; Prof. W. I. Thomas, Chicago; and Lillian D. Wald, New York.

45. *Proceedings of the National Negro Conference, 1909: New York, May 31 and June 1* (1909; reprint, James M. McPherson, ed., New York: Arno Press and the *New York Times,* 1969), 9–10.

46. Ibid., 14, 15–16, 17, 18, 20.

47. Ibid., 71, 72.

48. Ibid., 79, 80, 81–82, 86, 87.

49. Ibid., 174–77.

50. Charles Flint Kellogg, *NAACP: The History of the National Association for the Advancement of Colored People,* vol. 1, 1909–1920 (Baltimore: Johns Hopkins Univ. Press, 1967), 21–22.

51. *New York Age,* 10 June 1909.

CHAPTER 4. From the National Negro
Conference to the NAACP

1. Du Bois, *Souls of the Black Folk,* 614–15; "National Negro Conference," *Horizon* 5, no. 1 (Nov. 1909): 1–2.

2. For a list of the signers of the Call, see Ovington, "How the National Association for the Advancement of Colored People Began," 185.

3. On Wells-Barnett, Terrell, and black women's organizations, see Giddings, *When and Where I Enter;* "Ida Wells-Barnett (1862–1931)," in G. J. Barker-Benfield and Catherine Clinton, eds., *Portraits of American Women: From the Civil War to the Present* (New York: St. Martin's Press, 1991), 2:367–85; Dorothy Sterling, *Black Foremothers: Three Lives* (New York: Feminist Press, 1988); Beverly Washington Jones, *Quest for Equality: The Life and Writings of Mary Eliza Church Terrell, 1863,* vol. 13 of Darlene Clark Hine, ed., *Black Women in United States History* (Brooklyn: Carlson, 1990); and Dorothy C. Salem, "Black Women and the NAACP, 1909–1922: An Encounter with Race, Class, and Gender," in Kim Marie Vaz, ed., *Black Women in America* (London: Sage, 1995), 54–70.

4. Mary Church Terrell, *A Colored Woman in a White World* (Washington DC: Ransdell Press, 1940).

5. Wells-Barnett, *Crusade for Justice,* 327–28, 323; and Wells-Barnett, "Booker T. Washington and His Critics," *World Today* 6 (April 1904): 520.

6. Wells-Barnett, *Crusade for Justice,* 299, 322, 324.

7. Ibid., 324, 326.

8. Lewis, *W. E. B. Du Bois,* 396–97; and Mary W. Ovington, *Black and White Sat Down Together: The Reminiscences of an NAACP Founder* (New York: Feminist Press, 1995), 60.

9. Wells-Barnett, *Crusade for Justice,* 328.

10. Ovington, *Black and White Sat Down Together,* 58–59, 60; on the organizers' handling of Washington's invitation, see Lewis, *W. E. B. Du Bois,* 391.

11. Ovington, *Walls Came Tumbling Down,* 44–45, 63; Ovington, *Black and White Sat Down Together,* 32–33, 34–35; and Harlan, *Booker T. Washington,* 376–77.

12. Harlan, *Booker T. Washington,* 377, 378; on Du Bois's appearance and the *New York Age* quote, see Lewis, *W. E. B. Du Bois,* 429; see also Manning Marable, *W. E. B. Du Bois: Black Radical Democrat* (Boston: Twayne, 1986), 78–79.

13. On reconstruction of the event, see Harlan, *Booker T. Washington,*

379–84; Villard quoted in ibid., 383–84; on support for Washington from Low, Taft, Carnegie, and Roosevelt, see Harlan and Smock, eds., *Washington Papers*, 11:28–29, 10, 50; on Du Bois's reaction, see Lewis, *W. E. B. Du Bois*, 431–32; for the NAACP resolution, see Harlan and Smock, eds., *Washington Papers*, 11:69, and Kellogg, *NACCP*, 1:82.

14. Quotations are from Ovington, *Walls Came Tumbling Down*, 12, 6–8, 11; on her reactions to Douglass's speech, see Ovington, *Black and White Sat Down Together*, 3, 4; on the Greenpoint Settlement and the Social Reform Club, see ibid., 7–9; on the boys yelling at colored women, see ibid., 10.

15. On Du Bois's recommendation of Ovington's writings, see Lewis, *W. E. B. Du Bois*, 348; Franz Boas, foreword to Mary White Ovington, *Half a Man: The Status of the Negro in New York* (New York: Longmans, Green, 1911), vii; on the Greenwich House fellowship and the title of the book, see Ovington, *Black and White Sat Down Together*, 13–14, 72.

16. Ovington, *Half a Man*, 153–54, 144, 146, 148–49. Seventy-five percent of all colored unmarried working women lived with their employers or boarded.

17. By the time Matthews opened the White Rose Mission, she had already written for the leading papers of the country and had achieved some success in literature as the author of novels, textbooks, and teaching materials. See Majors, *Noted Negro Women*, 211–12.

18. Ovington, *Half a Man*, 151–52. On black women migrating north and their working and living conditions, see Jacqueline Jones, *Labor of Love, Labor of Sorrow: Black Women, Work, and the Family from Slavery to the Present* (New York: Basic Books, 1985), 152–95.

19. Ovington, "The Negro at Home in New York," *Charities* 15 (7 Oct. 1905): 26–27, 30. Fifty black families were chosen at random among those living in the most demoralizing neighborhoods of New York. Ovington's investigation showed that seventy percent of the mothers were known to be morally sound by the charity workers who had been in touch with them for a number of years.

20. Ovington, *Half a Man*, 156, 163–64; Jones, *Labor of Love, Labor of Sorrow*, 166–68; and Ovington, *Half a Man*, 158–59, 157.

21. On Ovington meeting Du Bois, see Ovington, *Walls Came Tumbling Down*, 54; on Ovington and Du Bois's friendship and political alliance, see Lewis, *W. E. B. Du Bois*, 347–50, 480–81, 494–95, 544–45.

22. Wells-Barnett, *Crusade for Justice*, 72–73; and Booker T. Washington, *Frederick Douglass* (1906; reprint, New York: Argosy-Antiquarian, 1969).

23. Wells-Barnett, *Crusade for Justice*, 64, 65–66, 70, 71; on Wells-Barnett's analysis of lynching as a frontal attack on southern values of white women's purity, see Hazel V. Carby, *Reconstructing Womanhood: The Emancipation of the Afro-American Woman Novelist* (New York: Oxford Univ. Press, 1987), 109–16.

24. Willard quoted in Wells-Barnett, "A Red Record," in *On Lynching:*

Southern Horrors, a Red Record, and Mob Rule in New Orleans (New York: Arno Press, 1969), 59, 80, 83.

25. Wells-Barnett, *Crusade for Justice*, 274–78, 321–22; on Addams at the Atlanta conference, see Lewis, *W. E. B. Du Bois*, 377–78.

26. Jane Addams, "Respect for Law," *Independent* (Jan. 1901), reprinted in Bettina Aptheker, ed., *Lynching and Rape: An Exchange of Views* (San Jose CA: San Jose University, 1977), 23–27.

27. Wells-Barnett, "Lynching and the Excuse for It," *Independent* (May 1901), reprinted in B. Aptheker, ed., *Lynching and Rape*, 29–34.

28. In his latest book Leon Litwack analyzes the phases of Sam Hose's lynching as a horrifying and yet emblematic public ritual staged by a southern crowd. Litwack observes that although versions of the planter's death varied, the "story of Sam Hose's fate did not." On Hose's lynching, see Litwack, *Trouble in Mind*, 280–83; for a thorough and insightful understanding of lynching as a public ritual, see chapter 6, "Hellhounds," 280–325.

29. Mary Church Terrell, "Lynching from a Negro's Point of View," *North American Review* 178 (June 1904): 172–73, 178–79, 180, 181.

30. Ovington, *Black and White Sat Down Together*, 66–68.

31. Lewis, *W. E. B. Du Bois*, 386–87; and "Resolutions," in *Proceedings of the National Negro Conference, 1909*, 223–24.

32. On Du Bois's switch from science to propaganda, see Lewis, *W. E. B. Du Bois*, 408; for quotations, see Du Bois, *Dusk of Dawn*, 136, 222, 67.

33. W. E. B. Du Bois, "Segregation," *Crisis* 1 (Nov. 1910): 28.

34. Franz Boas, "The Real Race Problem," *Crisis* 1, no. 2 (Dec. 1910): 23, 24–25.

35. Franz Boas, *Anthropology and Modern Life* (Westport CT: Greenwood Press, 1984), 228.

36. Du Bois, "The Races Congress," *Crisis* 2, no. 5 (Sept. 1911): 207, 200, 202, 206–7, 206, 204–5, 209; Lewis, *W. E. B. Du Bois*, 441; and Ovington, *Black and White Sat Down Together*, 78, 79–80.

37. W. E. B. Du Bois, "The African Roots of War," *Atlantic Monthly* 115 (May 1915): 707–14; Lewis, *W. E. B. Du Bois*, 503–4; and Du Bois, *Dusk of Dawn*, 232.

38. Du Bois, *Dusk of Dawn*, 95, 94, 95, 227.

39. "Annual Report of the Director of Publicity and Research for the Year 1913," and "N.A.A.C.P. Report of the Department of Publications and Research, from August, 1910, through November, 1915," in Aptheker, ed., *Pamphlets and Leaflets by Du Bois*, 137–38, 154–55, 159.

40. Marable, *W. E. B. Du Bois*, 78–79, 80.

41. Du Bois, *Dusk of Dawn*, 227.

42. Elliott Rudwick, *W. E. B. Du Bois: Propagandist of the Negro Protest*, 166; and Lewis, *W. E. B. Du Bois*, 478.

43. Mary White Ovington to W. E. B. Du Bois, 11 April 1914, Du Bois Papers, in Herbert Aptheker, ed., *The Correspondence of W. E. B. Du Bois*, vol.

1, *Selections*, *1877–1939* (Amherst: Univ. of Massachusetts Press, 1973), 192; and Lewis, *W. E. B. Du Bois*, 480.

CHAPTER 5. From Stage to Street

1. E. Franklin Frazier, *The Negro Church in America, 1894–1962* (New York: Schocken Books, 1963), 30, 31; and *New York Age*, 15 February 1919. Similar ads appeared at the beginning of the century throughout major African-American publications, such as the *Colored American Magazine*.

2. At the turn of the century, Charles W. Chestnutt made the character of the light-skinned Negro crossing over the color line central to his fiction, and Nella Larsen wrote the novel *Passing* in 1929. Black writers like George Schuyler in his novel *Black No More: Being an Account of the Strange and Wonderful Workings of Science in the Land of the Free* (1931) made "passing" a subject of social satire.

3. James Weldon Johnson, *The Autobiography of an Ex-Coloured Man* (1912; reprint, New York: Vintage Books, 1989), 190–91.

4. James Weldon Johnson, *Along This Way: The Autobiography of James Weldon Johnson* (1933; reprint, New York: Penguin Books, 1968), 238–39.

5. Henry Louis Gates Jr., introduction to Johnson, *Autobiography of an Ex-Coloured Man*, xvi.

6. It is impossible to generalize why certain fair-complexioned members of the black elite chose to pass as whites and others did not, as Gatewood has remarked. The occasional passing was a matter of convenience: to secure decent seats at theaters and accommodations at hotels, to avoid Jim Crow cars. See Willard B. Gatewood, *Aristocrats of Color: The Black Elite, 1880–1920* (Bloomington: Indiana Univ. Press, 1990), 175–76.

7. Lewis A. Erenberg, *Steppin' Out: New York Night Life and the Transformation of American Culture, 1890–1930* (Westport CT: Greenwood Press, 1981), 73.

8. The collection of black vaudeville and minstrel shows at the Schomburg Center of the New York Public Library includes *Bandanna Land, Dahomey, Abyssinia, Dat Watermillyon, The Gentlemen Coons' Parade,* and *Dat Famous Chicken Debate.*

9. Henry Collins Brown, *In the Golden Nineties* (New York: Hastings-on-Hudson, 1928), 173–74; and Johnson, *Along This Way*, 152–53.

10. Johnson, *Along This Way*, 122.

11. Ibid., 149, 150, 152, 172–73.

12. See Thomas L. Riis, *Just before Jazz: Black Musical Theater in New York, 1890–1915* (Washington DC: Smithsonian Institution Press, 1989), 35, 109–10.

13. Johnson, *Along This Way*, 154, 155.

14. Ibid., 218, 219.

15. Dudley in *Indianapolis Freeman*, 20 Sept. 1916, quoted in Riis, *Just be-*

fore Jazz, 160; and Jack Poggi, *Theatre in America: The Impact of Economic Forces* (Ithaca: Cornell Univ. Press, 1968), 28–30, 36, 45.

16. Poggi, *Theatre in America,* 259.

17. Gilbert Osofsky, *Harlem: The Making of a Ghetto; Negro New York, 1890–1930* (New York: Harper Torchbooks, 1963), 93–104; and David Levering Lewis, *When Harlem Was in Vogue* (New York: Oxford Univ. Press, 1979), 24, 26.

18. James Weldon Johnson, *Black Manhattan* (1930; reprint, New York: Da Capo, 1991), 118–19.

19. Ann Douglas, *Terrible Honesty: Mongrel Manhattan in the 1920s* (New York: Farrar, Straus & Giroux, 1995), 5–6.

20. *Sun* editorial quoted in Erenberg, *Steppin' Out,* 81; Belle Lindner Israels, "The Way of the Girl," *Survey* 22 (1909): 494; Michael M. Davis, *The Exploitation of Pleasure* (New York: Russell Sage Foundation, 1911), 12–17; Richard H. Edwards, *Popular Amusements* (New York: Association Press, 1915), 78; and Roger D. Abrahams, *Singing the Master: The Emergence of African American Culture in the Plantation South* (New York: Pantheon, 1992), 98, 99.

21. Walker quoted in Ovington, *Half a Man,* 123; and Ann Charters, *Nobody: The Story of Bert Williams* (New York: Macmillan, 1983), 35.

22. Johnson, *Autobiography of an Ex-Coloured Man,* 86–87.

23. Erenberg, *Steppin' Out,* 151; on ragtime, see E. L. Doctorow, *Ragtime* (New York: Ballantine Books, 1974). Also see Le Roi Jones, "Blues, Jazz and the Negro," in John P. Davis, ed., *The American Negro Reference Book* (Englewood Cliffs NJ: Prentice Hall, 1966), 762 n. 1; and Erenberg, *Steppin' Out,* 152.

24. Black music, according to a music historian, "ignores any division of time that follows the natural pulse of a regular metrical beat, and anticipates or holds over accents beyond their expected time." See Maud Cuney-Hare, *Negro Musicians and Their Music* (Washington DC: Associated, 1936), 133. Also see Douglas, *Terrible Honesty,* 364–76.

25. Lewis, *When Harlem Was in Vogue,* 30.

26. Johnson, *Black Manhattan,* 73.

27. Jones, billed as the "Black Patti," and her company of Troubadours toured for many years. Other women of the early black musical theater were Dora Dean, Belle Davis, Ada Overton, and Abbie Mitchell. See Langston Hughes, "The Negro and American Entertainment," in Davis, *American Negro Reference Book,* 831.

28. Loften Mitchell, *Black Drama: The Story of the American Negro in Theatre* (New York: Hawthorn Books, 1967), 46. Also see Eric Lott, *Love and Theft: Blackface Minstrelsy and the American Working Class* (New York: Oxford Univ. Press, 1993), for the period up to the Civil War.

29. Robert C. Toll, *Blacking Up: The Minstrel Show in Nineteenth-Century America* (New York: Oxford Univ. Press, 1974), 262, 205, 263.

30. Ibid., 218–19; and Ovington, *Half a Man,* 128.

31. Hughes, "Negro and American Entertainment," 829.

32. Johnson, *Black Manhattan,* 93; and *New York Dramatic Mirror,* 9 April 1898.

33. Unidentified review, 6 Feb. 1900, quoted in Riis, *Just before Jazz,* 77–78.

34. Mitchell, *Black Drama,* 44, 46–47; Riis, *Just before Jazz,* 41; and Johnson, *Along This Way,* 172–73.

35. Will Marion Cook, "Clorindy, the Origin of the Cakewalk," in Eileen Southern, ed., *Readings in Black American Music* (New York: Norton, 1983), 231–32; and Johnson, *Along This Way,* 151.

36. Charters, *Nobody: The Story of Bert Williams,* 8, 14.

37. Quoted in ibid., 14.

38. Ibid., 18, 19, 105.

39. Quoted in ibid., 29.

40. Riis, *Just before Jazz,* 91–92, 103; *New York Times,* 19 Feb. 1903; unidentified London review, 23 October 1903, cited by Riis, *Just before Jazz.*

41. Charters, *Nobody: The Story of Bert Williams,* 160; and Riis, *Just before Jazz,* 117, 121.

42. Historian of black musical theater Thomas L. Riis has listed for the first six months of 1909 some 110 different vaudeville acts employing between three and four hundred people, a number that continued to rise during the decade. See Riis, *Just before Jazz,* 166 n. 17, 219. Also see Ovington, *Half a Man,* 135–36; and Erenberg, *Steppin' Out,* 152.

43. William Lichtenwanger, in his essay on Jones, writes that with her Troubadours the Black Patti "fought a constant battle on the side of taste and artistic integrity." William Lichtenwanger, "Sissieretta Jones," in Edward T. James, ed., *Notable American Women* (Cambridge: Harvard Univ. Press, 1971), 289–90.

44. *Boston Transcript,* 18 April 1911, cited in William Estelle Daughtry, "Sissieretta Jones: A Study of the Negro's Contribution to Nineteenth Century American Concert and Theatrical Life" (Ph.D. diss., Syracuse University, 1968), 112.

45. Osofsky, *Harlem: The Making of a Ghetto,* 40.

46. Johnson, *Autobiography of an Ex-Coloured Man,* 104, 105, 106, 107.

47. *Variety,* 13 July 1907, cited in Riis, *Just before Jazz,* 168; and Toll, *Blacking Up,* 196, 200–201.

48. Johnson, *Black Manhattan,* 102; and Riis, *Just before Jazz,* 38.

49. Johnson, *Along This Way,* 159.

50. *New York Age,* 31 Jan. 1907; and Bert Williams, "The Comic Side of Trouble," *American Magazine* 85 (Jan. 1918): 33.

51. Ralph Ellison, *Invisible Man* (1952; reprint, New York: Vintage Books, 1972), 109.

52. Paul Laurence Dunbar, "We Wear the Mask," reprinted in Gates, ed., *Norton Anthology of African-American Literature,* 896.

53. *New York Times,* 9 Sept. 1900; Du Bois quoted in Osofsky, *Harlem: The Making of a Ghetto,* 40.

54. Johnson, *Along This Way,* 157–58.

55. *Dramatic Mirror* review quoted in Charters, *Nobody: The Story of Bert Williams,* 54; and *New York Herald,* 16 Aug. 1900.

56. Osofsky, *Harlem: The Making of a Ghetto,* 46–47; and *New York World,* 17 Aug. 1900.

57. Osofsky, *Harlem: The Making of a Ghetto,* 12–13; on the history of the assumption about black women being prostitutes, see Giddings, *When and Where I Enter,* and Carby, *Reconstructing Womanhood.*

58. *New York Daily Tribune,* 16 Aug. 1900.

59. Johnson, *Black Manhattan,* 127.

60. *New York Herald,* 16 and 17 Aug. 1900; and Citizens' Protective League, *Persecution of Negroes by Roughs and Policemen, in the City of New York, August, 1900: Statement of Proofs Written and Compiled by Frank Moss and Issued by the Citizens' Protective League* (New York: Citizens' Protective League, 1900), 15.

61. *New York Times, New York Herald, New York Daily Tribune,* 16 and 17 Aug. 1900; Scheiner, *Negro Mecca,* 122. The *New York Tribune* (19 Aug. 1900) described the behavior of the police during the riot as an example of the "abominable municipal government" of Tammany Hall. Similarly, the *New York Post* (16 and 18 Aug. 1900) repudiated a police force and a governmental system that "reeks throughout with corruption."

62. *New York Herald,* 17 Aug. 1900.

63. Citizens' Protective League, *Persecution of Negroes,* 2.

64. Ibid., 4–5.

65. Ibid., 68, 70–71, 72, 74.

66. Ibid., 23, 30–31, 50–51, 46–47.

67. *New York Herald,* 17 Aug. 1900. Excerpts from an article in the *Louisville Courier Journal* were reprinted in the *New York Herald,* 27 Aug. 1900.

68. *New York Herald,* 27 Aug. 1900.

69. *New York Times,* 24 Aug. 1900.

70. See Charters, *Nobody: The Story of Bert Williams,* 38, 54, 59; and Williams, interview in *New York Age,* quoted in ibid., 133.

71. Booker T. Washington, "Interesting People—Bert Williams," *American Magazine* 70 (Sept. 1910): 600.

CHAPTER 6. Myths of Economic Success

1. W. E. B. Du Bois, "The Black North in 1901," in Dan S. Green and Edwin D. Drive, eds., *On Sociology and the Black Community* (Chicago: Univ. of Chicago Press), 152.

2. Before the Civil War, African-American papers were in the hands of the religious leaders of the community and financially supported by white abolitionists—such as the *Colored American,* which was fully supported by Ar-

thur Tappan. After the war, however, the papers became more secular and connected to political parties. The *New York Globe* was discontinued in November 1884 due to an internal dispute between Thomas Fortune and the Reverend W. B. Derrick. In 1891 Fortune became the director of the *New York Age,* which in 1907 passed into the control of Booker T. Washington. See Martin E. Dann, ed., *The Black Press, 1827–1890* (New York: Putnam's Sons, 1971).

3. *New York Globe,* 24 Feb. 1883 and 8 March 1884.

4. Ibid., 24 Feb. 1883.

5. Gatewood, *Aristocrats of Color,* 61, 159.

6. William F. Ogburn, "The Richmond Negro in New York City: His Social Mind as Seen in His Pleasures" (master's thesis, Columbia University, 1909), 69–70.

7. Lewis, *When Harlem Was in Vogue,* 28.

8. *New York Globe,* 20 Jan. 1883.

9. Ibid.

10. W. E. B. Du Bois in his *Philadelphia Negro* used the term "respectable" for the small group of black aristocrats, which made respectability a virtue of the better-off members of the laboring classes. E. Franklin Frazier used respectability as an indicator to distinguish the old elite from the new elite that emerged at the turn of the century. For others, "respectable" means different things according to one's level in the community. See Du Bois, *Philadelphia Negro,* 310–11; E. Franklin Frazier, *Black Bourgeoisie* (New York: Free Press, 1962), 80, 102; David Gordon Nielson, *Black Ethos: Northern Urban Negro Life and Thought, 1890–1930* (Westport CT: Greenwood Press, 1977), 52–55.

11. Nielson, *Black Ethos,* 53.

12. Gatewood, *Aristocrats of Color,* 23–24, 28. According to Gatewood's analysis, the old black upper class in late nineteenth-century New York represented a fusion of three elements: those who bore Dutch names and who had appeared in the educational, religious, and civic life of black New Yorkers since the late eighteenth century; immigrants whose long residence in the city and achievements placed them at the top of the class structure; and a small group of West Indian immigrants. By the end of the century, these three elements had combined through marriage and formed an exclusive group. They belonged to the same social clubs, organizations, and churches (103–5). Also see Joel Williamson, *New People: Miscegenation and Mulattoes in the United States* (New York: New York Univ. Press, 1980), 130.

13. Gatewood, *Aristocrats of Color,* 188.

14. Kevin K. Gaines, *Uplifting the Race: Black Leadership, Politics, and Culture in the Twentieth Century* (Chapel Hill: Univ. of North Carolina Press, 1996), 3, 4.

15. *New York Globe,* 29 Jan. 1883.

16. Ibid.

17. Gatewood, *Aristocrats of Color,* 15.

18. *New York Globe,* 20 Jan. 1883.

19. *New York Times,* 18 Nov. 1898.

20. *New York Age,* 7 Feb. and 21 Nov. 1907.

21. Gatewood, *Aristocrats of Color,* 106.

22. Johnson, *Along This Way,* 202–3.

23. August Meier, *Negro Thought in America, 1850–1915* (Ann Arbor: Univ. of Michigan Press, 1966), 155–56; Du Bois, "Black North in 1901," 46; and Gatewood, *Aristocrats of Color.*

24. *New York Times,* 14 July 1895.

25. Ibid.

26. National Negro Business League, "First Meeting in Boston, Mass., August 23 and 24, 1900," *Proceedings of the National Negro Business League* (Boston: J. R. Hamm, 1901), in John H. Bracey Jr. and August Meier, eds., *Records of the National Negro Business League (1900–1923)* (Bethesda MD: University Publications of America, 1994), microfilm, reel no. 1, appendix, 59, 60, 61.

27. *Report of the Sixth Annual Convention of the National Negro Business League, Held at New York City, August 16, 17, 18, 1905* (Boston: S. Laing, 1906), 10–12, 65, 27, reprinted in Bracey and Meier, eds., *Records of the National Negro Business League.*

28. Ibid., 45, 54. For an insightful analysis of white complaints about the new generation of black servants, see Litwack, *Trouble in Mind,* 209–10.

29. Ibid., 55, 61.

30. Ibid., 66, 67.

31. Harlan, *Booker T. Washington,* 1:296–97; and *Report of the Seventh Annual Convention of the National Negro Business League, Held at Atlanta, Georgia, August 29, 20, 31, 1906,* compiled by William H. Davis, official stenographer, 18–20, in Bracey and Meier, eds., *Records of the National Negro Business League.*

32. *Report of the Seventh Annual Convention of the NNBL,* 61, 63, 64–65.

33. W. E. B. Du Bois, ed., *The Negro in Business: Report of a Social Study Made under the Direction of Atlanta University; Together with the Proceedings of the Fourth Conference for the Study of the Negro Problems, Held at Atlanta University, May 30–31, 1899* (Atlanta: Press of the Atlanta University, 1899), 7, 5.

34. Harlan, *Booker T. Washington,* 1:266; Louis R. Harlan, "Booker T. Washington and the National Negro Business League," in Raymond W. Smock, ed., *Booker T. Washington in Perspective: Essays by Louis R. Harlan* (Jackson: Univ. Press of Mississippi, 1988), 99; Lewis, *W. E. B. Du Bois,* 220–21; James Oliver Horton, *Free People of Color: Inside the African American Community* (Washington DC: Smithsonian Institution Press, 1993); and Lorini, "Public Rituals, Race Ideology," chapters 1 and 2.

35. Ovington, *Black and White Sat Down Together,* 23. For a vivid description of the rigid racial rituals in the post-Reconstruction South, see Litwack, *Trouble in Mind,* 230–37.

36. *New York Age,* 27 September 1906; on the Atlanta massacre, see Litwack, *Trouble in Mind,* 315–19.

37. *Atlanta Journal* editorial quoted in Walter White, *A Man Called White* (New York: Viking Press, 1948), 8.

38. On the gubernatorial election, see Dewey W. Grantham, *Hoke Smith and the Politics of the New South* (Baton Rouge: Louisiana State Univ. Press, 1958), 134; on the Atlanta riot, see Charles Crowe, "Racial Violence and Social Reform—Origins of the Atlanta Riot of 1906," *Journal of Negro History* 53 (April 1968): 234–56; and also Charles Crowe, "Racial Massacre in Atlanta, September 22, 1906," *Journal of Negro History* 54 (April 1969): 150–73.

39. *New York Evening Post,* 7 Sept. 1906.

40. Du Bois, "A Litany of Atlanta," in Gates and McKay, eds., *Anthology of African American Literature,* 609, 610, 611.

41. See Du Bois, *Autobiography,* 286.

42. *New York Age,* 27 Sept. 1906.

43. *New York Age,* 4 Oct. 1906.

44. Ibid.

45. Ibid.

46. Ibid.

CHAPTER 7. Pageants of American Racial Democracy

1. Hudson-Fulton Celebration Commission, *The Hudson-Fulton Celebration: The Fourth Annual Report of the Hudson-Fulton Celebration Commission Transmitted to the Legislature of the State of New York, May 20, 1910,* prepared by Edward H. Hall, vol. 1 (Albany: J. B. Lyon, 1910), 61–72. The complete program of this gigantic festival also appeared in the *New York Tribune,* 25 Sept. 1909.

2. Hudson-Fulton Celebration Commission, *Hudson-Fulton Celebration,* 3, 41. This large committee was divided into subcommittees that took charge of specific aspects of the festival. School principals, church ministers, settlement and playground workers, city clerks and managers, pageant masters, academics, and many representatives of reform groups joined the commission.

3. Ibid., 282, 283, 287, 289–92.

4. *New York Sun,* 29 Sept. 1909; and Marie Jastrow, *Looking Back: The American Dream through Immigrant Eyes* (New York: Vintage, 1986), 120, 121.

5. Hudson-Fulton Celebration Commission, *Hudson-Fulton Celebration,* 293, 295, 300, 301, 303.

6. Ibid., 362–63, 368–80. Although other floats appeared titled "The Jungle," "Egyptian Art," "The Queen of Sheba," and dedicated to Greek mythological figures, the procession's major theme was the folklore of German-speaking countries.

7. Ibid., 505. Local papers unanimously agreed.

8. The most influential work on this subject was Granville Stanley Hall's *Adolescence: Its Psychology and Its Relations to Physiology, Anthropology, Sociology, Sex, Crime, Religion and Education* (New York: D. Appleton, 1904). In what Hall and other social scientists called "recapitulation theory," ontogenesis followed phylogenesis, and children and primitive people shared the same characteristics.

9. "Children's Festivals, Hudson-Fulton Celebration," *Playground* 3 (Nov. 1909): 1, 5.

10. Hudson-Fulton Celebration Commission, *Hudson-Fulton Celebration,* 509.

11. If dancing is an important "identity maker," then the performance of the same dance all over the city had the double effect of creating cultural uniformity by maintaining an ethnic tradition. But interaction can become structured in such a way "that it takes place in terms of stereotypes." See Anya P. Royce, *The Anthropology of Dance* (Bloomington: Indiana Univ. Press, 1977), 155–57.

12. Clarence A. Perry, "School Playgrounds," *Playground* 4 (July 1910): 121.

13. *New York Age,* 23 and 30 Sept., 7 Oct. 1909.

14. On group self-presentation in public, see Hanna Fenichel Pitkin, *The Concept of Representation* (Berkeley: Univ. of California Press, 1967).

15. The exclusion of black seamen from the Hudson-Fulton parade exemplified a broader process of eliminating African Americans from the U.S. Navy. See Jack D. Foner, *Blacks and the Military in American History: A New Perspective* (New York: Praeger, 1974), 105–6. See also John R. Commons, *Races and Immigrants in America* (1907; reprint, New York: A. M. Kelley, 1967), 20.

16. Hudson-Fulton Celebration Commission, *Hudson-Fulton Celebration,* 5–7.

17. Ibid., 7–8, 12. The cost of the celebration (a little over one million dollars) was shared as follows: state government, 48 percent; New York City government, 24 percent; private organizations and free offers, 28 percent. No aid was received from the federal government.

18. On British influence, see Claude E. Dierolf, "The Pageant Drama and American Pageantry" (Ph.D. diss., University of Pennsylvania, 1953); see also "Pageants Better than Gunpowder," *Century* 58 (July 1910): 476; and Lady Blanche Murphy, "Glimpses of Old-Time Pageantry," *Southern Magazine* 9 (Feb. 1876): 134.

19. David Glassberg, *American Historical Pageantry: The Uses of Tradition in*

the Early Twentieth Century (Chapel Hill: Univ. of North Carolina Press, 1990), 4; on the history of pageantry, see also Naima Prevots, *American Pageantry: A Movement for Art and Democracy* (Ann Arbor MI: UMI Research Press, 1990).

20. William C. Langdon, *Suggestions for the Celebration of the Fourth of July by Means of Pageantry* (New York: Russell Sage Foundation, 1912), 36, 13–17.

21. Du Bois's pageant was also staged in Los Angeles at the Hollywood Bowl on 15 and 18 June 1925 by the Los Angeles branch of the NAACP.

22. W. E. B. Du Bois, "The Star of Ethiopia," *Crisis* 11 (Dec. 1915): 91; and *New York Times*, 15 Dec. 1913.

23. *New York Age*, 30 Oct. 1913. On 6 November the paper reported a heated argument over a trivial issue between Du Bois, referred to as the "master mind" of the organization committee, and the vice chair, an altercation that the paper sarcastically defined the "star exhibition" of the exposition. The vice chair of the commission "proceeded to call the professor a few names not known to sociology." On the difficult relationship between Du Bois and the African-American press, see Lewis, *W. E. B. Du Bois*, 349, 416.

24. Du Bois, "Star of Ethiopia," 91; and W. E. B. Du Bois, "The Drama among Black Folk," *Crisis* 12 (Aug. 1916): 171.

25. *New York Times*, 23 Oct. 1913; and W. E. B. Du Bois, "Conservation of Races," 5.

26. W. E. B. Du Bois to S. L. Smith, 10 May 1932, in Aptheker, ed., *Correspondence of Du Bois*, 1:457–58.

27. The following reconstruction of the pageant text is based on several drafts and comments included in Du Bois's papers and his article "The People of Peoples and Their Gifts to Men," *Crisis* 6 (Nov. 1913): 339–41.

28. "Bamboula" from West Africa, "Take Nabauji" from East Africa, and "The Imaginary Ballet" and "Motherless Child" were by British composer Coleridge-Taylor; "Big Indian Chief" and "Red Shawl" were by Cole and Johnson; and "Prelude Primitive," "Chant of the Savages," "When Darkness Descends," "The African Chant," and "The Welding Song" were by Young. See W. E. B. Du Bois, *The Papers of W. E. B. Du Bois, 1877–1963*, microfilm ed., University of Massachusetts collection, Amherst (Microfilm Corporation of America, 1981), reel no. 87.

29. W. E. B. Du Bois, editorial, *Crisis* 1 (Nov. 1910): 10.

30. Lewis, *W. E. B. Du Bois*, 461.

31. Du Bois quoted in Glassberg, *American Historical Pageantry*, 132, 179, 187.

32. Jane Addams, "The Progressive Party and the Negro," *Crisis* 5 (Nov. 1912): 30.

33. Du Bois, "Drama among Black Folk," 169; "To the Nations of the World," in Aptheker, ed., *Writings by Du Bois in Non-Periodical Literature Edited by Others*, 2:11; and W. E. B. Du Bois, *The Negro* (New York: Holt, 1915).

34. Du Bois, "African Roots of War," 704–14; and Du Bois, *Dusk of Dawn*, 240.

35. *Moving Picture World* 23 (13 March 1915): 1587; and Fred Silva, ed., *Focus on "The Birth of a Nation"* (Englewood Cliffs NJ: Prentice Hall, 1971), 28–29.

36. The original film consisted of 1,544 individual shots, or 13,058 feet, which later was cut down to 1,375 shots, or 12,000 feet. See Silva, ed., *Focus on "The Birth of a Nation,"* 4; and Larry May, *Screening Out the Past: The Birth of Mass Culture and the Motion Picture Industry* (New York: Oxford Univ. Press, 1980), 60–93. Also see Lewis Jacob, *The Rise of the American Film: A Critical History* (New York: Teachers College Press, 1968), 175.

37. Wilson quoted in Everett Carter, "Cultural History Written with Lightning: The Significance of *The Birth of a Nation,"* *American Quarterly* 12 (fall 1960): 347; on the resemblance between *Birth* and a pageant, see Glassberg, *American Historical Pageantry,* 155; see also *New York Times,* 7 March 1915.

38. Robert Henderson, *D. W. Griffith: His Life and Work* (New York: Oxford Univ. Press, 1972), 158; Seymour Stern, "The Birth of a Nation," *American Mercury* (March 1949); on the reaction *Birth* caused, see Thomas Cripps, "The Reaction of the Negro to the Motion Picture *Birth of a Nation,"* *Historian* 25 (1963): 344–62; and also Thomas Cripps, *Slow Fade to Black: The Negro in American Film, 1900–1942* (New York: Oxford Univ. Press, 1977), 45–69.

39. It was estimated than more than three million residents and visitors to New York saw the picture. See Harry M. Geduld, ed., *Focus on D. W. Griffith* (Englewood Cliffs NJ: Prentice Hall, 1971), 27; and Henderson, *D. W. Griffith,* 160.

40. Griffith's film built on contemporary historical interpretations of Reconstruction seen in the scholarship of Woodrow Wilson, William A. Dunning, James Ford Rhodes, and Walter Fleming. See Jack Temple Kirby, *Media-Made Dixie: The South in the American Imagination* (Baton Rouge: Louisiana State Univ. Press, 1978), 6–7; and Maxwell Bloomfield, "Dixon's *The Leopard's Spot*: A Study in Popular Racism," *American Quarterly* 16 (fall 1964): 387–401.

41. See Silva, ed., *Focus on "The Birth of a Nation,"* 12.

42. *Atlanta Journal,* 7 Dec. 1915; *Atlanta Constitution,* 7 Dec. 1915; for a sample of reviews of *Birth,* see Silva, ed., *Focus on "The Birth of a Nation,"* 22–40; see also *New York Variety,* 12 March 1915; and Ralph Ellison, *Shadow and Act* (1953; reprint, New York: Vintage Books, 1964), 275.

43. Hugo Münsterberg, *The Photoplay: A Psychological Study* (New York: D. Appleton, 1916), 95, 96.

44. "The Ubiquitous Moving Picture," *American Magazine* 75 (July 1913): 105; and Antonio Mangano, *Sons of Italy: A Social and Religious Study of the Italians in America* (New York: Missionary Education Movement of the United States and Canada, 1917), 6–7.

45. On the social history of early movies and audiences, see Robert Sklar, *Movie-Made America: A Cultural History of American Movies* (New York: Vintage

Books, 1975); and Garth Jowett, *Film: The Democratic Art* (Boston: Little, Brown, 1976); see also Elizabeth Ewen, "City Lights: Immigrant Women and the Rise of the Movies," *Signs* 5 (spring 1980): 46; May, *Screening Out the Past,* 35, 52, 44, 61; *Jewish Daily Forward* quoted in Irving Howe, *World of Our Fathers* (New York: Harcourt Brace Jovanovich, 1976), 117–18, 213.

46. Silva, ed., *Focus on "The Birth of a Nation,"* 4. The epilogue filmed at the Hampton Institute was temporary and no longer exists. See also Nickie-ann Fleener-Marzec, *D. W. Griffith's "The Birth of a Nation": Controversy, Suppression, and the First Amendment as It Applies to Filmic Expression, 1915–1973* (New York: Arno Press, 1980), 366, 367.

47. Du Bois, "The Clansman," *Crisis* 10 (May 1915): 98–99. On the violence, mob murders surrounding the movie, and the NAACP's campaign against it, see Kellogg, *NAACP,* 1:143.

48. W. E. B. Du Bois, "The Birth of a Nation," *Crisis* 10 (May–June 1915): 33; and Mary Childs Nerney to Major R. C. Wendall, 26 March 1915, file C302, NAACP Archives, quoted in Fleener-Marzec, *D. W. Griffith's "The Birth of a Nation,"* 383–84. The Nerney-Wendall letter is also available in Mark Fox, ed., *Papers of the NAACP* (Frederick MD: University Publications of America, 1981–86), microfilm, 89 reels.

49. W. E. B. Du Bois, "Fighting Race Calumny," *Crisis* 10 (May–June 1915): 40–42. On 30 March the following speakers appeared before the mayor: Frederick C. Howe, chair of the National Board of Censorship; William H. Brooks, pastor of St. Mark's Methodist-Episcopal Church; W. E. B. Du Bois, editor of the *Crisis*; Stephen S. Wise, rabbi of the Free Synagogue; Fred R. Moore, editor of the *New York Age;* George E. Wibecan, president of the Brooklyn Citizen's Club; and Oswald Garrison Villard, president of the New York Evening Post Company and vice president of the NAACP.

50. *New York Age,* 1 April 1915.

51. Du Bois, "Fighting Race Calumny," 87–88. In Des Moines, Iowa, the film could not be shown because an ordinance had previously been introduced prohibiting plays arousing racial feelings.

52. *New York Age,* 6 May 1915.

53. Du Bois, *Dusk of Dawn,* 240. On the controversial issue of censorship and how it split the leadership of the NAACP, see Langston Hughes, *Fight for Freedom: The Story of the NAACP* (New York: Norton, 1962), 29; Joyce Ross, *J. E. Spingarn and the Rise of the NAACP, 1911–1939* (New York: Atheneum, 1972), 738; and Kellogg, *NAACP,* 1:143. See also Du Bois, *Dusk of Dawn,* 240.

54. The fight against *Birth* reemerged in the early 1930s when the new sound-track version of the film was released. See Kellogg, *NAACP,* 1:144.

55. Griffith quoted in Michael Rogin, "'The Sword Became Flashing Vision': D. W. Griffith's *The Birth of a Nation,"* *Representations* (winter 1985): 156; Homer Croy, *Star Maker: The Story of D. W. Griffith* (New York: Dell, Sloan & Pearce, 1959), 106.

56. Editorial, *New York Globe,* 6 April 1915; for Griffith's response, see *New York Globe,* 10 April 1915; see also Silva, ed., *Focus on "The Birth of a Nation,"* 75–79.

57. Silva, *Focus on "The Birth of a Nation,"* 71.

58. *Boston Journal,* 26 April 1915.

59. David W. Griffith, *The Rise and Fall of Free Speech in America* (Los Angeles: [David W. Griffith], 1916), 1, 5.

60. The success of *Caliban* was such that the masque was repeated the following year at the Harvard Stadium for seventeen performances, from 2 July to 21 July 1917. See Claude E. Dierolf, "The Pageant Drama and American Pageantry" (Ph.D. diss., University of Pennsylvania, 1953), 102; on MacKaye's concept of art and democracy, see Prevots, *American Pageantry,* 68–87.

61. *New York Times,* 11 Jan. 1916.

62. *New York Times,* 3 June 1916.

63. Professional performers numbered only forty-seven out of fifteen hundred people participating in the masque. See *New York Times,* 22 May 1916.

64. *New York Times,* 15 April 1916; and Joyce Kilmer, "Percy MacKaye Predicts Communal Theatre," *New York Times,* 14 May 1916.

65. Percy MacKaye, *Caliban by the Yellow Sands* (Garden City NY: Doubleday, Page, 1916), xvii, xv.

66. Ronald Takaki, "The Tempest in the Wilderness: The Racialization of Slavery," *Journal of American History* (December 1992): 892; on "recapitulation theory," see Hall, *Adolescence,* 2:65–66; for a critique of *Caliban,* see Dominick Cavallo, *Muscles and Morals: Organized Playground and Urban Reform, 1880–1920* (Philadelphia: Univ. of Pennsylvania Press, 1981), 55–60; and Alessandra Lorini, "The Progressives' Rhetoric on National Recreation: The Play Movement in New York City, 1880–1917," *Storia Nord Americana* 1 (1984): 34–71.

67. Percy MacKaye, *The Civic Theatre in Relation to the Redemption of Leisure* (New York: M. Kennerley, 1912), 252–53, 256–58.

68. St. Louis's black population was about 6 percent of the total population. The only black performer in the St. Louis pageant was a local janitor, who appeared exotically dressed to represent Africa in a scene in which five figures—Europe, Asia, Australia, Oceania, and Africa—led new immigrant groups. See Glassberg, *American Historical Pageantry,* 179, 187.

69. Kilmer, "Percy MacKaye Predicts Community Theatre"; Percy MacKaye, *The Playhouse and the Play* (New York: Macmillan, 1909), 19; for a detailed analysis of MacKaye's works, see Glassberg, *American Historical Pageantry.*

70. *New York Times,* 25 and 26 May 1916.

71. *New York Times,* 2 June 1916.

72. These excerpts from the New York press are in the appendix of Percy MacKaye, *Community Drama: Its Motive and Method of Neighborliness* (Boston: Houghton Mifflin, 1917), 51–59.

73. Louise Burleigh, *The Community Theatre in Theory and Practice* (Boston: Little, Brown, 1917), 34, 43, 45.

74. Ibid., 5, 52–53, 113.

75. John Collier, "*Caliban of the Yellow Sands:* The Shakespeare Pageant and Masque Reviewed against a Background of American Pageantry," *Survey* 36 (July 1916): 343, 344, 347.

76. G. K. Chesterton, "A Meditation in Broadway," in Mike Marqusee and Bill Harris, eds., *New York: An Anthology* (Boston: Little, Brown, 1985), 141.

77. W. E. B. Du Bois, editorial, *Crisis* 14 (Sept. 1917): 216; and Johnson, *Along This Way*, 320.

78. *New York Times*, 24 Nov. 1901; and *New York Tribune*, 29 July 1917. The police estimated the crowd at twenty thousand, according to the *New York Times*, 29 July 1917. See also Johnson, *Along This Way*, 321.

79. Toni Morrison, *Jazz* (New York: Penguin Books, 1993), 53–54.

80. *New York Tribune*, 29 July 1917; and Johnson, *Along This Way*, 321.

81. The Reverend Dr. H. C. Bishop was president of the parade, the Reverend Dr. Charles Martin was secretary, and J. Rosamond Johnson was the first deputy marshal. See "The Negro Silent Parade," *Crisis* 14 (Sept. 1917): 244. Dr. W. E. B. Du Bois marched in the second rank behind the drummers, "walking stick in his left hand and suit coat unbuttoned to the summer heat." See Lewis, *W. E. B. Du Bois*, 539.

82. "The Negro Silent Parade," 241, 244.

83. NAACP, "The Massacre of East St. Louis," *Crisis* 14 (Sept. 1917): 219–20; and Lewis, *W. E. B. Du Bois*, 539.

84. NAACP, "Massacre of East St. Louis," 220, 221, 238.

85. *New York Age*, 2 Aug. 1917.

86. Ibid.

87. Cornel West, *Prophesy Deliverance! An Afro-American Revolutionary Christianity* (Philadelphia: Westminster Press, 1982), 85; Ovington, *Half a Man*, 197; and Michael Rogin, "Making America Home: Racial Masquerade and Ethnic Assimilation in the Transition to Talking Pictures," *Journal of American History* 79 (Dec. 1992): 1052–53.

88. Wilson's secretary quoted in Rogin, "'Sword Became a Flashing Vision,'" 155. Wilson even nominated a white ambassador to Haiti, a post traditionally given to a black American.

89. Ibid., 154; see Kathleen M. Blee, *Women of the Klan: Racism and Gender in the 1920s* (Berkeley: Univ. of California Press, 1991); Klan member quoted in ibid., 172.

90. As film director Sergei Eisenstein keenly observed, to understand Griffith, "one must visualize an America made up of more than visions of

speeding automobiles. . . . One is obliged to comprehend this second side of America as well—America the traditional, the patriarchal, the provincial." Sergei Eisenstein, *Film Form: Essays in Film Theory* (New York: Harcourt, Brace, 1949), 197.

91. Michael M. Davis, *The Exploitation of Pleasure: A Study of Commercial Recreations in New York City* (New York: Russell Sage Foundation, 1911); and Richard H. Edwards, *Popular Amusements* (New York: Association Press, 1915).

92. Between 1908 and 1917, more than three hundred pageants were performed in the United States with contents including fairy tales, classical themes, the Bible, and medieval and Renaissance legends. See Glassberg, *American Historical Pageantry,* 1; Prevots, *American Pageantry,* lists more than 340 pageants in appendix A, 177–99.

93. *New York Age,* 30 March 1918.

94. *The Presentation of Colors to the 367th Regiment of Infantry by the Union League Club and the Parade of the Regiment in New York City, March 23, 1918* (New York: Union League Club, 1918).

95. *Report of a Special Meeting of the Union League Club of New York with the Resolutions and Report Submitted by the Special Committee on Immediate Defense and National Service, New York, March 20, 1917* (New York: Union League Club, 1917), 19, 24, 26; and Irwin, May, and Hotchkiss, *History of the Union League Club,* 171.

96. *New York Age,* 30 March 1918.

97. W. E. B. Du Bois, "Returning Soldiers," *Crisis* 18 (May 1919): 13–14, reprinted in David Levering Lewis, *The Portable Harlem Renaissance Reader* (New York: Penguin Books, 1994), 5.

98. Du Bois, *Autobiography,* 274.

99. Franz Boas, letter to the editor, *New York Times,* 8 Jan. 1916, reprinted in Stocking, ed., *Franz Boas Reader,* 331–35; and Boas, letter to the editor, *Nation* 107 (1918): 331–35.

Index

public demonstrations, 2, 3, 12–13, 257 n.5. *See also* women, black; women, white

women, black: and the Call, 118–19; and the Chicago World's Fair, 48–49, 105; and domestic service, 129, 130–31; and morality, 48, 131, 272 n.19; and musical comedy, 163, 165; surplus of, 129; surveyed by Mary White Ovington, 129–32, 272 nn.16, 19; wealthy, 193

Women's Christian Temperance Union, 135

women's rights, xiii, 118. *See also* feminist movement

women's studies, xxii

women, white: and the Call, 119; and the Hudson-Fulton Festival, 216; influence for law and order of, 139–40; and the race riots of 1900, 175; relationships between

black men and, 134–35; at the Twentieth Regiment Colored Troops parade, 1–2, 3, 12–13

Wood, Fernando, 8

Wood, Robert N., 220

Woods, Granville T., 60

Wooley, Celia, 121

Workingman's Advocate, 25

World's Columbian Exposition. *See* Chicago World's Columbian Exposition

World's Conference of Representative Women, 48

World War I, xii, 14, 131

Wright, Richard, 172

Young, Charles, 223, 282 n.28

Zangwill, Israel, 146

Zionists, 107

Zulu tribe, 67, 85

Carter G. Woodson Institute Series in Black Studies

Michael Plunkett
Afro-American Sources in Virginia: A Guide to Manuscripts

Sally Belfrage
Freedom Summer

Armstead L. Robinson and Patricia Sullivan, eds.
New Directions in Civil Rights Studies

Leroy Vail and Landeg White
Power and the Praise Poem: Southern African Voices in History

Robert A. Pratt
The Color of Their Skin: Education and Race in Richmond, Virginia, 1954–89

Ira Berlin and Philip D. Morgan, eds.
Cultivation and Culture: Labor and the Shaping of Slave Life in the Americas

Gerald Horne
Fire This Time: The Watts Uprising and the 1960s

Sam C. Nolutshungu
Limits of Anarchy: Intervention and State Formation in Chad

Jeannie M. Whayne
A New Plantation South: Land, Labor, and Federal Favor in Twentieth-Century Arkansas

Patience Essah
A House Divided: Slavery and Emancipation in Delaware, 1638–1865

Tommy L. Bogger
Free Blacks in Norfolk, Virginia, 1790–1860: The Darker Side of Freedom

Robert C. Kenzer
Enterprising Southerners: Black Economic Success in North Carolina, 1865–1915

Midori Takagi
"Rearing Wolves to Our Own Destruction": Slavery in Richmond, Virginia, 1782–1865

Alessandra Lorini
Rituals of Race: American Public Culture and the Search for Racial Democracy